The Cultural Dimension
in EC Law

The Cultural Dimension
in EC Law

Matthias Niedobitek

Translated by James Benn and Robert Bray

KLUWER LAW
INTERNATIONAL
LONDON – THE HAGUE – BOSTON

Published by
Kluwer Law International Ltd
Sterling House
66 Wilton Road
London SW1V 1DE
UK

Sold and distributed in the
USA and Canada by
Kluwer Law International
675 Massachusetts Avenue
Cambridge MA 02139
USA

Kluwer Law International Ltd
incorporates
the publishing programmes of
Graham & Trotman Ltd,
Kluwer Law & Taxation Publishers
and Martinus Nijhoff Publishers

In all other countries, sold and distributed by
Kluwer Law International
P.O. Box 322
3300 AH Dordrecht
The Netherlands

ISBN 90-411-0685-5

© Kluwer Law International 1997
First published 1997

British Library Cataloguing in Publication Data
A catalogue record for this book is available from the British Library

Library of Congress Cataloguing-in-Publication Data is available

Typeset in 11pt Garamond by RTR Information Design, London
Printed and bound by Athenaeum Press Ltd, Gateshead, Tyne and Wear

PREFACE

This book comprises the English version of my doctoral thesis (Parts 2–4) plus a supplementary part (Part 1). The thesis won the Wolters Kluwer Award of 1993, a prize which made possible its translation into English. I would like to thank both Wolters Kluwer and the competition jury, especially its chairman, the then Advocate-General at the European Court of Justice, Prof. Walter Van Gerven, for providing me with this wonderful opportunity.

The research for this book was conducted at the Forschungsinstitut für öffentliche Verwaltung bei der Hochschule für Verwaltungswissenschaften Speyer (Research Institute for Public Administration at the Postgraduate School of Administrative Sciences Speyer). It contains results of the research project 'Pläne und Entwicklung eines Europas der Bürger' ('Plans and Development of a Europe of Citizens'), which I carried out from 1988 to 1991 under the academic supervision of Prof. Siegfried Magiera at the Research Institute. The study was accepted as a doctoral thesis by the Postgraduate School of Administrative Sciences Speyer in the 1991/92 winter semester, and was published in 1992 by Duncker & Humblot, Berlin, entitled *Kultur und Europäisches Gemeinschaftsrecht*. Taking account of the changes brought about by the Maastricht Treaty, I have added a part to the unchanged thesis on the Treaty on European Union which originally appeared in German as 'Die kulturelle Dimension im Vertrag über die Europäische Union' in the magazine *Europarecht* (EuR 1995, 349-376).

The translation was carried out by James Benn, lawyer-linguist at the European Court of Justice, and Robert Bray, lawyer-reviser at the European Court of Justice. No one could have done a better job of fulfilling this task, and I would like to take this opportunity to thank them for their outstanding work. I would also like to thank Karen Smith, freelance editor, for her careful preparation of the text for publication.

Matthias Niedobitek

CONTENTS

TABLE OF CASES

German cases

TABLE OF LEGISLATION

Regulations

TABLE OF ABBREVIATIONS

ABl. EG	*Amtsblatt der Europäischen Gemeinschaften* (German version of OJ)
AfP	*Archiv für Presserecht*
AK-GG	Reihe Alternativkommentare, *Kommentar zum Grundgesetz für die Bundesrepublik Deutschland* (see Bibliography)
AöR	*Archiv des öffentlichen Rechts*
ArbG	Arbeitsgericht (Labour Court)
Aufl.	Auflage (edition)
AWD	*Außenwirtschaftsdienst des Betriebsberaters*
BAföG	Bundesausbildungsförderungsgesetz (Federal Law concerning the Promotion of Education and Training)
BArbBl.	*Bundesarbeitsblatt*
BayVBl.	*Bayerische Verwaltungsblätter*
BGBl.	*Bundesgesetzblatt* (German *Official Gazette*)
BK	*Kommentar zum Bonner Grundgesetz/Bonner Kommentar* (see Bibliography)
BRITE	Basic Research in Industrial Technologies for Europe
BRRG	Beamtenrechtsrahmengesetz (Framework Law relating to Civil Service)
BR-Drs.	Bundesratsdrucksache (document of the German Federal Council)
BT-Drs.	Bundestagsdrucksache (document of the German Lower House)
Bull.	Bulletin
BVerfGE	Entscheidungen des Bundesverfassungsgerichts (official collection of the decisions of the German Federal Constitutional Court)
BVerwG	Bundesverwaltungsgericht (Federal Administrative Court)
CDE	*Cahiers de Droit Européen*
CJEL	*Columbia Journal of European Law*
CML Rev.	*Common Market Law Review*
Cmd., Cmnd.	Command paper
COM	Document of the Commission of the European Communities

COMETT	Action Programme of the Community in Education and Training for Technology
COST	European cooperation in the field of scientific and technical research
DÖV	*Die Öffentliche Verwaltung*
DUZ	*Deutsche Universitätszeitung*
DV	*Die Verwaltung*
DVBl.	*Deutsches Verwaltungsblatt*
EA	*Europa-Archiv*
EAEC	European Atomic Energy Community (EURATOM)
EC	European Community
ECHR	(European) Convention for the Protection of Human Rights and Fundamental Freedoms
ECR	*European Court Reports*
ECSC	European Coal and Steel Community
ECU	European Currency Unit
ed.	edition/editor
eds	editors
EEA	European Economic Area
EEC	European Economic Community
EFTA	European Free Trade Association
EIB	European Investment Bank
ELR	*European Law Review*
EP doc.	European Parliament, Committee document
EPC	European Political Cooperation
EPOCH	European Programme on Climatology and Natural Hazards
ERASMUS	European Community Action Scheme for the Mobility of University Students
ESPRIT	European Strategic Programme for Research and Development in Information Technology
EuGRZ	*Europäische Grundrechte-Zeitschrift*
EuR	*Europarecht*
EURAM	European Research in Advanced Materials
EURATOM	(see EAEC)
EUREKA	European Research Coordination Agency
EUROTECNET	European Technical Network
EuZW	*Europäische Zeitschrift für Wirtschaftsrecht*
FAST	Forecasting and Assessment in the Field of Science and Technology
FFG	Filmförderungsgesetz (Law on the promotion of films)
FG	Festgabe
FORCE	European Community Action Programme for the Development of Continuing Vocational Training
FR	*Frankfurter Rundschau*
FS	Festschrift
GATT	General Agreement on Tariffs and Trade
GBTE	von der Groeben, von Boeckh, Thiesing & Ehlermann, *Kommentar zum EWG-Vertrag* (3rd ed.) (see Bibliography)
GdWZ	*Grundlagen der Weiterbildung*
GG	Grundgesetz (Basic Law of the Federal Republic of Germany)

GTE	von der Groeben, von Thiesing & Ehlermann, *Kommentar zum EWG-Vertrag* (4th ed.) (see Bibliography)
HDTV	High-definition television
HER	von der Groeben, Thiesing & Ehlermann, *Handbuch des Europäischen Rechts* (see Bibliography)
HRG	Hochschulrahmengesetz (Framework Law on Universities)
J.W.T.L.	*Journal of World Trade Law*
JIR	*Jahrbuch für Internationales Recht*
JO	*Journal officiel des Communautés européennes*
JöR	*Jahrbuch des öffentlichen Rechts der Gegenwart*
JuS	*Juristische Schulung*
JZ	*Juristenzeitung*
LIEI	*Legal Issues of European Integration*
LINGUA	Action programme to promote foreign language competence
MDHS	Maunz, Dürig, Herzog & Scholz (see Bibliography)
MEDIA	Mesures pour encourager le développement de l'industrie audiovisuelle
MittHV	*Mitteilungen des Hochschulverbandes*
MONITOR	Strategic Analysis, Forecasting and Evaluation in Matters of Research and Technology
NJW	*Neue Juristische Wochenschrift*
NuR	*Natur & Recht*
NVwZ	*Neue Zeitschrift für Verwaltungsrecht*
NWVBl.	*Nordrhein-Westfälische Verwaltungsblätter*
NYIL	*Netherlands Yearbook of International Law*
NZZ	*Neue Zürcher Zeitung*
OJ	*Official Journal of the European Communities*
R.A.E.	*Revue des Affaires Européennes*
RabelsZ	*Rabels Zeitschrift für ausländisches und internationales Privatrecht*
RACE	Research and Development Programme in Advanced Communications Technologies for Europe
RdJB	*Recht der Jugend und des Bildungswesens*
RDP	*Revue du Droit Public*
RIW	*Recht der Internationalen Wirtschaft*
RMC	*Revue du Marché Commun*
RMUE	*Revue du Marché Unique Européen*
RTDE	*Revue Trimestrielle de Droit Européen*
RuF	*Rundfunk und Fernsehen*
SCIENCE	Stimulation des coopérations internationales et des échanges nécessaires aux chercheurs européens
SEA	Single European Act
SEW	*Sociaal-Economische Wetgeving*
SPES	Stimulation Plan for Economic Sciences
STEP	Science and Technology for Environmental Protection
TEMPUS	Trans-European Mobility Scheme for University Studies
TEU	Treaty on European Union
UNESCO	United Nations Organization for Education, Science and Culture
VOP	*Verwaltungsführung/Organisation/Personal*

VVDStRL	*Veröffentlichungen der Vereinigung der Deutschen Staatsrechtslehrer*
WEGS	Wohlfahrt, Everling, Glaesner & Sprung (see Bibliography)
WissR	*Wissenschaftsrecht/Wissenschaftverwaltung/ Wissenschaftsförderung* (since 1994: *Wissenschaftsrecht*)
WiVerw	*Wirtschaft und Verwaltung*
WUR	*Wirtschaftsverwaltungs- und Umweltrecht*
YEL	*Yearbook of European Law*
ZaöRV	*Zeitschrift für ausländisches öffentliches Recht und Völkerrecht*
ZAR	*Zeitschrift für Ausländerrecht und Ausländerpolitik*
ZBR	*Zeitschrift für Beamtenrecht*
ZfW	*Zeitschrift für Wasserrecht*
ZG	*Zeitschrift für Gesetzgebung*
ZHR	*Zeitschrift für das gesamte Handelsrecht und Wirtschaftsrecht*
ZRP	*Zeitschrift für Rechtspolitik*
ZSR	*Zeitschrift für Schweizerisches Recht*
ZStW	*Zeitschrift für die gesamte Staatswissenschaft*
ZUM	*Zeitschrift für Urheber- und Medienrecht*

INTRODUCTION

The thematic linking of culture with European Community law may prompt a variety of reactions amongst readers. On the one hand, it might be objected that such a subject does not warrant the production of a monograph, and that culture and EC law have little to do with one another, since the three European Communities[1]- the European Community,[2] the European Coal and Steel Community[3] and the European Atomic Energy Community[4] – constitute associations of European States pursuing essentially economic goals. On the other hand, the vagueness and elasticity of the notion of culture[5] might prompt doubts as to whether it is at all meaningful to link culture with EC law and whether such a link is capable of forming the basis of an academic inquiry.

I would answer the first of these objections by saying that the connections between Community law and the cultural sphere are – as will be demonstrated – more extensive than they may appear at first sight. Those who harbour doubts by reason of the imprecise nature of the notion of culture overlook the fact that it is not possible to base a study grounded in the science of public administration, particularly its legal aspects, on just any definition of culture. Instead, it is necessary to proceed from the *descriptive* idea familiar from German public law, which breaks culture down into education, science and art,[6] thus defining the sphere '*in which the State enters into a particularly close association with the domain of the intellect* in its manifold manifestations within society'.[7] Not only does this descriptive concept of culture have the advantage of being legally manageable,[8] it is also characterized by the fact that 'it can attach to a widespread, everyday understanding of the word "culture" '.[9] For the purposes of this work, however, the

---

1 The three Communities are hereinafter collectively referred to as 'the European Community'.

2 Treaty establishing the EEC of 25 March 1957, Cmnd. 4864.

3 Treaty establishing the ECSC of 18 April 1951, Cmnd. 4863.

4 Treaty establishing the EAEC of 25 March 1957, Cmnd. 4865.

5 e.g. see Gau, pp. 17 *et seq.*

6 See Häberle, *Verfassungslehre als Kulturwissenschaft*, pp. 10 *et seq.*; Oppermann, *Kulturverwaltungsrecht*, p. 9; Ischreyt, p. 16.

7 Oppermann, *op. cit.*, p. 8.

8 Häberle, *op. cit.*

9 *ibid.*

third element of the chosen definition, that of art, is too restricted, and gives way
to the concept of culture in a narrower sense.[10]

The definition of culture underlying this work has two functions: first, from
the point of view of form, it narrows down the subject-matter under investigation;
and secondly, it characterizes that subject-matter, substantively, as the area
covered by 'those manifestations of life in society which cannot be measured by the
yardstick of economic efficiency'[11] - a characterization which links together all
three areas comprising the field of culture: education, science and culture in the
narrower sense.[12]

The general questions dealt with in this investigation arise from the association
of culture, as delineated above, with EC law. Those questions concern the options
and powers which exist at Community level for taking action in the spheres of
education, science and culture in its narrower sense - ultimately, therefore, the
question of the 'Kulturhoheit der EG',[13] that is to say, the EC's cultural
sovereignty.

Individual aspects of these questions have previously been dealt with in varying
degrees of detail in the literature, prompted by decisions of the Court of Justice or
the adoption of legislation by the Community institutions. Particular attention
has been paid in the literature to the question of the EC's powers in the field of
broadcasting. General investigations encompassing the various individual
problems and the principles of the relationship between culture and EC law are
few and far between[14] and some lack the necessary depth on account of their
approach.[15] This study attempts to close the *lacuna* which has been found to exist
in the literature on European Community law.

The inquiry into the question of the options and powers for taking action in the
cultural sphere which exist at Community level is pursued in four stages.

Part 1 describes the changes in the cultural field which have been brought
about by the Treaty on European Union.

Next, Part 2 takes stock of Community practice in the three sectors of the
cultural sphere, as it presented itself in the period prior to the Treaty on European
Union. The subdivision of individual activities within each sector, according to
those who initiate them, affords an insight into the interaction and transitions
taking place between national and supranational options for action at Council
level, and provides information about the view prevailing in the Council
regarding the division of powers between the Community and the Member
States in the cultural sphere.

Part 3 deals with the most significant individual questions of Community law
in the cultural sphere. The problems here arise principally in the fields of
education and of culture in the narrower sense, but not - it would appear - in the

---

10 For further details, see 'Introduction', pp. 63 *et seq.*
11 Tomuschat, *F.I.D.E. Reports*, p. 20.
12 See also de Witte, *Cultural linkages*, p. 193: this concept of culture 'is based on the
assumption that the objects and processes brought under the heading "culture" have some
unifying characteristics'.
13 As to this term, see Köstlin.
14 But see Wemmer; Loman et al.; Ress, *Kultur und Europäischer Binnenmarkt.*
15 e.g. see Schweitzer, *EG-Kompetenzen*; Fiedler.

field of science. In this part, as in Part 4, the legal position is likewise shown as it was prior to the entry into force of the Treaty on European Union.

Finally, Part 4 of the work elaborates the principles of the relationship between Community law and the cultural sphere; in addition, the possibility that Community law will develop further on the basis of Article 235 of the EEC Treaty is considered.

In principle, the study encompasses all three European Communities. The fact that the legal discussion in Parts 1, 3 and 4 relates solely to the EEC/EC simply reflects the lack of significance of the other Communities for the cultural sphere.

Part 1

THE CULTURAL DIMENSION
IN THE
TREATY ON EUROPEAN UNION

I. INTRODUCTION

The Treaty on European Union[1] pursues the general objective of '(marking) a new stage in the process of European integration'.[2] Having regard to all the amendments, additions and extensions to primary Community law brought about by the Treaty, it is not unreasonable to speak of 'the most important change since the signature of the Rome Treaties'[3] and of a 'qualitative leap forward'.[4] Consequently, whilst it remains open to debate whether the European Union can still be said to be an international institution within the meaning of Article 24(1) of the German Basic Law,[5] it nevertheless seems clear that the declared qualitative leap has not resulted in the transformation of the European Communities into a European State.[6]

On the other hand, the European Union has at its disposal an arsenal of powers, deriving in particular from the European Communities on which it is founded,[7] from which, in terms of subject-matter, no important aspect of State activity remains absent. In all three sectors of the cultural field – education and training, science, and culture in the narrower sense[8] – characterized, even now, by their 'great proximity to the core of national identity',[9] the EC Treaty henceforth provides for action to be taken at Community level.

From the very start of the Inter-Governmental Conference on Political Union, there was agreement that the cultural dimension should expressly be extended beyond the areas of vocational training and research and technological development already covered by the EEC Treaty. At its meeting in Rome on 14-15 December 1990, the European Council requested the Inter-Governmental Conference inter alia to have regard to 'the preservation of the multiplicity of the European heritage and the promotion of cultural exchanges and education'.[10]

The shape of the Treaty provisions finally adopted was already apparent from the 'non-paper' of 12 April 1991[11] prepared by the Luxembourg presidency, but more evident still from the draft Treaty on Union submitted by the Luxembourg presidency on 20 June 1991, which determined the further course of the

---

1 OJ 1992 C 191; the Treaty entered into force on 1 November 1993.
2 First recital in the preamble; see also the second para. of Art. A of the Treaty on European Union.
3 German Federal Government, Draft Law on the Treaty on European Union of 7 February 1992, BT-Drs. 12/3334, p. 82.
4 Select Committee on 'European Union (Maastricht Treaty)'. Recommended decision and report on a Draft Law amending inter alia the German Basic Law, BT-Drs. 12/3896, p. 16.
5 See the Draft Law amending the German Basic Law, BT-Drs. 12/3338, p. 6; BT-Drs. 12/3896, op. cit., pp. 16 et seq.
6 See BVerfGE 89, p. 155 (at p. 188); previously the subject of a detailed analysis by Blanke, DÖV 1993, p. 412 (at pp. 414 et seq.).
7 See the third para. of Art. A of the Treaty on European Union.
8 A more detailed analysis of this classification appears in the Introduction, above.
9 Beutler et al., 4th ed., p. 496.
10 Conclusions of the presidency, approved by the European Council, EC Bulletin 12/1990, para. I.8.
11 Europe Documents Nos 1709 and 1710, 3 May 1991.

negotiations.[12] Even the draft Treaty submitted by the Netherlands presidency,[13] although rejected in its entirety on grounds of principle on 30 September 1991,[14] did not differ in any far-reaching respect from the Luxembourg text as regards the cultural dimension.

By and large, there would seem to be good reason for thinking that there was never really any danger at any stage in the Treaty negotiations that the cultural dimension of the European Union would not be recognized and given shape. Apparently, no serious attempt was made to prevent this, not even by the German *Länder.*[15]

II. SURVEY OF THE CHANGES BROUGHT ABOUT BY THE TREATY

1. THE FIELD OF EDUCATION

Even before the Treaty on European Union entered into force, primary Community law contained a considerable number of provisions specifically relating to education and training.[16] As we know, the focus for academic interest was Article 128 of the EEC Treaty, which empowered the Council to lay down general principles for implementing a common vocational training policy. The position occupied by that provision within Title III, entitled 'Social policy', as the final article in the chapter containing the rules on the Social Fund, did not do justice to its development potential.

The Treaty on European Union therefore has a special chapter bringing vocational training together with the rules on education and youth. The continuing connection between vocational training and social policy can still be seen in the fact that the chapter in question has been placed in Title VIII, entitled 'Social policy, education, vocational training and youth'. The link between social policy and vocational training policy, made possible by Article 127 of the EC Treaty, becomes particularly clear when the objectives of the two policy fields are compared. Above all, the prime objective of Community activity in the field of vocational training – which aims to 'facilitate adaptation to industrial changes, in particular through vocational training and retraining' (Article 127(2) of the EC Treaty, first indent) – accords, in terms of its wording, with the new objective of the European Social Fund inserted in Article 123 of the EC Treaty.

In addition to being empowered to pursue a vocational training policy, the Community is assigned the task, in Article 126 of the EC Treaty, of contributing to the development of quality education. Thus the field of general education is also

---

12 Europe Documents Nos 1722 and 1723, 5 July 1991; see also Laursen & Vanhoonacker, pp. 358 *et seq.*

13 Europe Documents Nos 1733 and 1734, 3 October 1991.

14 For the reasons why it was rejected, see Dehousse, *From Community to Union*, pp. 6 *et seq.*

15 e.g. see J. Böhm, p. 545 (at p. 547), who goes so far as to contend that, in the field of education and culture in the narrower sense, the *Länder* could 'perfectly well have caused their ideas to prevail within the EC'; a somewhat different view is taken by Berggreen, *RdJB 1992*, p. 436 (at p. 442); Berggreen & Hochbaum, pp. 50 *et seq.*

16 See 'Introduction', pp. 31 *et seq.*, below.

subject to independent action on the part of the Community institutions which does not arise by virtue of any other Treaty provisions.[17]

2. The Field of Science

The rules on Community policy in the field of research and technological development, which were introduced by the Single European Act, do not appear at first sight to have been radically changed by the Treaty on European Union; however, 'the small differences may well have considerable repercussions'.[18] This is especially true of the new objective, inserted into Article 130f(1) of the EC Treaty, of 'promoting all the research activities deemed necessary by virtue of other Chapters of this Treaty'. According to the prevailing – and correct – view, the result of this is that 'European research policy has been extended to cover the entire field of Community policy'[19] and the restriction of the objective to the strengthening of industry has been abandoned.[20]

However, reinforcing the scientific and technological underpinnings of Community industry and improving its international competitiveness continue to constitute a key concern of Community research policy. Formerly, this was the only express Community competence in the sphere of industrial policy, but it has now been supplemented and 'more precisely defined'[21] by Article 130 of the EC Treaty. Article 130 of the EC Treaty, for its part, refers to Article 130f of the EC Treaty, by stipulating, in paragraph 1, that Community industrial policy is to be aimed at 'fostering better exploitation of the industrial potential of policies of innovation, research and technological development'.

3. The Field of Culture in the Narrower Sense

There was no precedent in Community law for Article 128 of the EC Treaty, which is the most important of the new provisions relating to the field of culture in the narrower sense. Article 128(1) assigns to the Community the task of '(contributing) to the flowering of the cultures of the Member States, while respecting their national and regional diversity and at the same time bringing the common cultural heritage to the fore'.

The power of the Community itself to take measures in the narrower cultural field under Article 128 of the EC Treaty is supplemented by the Commission's

---

17 See in that regard, for example, Art. 12 of Regulation No. 1612/68 on freedom of movement for workers within the Community (OJ, English Special Edition 1968 (II), p. 475); Council Directive 77/486/EEC of 25 July 1977 on the education of the children of migrant workers (OJ 1977 L 199, p. 32).

18 According to the Preface of the then Vice-President of the Commission, Commissioner Pandolfi, in 'Research after Maastricht: An Assessment, a Strategy', *EC Bulletin* Supplement 2/92.

19 Trute & Groß, p. 205.

20 As is rightly stated by Geißler, p. 217; by contrast, the narrow view taken by Konow, *WissR 1993, Beiheft 11*, p. 49, is not convincing.

21 Commission document, op. cit., n. 18, p. 8.

right, now expressly provided for in Article 92(3)(d) of the EC Treaty, to permit, subject to detailed conditions, grants of aid by individual Member States for the promotion of culture and heritage conservation.[22] No change in the practice for approving aid is generally anticipated: it is said that the Commission has in the past shown broad-mindedness in relation to individual State aids in the field of culture.[23]

Tourism is addressed in Article 3(t) of the EC Treaty, but the 'activities of the Community' provided for in that article are not further dealt with in the EC Treaty. The 'Declaration on civil protection, energy and tourism' annexed to the Treaty on European Union contemplates – as did the Luxembourg draft of the Treaty before it[24] – the possible introduction into the Treaty of a separate Title on 'Tourism', in the context of the Inter-Governmental Conference on the revision of the Treaty which is planned for 1996.[25]

In the meantime, the Community will carry on its activities in that field in accordance with the Declaration referred to above, on the basis of the rules hitherto applying. Particular attention must be paid to the 'horizontal Treaty provisions' contained in Articles 100a and 235 of the EC Treaty.[26]

There is also the possibility, however, that Community activities in that field may be based on other provisions of the Treaty, the application of which enables aspects of tourism to be taken into account. Thus, for example, Council Directive 95/57/EC of 23 November 1995 on the collection of statistical information in the field of tourism is based on Article 213 of the EC Treaty.[27] Tourism – which straddles many policy areas – may also conceivably be taken into account in the context, for example, of Community environmental policy, research and technology policy, and the development of trans-European networks.[28]

---

22   The *Länder* did not prevail with their contention that cultural aid 'cannot, by definition, constitute aid within the meaning of EC law'; see Berggreen & Hochbaum, p. 59; Ress, *Kulturbeihilfen*, p. 621, likewise considers that it would have been rational for cultural aid to have been covered by Art. 92(2) of the EC Treaty, which provides that certain aid is compatible with the Common Market, without the Commission having any discretion in that regard; see also Slot.

23   Loman et al., p. 187; Rawlinson in: Lenz, *EG-Vertrag*, Art. 92, n. 33.

24   Title XV of the draft, op. cit., n. 12.

25   At its sitting on 17 May 1995, the European Parliament called for tourism 'in its European aspects' to be embodied as an autonomous common policy; see 'Resolution on the Functioning of the Treaty on European Union with a View to the 1996 Intergovernmental Conference – Implementation and Development of the Union', OJ 1995 C 151, p. 56.

26   See von Borries, p. 36.

27   OJ 1995 L 291, p. 32; in its judgment of 9 November 1995 in Case C-426/93 *Germany* v. *Council* [1995] ECR I-3723, the Court of Justice held that Art. 213 of the EC Treaty is capable of serving as an autonomous legal basis for the adoption of acts of the Council.

28   For a more detailed analysis, with further examples, see the Commission document entitled 'The Role of the Union in the Field of Tourism', COM(95) 97, pp. 10 *et seq.*

III. THE OBJECTIVE OF THE MAINTENANCE AND DEVELOPMENT OF THE *ACQUIS COMMUNAUTAIRE*

The great majority of academic legal authors, in comparing the new Treaty provisions in the cultural field with the previous provisions, arrive at the somewhat cautious conclusion that the Community action hitherto taken is now founded on a clearer legal basis and, at the same time, that any further 'proliferation'[29] has been checked by the precise formulation of the individual provisions.[30]

Some authors even go so far as to express the view – although it is less frequently advanced – that, under the new legal regime, certain measures taken in the past would no longer be permissible. Wittkowski maintains, for example, that the harmonization measures allegedly[31] taken in the case of the ERASMUS programme 'would appear to be no longer permissible in that form under the new rules'.[32] Dehousse likewise considers, with regard to the exclusion of harmonization contained in Articles 126-129 of the EC Treaty, that 'a whole range of activities which were previously possible under Article 235 or other general heads are now explicitly excluded'.[33] Dehousse states, by way of example, that the directive on the approximation of the laws, regulations and administrative provisions of the Member States concerning the labelling of tobacco products[34] could not be based on Article 129 of the EC Treaty.[35] Lastly, Classen concludes from a comparison between the new Articles 126 and 127, on the one hand, and Article 128 of the EEC Treaty, on the other, that the competence of the EC has been curtailed generally in the field of education.[36]

A feature common to both the views described above is their contention that the new Treaty provisions may possibly reduce the competence of the Community – in the first case, as a result of a curtailment of the dynamic *potential* inherent in the former provisions, and in the second, as a result of the curtailment of competences which *have already* been exercised.

It is not possible to undertake here a detailed examination of the extent to which the Treaty on European Union actually gives rise to such a reduction in

---

29 See Everling, *Kompetenzordnung*, p. 170; a similar view is expressed by Loman et al. who refer to 'an attempt to block the more or less spontaneous further expansion of Community law in this area'.

30 e.g. see Blanke, *Bildungs- und Kulturgemeinschaft*, p. 65, who refers to a 'legislative straitjacket'; Hilf, *VVDStRL 1994*, p. 11, speaks of the 'designation and demarcation of competence'; Pernice, *DV 1993*, p. 460, refers to 'restrictive specification'; whilst Klein & Haratsch, p. 794, speak of the creation of express legal bases simultaneously with the erection of barriers.

31 Cludius, pp. 104 *et seq.*, concludes in his study (at p. 113) that the programmes undertaken in the educational field, and the ERASMUS programme in particular, do not involve any harmonization of the laws and regulations of the Member States.

32 Wittkowski, p. 323; see also, to the same effect, Lambers, p. 231.

33 Dehousse, *Community Competences*, p. 106.

34 Council Directive 89/622/EEC of 13 November 1989 (OJ 1989 L 359, p. 1); amended by Directive 92/41/EEC of 15 May 1992 (OJ 1992 L 158, p. 30).

35 Dehousse, *Community Competences*, p. 106.

36 Classen, *ZRP 1993*, p. 58; Zuleeg states less categorically in *DVBl. 1992*, p. 1334, that the Treaty on European Union *limits* the powers of the Community in the field of education.

Community competence; in any event, this cannot be reliably determined until the Court of Justice has pronounced on the scope of the new Treaty provisions.[37] Furthermore, the Treaty on European Union has not merely amended previously existing Treaty provisions: had it done so, comparison would have been easier. Instead, it has to some extent reformulated the Community powers anew in considerably more detail. Nevertheless, it appears that it cannot be ruled out that the powers formerly conferred on the Community in the cultural field have been reduced in one way or another.

This raises the question of the interrelation between such a finding and the fifth indent in the first paragraph of Article B of the Treaty on European Union. According to that provision, the Union sees it as one of its objectives 'to maintain in full the *acquis communautaire* and build on it'.[38]

Extensive agreement exists on the substantive meaning of the term *acquis communautaire* contained in that provision. Most commentators assume expressly or tacitly that the *acquis communautaire* includes 'all primary, secondary and unwritten Community law as it has been interpreted by the Court of Justice'[39] and, consequently, that 'the amendment of the Treaty is not intended to reduce existing Community powers'.[40] This is also the thrust of the finding, in respect of the field of education, that Articles 126 and 127 of the EC Treaty must be interpreted in such a way 'that at least the corpus of legislation prepared on the basis of Article 128 EEC should fall under, and should be able to be built upon pursuant to, the new provisions'.[41]

If this view is followed, a conflict clearly can be seen to exist between the objective of maintaining and building upon the *acquis communautaire* and the idea of the curtailment of Community powers. Thus, in considering the new system of powers, Berggreen finds that fixing the *acquis communautaire* is inconsistent.[42] Faced with that inconsistency, her summary of the situation reflects a certain helplessness when she says, focusing purely on results, that the situation has changed following Maastricht and that the inferences to be drawn from the new rules cannot be squared with the reference to the *acquis communautaire*.[43] Hablitzel likewise takes the view that the *acquis communautaire* cannot be raised to the status of an immutable constant in such a way as to render it impervious even to an amendment of the Treaty, and it cannot form a self-imposed straitjacket with the aim of setting European law in stone.[44]

---

37   Zuleeg, op. cit., n. 36, also considers that it is too early to say where precisely the limits of Community competence are to be drawn.

38   That objective is also expressly referred to in the first para. of Art. C of the Treaty on European Union and the preamble to the Protocol on social policy.

39   As Dohms puts it at p. 452.

40   Dohms, p. 459; that view is clearly shared by Advocate-General Van Gerven, who states in section 23 of his Opinion of 28 April 1993 in Case C-109/91 *Ten Oever* [1993] ECR I-4879 that the *acquis communautaire* comprises the entire body of the existing Community rules as interpreted and applied by the Court; a similar view is expressed, albeit less clearly, by Schima, p. 48, who states that no restoration of powers is to be expected, on account of the fact that the *acquis communautaire* has been enshrined in the Treaty.

41   Lenaerts, *CML Rev. 1994*, p. 8.

42   Berggreen, *RdJB 1992*, p. 442.

43   *ibid.*

44   Hablitzel, p. 22.

There are two conceivable ways of resolving this conflict between the fixing of the *acquis communautaire* and a possible reduction of Community powers, one procedural, the other substantive.

First, the view might be taken that the problem is simply academic: the relevant provisions of the Treaty on European Union concerning the *acquis communautaire* – the fifth indent of the first paragraph of Article B and the first paragraph of Article C – fall, according to Article L, outside the jurisdiction of the Court of Justice.[45] However, that view is not entirely correct, since, even though it is certainly not possible for the Court of Justice to interpret Article B or Article C of the Treaty on European Union in proceedings for a preliminary ruling,[46] or to gauge the acts of the Community institutions or the Member States directly against those provisions, that does not preclude the Court of Justice from interpreting the provisions of the EC Treaty coming within its jurisdiction in the light of the objective laid down in the fifth indent of the first paragraph of Article B of the Treaty on European Union – indeed, it may even be said to be under a duty to do so.[47] However, such an 'interpretation in accordance with the *acquis communautaire*' must remain within the limits imposed by the wording and meaning of the relevant provisions, and is thus capable in practice of mitigating, but not of overcoming, the conflict which has been found to exist.

The starting-point for any substantive resolution of the conflict must be the concept of the *acquis communautaire*. That concept, never before used in primary Community law, has been approached unhesitatingly by commentators conceptually from the point of view of the situation in which new Member States accede to the Community.[48] That idea suggested itself because, before the term was employed in the Treaty on European Union (and even afterwards), it was used to describe the complete corpus of primary and secondary written and unwritten[49] legal rules[50] binding on the new Member States, as well as other declarations

---

45   In its order of 7 April 1995 in Case C-167/94 *Juan Carlos Grau Gomis and Others* [1995] ECR I-1023, the Court of Justice declined to interpret Art. B of the Treaty on European Union in the context of a reference for a preliminary ruling, stating (at p. 1027) that, according to Art. L of that Treaty, the Court 'clearly has no jurisdiction to interpret that article in the context of such proceedings'; see also the order of the Court of First Instance of 14 July 1994 in Case T-584/93 *Roujansky* v. *Council* [1994] ECR II-585, in which the Court relied *inter alia* on Art. L of the Treaty on European Union in support of its view that it has no jurisdiction to review the legality of a declaration of the European Council (at p. 592).

46   See the order in *Juan Carlos Grau Gomis and Others*, op. cit.

47   See, to the same effect, Lenaerts, *CML Rev. 1994*, p. 8; Durand, p. 375; also (albeit without any express reference to Art. B of the Treaty on European Union), Feuchthofen & Brackmann, p. 469; Demaret, p. 7, is unclear on the point, stating that the *acquis communautaire* is 'subject to the control of the Court of Justice'; in his Opinion in Case C-7/93 *Beune* [1994] ECR I-4471, Advocate-General Jacobs has likewise interpreted the Protocol on Art. 119, annexed to the EC Treaty by virtue of the Treaty on European Union, in a way which accords with the *acquis communautaire*.

48   e.g. see Schima, pp. 47 *et seq.*; Hablitzel, p. 22; a differentiating view is taken by Cloos et al., p. 307.

49   Streinz, *Europarecht*, n. 80.

50   See Art. 2 of the Act of Accession of Spain and Portugal (OJ 1985 L 302, p. 23) and Art. 2 of the Act of Accession of Austria, Finland and Sweden (OJ 1994 C 241, p. 21, in conjunction with OJ 1995 L 1, p. 1).

concerning the Community made by the Council and the Member States.[51] It was so described not only by academic commentators[52] but also in acts of Community secondary legislation[53] and judgments of the Court of Justice.[54]

On this view, it is logical to regard the complete corpus of primary and secondary Community law as being protected by the fifth indent of the first paragraph of Article B of the Treaty on European Union. It should not be overlooked, however, that it is only this approach which gives rise to a conflict between the objective of maintaining the *acquis communautaire* and the newly created system of powers in so far as it includes within the concept of the *acquis communautaire* each and every provision of secondary Community law, be it marginal or of limited temporal validity. This point of view is misleading and incorrect. The concept of the *acquis communautaire* in the Treaty on European Union is a narrower one.

It is, admittedly, quite clear that, as regards the accession of new Member States, it is necessary to proceed on the basis of a comprehensive, purely *quantitative* conception of the *acquis communautaire*. Upon its accession, a new Member State should in principle – subject to any transitional provisions – be in the same position in every respect as the original Member States. However, that objective plays no part in any amendment made to the Treaty as between States which are already Member States of the Community. In such circumstances, a *qualitative* meaning attaches to the concept of the *acquis communautaire*.

This is already apparent from the fact that the *acquis communautaire* is to be not merely maintained but also built upon. Doubtless, the phrase 'built upon' is not intended to signify merely more Community legislation. It is, moreover, apparent from the reasons which prompted the insertion in the Treaty on European Union of the objective of maintaining and building on the *acquis communautaire* that the intention was not to prevent retrogression in all such fields of Community law as are merely conceivable. Rather, as Corbett reports, the Luxembourg presidency undertook the insertion of the *acquis communautaire* provision in order 'to reassure the majority that the pillar structure would not be the beginning of the end of the Community system, but on the contrary, could represent a step towards communautarization of the two non-Community pillars'.[55] Constantinesco likewise surmises that the emphasis placed on the *acquis communautaire* and the

---

51   See Art. 3(3) of the Act of Accession of Spain and Portugal and Art. 4(3) of the Act of Accession of Austria, Finland and Sweden.

52   e.g. see Streinz, op. cit., n. 49; Oppermann, *Europarecht*, nn. 1846, 1856.

53   Sixth recital in the preamble to Council Regulation (EEC) No. 1721/91 of 13 June 1991 fixing the production target price, the production aid and the intervention price for olive oil for the 1991/92 marketing year as well as the maximum guaranteed quantity (OJ 1991 L 162, p. 29); third recital in the preamble to Council Regulation (EC) No. 1275/94 of 30 May 1994 on adjustments to the arrangements in the fisheries chapters of the Act of Accession of Spain and Portugal (OJ 1994 L 140, p. 1).

54   e.g. see the judgments of 13 October 1992 in Joined Cases C-63 and C-67/90 *Portugal and Spain* v. *Council* [1992] ECR I-5073 (at pp. 5154, 5156) and of 15 January 1986 in Case 44/84 *Hurd* [1986] ECR 29 (at p. 79).

55   Corbett, p. 37; as to this background, see also Wyatt & Dashwood, pp. 655 *et seq.*; Dehousse, *From Community to Union*, p. 10.

building on it was intended to express the transitional nature of the cooperation procedures introduced by the second and third pillars.[56]

The concept of the *acquis communautaire* denotes in the Treaty on European Union the 'philosophy of the system'[57] and therefore is certainly not the *'acquis communautaire* with relation to vegetable oils and fats'.[58] It involves – as Pescatore has put it[59] – the 'acquis de caractère fondamental, c'est-à-dire de rang constitutionnel' (the fundamental Community patrimony, that is to say, that of a constitutional rank),[60] which must also be observed, according to Article N(2) of the Treaty on European Union, if and when that Treaty is revised in accordance with that article.

It is not appropriate here to undertake a detailed analysis of the individual matters falling within the ambit of the *acquis communautaire* as characterized above. They certainly include the principles of the primacy and direct effect of provisions of Community law[61] and – more generally – the principle of the 'autonomy of the Community legal order'.[62] The exclusive jurisdiction of the Court of Justice by which that autonomy is ensured, in accordance with Article 164 of the EC Treaty, should also be mentioned in this context.[63] In addition, it is also necessary to regard the basic freedoms enshrined in the Treaty, the general prohibition of discrimination and the protection of fundamental rights under Community law, or at least their basic tenets, as forming part of the *acquis communautaire.*[64]

It is clear, however, that, in view of the significance attaching to the principles covered by the *acquis communautaire* as thus defined, there can scarcely be any question of the new Treaty provisions in the cultural field conflicting with them.

IV. CLASSIFICATION OF THE NEW PROVISIONS WITHIN THE TREATY STRUCTURE

1. The Principle of Subsidiarity in the Cultural Field

The principle of subsidiarity can be applied in the cultural field only if the Treaty provisions relating to that field[65] do not fall within the exclusive competence of the Community (second paragraph of Article 3b of the EC Treaty). Since the EC Treaty does not specify the exclusively Community powers, it may be difficult in individual cases to determine the field of application of the principle of

---

56 Constantinesco, *CDE 1993*, p. 266.
57 Denys Simon, in: Constantinesco et al., Art. B TEU, n. 2.
58 See the sixth recital in the preamble to Regulation No. 1721/91, op. cit., n. 53.
59 Pescatore, *RDTE 1981*, p. 620.
60 See also, to the same effect, da Cruz Vilaça & Piçarra, pp. 37 *et seq.*
61 In its first opinion on the EEA Agreement, the Court of Justice described those principles as the 'essential characteristics of the Community legal order which has been thus established': see Opinion 1/91 of 14 December 1991, [1991] ECR I-6079 (at p. 6102).
62 *ibid.*, at p. 6105.
63 *ibid.*, at pp. 6105 and 6111.
64 According to da Cruz Vilaça & Piçarra, pp. 38 *et seq.*
65 See 'Survey of the changes brought about by the Treaty', pp. 4 *et seq.*, above.

subsidiarity. As regards provisions relating to the cultural field, however, it is agreed that they do not confer exclusive competence on the Community,[66] without there being any need to consider in any more detail how those spheres of competence are to be characterized.[67]

In the light of the wording of the new provisions in the cultural field, in particular Articles 126-128 of the EC Treaty, however, the question arises as to the extent to which it is meaningful to apply the principle of subsidiarity in addition to considering the individual criteria governing the application of the relevant provisions. The restrictive wording of those provisions, by which the Community is confined merely to making a 'contribution' in the relevant fields by means of 'supporting' and 'supplementing' measures (such contribution being further qualified, in the case of Articles 126 and 128 of the Treaty, by the words 'if necessary'), appears in itself to take adequate account of the matters addressed in the second paragraph of Article 3b of the EC Treaty. It is not surprising, therefore, that the wording used (both that already mentioned and other[68] formulations) is extensively regarded in the literature as reflecting the principle of subsidiarity.[69] Only occasionally, however, is the obvious inference drawn from this, namely that Articles 126-128 of the EC Treaty must be regarded, in relation to the second paragraph of Article 3b of the Treaty, as *leges speciales*.[70]

However, the wording of the provisions in question affords no support for the idea that the relationship which those provisions bear to each other constitutes a *lex generalis/lex specialis* relationship in the technical legal sense, since a special rule must possess all the characteristics of the general rule plus at least one further characteristic.[71] As regards the relationship between Articles 126-128 and the second paragraph of Article 3b of the EC Treaty, that is clearly not the case. The fact that the conditions for the application of Articles 126-128 operate *in the final analysis* to render any additional application of the principle of subsidiarity

---

66   See generally, with regard to the 'new' fields of policy and action, von Borries, p. 28; Constantinesco, *CDE 1993*, p. 278; as regards the provisions in respect of education and culture, Loman et al., p. 207; Lafay, in: Constantinesco et al., Art. 126 of the EC Treaty, n. 6, Art. 127, n. 4, Art. 128, n. 8; in relation to the field of research and technological development, see the Commission document, op. cit., n. 18, at pp. 26 *et seq.*; Konow, *WissR 1993, Beiheft 11*, p. 48.

67   Stauffenberg & Langenfeld, p. 255, refer to a 'system of parallel competences'; their view is supported by Blanke, *Bildungs- und Kulturgemeinschaft*, p. 68; in opposition to this, Nanclares, p. 40, regards Art. 128 of the EC Treaty as conferring 'concurrent' competence; that view is rightly contested by Schwartz, *AfP 1993*, p. 417, who speaks of 'complementary' competence; the attempt by Emiliou, p. 400, and Konow, op. cit., p. 49, to equate non-exclusive competence with concurrent competence must therefore be rejected.

68   Some authors further regard the *prohibition* of harmonization contained in Arts 126-128 of the EC Treaty as an expression of the principle of subsidiarity; e.g. see Cludius, pp. 86 *et seq.* and pp. 113 *et seq.*; Lafay, in: Constantinesco et al., Art. 127 of the EC Treaty, n. 10; this seems fallacious, since, as the second para. of Art. 3b of the EC Treaty clearly shows, the principle of subsidiarity in fact guarantees the protection of the Member States not in unconditional and absolute terms but only having regard to the capabilities of the Member States and any 'added value' which the Community may provide: what is involved is a 'dynamic' principle; see the conclusions of the presidency of the European Council meeting in Edinburgh on 11–12 December 1992, published in *EC Bulletin* 12/1992, point I.15.

69   e.g. see Staudenmayer, *BayVBl. 1995*, p. 330; Beckedorf & Henze, pp. 127 *et seq.*; Cornu, p. 159; Klein & Haratsch, p. 794; Wittkowski, p. 322.

70   As in the case of Bekemans & Balodimos, p. 108.

71   Larenz, p. 267.

superfluous is not enough. Had it been intended to exclude the application of the principle of subsidiarity in the cultural field, an express direction providing for that legal consequence would have been necessary.[72]

2. THE RELATIONSHIP BETWEEN THE NEW PROVISIONS AND OTHER COMPETENCE-CONFERRING PROVISIONS

According to paragraph 1 of Article 3b of the EC Treaty, the Community is to 'act within the limits of the powers conferred upon it by this Treaty and of the objectives assigned to it therein'. Under the principle of restricted powers, which was given concrete form for the first time in that wording but which had been previously recognized,[73] all binding legal acts of the Community institutions must be attributable to specific competence-conferring provisions of the Treaty. As the Court of Justice has consistently held, the choice of the legal basis for a measure 'must be based on objective factors which are amenable to judicial review'.[74] Those factors include in particular the aim and content of the measure, as expressed in the act itself.[75]

It is clear from the foregoing that the greatest possible care should be taken in differentiating between individual competence-conferring provisions and in attributing Community acts to individual competence-conferring provisions. However, where a legal act is objectively based on more than one provision of the Treaty, either because it combines different measures or because one indivisible measure aims to achieve more than one objective, the Community institutions are in principle bound to adopt the act in question on the basis of all the relevant provisions.[76] This may give rise to problems, particularly where the various legal bases contain different procedural rules. In those circumstances, it may be necessary to specify one appropriate legal basis from amongst those falling to be considered.[77]

(a) The relationship with provisions concerning the internal market

A problem theoretically arises in relation to provisions concerning the internal market, particularly Article 100a of the EC Treaty, where a legal act contains measures making it necessary to refer at the same time to both Articles 100a and 128. Whilst it is true that both those articles provide that the co-decision procedure of the European Parliament and the Council (Article 189b of the EC Treaty) must be followed, Article 128 of the Treaty differs from Article 189b in

---

72 See also, to that effect, point 4 of the resolution of the Bundesrat (German Federal Council) on the Commission of the European Communities' Green Paper on the European Dimension in Education, BR-Drs. 769/93 (resolution).

73 For a more detailed analysis, see 'The institutional competence of the Community institutions', pp. 196 et seq., below; the point is exhaustively dealt with by Kraußer.

74 Judgment of 28 June 1994 in Case C-187/93 European Parliament v. Council [1994] ECR I-2857 (at p. 2880).

75 ibid.

76 Judgment of 11 June 1991 in Case C-300/89 Commission v. Council [1991] ECR I-2867 (at p. 2900).

77 ibid., at p. 2901.

that it invariably requires a unanimous vote in the Council. No problems should arise, by contrast, where Article 100a of the EC Treaty is used as the legal basis together with Article 126 or Article 127, in the first case because, in principle,[78] the same procedure is applicable, and in the second case because, in the event of conflict between the co-decision procedure provided for by Article 189b of the Treaty and the cooperation procedure provided for by Article 189c, the former prevails.[79]

Those problems seem likely, however, to remain completely academic, since the substantive design of the new provisions in the cultural field, particularly Articles 126-128 of the EC Treaty, ensures that a conflict of this type will scarcely ever arise. Admittedly, an act may conceivably provide for several different (divisible) measures, with the result that the possibility of Article 100a of the EC Treaty and, for example, Article 128 both being the legal basis cannot be ruled out. In such a case, however, the more natural course would be to adopt two different acts. By contrast, it is virtually inconceivable that a uniform (indivisible) measure should need to be based simultaneously on Articles 100a and 128 of the Treaty. Even the example advanced by Ress,[80] namely the television directive, which is based on Articles 57(2) and 66 of the EEC Treaty, does not hold water. Ress regards it as conceivable that the part of the directive which concerns the so-called quota system should now have been based on Article 128 of the EC Treaty. However, he overlooks the fact that, by reason of the prohibition of harmonization contained in Article 128(5), a measure such as the quota system would not even be permissible under Article 128 of the EC Treaty. It follows that the Commission was right once again to base its proposal for a directive amending the television directive[81] solely on Articles 57(2) and 66 of the EC Treaty.

One is bound, therefore, to share the view of the overwhelming majority of academic commentators that the new provisions in the cultural field do not affect the possible exercise of other competences - except as regards Article 235 of the EC Treaty, which will be considered in the next section.[82] The new provisions create *additional* scope for action by the Community institutions in relation to the unamended Treaty provisions - although not necessarily in relation to the provisions replaced or amended by them.

---

78   Art. 126 additionally requires consultation of the Committee of the Regions.
79   Decision No. 819/95/EC of the European Parliament and of the Council of 14 March 1995 establishing the 'Socrates' Community action programme (OJ 1995 L 87, p. 10) had as its legal basis both Arts 126 and 127 of the EC Treaty and was adopted in accordance with the co-decision procedure by the European Parliament and the Council. Decision No. 2493/95/EC of the European Parliament and of the Council of 23 October 1995 establishing 1996 as the 'European Year of Lifelong Learning' (OJ 1995 L 256, p. 45) was adopted in the same way.
80   Ress, *Kulturbeihilfen*, pp. 626 *et seq.*
81   COM(95) 86.
82   e.g. see Wägenbaur, *Bildungs- und Kulturgemeinschaft*, pp. 859, 865; Pernice, *DVBl. 1993*, p. 913; as regards education and training, see Cludius, p. 139; Zuleeg also takes this view in *DVBl. 1992*, p. 1335; Dörr, *VVDStRL 1994*, p. 125, also assesses the point correctly; a different view is taken by Bekemans & Balodimos, p. 132, with regard to the prohibition of harmonization contained in Arts 126-128 of the EC Treaty; they submit that harmonization measures in fields covered - as to their subject-matter? - by the new provisions in the cultural field cannot be based on Arts 100 or 100a of the EC Treaty; there exists an 'interdiction absolue de toute mesure d'harmonisation' (absolute prohibition of all harmonization measures).

Furthermore, any other interpretation would conflict with Article M of the Treaty on European Union, according to which, 'nothing in this Treaty shall affect the Treaties establishing the European Communities or the subsequent Treaties and Acts modifying or supplementing them', save in so far as it contains express provisions amending those Treaties. This provision safeguards the *acquis communautaire* in a further sense.[83]

It follows that, in the case of the new provisions in the cultural field, the position cannot be otherwise than as determined by the Court of Justice in relation to the powers introduced by the Single European Act in the environmental field: they 'leave intact the powers held by the Community under other provisions of the Treaty, even if the measures to be taken under the latter provisions pursue at the same time any of the objectives of environmental protection'.[84] Consequently, even the '(exclusion of) any harmonization of the laws and regulations of the Member States' laid down in Articles 126(4), 127(4) and 128(5) of the EC Treaty cannot stand in the way of harmonization measures adopted on the basis of other Treaty provisions, even where, as regards their subject-matter, those measures fall within the sphere of education and the field of culture in the narrower sense.[85] The prohibition of harmonization limits only *additional* powers, not the *acquis communautaire* (in its further sense).

(b) The relationship with Article 235 of the EC Treaty

Use of Article 235 of the EC Treaty is conditional on, *inter alia*, there being no other provision of the Treaty giving the Community the necessary powers to act.[86] It might be thought, therefore, that the incorporation of express powers, particularly in the fields of education and of culture in the narrower sense, has reduced the scope of application of Article 235 of the Treaty.[87] However, the

---

83   Advocate-General Van Gerven regards Art. M of the Treaty on European Union as embodying an expression of the aim of maintaining the *acquis communautaire*, but – in contradistinction to the point of view advanced here – does not differentiate between the fifth indent of the first para. of Art. B and Art. M of the Treaty on European Union; see his Opinion in Case C-57/93 *Vroege* [1994] ECR I-4541 (at p. 4561, n. 49); see also his Opinion in Case C-18/93 *Corsica Ferries* [1994] ECR I-1783 (at p. 1808).

84   Judgment of 29 March 1990 in Case C-62/88 *Greece* v. *Council* [1990] ECR I-1527 (at p.1550).

85   The correct view is stated by Stein, *Querschnittsklausel*, p. 1451: 'From a systematic standpoint, it would scarcely be tenable to contend that the "transverse" clause operates to transfer the exclusion of harmonization – like a mortgage, so to speak – into other legal bases'; a different view is taken by Bekemans & Balodimos, p. 132, and Blanke, *Bildungs- und Kulturgemeinschaft*, p. 74, with regard to the Treaty objectives described in Arts 126(2) and 127(2) of the EC Treaty; slightly further on, however, Blanke expresses the view that the prohibition of harmonization applies 'only in cases in which the objectives of Articles 126 and 127 of the EC Treaty are sought to be achieved by the instruments and procedures provided for in those two articles'.

86   This has been confirmed by the Court of Justice in a consistent line of cases; e.g. see the judgment in Case C-62/88 *Greece* v. *Council* [1990] ECR I-1527 (at p. 1551); for a more detailed analysis of the significance and limits of Art. 235 of the EC Treaty, see Magiera, *FS Rudolf Morsey*, pp. 218 *et seq.*

87   This is the view taken by, e.g., Dittmann & Fehrenbacher, p. 488; Blanke, *Bildungs- und Kulturgemeinschaft*, p. 79.

Treaty on European Union has not only created special provisions in those fields but has also inserted a subparagraph (p) in the general provision contained in Article 3 of the EC Treaty, designating as one of the activities of the Community making 'a contribution to education and training of quality and to the flowering of the cultures of the Member States'. According to Article 3(t) of the EC Treaty, the activities of the Community additionally include measures in the sphere of tourism. These constitute new objectives of the Community which may considerably extend the scope of application of Article 235 of the EC Treaty.[88]

This result frequently fails to find acceptance amongst academics, and consequently, attempts are made to find approaches enabling the danger of the Community's potentially trespassing on to areas of national cultural sovereignty and arrogating to itself far-reaching powers to be averted.[89]

The attempt to argue that Articles 126–128 of the EC Treaty constitute *once and for all* the only provisions which give concrete shape to Article 3(p) of the Treaty, is neat from the point of view of legal theory yet unsustainable in the final analysis.[90] No support for it can be found in the Treaty, and no further justification is given for it. The only argument to support it, namely that Article 3 of the Treaty provides that the activities of the Community are to be carried on 'as provided in this Treaty', is refuted by the fact that Article 235 of the EC Treaty is a 'provision of this Treaty' and that it presupposes by its very nature an objective of the Community going beyond the individual Treaty provisions.

A further attempt to base an argument to this effect on the text of the Treaty is nevertheless to be found in the view that activity on the part of the Community in the field of education no longer takes place 'in the course of the operation of the common market', within the meaning of Article 235 of the EC Treaty. On this view, the Community is no longer engaged, as a result of the amendments made by the Treaty on European Union, in the pursuit only of economic objectives, but also of non-economic objectives falling outside the operation of the Common Market.[91] This disregards the fact that the Community pursued non-economic objectives even before the amendments brought about by the Treaty on European Union were introduced.[92] In addition, the argument is based on an incorrect interpretation of the phrase 'in the course of the operation of the common market'.[93]

Finally, the least convincing argument is the attempt to 'read into' the

---

88   This is also the view of Klein & Haratsch, p. 794; Berggreen, *RdJB 1992*, p. 443; Loman et al., p. 191; also, apparently, Konow, *RdJB 1992*, p. 430 in conjunction with n. 13; see, generally, Borchmann, p. 105.

89   See, to that effect, Klein & Haratsch, *ibid.*

90   That is the view taken by, e.g., Lenaerts, *CML Rev. 1994*, p. 36; Wittkowski, p. 324; also, it would appear, in the final result, J. Böhm, p. 548.

91   See, to that effect, Dohms, p. 461.

92   In its judgment in Case 242/87 *Commission* v. *Council* [1989] ECR 1425 (at p. 1456), for example, the Court of Justice regarded the achievement of a people's Europe as one of the general objectives of the Community. Even before that judgment was delivered, Magiera, *DÖV 1987*, pp. 221 *et seq.*, underlined how important that objective is for the development of the Community (especially at pp. 230 *et seq.*); see also the views expressed by the same author in: Dauses, *Hdb. EG-WirtschaftsR*, D. IV., esp. n. 7.

93   For further details, see 'The attainment of objectives "in the course of the operation of the Common Market" ', pp. 295 *et seq.*, below.

conditions for the application of Article 235 of the EC Treaty the constraints of Articles 126–128, in order to bring about a restrictive application of that provision.[94] Quite apart from the fact that it is wholly unclear who, in the light of the unanimity required by Article 235, might have any interest in so doing, there are no grounds for believing that to 'read in' such conditions represents a recognized method of interpretation.

Having established that Article 235 of the EC Treaty remains, in principle, applicable in the cultural field, it is still necessary to examine whether the prohibition of harmonization contained in Articles 126–128 of the Treaty is capable of operating as a restriction in some circumstances where Article 235 is sought to be applied. The only reasonable answer is that it is capable of operating in that way. Accordingly, harmonization measures may not be adopted on the basis of Article 235 of the Treaty *simply on the ground that* they cannot be based on Articles 126, 127 or 128 because they are precluded by those provisions. Otherwise, it would be possible to circumvent the exclusion of harmonization at will and thereby restrict its *'effet utile'*.[95] In any event, this cannot be justified by the fact that, unlike Articles 126 and 127, Article 235 requires a unanimous vote in the Council.[96] Consequently, it is likewise necessary to reject what may well be termed the sophistical view that the prohibition of harmonization precisely proves that 'this Treaty has not provided the necessary powers' (Article 235).[97]

In the field of research and technological development, it must be assumed that recourse to Article 235 is no longer possible. This is because, according to Article 130f(3) of the EC Treaty, contained in the Title headed 'Research and technological development', 'all Community activities under this Treaty in the area of research and technological development ... shall be decided on and implemented in accordance with the provisions of this Title'. That formulation has binding force even as regards the objective of 'the promotion of research and technological development' laid down in Article 3(m) of the EC Treaty. However, there are no grounds for fearing that, as a result, research measures previously implemented outside the ambit of the Title 'Research and technological development' will in future have no legal basis under the Treaty, since, simultaneously with the incorporation in Article 130f of paragraph (3), quoted above, the aims of the Community's research policy have been extended by the addition, in paragraph (1) of that article, of the objective of 'promoting all the research activities deemed necessary by virtue of other Chapters of this Treaty'.

---

94 See, to that effect, Klein & Haratsch, p. 795; followed by Blanke, *Bildungs- und Kulturgemeinschaft*, p. 79.

95 The Court of Justice has applied the principle of safeguarding of the *'effet utile'* of provisions of the Treaty *inter alia* to the interpretation of Art. 128 of the EEC Treaty; see the judgment in Case 242/87 *Commission* v. *Council* [1989] ECR 1425 (at p. 1453).

96 See also, to the same effect, Lenaerts, *CJEL 1994/95*, p. 17.

97 An express argument to that effect is to be found in Dittmann & Fehrenbacher, p. 489; the point is left open by Wägenbaur, *Bildungs- und Kulturgemeinschaft*, p. 855.

V. INDIVIDUAL ASPECTS OF THE NEW PROVISIONS

1. THE FIELD OF EDUCATION

(a) The relationship between Articles 126 and 127 of the EC Treaty

Prior to the entry into force of the Treaty on European Union, it was necessary to make a sharp distinction between education and vocational training, in the Community sense,[98] because, unlike vocational training, (general) education did not, in principle, fall within the scope of the EEC Treaty. As recently as 27 September 1988, in its judgment in Case 263/86 *Humbel*, the Court of Justice held that, irrespective of any special Community rules, discrimination on grounds of nationality in relation to access to ordinary schooling was permissible.[99] The question whether, following the amendments made by the Treaty on European Union, the issue of equality of entitlement to access to general education now falls to be determined differently, will be considered below.[100] At all events, it is now clear that, in principle, general education is 'not unconnected with Community law',[101] and, moreover, that it clearly falls to a certain extent within the scope of the EC Treaty.[102] Thus the demarcation problem has shifted from the question of the scope of the Treaty to that of interpreting and distinguishing two Treaty provisions – Articles 126 and 127 of the EC Treaty – thereby becoming decisively less important.

The interrelationship between Articles 126 and 127 of the EC Treaty has given rise to highly divergent views. Many commentators advocate a clear demarcation between the two articles, arguing that Article 126 concerns general education and Article 127 vocational training.[103] That view is based in some instances on the supposition that the new rules on education have introduced into Community law the current German legal terminology in that sector.[104] It is also submitted by some that Article 127 of the EC Treaty is the successor to the old Article 128 of the EEC Treaty, whilst Article 126 confers new, additional powers on the Commu-

---

98   Academic commentators frequently fail to indicate with sufficient clarity whether the statements made by them are based on Community terminology or on national terminology.

99   [1988] ECR 5365 (at pp. 5388 *et seq.*).

100   See 'The prohibition of discrimination in the field of education', pp. 23 *et seq.*, below.

101   As the Court of Justice had already held in its judgment in Case 293/83 *Gravier* [1985] ECR 593 (at p. 612), with regard to access to and participation in courses of instruction and apprenticeship.

102   It follows from the analysis undertaken by the Court of Justice in Case 293/83 *Gravier* that not every field which is 'not unconnected with Community law' necessarily falls at the same time within the scope of the EC Treaty and is thus covered by the general prohibition of discrimination laid down in Art. 6.

103   That is the view advanced by, for example, Hablitzel, pp. 21, 26; Beckedorf & Henze, p. 127; Dittmann & Fehrenbacher, p. 430; Konow, *RdJB 1992*, p. 430; see also, to that effect, the seventh recital in the preamble to Decision No. 819/95/EC of the European Parliament and of the Council of 14 March 1995 establishing the 'Socrates' Community action programme (OJ 1995 L 87, p. 10), according to which some of the measures provided for in that decision concern vocational training and therefore 'go beyond general education (including higher education) as covered by Article 126'.

104   See, to that effect, Hablitzel, p. 27; Dittmann & Fehrenbacher, p. 485.

nity.[105] Lastly, a considerable number of commentators suggest that Article 126 of the EC Treaty should be regarded as governing the field of education generally and that Article 127 is intended to cover the specific field of vocational training;[106] it is sometimes even assumed in that regard that the relationship between the two articles is that between a *lex generalis* and a *lex specialis*.[107]

The diversity of the views advanced reflects only to some extent the areas which are unclear in the text of the Treaty; it is also due to a considerable extent to preconceptions for which the text of the Treaty affords no basis. This is particularly true of the view that the split between general education and vocational training made in German law is reflected in the new provisions on education. It is true that Article 3(p) of the EC Treaty and the headings of Title VIII and of Chapter 3 of that Title refer, in the German version,[108] to 'allgemeine und berufliche Bildung', (general education and vocational training) but, as we know, the terms used in the Treaty have a particular meaning in Community law which may diverge from the meaning given them in national law.[109]

Not even the areas covered by the terms 'general education' and 'vocational training' as they are understood in Community law can be ascribed unequivocally to Articles 126 and 127 of the EC Treaty respectively. Any attempt to do so is doomed to failure from the outset, since even the German text of Article 126 no longer refers to 'allgemeine' Bildung ('general' education), but to 'Entwicklung einer qualitativ hochstehenden Bildung' ('development of quality education'). Thus it certainly encompasses the field of general education, from which the Community institutions were previously excluded, but additionally covers aspects of university education, as is apparent from the second indent of Article 126(2).[110]

That is not to say, however, that university education is excluded from Article 127 of the EC Treaty. It is necessary to reject *a priori* any attempt to infer from the difference between the German wording of Article 127 of the EC Treaty and that of Article 128 of the EEC Treaty (Article 127 of the EC Treaty refers to 'berufliche Bildung', whilst Article 128 of the EEC Treaty concerned 'Berufsausbildung') that Article 127 of the EC Treaty is intended to signify only 'specifically vocational training and further training in the narrower sense'.[111] That view

---

105 See, to that effect, Staudenmayer, *BayVBl.* 1995, p. 326; R. Geiger, *EG-Vertrag*, Art. 127, n. 1.

106 Feuchthofen & Brackmann, p. 472; that is also the view to which Blanke, *Bildungs- und Kulturgemeinschaft*, p. 67, inclines.

107 That view is expressly postulated by Lenaerts, *CML Rev. 1994*, p. 26; see also, by the same author, *CJEL 1994/95*, p. 11; Strohmeier, p. 70.

108 The English and French versions respectively refer, by contrast, merely to '*education* and (vocational) training' and '*éducation et une formation (professionnelle)*', although the terms 'general education' and 'éducation générale' are perfectly well known in those languages; see the English and French versions of the seventh recital in the preamble to the 'Socrates' action programme (OJ 1995 L 87, p. 10).

109 As is correctly noted by Loman et al., p. 181.

110 As the German Government rightly concludes in its *Denkschrift zum Vertrag vom 7. Februar 1992 über die Europäische Union*, BT-Drs. 12/3334, p. 97.

111 See Beckedorf & Henze, p. 125 (at p. 127); Staudenmayer, *BayVBl. 1995*, p. 321 (at p. 326), likewise does not regard that argument as erroneous; a similar view is taken, in the final analysis, by Dohms, p. 454, who focuses on the 'industrial motivation' of the training measures.

overlooks the fact that the linguistic difference appears only in the German version of the text. The English and French versions of the Treaty, for example, refer in both instances to 'vocational training policy' and 'politique de formation professionnelle' respectively, whilst Article 128 of the EEC Treaty also contained the words 'common' and 'commune' respectively. Even apart from that, it is not clear why the concept of 'berufliche Bildung' in Community law should be generally narrower than that of 'Berufsausbildung'. Only in the special case of the first indent of Article 127(2) is it necessary to accept that a narrower meaning attaches to the term 'berufliche Bildung'; that provision refers to 'Erleichterung der Anpassung an die industriellen Wandlungsprozesse, insbesondere durch berufliche Bildung und Umschulung' ('(facilitating) adaptation to industrial changes, in particular through vocational training and retraining'). Since this is an objective falling within the framework of the 'Politik der beruflichen Bildung' ('vocational training policy') referred to in Article 127(1) of the EC Treaty, which also covers retraining measures, the term 'berufliche Bildung' in the first indent of Article 127(2), juxtaposed as it is with 'Umschulung' (retraining), cannot have the same meaning as in Article 127(1).

All in all, there is much to be said for the view that Article 126 of the EC Treaty represents the basic norm in respect of education and that Article 127 confers additional powers in the field of vocational training. However, this by no means signifies that the relationship of the two provisions is that between a *lex generalis* and a *lex specialis* in the technical legal sense.[112] Consequently, it is also possible to consider, for example, that the second indent of Article 126(2) of the EC Treaty is the more specific provision as regards student mobility compared with the third indent of Article 127(2).[113]

The theoretically difficult demarcation between Articles 126 and 127 of the EC Treaty will be clarified by the practice followed by the Community institutions and the case-law of the Court of Justice. The question whether the Court of Justice will confirm its case-law on the concept of vocational training contained in Article 128 of the EEC Treaty on the basis of Article 127 of the EC Treaty[114] appears to be of secondary importance in comparison with the indisputable conclusion that access to vocational training, as hitherto ensured by the case-law of the Court of Justice, will continue in the future to fall within the scope of the EC Treaty, within the meaning of the first paragraph of Article 6 of that Treaty.

(b) The powers conferred on the Community by Articles 126 and 127 of the EC Treaty

(i) Instruments

The Community institutions may adopt only limited measures on the basis of Articles 126 and 127 of the EC Treaty. The first indent of Article 126(4), to which the co-decision procedure laid down in Article 189b of the EC Treaty applies,

---

112 See in this regard Larenz, p. 267.
113 This is the view advanced by Cludius, p. 79.
114 Various authors form conjectures in this regard; e.g. see Berggreen & Hochbaum, p. 56; Bekemans & Balodimos, p. 131; by implication, R. Geiger, *EG-Vertrag*, Art. 127, n. 3.

permits the Council to adopt 'incentive measures', whilst Article 127(4), which is subject to the cooperation procedure provided for by Article 189c, permits the adoption of 'measures to contribute to the achievement of the objectives referred to in this Article'. In both cases, the powers conferred may be exercised only subject to the exclusion of 'any harmonization of the laws and regulations of the Member States'.

Although the term 'incentive measures' ('Fördermaßnahmen' in German, 'actions d'encouragement' in French) is new to Community law, the concept of 'measures' ('Maßnahmen' or 'mesures') forms an established element of Community legal terminology.[115] The conclusion has been drawn in part from the divergent wording of the two articles that Article 126 of the Treaty allows the Community to undertake only 'activities of a more or less symbolic nature'.[116] It is contended that the Community is restricted to the creation of incentives; obligations cannot be imposed unilaterally.[117] On that view, it is only the term 'measures' in Article 127(4) of the Treaty which refers to the machinery of Article 189 of the EC Treaty, not the term 'incentive measures' in Article 126(4).[118]

This appears to be wrong. The only thing which may be inferred from the linguistic difference between 'measures' and 'incentive measures' lies in the fact that the latter term specifies the objective of the measures to be adopted.[119] No conclusions can be drawn from the linguistic difference as regards the applicable machinery; nor does it give any indications regarding the degree of binding legal force attaching to the measures which may be taken.

Not even the term 'measures' itself refers to the machinery of Article 189 of the EC Treaty, as many commentators consider to be the case. Rather, it is neutral as regards the form of the measures to be adopted. It is true that it does not exclude recourse to the instruments provided for by Article 189 of the Treaty, but, in addition to the formal acts provided for by Article 189,[120] it also permits other legal acts[121] to be adopted, as well as acts without binding legal force, such as resolutions[122] or conclusions.[123]

---

115 e.g. see the first para. of Art. 7a, Arts 49 and 51, the first sentence of Art. 70(1) and Art. 100a(1) of the EC Treaty.

116 Loman et al., pp. 196 *et seq.*

117 Dittmann & Fehrenbacher, p. 484; a similar view is expressed by Beckedorf & Henze, p. 127.

118 Blanke, *Bildungs- und Kulturgemeinschaft*, p. 66; see also, to the same effect, Loman et al., p. 196 in conjunction with n. 43; Bekemans & Balodimos, p. 133; also, arguably, Lenaerts, *CJEL 1994/95*, p. 9.

119 As is rightly stated by Berggreen & Hochbaum, p. 56.

120 For further details, see Magiera in: Hailbronner et al., Art. 189 of the EEC Treaty, nn. 2, 5 *et seq.*

121 See in that regard Magiera, op. cit., Art. 189, n. 3.

122 Whether resolutions constitute 'appropriate measures' ('geeignete Vorschriften') within the meaning of Art. 235 of the EC Treaty is a matter of debate; an affirmative answer is given by Grabitz, in: Grabitz & Hilf, *Kommentar zur EU*, Art. 235 of the EEC Treaty, n. 83; a contrary view is taken by Schwartz in: GTE, *Kommentar zum EWGV*, Art. 235, n. 199; in all events, the concept of 'measures' appears to be wider than that of 'appropriate measures'.

123 Even Ress, *DÖV 1992*, p. 947 in conjunction with fn. 27, appears in the final analysis to subscribe to that view, contending that the term 'incentive measures' is not limited to the legal acts listed in Art. 189 of the EC Treaty.

It is impossible in this respect to evaluate the term 'incentive measures' in any other way. If it were taken to signify only measures having no binding legal force, the prohibition of harmonization would be inexplicable. One is bound, therefore, to subscribe to the view that programmes such as ERASMUS, which may impose legal obligations on the Member States, can 'no longer give rise to any objections, or not, in any event, following Maastricht'.[124]

see footnote

(ii) The prohibition of harmonization

According to paragraph (4) of both Articles 126 and 127 of the EC Treaty, measures may be adopted under those articles only '(subject to the exclusion of) any harmonization of the laws and regulations of the Member States'. That wording leaves open the question whether the prohibition covers only measures which are principally aimed at such harmonization[125] or whether it also covers measures which primarily pursue a different aim but which may result in the approximation of certain aspects of national provisions.[126]

No further light is cast on this issue by the argument that Articles 126(4) and 127(4) prohibit *any* harmonization. That wording only excludes a *de minimis* rule, without clarifying the concept of harmonization in any way.

There are at least two reasons for rejecting the wide view referred to above. First, in the case of measures which are not primarily aimed at the harmonization of national rules, it is almost impossible to predict whether any adaptation of national law will be required in an individual case. Such a requirement will often not become apparent until the measure in question is implemented. Secondly, to interpret harmonization in such a broad way would cause its meaning to become blurred, since any adaptation of national law to higher-ranking Community law would have to be described as 'harmonization' within the meaning of the specific Treaty provisions.

It follows that the correct view seems to be that the exclusion of any harmonization measures relates only to such measures which have as their primary aim the harmonization of national laws and administrative provisions.

In so far as the prohibition of harmonization applies, it prohibits measures of *any* intensity whatever for the approximation of laws. It is not possible, for example, to regard 'directives de coordination' (coordinating directives) as permissible and to

---

124 Klein, *MittHV 1992*, p. 264; a different view is taken by Hablitzel, p. 24, who contends that, following Maastricht, the Member States could not be compelled to take part in any collaborative action initiated by the Community.

125 e.g. Council Directive 93/98/EEC of 29 October 1993 harmonizing the term of protection of copyright and certain related rights (OJ 1993 L 290, p. 9); Council Directive 93/15/EEC of 5 April 1993 on the harmonization of the provisions relating to the placing on the market and supervision of explosives for civil uses (OJ 1993 L 121, p. 20); Council Directive 92/81/EEC of 19 October 1992 on the harmonization of the structures of excise duties on mineral oils (OJ 1992 L 316, p. 12).

126 As is conceivable, for example, in the case of the ERASMUS programme; see Lenaerts, *CML Rev. 1994*, p. 24; a contrary view is taken by Cludius, pp. 104 *et seq.*

contrast them with impermissible 'véritable harmonisation' (true harmonization).[127] There is nothing in Community law to justify such a distinction.[128]

(c) The prohibition of discrimination in the field of education

The first paragraph of Article 6 of the EC Treaty provides that, within the scope of application of that Treaty and without prejudice to any special provisions contained therein, any discrimination on grounds of nationality is prohibited. Even before the Treaty on European Union entered into force, the general prohibition of discrimination applied to access to vocational training.[129] This necessarily gave rise to a right of residence in the Member State within the territory of which the vocational training took place.[130] On the other hand, the Court of Justice held that, provided that they were not concerned solely with meeting the fees payable for access to vocational training, maintenance grants were not covered by the Treaty.[131] Moreover, the prohibition of discrimination did not apply to the field of general education.[132]

Following the changes introduced by the Treaty on European Union, many commentators have drawn what is at first sight, perhaps, the obvious conclusion that both maintenance grants and access to general education fall henceforth within the scope of the Treaty, and that discrimination on grounds of nationality is therefore prohibited under the first paragraph of Article 6 of the EC Treaty.[133]

That appears to be a hasty conclusion. In order for a subject to fall within the scope of the Treaty, it is not enough for it to be addressed in general terms in the Treaty. In its judgment in Case 293/83 *Gravier*,[134] the Court of Justice did not confine itself to referring to Article 128 of the EEC Treaty and the concept of vocational training contained in that article in order to substantiate its finding that access to vocational training falls within the scope of the Treaty. Only after it had first considered further (legal) acts adopted by the Council and by the Council

---

127 Although Lafay does so, in: Constantinesco et al., Art. 126 of the EC Treaty, n. 9 in conjunction with fn. 4.

128 Langeheine, in: Grabitz & Hilf, *Kommentar zur EU*, Art. 100 of the EC Treaty, n. 8; for a detailed analysis based on the original Treaties, see Lochner, pp. 35 *et seq.*

129 For a more detailed analysis, see 'Equality of access to education in other Member States', pp. 115 *et seq.*, below.

130 This has been confirmed by the Court of Justice *inter alia* in its judgment of 7 July 1992 in Case C-295/90 *European Parliament* v. *Council* [1992] ECR I-4193 (at pp. 4234 *et seq.*); following delivery of that judgment, the Council changed the legal basis of the directive on the right of residence for students, which had been annulled, from Art. 235 of the EEC Treaty (see the original directive of 28 June 1990, OJ 1990 L 180, p. 30) to the second para. of Art. 7 of the EEC Treaty (Directive 93/96/EEC of 29 October 1993, OJ 1993 L 317, p. 59).

131 For more details, see 'Equal treatment in the award of educational grants', pp. 120 *et seq.*, below.

132 See 'The relationship between Articles 126 and 127 of the EC Treaty', pp. 18 *et seq.*, above.

133 See, with regard to maintenance grants, Staudenmayer, *WissR 1994*, pp. 256 *et seq.*; as regards access to general education, see Dohms, p. 457; Lenaerts, *CML Rev. 1994*, p. 9 in conjunction with n. 7; Engelhard & Müller-Solger, in: Lenz, *EG-Vertrag*, preliminary observation concerning Arts 126 and 127, n. 6; also, apparently, in the final analysis, Everling, *CML Rev. 1992*, pp. 1068 *et seq.*

134 [1985] ECR 593.

and the Education Ministers did it regard itself as justified in ruling that access to vocational training was subject to the prohibition of discrimination.[135]

It is necessary, therefore, to consider more closely whether, following the changes introduced by the Treaty on European Union, maintenance grants and access to general education are covered by the prohibition of discrimination laid down by the first paragraph of Article 6 of the EC Treaty.

Staudenmayer's arguments in favour of the inclusion of maintenance grants within the scope of the Treaty[136] appear artificial and, moreover, incorrect, since, in order for the prohibition of discrimination laid down by the first paragraph of Article 6 of the EC Treaty to apply, the fact that a given field does 'not fall outside the ambit of Community law' is not enough. The matter in question must in addition fall *positively* within the scope of the EC Treaty.[137]

It is, moreover, questionable whether access to general education comes within the scope of the EC Treaty. That it does not is suggested by the fact that the aim of Community action specified in the second indent of Article 126(2) of the EC Treaty is restricted merely to 'encouraging mobility of students and teachers', whereas the third indent of Article 127(3) additionally refers to the aim of '(facilitating) access to vocational training'. On the other hand, Article 2(1) of Decision No. 2493/95/EC of the European Parliament and of the Council of 23 October 1995 establishing 1996 as the 'European Year of Lifelong Learning'[138] includes 'the importance of a high quality general education, open to all without discrimination of any kind' as one of its themes. Whether this is enough on its own to justify the inclusion of access to general education within the scope of the Treaty remains an open question. It is probable that the Court of Justice would require the existence of further acts expressing a corresponding tendency. In the context of considering this, the Court might then attach legal significance, in particular, to recommendations adopted pursuant to Article 126(4) of the EC Treaty which have no binding legal force in their own right.

2. THE FIELD OF CULTURE IN THE NARROWER SENSE

(a) The powers conferred on the Community by Article 128 of the EC Treaty

Article 126 of the EC Treaty, relating to education, and Article 128, which is the sole provision contained in the Title headed 'Culture', have a number of features in common. Not only are both provisions extensively concerned, as a matter of fact, with 'new' powers; there are also, as regards their content, far-reaching links between the two provisions, so that it is possible to concur with the statement that it is 'quite surprising that the relevant provisions were not placed in the same Title'.[139]

A further feature common to the two provisions is to be found in the powers conferred on the Community institutions. Both provisions (Articles 126(4) and

---

135 For a more detailed analysis, see 'The scope of the EEC Treaty', pp. 115 *et seq.*, below.
136 Staudenmayer, *WissR 1994*, pp. 256 *et seq.*
137 See, with regard to this distinction, n.102, above.
138 OJ 1995 L 256, p. 45.
139 Loman et al., p. 201.

128(5) of the EC Treaty) restrict the Council to the adoption of 'incentive measures, excluding any harmonization of the laws and regulations of the Member States'. In both cases, the co-decision procedure (Article 189b of the EC Treaty) involving the European Parliament and the Council is to apply. Lastly, special rules, derogating from Article 148(1) of the EC Treaty, are applicable in both cases to the adoption of recommendations by the Council.

By contrast with Article 126(4), however, Article 128(5) presents a number of further obstacles to Community action, which have prompted complaints that, as regards the transfer of cultural powers, the Member States were 'tight-fisted'[140] and 'perhaps overdid it in seeking to do the right thing'.[141] This is because, according to Article 128(5), unanimity is invariably required in the context of the co-decision procedure; this derogates from Article 189b of the Treaty and constitutes a procedural anomaly[142] the insertion of which can plainly be laid at the door of the German *Länder*.[143] The same is true of the requirement for recommendations to be adopted unanimously.

In contrast, there is little consolation to be found in the widely held view that the Community institutions enjoy, in terms of subject-matter, 'practically unlimited terrain for activities in the cultural sphere'.[144]

(b) The significance of the 'transverse' clause

Article 128(4) of the EC Treaty provides that the Community 'shall take cultural aspects into account in its action under other provisions of this Treaty'. This 'transverse' provision, for which the inelegant term 'Kulturverträglichkeitsklausel' (culture tolerance clause) has also been coined,[145] has been the subject of widespread misunderstanding and has, in some cases, led to a number of astonishing interpretations. It is necessary, therefore, to make a few observations by way of clarification.

First of all, it should be noted that Article 128(4) neither creates new powers nor curtails powers which were already in existence.[146] Its significance is greatly overestimated. First, it merely refers to other competence-conferring provisions of the Treaty and to the fact that cultural aspects should be taken into account when applying them. In that respect, it signifies no change in the legal position by comparison with the situation as it stood before the Treaty on European Union entered into force, and is thus declaratory only. This is because, even on the basis of the legal position previously applying, the Community was empowered to take

---

140 See Cloos et al., p. 332: 'les Etats membres se sont montrés parcimonieux' (the Member States proved to be parsimonious).
141 Wägenbaur, *Bildungs- und Kulturgemeinschaft*, p. 858.
142 *ibid.*
143 See Berggreen & Hochbaum, pp. 51 *et seq.*
144 Engelhard, in: Lenz, *EG-Vertrag*, Art.128, n. 4; a similar view is expressed by Blanke, *Bildungs- und Kulturgemeinschaft*, p. 102.
145 e.g. see Blanke, *Bildungs- und Kulturgemeinschaft*, p. 103; Flesch, *EG-Informationen 10/1992*, p. 2; the term appears even in the literature in French; see Bekemans & Balodimos, p. 134.
146 For a concurring view, see Schwartz, *AfP 1993*, p. 418.

cultural aspects into account when carrying out its activities.[147] The Community institutions did in fact make use of that power – moreover, to a greater extent 'in recent years'.[148]

Cultural aspects have been taken into account in a positive way in, for example, Directive 92/100/EEC of 19 November 1992 on rental right and lending right and on certain rights related to copyright in the field of intellectual property,[149] the adoption of which was justified by the Council *inter alia* on the ground that 'the creative and artistic work of authors and performers necessitates an adequate income as a basis for further creative and artistic work'.[150] The same may be said of Council Directive 93/98/EEC of 29 October 1993 harmonizing the term of protection of copyright and certain related rights.[151] In the preamble to that directive, the Council cites a communication from the Commission stressing the need to harmonize copyright and the related rights at a high level of protection, since these rights are fundamental to intellectual creation.[152] That high level of protection, the Council itself continues, must be one which 'at the same time meets the requirements of the internal market and the need to establish a legal environment conducive to the harmonious development of literary and artistic creation'.[153] Even Council Directive 92/77/EEC of 19 October 1992 supplementing the common system of value added tax and amending Directive 77/388/EEC (approximation of VAT rates)[154] takes account of cultural aspects by allowing the Member States to apply reduced rates of tax to supplies of cultural goods (books, for example) or cultural services (such as the offerings of writers, composers and performing artists).[155]

The only addition made by Article 128(4) of the EC Treaty to the Community institutions' pre-existing power (and duty[156]) to have regard to cultural aspects is the obligation which it imposes to give greater weight to the cultural dimension in balancing interests. This certainly does not involve any 'obligation de résultat' (obligation to achieve any specific result),[157] but that does not mean that Article 128(4) lacks binding legal force.[158]

Above all, therefore, it is necessary to reject the view that Article 128(4) of the EC Treaty requires the sphere of competence of the Member States in the cultural

---

147 For further details, see 'The modalities of the exercise of Community competence in the cultural field', pp. 205 *et seq.*, below; a different view is taken by Ress, *Kultur und Europäischer Binnenmarkt*, p. 31, who contends that all individual powers fall to be construed in accordance with the economic objectives of the Community. Ress describes this method of construction as the 'principle of a-cultural interpretation'.

148 Conclusions of the Ministers of Culture meeting within the Council of 12 November 1992 on guidelines for Community cultural action (OJ 1992 C 336, p. 1).

149 OJ 1992 L 346, p. 61.

150 *ibid.*, seventh recital in the preamble.

151 OJ 1993 L 290, p. 9.

152 *ibid.*, tenth recital in the preamble.

153 *ibid.*, eleventh recital in the preamble.

154 OJ 1992 L 316, p. 1.

155 *ibid.*, Art. 1(1) in conjunction with the Annex.

156 See 'Permissibility of taking into consideration the cultural aspects of a matter which is to be regulated', pp. 206 *et seq.*, below, *in fine*.

157 As is rightly stated by Bekemans & Balodimos, p. 135.

158 Lane, pp. 947 *et seq.*, regards this as a possibility; Schwartz, *AfP 1993*, p. 417, rightly disagrees.

field to be taken into account.[159] The only provision of the EC Treaty which pursues – along with others, at least – the objective of protecting the sphere of competence of the Member States is the second paragraph of Article 3b.[160] No such tendency to safeguard national competence can be inferred from Article 128(4) of the Treaty, even if the term 'cultural aspects' is interpreted in the light of the general objectives laid down in Article 128(1). The latter provision refers to 'the cultures of the Member States' and to 'their national and regional diversity', but not to the 'cultural *sovereignty* of the Member States'.[161] Only if 'culture' is equated with 'cultural *policy*' and/or 'cultural *sovereignty*' is it possible to arrive at the erroneous view that the aim of Article 128(4) of the Treaty is to restrict the exercise of Community powers in favour of action by the Member States.

However, that does not rule out the possibility that, in individual cases, Article 128(4) *may* have the effect of protecting the sphere of competence reserved to the Member States, since it provides that cultural aspects are to be taken into account in *all* the actions taken by *all* the Community institutions – hence not only in the case of legislative acts but also in the case of supervisory measures adopted by the Commission. A specific expression of this possibility is to be found in Article 92(3)(d) of the Treaty, which allows the Commission in certain circumstances to authorize grants of aid to promote national culture.

Admittedly, it seems logical, on the basis of the interpretation of Article 128(4) rejected above, that the Commission should be required to exercise its discretion under Article 92(3) of the Treaty 'in such a way as to favour, in principle, the permissibility of the promotion of national culture', and that its discretion would tend as a result to be reduced to zero.[162] This shows once again, however, that the view referred to is misconceived, since the German *Länder* were unsuccessful in their attempt to secure the inclusion of cultural aid within the matters covered by Article 92(2) of the EC Treaty.[163]

Nor is there any justification for the fear, expressed by another school of thought, that the transverse clause could make it possible 'to break free from the fetters of express restrictions on action or prohibitions of harmonization'[164] or, indeed, to circumvent a prohibition of harmonization.[165]

First of all, that assumption is based on the notion – which, as has been shown, must be rejected – that, without the transverse clause, the Community institutions would not be in a position to take cultural aspects into account.[166]

In addition, it seems problematical to refer to 'circumvention', since – as has

---

159 That view is primarily advanced by Ress, *DÖV* 1992, pp. 947 *et seq.*; Blanke, *Bildungs- und Kulturgemeinschaft*, p. 103, concurs with him; a similar view is taken by Eberle, p. 426; it is rightly criticized by Stein, *Querschnittsklausel*, pp. 1442 *et seq.*

160 Ress, *DÖV* 1992, p. 948, considers – proceeding logically from his starting-point that a dividing line must be drawn between Art. 128(4) of the Treaty and the principle of subsidiarity.

161 Although that is contended by Blanke, *Bildungs- und Kulturgemeinschaft*, p. 103; Häberle, *DVBl.* 1995, p. 762, concurs; his view is rightly opposed by Schwartz, *AfP* 1993, p. 418, who contends that Art. 128(4) of the Treaty does not express any cultural proviso in favour of the individual Member States.

162 See Ress, *Kulturbeihilfen*, p. 602.

163 See n. 22, above.

164 Stein, *Querschnittsklausel*, p. 1444.

165 *ibid.*, pp. 1449 *et seq.*

166 *ibid.*, p. 1441, referring to the 'liberalizing effect' of the transverse clauses.

been shown elsewhere[167] – the new provisions do not in any way affect the application of the provisions of the Treaty, in particular those relating to the internal market. Consequently, where a harmonization measure is based on, for example, Article 100a of the EC Treaty, that does not amount to a 'circumvention' of a prohibition of harmonization provided for in another provision. The view described fails to take adequate account of the fact that a functional power such as that conferred by Article 100a of the Treaty invariably needs to be bolstered from a substantive standpoint.[168]

It is also necessary, therefore, to reject the approach suggested in this connection, to the effect that the cultural aspects of an activity should be allowed to be taken into account on the basis of other provisions, in accordance with the 'transverse' clause, only where the main thrust of the proposed measures lies not in the cultural field but in some other policy area. According to that view, where the main thrust of the measures is in the cultural field, the Court of Justice must keep the Community 'within the confines laid down for action in that field'.[169] That approach, which has previously been put forward in order to deny any Community competence in the cultural field,[170] must in any event fail in the sphere of functional Community powers such as those conferred by Article 100a of the EC Treaty, since the substantive thrust in this case is invariably focused on a field other than the 'establishment of the internal market', which is not an autonomous substantive area.

---

167   See 'The relationship with provisions concerning the internal market', pp. 13 *et seq.*, above.
168   See 'Permissibility of taking into consideration the cultural aspects of a matter which is to be regulated', pp. 206 *et seq.*, below.
169   Stein, op. cit., n. 164, pp. 1452 *et seq.*
170   See 'Conclusions in relation to the cultural field', pp. 193 *et seq.*, below.

Part 2

COMMUNITY PRACTICE
IN THE
CULTURAL SPHERE

Chapter 1

THE FIELD OF EDUCATION

I. INTRODUCTION

The field of education comprises all sectors of education: pre-school, general and vocational, higher and further education.[1] This applies irrespective of the content or length of the training and of the stage of life at which it is taken.[2] Education as a part of national culture[3] appeared originally to belong to the 'inviolable private domain'[4] of Member States, and thus to be beyond the reach of the Community institutions. Consequently, even the Treaties establishing the European Communities contain only isolated provisions permitting the implementation by the EC of measures in the field of education.

In the ECSC Treaty, Article 56(1)(c) authorizes, subject to certain conditions, the provision of aid towards 'the financing of vocational retraining for workers having to change their employment'. Article 9(1) of the Euratom Treaty assigns to the Commission the task, within the framework of the Joint Research Centre, of setting up schools for the training of specialists; under Article 9(2), the Council is to establish an institution with university status.

More extensive provisions concerning the field of education are to be found in the EEC Treaty. Article 41 of the EEC Treaty provides for 'an effective coordination of efforts in the spheres of vocational training' as one of the measures to be taken in connection with the Common Agricultural Policy. According to Article 57(1) of the EEC Treaty, the Council is empowered, for the purpose of making it easier for persons to take up and pursue their right of establishment, to issue directives for the mutual recognition of diplomas, certificates and other evidence of formal qualifications. For the same purpose, it may, under Article

---

1 See the sixth recital in the preamble to the resolution of the Council and of the Ministers of Education meeting within the Council on environmental education of 24 May 1988, OJ 1988 C 177, p. 8.

2 See para. 9.1. of the Opinion of the Economic and Social Committee on education in the European Community, drawn up at its plenary session on 23 and 24 April 1975, OJ 1975 C 255, p. 9.

3 See Buss, p. 18.

4 *ibid.*

57(2), issue directives for the coordination of the provisions laid down under the legislation of Member States concerning the taking up and pursuit of activities as self-employed persons. Those powers are also vested in the Council by Article 66 of the EEC Treaty for the purpose of the implementation of freedom to provide services.

Furthermore, Article 118 of the EEC Treaty imposes on the Commission the task of promoting close cooperation between Member States in the social field, particularly in matters relating to basic and advanced vocational training. According to Article 125 of the EEC Treaty, which has in the interim ceased to be relevant,[5] the European Social Fund could finance up to 50 per cent of the expenditure incurred by a Member State or by a body governed by public law in the vocational retraining of unemployed workers. Article 128 of the EEC Treaty, which, like the two provisions previously referred to in this paragraph, is contained in Title III of Part Three of the Treaty ('Social Policy'), requires the Council to lay down general principles for implementing a common vocational training policy 'capable of contributing to the harmonious development both of the national economies and of the common market'. Finally, Article 130g(d) of the EEC Treaty empowers the Community, complementing the activities carried out in Member States, to take action for the 'stimulation of the training and mobility of researchers in the Community'.

As against this apparently narrowly circumscribed competence, activities at Community level have developed in the field of education which, although initially hesitant, have subsequently increased. These are described below.

II. THE BEGINNINGS OF COMMUNITY ACTION IN THE FIELD OF EDUCATION

1. The Council and the Representatives of the Governments of the Member States

(a) The government representatives meeting within the Council

On 16 November 1971 the Education Ministers of the Member States met within the Council for the first time[6] and adopted, as 'the Ministers of Education meeting within the Council', a resolution on cooperation in that field.[7] They declared that there was a need, in addition to the measures already provided for in the Community Treaties, for greater collaboration in the field of education, the ultimate objective being 'the definition of a European cultural model in the context of European integration'.[8] That resolution clearly expresses the Ministers' intention to take action, not as the Council itself, but nevertheless within the framework of the Council, particularly since the group of experts set up by the resolution was given the task of reporting on their activities to the Education

---

5   Jansen in: Grabitz, *Kommentar zum EWGV*, Art. 125, n.1.
6   *EC Bulletin* 12/1971, p. 28.
7   See EC Council, *European Educational Policy Statements* (2nd ed., 1986), p. 9.
8   *ibid.*, fourth recital.

Ministers 'in their capacity as the representatives of the Member States meeting within the Council'.[9]

At their second session on 6 June 1974,[10] the Education Ministers again met, not as the Council itself, but as the ministers meeting within the Council, where they passed a further resolution on cooperation in the field of education.[11] The ministers laid down three principles and seven priority spheres of action for such cooperation. Particular mention should be made of the second principle, according to which 'on no account must education be regarded merely as a component of economic life', and the third principle, which emphasizes the value in itself of the diversity of the respective educational systems of each individual country and expressly provides that the harmonization of national education policies and systems cannot be regarded, for the purposes of the cooperation, as an end in itself. The cooperation was to take place at the level of the Member States. The ministers, conscious of the potential conflicts of competence which might arise in that connection between the EC and the Member States, declared that it must not hinder the exercise of the powers conferred on the institutions of the European Communities.

(b) The Council and the governmental representatives acting jointly

On 10 December 1975, the Education Ministers met for their third[12] conference in their joint capacity as the Council and as the government representatives meeting within the Council. They adopted a resolution comprising an action programme in the field of education,[13] which was formally passed by them on 9 February 1976.[14] That resolution is important for a number of reasons regarding the further development of cooperation in the field of education. First, the action programme provides for measures to be taken both at Member State level and at Community level, thereby justifying the 'mixed' decision-making whereby the role of the Community in the field of general education came to be recognized for the first time. Next, a standing Education Committee, consisting of representatives of the Member States and of the Commission, was set up to coordinate the action programme. Lastly, the Council and the Education Ministers agreed henceforth to meet periodically 'to follow the implementation of the action programme, to establish further guidelines, and to compare their policies'.[15]

The action programme covers a broad spectrum of cooperation in the field of

---

9   EC Council, *European Educational Policy Statements* (2nd ed., 1986), para. 2.

10   *EC General Report* 8/1974, para. 323. The previous establishment, on 19 April 1972, of the European University Institute in Florence was based not on a resolution of the Ministers of Education meeting within the Council but on an international convention concluded between the Member States; see OJ 1976 C 29, p. 1. The publication of the convention in the *Official Journal* is, however, an indication of its Community dimension.

11   OJ 1974 C 98, p. 2. In its draft resolution (OJ 1974 C 58, p. 20), the Commission had previously proposed that it should be adopted jointly by the Council and the Ministers of Education meeting within the Council.

12   See Maaß, p. 11.

13   *EC Bulletin* 12/1975, para. 1101.

14   OJ 1976 C 38, p. 1; see also *EC Bulletin* 2/1976, para. 2252.

15   *ibid.*, point III of the resolution.

education policy. By way of example, it deals with general opportunities for education and training in other Member States, the improvement of the correspondence between the individual education systems, cooperation in the field of university education, the promotion of foreign language teaching and the achievement of equal opportunity for free access to all forms of education.

The latter objective involves *inter alia* measures 'to prepare young people for work, [and] to facilitate their transition from study to working life, ... thereby reducing the risks of unemployment'.[16] With reference thereto, the Council and the Education Ministers passed a resolution on 13 December 1976,[17] having taken note of the report of the Education Committee on the 'preparation of young people for work and for their transition from education to working life'.[18] That resolution again provides for measures to be taken by the Member States and at Community level.

(c) The Council

(i) Vocational training

The activities of the Council in the field of education, which relate almost exclusively to vocational training, can be traced back to the early 1960s. On 2 April 1963 the Council adopted a decision 'laying down general principles for implementing a common vocational training policy',[19] thereby availing itself of the power conferred on it by Article 128 of the EEC Treaty. According to the second principle[20] laid down in that decision, the fundamental objectives of the common vocational training policy are *inter alia* to bring about conditions that will guarantee adequate vocational training for all, to avoid any harmful interruption between completion of general education and commencement of vocational training, and to offer to every person the opportunity to gain promotion. However, the scope of the decision is restricted by the first principle to 'the training of young persons and adults who might be or already are employed in posts up to supervisory level'.

The 'General guidelines for drawing up a Community programme on vocational training' were adopted by the Council on 26 July 1971[21] with a view to reinforcing and rendering more effective the work already undertaken in all aspects of vocational training. In those guidelines, the Council emphasized the connection between general and vocational training, by stating that vocational training must not and cannot be an isolated and independent project but should be

---

16   OJ 1976 C38, p. 1, point IV, para. 22.

17   Resolution concerning measures to be taken to improve the preparation of young people for work and to facilitate their transition from education to working life, OJ 1976 C 308, p. 1.

18   *EC Bulletin* Supplement 12/76.

19   OJ, English Special Edition 1963-1964, p. 25; OJ 1963 No. 63, p. 1338 in other language versions.

20   The decision comprises a total of 10 principles.

21   OJ, English Special Edition, Second Series IX, p. 50; OJ 1971 C 81, p. 5, in other language versions.

based on the achievements of a general education 'adapted at all its levels to the requirements of modern society'.[22]

The 'foundation stone of an individual vocational training policy'[23] was laid by the Council on 10 February 1975. It established, by a regulation adopted pursuant to Article 235 of the EEC Treaty, the European Centre for the Development of Vocational Training, having its seat in Berlin.[24] Article 2(1) of the regulation provides that the aim of the Centre, which enjoys full legal capacity by virtue of Article 1, is to assist the Commission 'in encouraging, at Community level, the promotion and development of vocational training and of in-service training', particularly by promoting the exchange of information and the comparison of experience in the field of vocational training.

(ii) General education

Not only vocational training but also general education formed the subject-matter of legislation adopted at an early stage by the Council, although its legislative activities in that regard were few and far between. Under the first paragraph of Article 12 of Regulation No. 1612/68 of 15 October 1968 on freedom of movement for workers within the Community,[25] adopted pursuant to Article 49 of the EEC Treaty, the children of migrant workers employed in another Member State are entitled to be admitted to that State's 'general educational ... courses under the same conditions as the nationals of that State'. That right is supplemented from a financial standpoint by the Council Directive of 25 July 1977 on the education of the children of migrant workers,[26] which is likewise founded on Article 49 of the EEC Treaty. Member States are obliged by Article 2 of that directive to offer such children in their territory free tuition to facilitate initial reception, including, in particular, the teaching of the official language of the host State. Under Article 3 of the directive, Member States are to promote the teaching to such children of the mother tongue and culture of their country of origin.

(iii) Recognition of evidence of occupational qualifications

The rules laid down by Article 57 of the EEC Treaty for the mutual recognition of diplomas, certificates and other evidence of formal qualifications and for the coordination of national legislation on training are concerned with a special field connected with vocational training. The first reference found in secondary legislation to those problems is to be found in the Council's General Programmes

---

22 *ibid.*, para. 2.
23 See Maaß, p. 27.
24 OJ 1975 L 39, p. 1.
25 OJ, English Special Edition 1968 (II), p. 475 (OJ 1968 L 257, p. 2, in other language versions); see the Commission proposal for the amendment thereof, submitted in January 1989, OJ 1989 C 100, p. 6, as modified by a proposal submitted in April 1990, OJ 1990 C 119, p. 10.
26 OJ 1977 L 199, p. 32.

for the abolition of restrictions on freedom to provide services and freedom of establishment of 18 December 1961.[27]

The Council addressed this question in principle in its resolution of 6 June 1974 on the mutual recognition of diplomas, certificates and other evidence of formal qualifications.[28] It formulated the guideline that the recognition and coordination directives should lay down training requirements which are as non-specific as possible, given that, despite the differences between training courses in the Member States, 'the final qualifications giving access to similar fields of activity are in practice broadly comparable'.[29] The Council subsequently adopted a number of directives aimed at the mutual recognition of evidence of occupational qualifications and the coordination of training provisions, particularly in the field of medicine.[30]

2. The Commission

The Commission's initial efforts in relation to education were concentrated on the field of vocational training, and thus in 1965 it adopted two action programmes in pursuance of the common vocational training policy.[31] In the early 1970s, however, it began to pursue a wider approach, aimed at the development of a general educational policy. On 19 July 1972 it commissioned the former Belgian Minister of Education, Henri Janne, to establish the essential elements of an education policy at Community level.[32] His report, which was based on questions put to experts and other appropriate persons, was submitted to the Commission on 27 February 1973.[33]

From an organizational standpoint, the new importance attached to the field of education was reflected in the fact that in 1973 education was for the first time expressly assigned to the sphere of activity of a Commissioner. From 1 January 1973 the fields of research, science and education were combined in a directorate-general.[34]

On 11 March 1974 the Commission, under the auspices of the competent Commissioner, Ralf Dahrendorf, submitted to the Council a communication entitled 'Education in the European Community'.[35] Following an analysis of the

27 OJ, English Special Edition 1959–1962, pp. 3 and 7 (OJ 1962 No. 2, pp. 32 and 36, in other language versions), Titles VI and V respectively.

28 OJ 1974 C 98, p. 1.

29 ibid., point II.

30 e.g. see the directive of 16 June 1975 on the mutual recognition of doctors' qualifications, OJ 1975 L 167, p. 1, and the corresponding coordination directive of the same date, OJ 1975 L 167, p. 14; the directive on nurses of 27 June 1977, OJ 1977 L 176, p. 1, and the corresponding coordination directive of the same date, OJ 1977 L 176, p. 8; as regards the non-medical field, see, for example, the directive on goods haulage operators and road passenger transport operators of 12 December 1977, OJ 1977 L 334, p. 37.

31 One laying down general objectives, and one aimed at agriculture; see *EEC Bulletin* 7/1965, para. 25.

32 See the report entitled 'For a Community Policy on Education', *EC Bulletin* Supplement 10/73, p. 5.

33 *ibid.*

34 See *EC General Report* 7/1973, para. 369.

35 *EC Bulletin* Supplement 3/74.

situation at that time,[36] it explained the priority spheres of action, namely 'Mobility in Education',[37] 'The education of children of the migrant workers',[38] 'Towards a European dimension in education'[39] and 'Relations with the Council of Europe, OECD and UNESCO'.[40] According to the Commission, account had been taken, in formulating those spheres of action, of the opportunities which presented themselves in the context of the Treaty provisions; in addition, it indicated with particular emphasis the role to be played by education in the process of European unification.[41] It is clear from that formulation that the Commission's approach to education policy is dictated not so much by the formal limitations of the Treaty provisions as by the need for European integration.

3. THE EUROPEAN PARLIAMENT

As in the case of the Commission, the interest shown by the European Parliament towards educational policy during the 1960s was focused on the field of vocational training;[42] from the early 1970s,[43] however, it was increasingly directed towards the requirements of a general education policy at Community level. At its sitting on 8 February 1972 it expressly called for the formulation of a coherent policy on youth and education.[44] In that connection, it was thought to be particularly necessary for European education policy to foster the democratization of education and to centre attention on the idea of cultural diversity.[45]

Just over two years later, the Parliament again emphasized the need for 'a coherent Community policy on youth, education and culture'.[46] During the ensuing period, it explained its view that collective competence for the common education policy lay with the Community and that the Education Ministers should act in their capacity as the Council, that is to say, without the ministers acting as an intergovernmental conference.[47] Following the adoption of the resolution of the Council and of the Ministers of Education meeting within the Council of 9 February 1976 comprising an action programme in the field of

---

36 *EC Bulletin* Supplement 3/74, pp. 5 *et seq.*
37 *ibid.*, pp. 18 *et seq.*
38 *ibid.*, pp. 11 *et seq.*
39 *ibid.*, pp. 12 *et seq.*
40 *ibid.*, pp. 16 *et seq.*
41 *ibid.*, p. 5.
42 e.g. see the resolution of 11 March 1966 on the action programme of the EEC Commission in the field of the common vocational training policy in general and with regard to agriculture, OJ 1966 No. 53, p. 784.
43 But see, prior to that, the resolution of 7 October 1969 on academic research and its importance for the youth of Europe, OJ 1969 C 139, p. 16.
44 See para. 2 of the resolution of 8 February 1972 for a policy on youth and education within the European Communities, OJ 1972 C 19, p. 20.
45 *ibid.*, para. 11.
46 See the resolution of 22 April 1974 on the communication from the Commission of the European Communities to the Council on education in the European Community, OJ 1974 C 55, p. 22.
47 See the resolution on education in the European Community of 22 September 1975, OJ 1975 C 239, p. 15.

education,[48] the Parliament, whilst welcoming the adoption by the Council for the first time of a resolution in the field of education, nevertheless expressed surprise 'that the title of the resolution also refers to the "Ministers of Education meeting within the Council" which reduces its Community status and its scope' and reiterated its belief that cooperation in the field of education 'should lead eventually to a genuine Community education policy within the framework of the European Community'.[49] Thus the Parliament ignored the role played in the adoption of the resolution by the Education Ministers meeting within the Council as adverted to in its title.[50]

III. THE INTENSIFICATION OF COMMUNITY ACTIVITY IN THE FIELD OF EDUCATION

1. THE COUNCIL AND THE REPRESENTATIVES OF THE GOVERNMENTS OF THE MEMBER STATES

(a) The Council and the governmental representatives acting jointly

The sharp increase, by comparison with the previous decade, in the number of resolutions and conclusions adopted in 'mixed' form in the 1980s represents a clear indication of the consolidation of Community activity in the field of education. This finding is confirmed by the lack of decisions in the field of education attributable solely to the ministers meeting within the Council: in every instance, the Council is recorded as having participated in their adoption. It may be stated that henceforth the adoption of decisions in 'mixed' form represents the typical manner of proceeding at Council level where the field of general education is concerned or at least involved.

(i) Education in schools

Scholastic education forms the sole subject-matter of the conclusions of 17 September 1985 concerning the reappraisal of the European dimension in education,[51] the resolution of 9 June 1986 on consumer education in primary and secondary schools,[52] the conclusions of 14 May 1987 on in-service training for

---

48 OJ 1976 C 38, p. 1; see in that regard 'The Council and the governmental representatives acting jointly', pp. 33 *et seq.*, above.

49 Resolution of 8 April 1976 on a resolution of the Council of the European Communities comprising an action programme in the field of education, OJ 1976 C 100, p. 29.

50 In a later resolution, on the other hand, the European Parliament attributed to the 'Education Ministers meeting within the Council' alone the action programme on education which had been adopted in a 'mixed' form; see the resolution of 16 November 1979 on the meeting of the Council of Education Ministers, OJ 1979 C 309, p. 59.

51 See EC Council, *European Educational Policy Statements* (2nd ed., 1986), p. 153.

52 OJ 1986 C 184, p. 21. The Commission had drafted the resolution on the basis that it was to be adopted by the Council alone; see OJ 1985 C 238, p. 7.

teachers[53] and the resolution of 23 November 1988 concerning health education in schools. [54] Mention should also be made in this connection of the resolutions of 22 May 1989 on school provision for children of occupational travellers[55] and on school provision for gypsy and traveller children,[56] and the resolution of 14 December 1989 on measures to combat failure at school[57] and also, lastly, of the conclusions of 31 May 1990 on the enhanced treatment of equality of educational opportunity for girls and boys in the initial and in-service training of teachers.[58]

Other resolutions and conclusions relate to all areas of education, thus including scholastic education, for instance the conclusions of the Council and of the Ministers for Education of 4 June 1984,[59] which are primarily devoted to the various aspects of scholastic education, for example, the teaching of foreign languages,[60] school provision for children of migrant workers[61] and the integration in schools of handicapped pupils,[62] and also the resolution of 3 June 1985 containing an action programme on equal opportunities for girls and boys in education,[63] as well as the resolution on the European dimension in education[64] and the resolution on environmental education,[65] both dated 24 May 1988.

(ii) Transition from education to working life

A further series of resolutions of the Council and of the Education Ministers meeting within the Council is devoted to the preparation of young people for work and to measures to facilitate their transition from education to working life. On 12 July 1982 the Council and the Education Ministers meeting within the Council adopted a second programme of pilot projects in that field,[66] following the extension of the first programme[67] to 31 December 1982 by resolution adopted on 15 January 1980.[68] The duration of the second programme was likewise extended, by resolution dated 5 December 1985,[69] for one year to 31 December 1987. The transition from education to working life is also dealt with in the conclusions of the Council and of the Education Ministers of 14 December 1989

---

53 OJ 1987 C 211, p. 5.
54 OJ 1989 C 3, p. 1
55 OJ 1989 C 153, p. 1.
56 OJ 1989 C 153, p. 3.
57 OJ 1990 C 27, p. 1.
58 OJ 1990 C 162, p. 6.
59 See *European Educational Policy Statements*, op. cit., n. 51, p. 123.
60 *ibid.*, p. 126.
61 *ibid.*, p. 129.
62 *ibid.*, p. 132.
63 OJ 1985 C 166, p. 1.
64 OJ 1988 C 177, p. 5.
65 OJ 1988 C 177, p. 8.
66 OJ 1982 C 193, p. 1.
67 OJ 1976 C 308, p. 1; see in that regard 'The Council and the governmental representatives acting jointly', pp. 33 *et seq.*, above.
68 OJ 1980 C 23, p. 1.
69 OJ 1985 C 328, p. 3.

on technical and vocational education and initial training.[70] It should be pointed out that those conclusions expressly mention the principle of subsidiarity as a guideline for EC measures.[71]

(iii) The field of education in general

With regard to education in general, the conclusions of 6 October 1989 on cooperation and Community policy in the field of education in the run-up to 1993[72] are of fundamental importance. The essential principles of such cooperation are stated to be respect for linguistic and cultural diversity and, once again, the subsidiarity of Community activities,[73] and five objectives shared by the Community Member States are identified as contributing to 'bringing about a Europe of knowledge and culture':[74] (1) a multicultural Europe, (2) a mobile Europe, (3) a Europe of training for all, (4) a Europe of skills, and (5) a Europe open to the world.

(b) The Council

We have established above that the 'mixed' formula is typically applied in the case of decisions referring to the field of general education; as regards decisions adopted by the Council alone, it is possible to make the complementary finding that these concern primarily the field of vocational training in general and the mutual recognition of diplomas.

(i) Vocational training

The way forward for vocational training policies in the European Community in the 1980s was indicated by a similarly entitled Council resolution of 11 June 1983.[75] In that resolution, the Council describes vocational training policy in the Community as an instrument of an active employment policy and as a means of ensuring the preparation of young people for working life,[76] and it lays down measures to be taken both by Member States and at Community level. These require the Member States to implement not only measures of a general nature but also specific measures to assist young people.

The special position occupied by vocational training for young people[77] is also expressed in a series of further measures enacted by the Council, such as the resolution of 18 December 1979 on linked work and training for young persons,[78] the conclusions of 9 March 1987 concerning vocational training for young people

---

70   OJ 1990 C 27, p. 4.
71   *ibid.*, seventh recital in the preamble.
72   OJ 1989 C 277, p. 5.
73   *ibid.*, point 2.
74   *ibid.*, point 3.
75   OJ 1983 C 193, p. 2.
76   *ibid.*, point I.
77   The vocational training of women also forms the subject-matter of conclusions reached by the Council; see OJ 1987 C 178, p. 3.
78   OJ 1980 C 1, p. 1.

in the European Community[79] and the decision of 1 December 1987 concerning an action programme for the vocational training of young people and their preparation for adult and working life.[80] Unlike the previous activities in that field, which were based on resolutions adopted by the Council and the Education Ministers meeting within the Council,[81] the action programme was adopted as a decision by the Council alone on the basis of Article 128 of the EEC Treaty. An application brought by the United Kingdom for the annulment of the programme, on the grounds that it was founded on a defective legal basis, was dismissed by the Court of Justice by judgment of 30 May 1989.[82]

On 22 July 1991 the Council decided to extend and amend the action programme.[83] Article 1 of the amended programme states that its primary objective is to support the efforts of the Member States, 'which are doing their utmost to ensure that all young people in the Community who so wish receive one or, if possible, two or more years' initial vocational training in addition to their full-time compulsory education, leading to a vocational qualification recognized by the competent authorities of the Member State in which it is obtained'. According to paragraph 3 of Article 1, as amended, the concept of initial vocational training is expressly stated not to denote university education. In addition, the action programme was enlarged by the integration of the previously separate programme to encourage the exchange of young workers within the Community.[84] That measure forms part of the efforts of the Commission to rationalize and coordinate the various Community programmes in the field of education.[85]

The Council has dealt not only with initial vocational training but also with continuing vocational training. First of all, in its conclusions of 15 June 1987,[86] it took note of the Commission's intention to propose a Community programme for the development of continuing vocational training, and subsequently, on 5 June 1989, it requested the Commission 'to lay before it as soon as possible an action programme on continuing vocational training'.[87] It stated that continuing vocational training played an important role in the strategy for achieving, by 1992, both the internal market and economic and social cohesion as a determining factor in economic and social policy.[88] Investment in 'the Community's human resources' was one of the most important preconditions for the achievement of those objectives.[89] Following the subsequent formulation by the Commission in

---

79   OJ 1987 C 73, p. 2.
80   OJ 1987 L 346, p. 31.
81   See 'Transition from education to working life', pp. 39 et seq., above.
82   Case 56/88 *United Kingdom* v. *Council* [1989] ECR 1615.
83   OJ 1991 L 214, p. 69.
84   See the latest extension of that programme, effected by decision of the Council of 29 May 1990, OJ 1990 L 156, p. 8.
85   See the Commission's memorandum, COM(90) 334; Written Questions Nos 201/91 and 210/91 of 18 February 1991 to the Commission, OJ 1991 C 144, p. 26.
86   Conclusions on the development of continuing vocational training for adult employees in undertakings, OJ 1987 C 178, p. 5.
87   Point II of the resolution on continuing vocational training, OJ 1989 C 148, p. 1.
88   *ibid.*, second recital in the preamble.
89   *ibid.*, third recital in the preamble.

late 1989 of a proposal for a Community programme,[90] the Council adopted on 29 May 1990, on the basis of Article 128 of the EEC Treaty, the action programme for the development of continuing vocational training in the European Community (FORCE).[91]

The promotion of foreign language competence forms the subject-matter of the LINGUA action programme of 28 July 1989;[92] this makes provision, however, not only for measures relating to the vocational training of foreign language teachers but also for general measures and the like in the field of education in schools for the promotion of foreign language competence, and is thus based on both Articles 128 and 235 of the EEC Treaty.[93]

Vocational training policy in relation to technological change is shaped by the Community programmes COMETT and EUROTECNET, both of which concern not only initial vocational training but also continuing vocational training. The second phase of the COMETT programme,[94] which seeks to promote cooperation between universities and enterprises primarily with regard to training in the field of technological progress, was based solely on Article 128 of the EEC Treaty, whereas recourse was also had to Article 235 of the EEC Treaty for the purposes of the first phase, because the Council was not certain that the EEC Treaty had provided for all the powers required in order to adopt the programme: for reasons of legal certainty, recourse was also made to Article 235 of the EEC Treaty.[95] The majority of the members of the Council clearly no longer had any such doubts upon the adoption of the second phase on 16 December 1988, but reservations were felt by the United Kingdom, France and Germany, which brought actions against the choice of legal basis in the Court of Justice. By judgment of 11 June 1991 the Court dismissed the joined applications.[96] In particular, the Court was unwilling to classify the programme as a research programme on account of its necessarily close connection with scientific research.[97]

The second phase of the COMETT programme was opened up to participation by EFTA countries. In the meantime, almost all of those countries have availed themselves of this possibility by entering into cooperation agreements with the EEC.[98]

The EUROTECNET programme of 18 December 1989,[99] which is also based solely on Article 128 of the EEC Treaty, is intended to promote innovation in the field of vocational training, 'with a view to taking account of current and future

---

90   OJ 1990 C 12, p. 16.
91   OJ 1990 L 156, p. 1.
92   OJ 1989 L 239, p. 24.
93   By reason of these two distinct aspects of the LINGUA programme, the Commission had proposed two separate decisions, one of them being based on Art. 128 of the EEC Treaty, OJ 1989 C 51, p. 7, and the other on Art. 235 of the EEC Treaty, OJ 1989 C 51, p. 13.
94   Phase 1, OJ 1986 L 222, p. 17; Phase 2, OJ 1989 L 13, p. 28.
95   ibid., first phase, second recital in the preamble.
96   Joined Cases C-51, C-90 and C-94/89 United Kingdom and Others v. Council [1991] ECR I-2757.
97   ibid., para. 27.
98   See, in respect of all EFTA States except Liechtenstein, OJ 1990 L 102.
99   OJ 1989 L 393, p. 29.

technological changes and their impact on employment, work and necessary qualifications and skills'.[100]

Mobility in the field of university studies is also the subject of promotion by the Community on the basis of Article 128 of the EEC Treaty.[101] Like the COMETT programme, the European Community Action Scheme for the Mobility of University Students (ERASMUS) had originally[102] been based in addition on Article 235 of the EEC Treaty. This was held to be correct by the Court of Justice in the context of the action brought for its annulment by the Commission, because the decision concerned not only vocational training but also scientific research.[103] The decision of 14 December 1989[104] amending the ERASMUS decision is based solely on Article 128 of the EEC Treaty. Article 1 of the decision as amended expressly states that the ERASMUS programme does not cover research and technological development activities. The main aim of the programme is the establishment of a European University Network for student exchanges, the grant of mobility stipends and the voluntary academic recognition of diplomas and periods of study.[105]

The Council directive of 28 June 1990 on the right of residence for students[106] represents a further measure to secure mobility in the field of vocational training generally. That directive forms part of a comprehensive package of Community measures aimed at extending the right of residence to all Community nationals.[107] This culminated in secondary legislation bringing to a temporary conclusion the efforts of the Commission over a period in excess of 10 years in relation to the general right of residence.[108] The stage has not yet been reached at which it is possible to speak of a final conclusion, since the European Parliament has brought an action for the annulment of the directive on the right of residence for students on the ground that the directive should not have been based on Article 235 of the EEC Treaty but on the second paragraph of Article 7.[109]

Lastly, on 7 May 1990 the Council, with a view to providing support for the

---

100   *ibid.*, Art. 2 of the decision.

101   However, the TEMPUS mobility scheme for university studies, relating to the countries of central and eastern Europe, of 7 May 1990, OJ 1990 L 131, p. 21, is based on Art. 235 of the EEC Treaty.

102   OJ 1987 L 166, p. 20.

103   Judgment in Case 242/87 *Commission* v. *Council* [1989] ECR 1425 (at p. 1458); see more particularly in that regard 'Programmes in the field of education', pp. 125 *et seq.*, below. The ERASMUS decision was enacted on 15 June 1987, i.e. before the Single European Act came into force, so that Art. 130f–q of the EEC Treaty was not yet applicable.

104   OJ 1989 L 395, p. 23.

105   *ibid.*, see the Annex thereto; see also, most recently, the call by the Commission for action in relation to the European Community Course Credit Transfer System (ECTS), OJ 1991 C 116, p. 19.

106   OJ 1990 L 180, p. 30.

107   See the further Council directives of 28 June 1990 on the right of residence for employees and self-employed persons who have ceased their occupational activity, OJ 1990 L 180, p. 28, and on the right of residence, OJ 1990 L 180, p. 26.

108   See the proposal for a directive of 31 July 1979, OJ 1979 C 207, p. 14, which the Commission withdrew on 3 May 1989, submitting instead three new proposals founded on different legal bases; see OJ 1989 C 191, pp. 2 *et seq.*

109   Case C-295/90 *European Parliament* v. *Council* [1992] ECR I-4193; action brought on 28 September 1990: see the notice in OJ 1990 C 285, p. 13; for further details, see 'The right of residence for educational purposes', pp. 122 *et seq.*, below.

countries of central and eastern Europe and to promoting cooperation with them, adopted a decision establishing the TEMPUS trans-European mobility scheme for university studies[110] and a regulation establishing the European Training Foundation,[111] which is intended to contribute to the development of the vocational training systems of those countries. Both measures are based on Article 235 of the EEC Treaty.

(ii) Recognition of evidence of occupational qualifications

In the field of the mutual recognition of diplomas, certificates and other evidence of formal qualifications, the Council initially pursued its policy of vertical measures in respect of individual occupations by adopting, for example, directives in the medical field in relation to the professions of midwifery[112] and pharmacy,[113] and also finally adopted on 10 June 1985, in the non-medical field, the directive, proposed as far back as May 1967,[114] on the profession of architecture.[115]

Subsequently, with its directive of 21 December 1988 'on a general system for the recognition of higher education diplomas awarded on completion of professional education and training of at least three years' duration',[116] the Council applied for the first time a horizontal approach, that is to say, one not limited to specific occupations, without at the same time coordinating training requirements.

2. THE COMMISSION

(a) The field of education in general

The definition of an education policy at Community level, which began during the 1970s, was continued by the Commission in the following decade. It drew up three documents in which it dealt with vocational training and general education in like measure, thereby letting it be known once more that it was taking a comprehensive approach to the education field. It submitted the first document, a report on education and vocational training within the European Community,[117] to the Council in April 1985. That document principally contains information on the measures taken at Community level to implement the action programme in the field of education[118] in 1983 and 1984.

---

110   OJ 1990 L 131, p. 21.
111   OJ 1990 L 131, p. 1.
112   Recognition directive of 31 January 1980, OJ 1980 L 33, p. 1; coordination directive of 31 January 1980, OJ 1980 L 33, p. 8.
113   Recognition directive of 16 September 1985, OJ 1985 L 253, p. 37; coordination directive of 16 September 1985, OJ 1985 L 253, p. 34.
114   OJ 1967 No 239, p. 15.
115   OJ 1985 L 223, p. 15.
116   OJ 1989 L 19, p. 16.
117   COM(85) 134.
118   See in that regard 'The Council and the governmental representatives acting jointly', pp. 33 *et seq.*, above.

That was followed in May 1988 by a communication entitled 'Education in the European Community – Medium-term perspectives: 1989-1992',[119] which prepared the way for the communication, submitted about a year later, on 'Education and training in the European Community – Guidelines for the medium term: 1989-1992'.[120] In the latter document the Commission undertakes a comprehensive survey of the field of education and promises specific measures in relation to individual areas, confirming its decision 'to place education and training at the forefront of its priorities'.[121] It promises in the process to have regard to the principles of respect for the diversity of the educational traditions of individual States and of subsidiarity.[122]

(b) Education in schools

In the field of education in schools, the Commission reported on the implementation of the directive on the education of the children of migrant workers in the individual Member States[123] and on consumer education in primary and secondary schools[124] in accordance with the resolution of the Council and the Ministers for Education meeting within the Council of 9 June 1986.[125] In addition, it developed a work programme relating to the promotion of innovation in secondary education,[126] with a view to adapting the 'strategies and methods of cooperation ... to the evolving situation of the 1990s'.[127]

(c) Vocational training

Specific activity on the part of the Commission may also be noted in the field of vocational training. With regard to vocational training for women, it addressed to the Member States on 24 November 1987 a recommendation[128] designed primarily to ensure the adoption by the Member States of 'specific measures, particularly as regards training, for occupations where women are underrepresented'.[129] A further measure undertaken by the Commission in favour of women was the NOW Community initiative adopted on 18 December 1990 to promote equal opportunities for women in the field of employment and vocational training,[130] which – like the HORIZON initiative concerning handicapped and disadvantaged persons[131] and the EUROFORM initiative concerning vocational

---

119 COM(88) 280.
120 COM(89) 236.
121 *ibid.*, p. 1.
122 *ibid.*, pp. 5 *et seq.*
123 COM(88) 787.
124 COM(89) 17.
125 OJ 1986 C 184, p. 21.
126 COM(88) 545.
127 *ibid.*, p. 3.
128 OJ 1987 L 342, p. 35; see also the Commission's communication on vocational training for women, COM(87) 155.
129 *ibid.*, Art. 1 of the recommendation.
130 OJ 1990 C 327, p. 5.
131 *ibid.*, p. 9.

training generally,[132] which were adopted on the same date – were to be co-financed by the Community from the Structural Funds.

The proposal requested by the Council[133] for an action programme for the development of continuing vocational training was submitted by the Commission in late 1989.[134] In its communication in connection with the proposal for a decision, the Commission specifies three tasks to be fulfilled by continuing vocational training, namely (1) constant adaptation to changes in occupations, (2) the promotion of social advancement and (3) the performance of a preventive function, in order to be able to forestall and overcome the difficulties to which the internal market may be expected to give rise.[135]

A further significant measure on the part of the Commission in the field of vocational training concerns the rationalization and coordination of vocational training programmes at Community level. In a similarly entitled memorandum submitted by the Commission in mid-1990,[136] it developed a frame of reference 'which can be used in future in locating and managing all Community initiatives and actions in the context of the development of the common vocational training policy, based on Article 128 of the Treaty'.[137] The concept pursued by the Commission is intended, *inter alia*, 'to avoid fragmentation of the Community effort' and 'to modify the machinery for following the programmes by simplifying the committee structures involved, thus economising in the number of committees and meetings'.[138] At the end of 1990 the Commission submitted a proposal, in the context of those objectives, for the consolidation in a single committee of the advisory committees established by the EUROTECNET and FORCE programmes.[139]

(d) Recognition of evidence of occupational qualifications

Although, as mentioned above, the Council adopted on 21 December 1988 a horizontal measure for the recognition of higher education diplomas,[140] it concerns only diplomas awarded on completion of professional education and training of at least three years' duration. Consequently, the Commission submitted in mid-1989 a supplementary proposal for a directive,[141] which it subsequently amended.[142] In its amended version, the proposal for a directive concerns occupational diplomas and certificates awarded on completion of a higher education course of a shorter duration than that required by the directive referred to above, or of a longer course of paramedical training in a specialist professional training establishment, or of a combined course of occupational

---

132   OJ 1990 C 327, p. 3.
133   See Point II of the resolution on continuing vocational training, OJ 1989 C 148, p. 1.
134   OJ 1990 C 12, p. 16; COM(89) 567.
135   *ibid.*, p. 2 of the Commission document.
136   COM(90) 334.
137   *ibid.*, p. 2.
138   *ibid.*, p. 4.
139   OJ 1991 C 24, p. 6.
140   See 'Recognition of evidence of occupational qualifications', p. 44, above.
141   OJ 1989 C 263, p. 1; COM(89) 372.
142   OJ 1990 C 217, p. 4; COM(90) 389.

training, or on completion of a study course in a secondary educational establishment.[143] In submitting that proposal, the Commission advocated, while incorporating the occupational qualifications covered by the directive of 21 December 1988, that, within certain limits, the various training levels should be permeable in an upward direction and, in 'accordance with the principle of "he who can do more can do less" ', without restriction in a downward direction.[144]

3. The European Parliament

The consolidation of Community education policy has also received support from the European Parliament, in the form of resolutions adopted in relation to all fields of education. The Parliament set out general development guidelines in its resolution of 11 March 1982 'on a Community programme in the field of education', [145] in which it called both for systematic cooperation on education policy by the Member States[146] and for action at Community level.[147] It emphasized in that regard that such action should not be construed as being at odds with the national governments' competence in matters of education policy.[148] A further resolution of a general nature was adopted by the Parliament on 17 February 1989,[149] prompted by the Commission's communication regarding medium-term prospects in the field of education.[150] The tenor of that resolution is characterized by the imminent completion of the internal market, the importance of education in that connection and the needs which will arise as a result of the new environment that the internal market will bring about.

Other resolutions adopted by the European Parliament[151] are devoted to miscellaneous aspects of education, for example, higher education and cooperation between universities in the EC,[152] student and teacher mobility,[153] education in the field of new technologies,[154] the European dimension in schools,[155] equal opportunities for boys and girls in education,[156] and illiteracy.[157] In addition, the Parliament has not only adopted a resolution on the recognition of higher education diplomas for professional and vocational purposes[158] but has also dealt with the need for the recognition of diplomas for academic purposes.[159]

---

143   OJ 1990 C 217, p. 4, Art. 1 of the amended proposal.
144   See COM(90) 389, p. 3.
145   OJ 1982 C 87, p. 90.
146   *ibid.*, point 1.
147   *ibid.*, point 2.
148   *ibid.*, point 3.
149   OJ 1989 C 69, p. 208.
150   See 'The field of education in general', pp. 44 *et seq.*, above.
151   These are summarized in the resolution of 17 February 1989, op. cit., n. 149.
152   Resolution of 13 March 1984, OJ 1984 C 104, p. 50.
153   Resolution of 25 January 1991, OJ 1991 C 48, p. 216.
154   Resolution of 11 November 1986, OJ 1986 C 322, p. 55.
155   Resolution of 20 November 1987, OJ 1987 C 345, p. 212.
156   Resolution of 8 July 1988, OJ 1988 C 235, p. 189.
157   Resolution of 17 March 1989, OJ 1989 C 96, p. 250.
158   Resolution of 14 November 1985, OJ 1985 C 345, p. 80.
159   Resolution of 14 March 1984, OJ 1984 C 104, p. 64; resolution of 18 April 1985, OJ 1985 C 122, p. 121.

The characteristic feature of the resolutions adopted by the European Parliament, as in the case of the action taken by the Commission, is that they incorporate measures in the field of general education, as well as measures in the field of vocational training, into a uniform concept of education policy.

Chapter 2   → Skip → Ch. 3.

THE FIELD OF SCIENCE

I. INTRODUCTION

It is not possible to draw a clear dividing line between the fields of science or knowledge and education. The institution of the university reflects this fact, since according to Article 2(1) of the German Hochschulrahmengesetz (Framework Law on Universities), their function is to promote the cultivation and development of knowledge by means of research, teaching and study. There is no compelling reason, therefore, to ascribe Community programmes relating to universities, such as ERASMUS or COMETT, to the field of education; yet it is justified by the emphasis which such programmes place on training, and not least by the legal basis chosen for them.[1] Consequently, the field of science discussed in this section is confined to scientific research.[2]

The three treaties establishing the European Community each contain, to varying degrees, provisions which directly confer a role upon the EC in the field of research. The ECSC Treaty (Article 55(1)) merely assigns to the Commission[3] the task of promoting 'technical and economic research relating to the production and increased use of coal and steel and to occupational safety in the coal and steel industries'. The EAEC Treaty, on the other hand, provides that the EC is to have comparatively extensive competence in the field of research.[4] This is clear from Article 2(a) of the EAEC Treaty, which expressly confers upon the EAEC the task of promoting research as provided in the Treaty. That task is given concrete form by Articles 4-11, which together form the chapter of Title 2 of the Treaty entitled

---

1 Both programmes are based, in their present form, solely on Art. 128 of the EEC Treaty; see the ERASMUS programme, OJ 1989 L 395, p. 23; COMETT programme, OJ 1989 L 13, p. 28.

2 The terms 'science' and 'research' are frequently used synonymously; e.g. see Glaesner, *Gemeinschaftspolitik*, p. 55; Schuster, pp. 1528 *et seq.*

3 As a result of the first para. of Art. 9 of the Treaty establishing a Single Council and a Single Commission of 8 April 1965, OJ 1967 No. 152, p. 2 (BGBl. II 1454), the Commission replaced the High Authority of the ECSC.

4 See also, in that regard, Beutler et al., *3rd ed.*, p. 483.

'Promotion of Research'. According to Article 6 of the EAEC Treaty, the Commission may support the research carried out in the Member States in various ways. The first paragraph of Article 7 of the EAEC Treaty confers on the Council responsibility for determining the Community's research programmes; according to Article 8(1), those programmes are to be carried out by the Joint Nuclear Research Centre to be established by the Commission.

Prior to its amendment by the Single European Act, the only relevant provision of the EEC Treaty was Article 41 on the attainment of the objectives of the Common Agricultural Policy, which expressly provided for 'an effective coordination of efforts in the sphere(s) ... of research'. Article 24 of the Single European Act added to Part 3 of the EEC Treaty a Title VI entitled 'Research and Technological Development' (Articles 130f-q)[5], thereby creating a new 'Policy of the Community'.[6] According to Article 130f(1) of the EEC Treaty, the aim of the research and technology policy is 'to strengthen the scientific and technological basis of European industry and to encourage it to become more competitive at international level'. Article 130g of the EEC Treaty affords the Community various possible courses of action in order to pursue those objectives, particularly the implementation of research programmes pursuant to paragraph (a).

II. THE BEGINNINGS OF COMMUNITY ACTION IN THE FIELD OF SCIENCE

1. THE COUNCIL AND THE REPRESENTATIVES OF THE GOVERNMENTS OF THE MEMBER STATES

(a) The Council and the governmental representatives acting jointly

The starting point for activity with regard to research at Council level may be regarded as 31 October 1967. It was then that the national ministers responsible for research met within the Council for the first time.[7] The resolution adopted at that meeting on questions relating to scientific and technical research in the Communities[8] has the particular characteristic that it was adopted not only by the Council and by the Member States' representatives meeting within the Council but also with the participation of the Commission. The Working Party on Scientific and Technical Research Policy of the Medium-Term Economic Policy Committee was given the task of examining the possibilities for Community cooperation in six areas of research to begin with.[9] In addition, it was considered desirable to promote 'the participation of other European States in the measures taken and cooperation given in the areas specified'.[10] That resolution accordingly

---

5   The Single European Act entered into force on 1 July 1987; see OJ 1987 L 169, p. 1 (at p. 29).
6   See the heading of Part 3 of the EEC Treaty.
7   See *EEC Bulletin* 12/1967, p. 28.
8   *ibid.*, p. 5.
9   *ibid.*
10   *ibid.*, p. 6.

marks the beginning of 'European Cooperation in the Field of Scientific and Technical Research' (COST[11]).[12]

The desire of the Council, the Governments of the Member States and the Commission for the implementation of the resolution of 31 October 1967 was strengthened in the introduction to a further resolution on cooperation in scientific and technical research dated 10 December 1968.[13] Most of the remainder of the resolution, specifying the concrete steps to be taken, is attributable only to the Council. Apart from a resolution adopted on 24 June 1971 with a view to coordinating the action of the Member States regarding scientific and technical information and documentation,[14] no further joint activities on the part of the Council and the representatives of the Governments of the Member States appear to have been undertaken in the field of science.

(b) The Council

The 'mixed' form of adoption of decisions has been used only exceptionally in the field of Community research policy. From the very outset, it has been the Council alone which has determined that policy. The first really important resolution was adopted by the Council at its meeting on 6 December 1969,[15] which basically resolved to open up the Joint Nuclear Research Centre to non-nuclear scientific and technical research,[16] and was intended to overcome the so-called EURATOM crisis, which had existed since the mid-1960s.[17] Further developments culminated on 14 January 1974 in four resolutions of the Council which may be described as forming the basis of Community research and technology policy.[18] Of particular significance in that regard are the resolutions on the coordination of national policies and the definition of projects of interest to the Community in the field of science and technology[19] and on an initial action programme of the European Communities in the field of science and technology.[20]

The first of those resolutions is striking from a formal standpoint, in that – unusually – it is divided into six articles. As to its contents, one significant feature is the setting up of a Scientific and Technical Research Committee to replace the above-mentioned Working Party on Scientific and Technical Research Policy of

---

11 Coopération européenne dans le domaine de la recherche scientifique et technique; see Gerold, p. 70, n. 12.

12 See *EC Bulletin* 12/1969, p. 47.

13 *EC Bulletin* 2/1969, p. 81.

14 OJ, English Special Edition, Second Series IX, p. 61 (OJ 1971 C 122, p. 7, in other language versions).

15 *EC Bulletin* 1/1970, p. 54.

16 *ibid.*, p. 55.

17 As to the 'EURATOM crisis', see Stremmel, pp. 16 *et seq.*; Fischer-Dieskau, pp. 36 *et seq.*

18 e.g. see Stremmel, p. 41; *EC Bulletin* 1/1974, para. 1401.

19 OJ 1974 C 7, p. 2.

20 OJ 1974 C 7, p. 6; the other resolutions concern the participation of the European Communities in the European Science Foundation (OJ 1974 C 7, p. 5) and a programme of research as an instrument of forecasting, assessment and methodology in the European Communities (OJ 1974 C 7, p. 7).

the Medium-Term Economic Policy Committee, which was dissolved.[21] This gave formal expression to the desire to pursue an independent research and technology policy. That desire was clarified by the second resolution, by means of two statements: first, the Council emphasized 'that, with the exception of matters militarily or industrially classified as secret, no sphere of action in the field of science and technology should be excluded *a priori*',[22] and, secondly, it expressed the view 'that the various research programmes currently being carried out within the Communities and the various projects to be undertaken in the future should be gradually integrated in the development of the common policy referred to by the Paris Summit'.[23]

A number of different research programmes had been agreed to by the Council in mid-1973, even before the adoption of the four resolutions of 14 January 1974. For example, on 14 May 1973 it adopted an EEC research programme in the field of standards and reference substances[24] and on 18 June 1973 a programme of research in new technologies for the EEC (use of solar energy and recycling of raw materials),[25] together with two programmes on the protection of the environment.[26] A feature common to those programmes is that they are all based on Article 235 of the EEC Treaty. This is indicative of a new policy on the application of Article 235 of the EEC Treaty, decided upon at the Summit Conference in Paris on 19 and 20 October 1972. In the final declaration made at that conference,[27] the Heads of State or of Government of the Member States had given the signal for a broad interpretation of the provisions of Article 235 of the EEC Treaty, by calling for moves 'to make the fullest possible use of all provisions of the Treaties, including Article 235 of the EEC Treaty'.[28]

Three of the four research programmes dating from 1973, referred to by way of example above, took the opportunity to use the Joint Nuclear Research Centre, which soon became known simply as the Joint Research Centre,[29] for non-nuclear research. Thus the Annex to the programme of research in new technologies[30] describes the programme as 'Direct Project – Non-Nuclear Project' and designates the Ispra Establishment as the organization by which it is to be carried out.[31] All of the programme decisions referred to give concrete form to the third Community multi-annual research programme, which had been awaited since 1968 and which was decided on by the Council on 6 February 1973.[32]

---

21 That Working Party was dissolved by Art. 5 of the resolution; the working parties and committees previously answerable to it were taken over by the new Committee.
22 See n. 20, point 3 of the resolution.
23 *ibid.*, point 6 of the resolution.
24 OJ 1973 L 153, p. 9.
25 OJ 1973 L 189, p. 34.
26 OJ 1973 L 189, pp. 30 and 43.
27 *EC Bulletin* 10/1972, p. 15.
28 *ibid.*, p. 24; as to this development, see Everling, *EuR 1976, Sonderheft*, pp. 6 *et seq.*
29 e.g. see Art. 3 of the Council Decision of 18 June 1973 adopting an EEC research programme in the field of standards and reference substances (OJ 1973 L 189, p. 32).
30 See n. 25, above.
31 In addition to the Research Establishment in Ispra (Italy), the Joint Research Centre maintains establishments in Geel (Belgium), Petten (Netherlands) and Karlsruhe (Germany); see Beutler et al., *3rd ed.*, p. 485.
32 See *EC Bulletin* 2 /1973, para. 2231; *EC General Report* 7/1973, para. 363.

In the ensuing period, Article 235 of the EEC Treaty was used by the Council to extend the EC's research policy.[33] Thus it was on that basis that it adopted, for example, on 14 April 1975 a research programme in the textile sector,[34] on 15 March 1976 a research programme in the environmental field,[35] on 13 February 1978 a concerted project in the field of the registration of congenital abnormalities[36] and on 7 December 1981 a multi-annual research and training programme in the field of biomolecular engineering.[37]

In the field of EURATOM research, particular mention should be made of the establishment of the Community undertaking JET (Joint European Torus) by Council decision of 30 May 1978.[38] The aim of the undertaking, established with legal personality pursuant to the second paragraph of Article 49 of the EAEC Treaty, is the setting up the world's largest nuclear fusion experiment installation.[39]

2. THE COMMISSION

The Commission's participation in the development of a Community research policy has chiefly taken the form of communications in which it has drawn up the basic outlines of that policy and submitted draft resolutions to the Council.

The beginning was marked by a memorandum prepared by the Commission for the Council on comprehensive Community action in the field of scientific and technological research and development, dating from 1971.[40] In the introductory part, the Commission described the document submitted by it as 'the basis for all initiatives in the field of scientific and technological research and development' to be undertaken by it in the ensuing years.[41] It went on to note the 'inadequacy of the current structures'[42] and made proposals *inter alia* for the elimination of the crisis in the Joint Research Centre, and in particular for it to be restructured.[43] For the rest, the Commission specified five areas of activity to be covered by Community action, namely basic research, applied research, public services, industrial development, and environmental protection.[44]

On 14 June 1972 there followed a communication from the Commission to the Council on the aims and means of achieving a common policy in the field of

---

33 See Fischer-Dieskau, p. 36.
34 OJ 1975 L 111, p. 34.
35 OJ 1976 L 74, p. 36.
36 OJ 1978 L 52, p. 20.
37 OJ 1981 L 375, p. 1.
38 OJ 1978 L 151, p. 10.
39 See European Documentation 2/1988, *Die Politik auf dem Gebiet der Forschung und der technologischen Entwicklung*, p. 51.
40 *EC Bulletin* Supplement 1/71.
41 *ibid.*, p. 4.
42 *ibid.*, p. 8.
43 On 13 January 1971 the Commission adopted a decision on the reorganization of the Joint Nuclear Research Centre, the aim of which, according to the only recital in the preamble to the decision, was to provide it 'with an organization and powers appropriate to its tasks'; see OJ, English Special Edition, Second Series V, p. 14 (OJ 1971 L 16, p. 14, in other language versions).
44 *EC Bulletin* Supplement 1/71, p. 15.

scientific research and technological development.[45] In the foreword thereto, the then Commissioner Altiero Spinelli explained that the Commission's approach was that, instead of examining what was possible within the framework of the structures then in existence, what was needed was to determine the sort of research and development policy the Community required. Once that point was clear, a concrete programme could be worked out, for the achievement of which it would be necessary to apply 'the treaties as they stand, partly by using the procedure under Article 235 of the EEC Treaty and partly the more complex procedure laid down by Article 236'.[46]

The communication concluded with a draft resolution of the Council and the representatives of the governments of the Member States on the gradual introduction of a common policy for scientific and technical research in the Community.[47] That draft resolution was replaced by four draft decisions and resolutions of the Council alone which were submitted to it by the Commission on 1 August 1973 in a communication entitled 'Action Programme for Scientific and Technological Policy'[48] and constituted the basis[49] for the Council resolution of 14 January 1974.[50]

There followed on 3 November 1975 a further communication to the Council regarding the objectives, priorities and resources for a common policy in the field of research and development.[51] The Commission formulated medium-term objectives[52] and specified the following possibilities for the implementation of Community measures: (1) direct action, (2) indirect action, (3) concerted action, and (4) coordination of national programmes.[53]

In June 1977, three years after the inception of a 'comprehensive Community research and technology policy',[54] the Commission drew up an initial review of developments to date and submitted to the Council guidelines for 1977 to 1980.[55] However, the Commission also considered that it was essential to formulate long-term objectives and priorities and proposed, by way of contribution to the definition of such objectives and priorities, a programme for them for the purposes of forecasting and evaluation.[56]

3. THE EUROPEAN PARLIAMENT

Long before the first steps were taken towards a Community research and technology policy, the European Parliament had voiced the need for a compre-

---

45 *EC Bulletin* Supplement 6/72.
46 *ibid.*, p. 7.
47 *ibid.*, p. 51.
48 *EC Bulletin* Supplement 14/73.
49 See *EC Bulletin* 1/1974, para. 1401.
50 See 'The Council', pp. 51 *et seq.*, above.
51 *EC Bulletin* Supplement 4/76.
52 *ibid.*, pp. 6 *et seq.*
53 *ibid.*, p. 9; as to the first three modalities, see Fischer-Dieskau, pp. 39 *et seq.*; Glaesner, *Gemeinschaftspolitik*, pp. 65 *et seq.*
54 See *EC Bulletin* Supplement 3/77, p. 11.
55 *EC Bulletin* Supplement 3/77.
56 *ibid.*, p. 36.

hensive approach. At its sitting on 18 October 1966, it adopted two resolutions on that subject, one of which concerned technological progress and scientific research within the framework of the EC[57] and the other a common European science policy.[58]

In the first of those resolutions, the Parliament expressed the view that lasting and comprehensive cooperation in the field of science was needed in order to promote the continuous and harmonious development of science within the Community;[59] in so saying, the Parliament used a turn of phrase which echoes the description, in Article 2 of the EEC Treaty, of one of the tasks of the EEC. However, at that time the European Parliament apparently did not yet regard the application of Article 235 of the EEC Treaty as a possible means of promoting the development of a Community science policy, since in the same resolution it expressed its regret 'that, according to the letter of the Community treaties, they allow only limited scope for the creation of a comprehensive common science policy'.[60] Nevertheless, at its sitting on 27 November 1967 it again called for a switch 'from disjointed individual measures to a uniform policy which proceeds from basic research, applied research and development work and is integrated into a programme for the expansion of the European economy'.[61]

The resolutions adopted in the ensuing years were concentrated upon the development of the EURATOM research programme and of the Joint Research Centre.[62] In addition, the Parliament regularly expressed its opinions on the Commission's activities in the field of research policy.[63] In a resolution of 17 November 1977, it again voiced in that regard, in critical tones, its regret that previous attempts at cooperation and coordination in the field of research and development policy had not yet been crowned with any real success;[64] the Member States must abandon, it said, their pursuit of national interests, 'a practice that has been witnessed far too often'.[65]

---

57   OJ 1966 No. 201, p. 3455.

58   OJ 1966 No. 210, p. 3457.

59   See OJ 1966 No. 201, p. 3455, point 1 of the resolution.

60   *ibid.*, point 4 of the resolution.

61   Point 4 of the resolution on a European policy for scientific and technological research (OJ 1967 No. 307, p. 6).

62   e.g. see the resolution of 10 October 1972 on the future of the Joint Research Centre and the setting up of a multi-annual programme for research and training (OJ 1972 C 112, p. 19); resolution of 15 February 1973 on the development of the joint research programme (OJ 1973 C 14, p. 47); resolution of 11 May 1976 on the conditions for a fresh start in Community research at the Joint Research Centre (OJ 1976 C 125, p. 16).

63   e.g. see the resolution of 11 May 1976 on the communication from the Commission of the European Communities to the Council on the objectives, priorities and resources for a common research and development policy (OJ 1976 C 125, p. 18); resolution of 17 November 1977 embodying the opinion of the European Parliament on the communication from the Commission of the European Communities to the Council on the common policy in the field of science and technology (OJ 1977 C 299, p. 41).

64   OJ 1977 C 299, p. 41, point 11.

65   *ibid.*, point 12.

III. THE INTENSIFICATION OF COMMUNITY ACTIVITY IN THE FIELD OF SCIENCE

1. THE COUNCIL

(a) Framework programmes

The latest date by which an intensification of Community activity in the field of science may be said to have taken place is the middle of 1983. On 25 July 1983 the Council adopted a resolution on framework programmes for Community research, development and demonstration activities and a first framework programme for 1984–1987.[66] That resolution is unusual in that it is based on specific Treaty provisions, namely Article 235 of the EEC Treaty and Article 7 of the EAEC Treaty, was not adopted until after the European Parliament and the Economic and Social Committee had delivered their opinions, and is divided up into articles.[67]

In that resolution, the Council took the fundamental decision to adopt framework programmes in future; at the same time, it sanctioned the first framework programme, the scientific and technical objectives of which are described in Annex I to the resolution. Annex III contains 'Financial indications' for the individual objectives, amounting to a total of 3,750 million ECU. The second framework programme in the field of research and technological development (1987–1991) was adopted by a decision of the Council of 28 September 1987.[68] As regards the area covered by the EEC Treaty, it was possible to base the decision on Article 130q(1) of the Treaty, which had in the meantime been added by the Single European Act, whereas, in relation to that covered by the EAEC Treaty, Article 7 continued to be the only appropriate provision. A total of 5,396 million ECU was approved for the implementation of the programme.[69]

The third and latest framework programme was adopted by decision of the Council of 23 April 1990.[70] It concerns the period from 1990–1994, and thus overlaps to some extent with the second framework programme. Accordingly, Article 1(1) of the decision provides that the decisions adopted in order to implement the second framework programme are to remain unaffected and that the remaining decisions necessary to complete that implementation may be adopted. The ninth recital in the preamble to the decision states that activities at Community level must be based on the principle of subsidiarity. According to that

---

66 OJ 1983 C 208, p. 1.
67 For further details regarding that resolution, see 'Characteristics of the resolutions in question', pp. 261 *et seq.*, below.
68 OJ 1987 L 302, p. 1.
69 *ibid.*, Art. 1(3) of the decision; see also the supplemental decision of 28 March 1988 (OJ 1988 L 89, p. 35). If one also takes into account the sum of 1,084 million ECU specified in Art. 1(3) of the decision in respect of research programmes already decided on or under way, as Damiani does at p. 369, the resulting total sum amounts to 6,480 million ECU.
70 OJ 1990 L 117, p. 28.

recital, such activities 'must thus provide added value in relation to activities carried out at national and other levels'.

The resources deemed necessary for the implementation of the programme have been fixed at a total of 5,700 million ECU, of which 2,500 million ECU has been earmarked for 1990-1992 and 3,200 million ECU for 1993-1994.[71] The catalogue of measures, which is systematized to a more marked degree than was the case in the preceding framework programmes, is divided into three parts, entitled 'Enabling technologies', 'Management of natural resources' and 'Management of intellectual resources'. The first part comprises information and communications technologies, and industrial and materials technologies, whilst the second part covers the environment, life sciences and technologies, and energy. The third part is encapsulated by the words 'human capital and mobility'. The largest share of the financial resources, amounting to approximately 39 per cent, is allocated, as in the second programme, to new information and communications technologies. The first framework programme was dominated, as to 47.2 per cent, by research in the energy sector,[72] but only 14 per cent is allocated for that purpose in the third framework programme.[73]

In sum, therefore, a shift of emphasis will be noted; yet there has not been any increase in expenditure on research, if one takes into account inflation and the enlargement of the Community,[74] as well as the fact that the duration of the programme is one year longer than the first framework programme.[75]

(b) Specific programmes

The framework programmes were followed by the adoption of such a number of specific programmes based on Article 130q(2) of the EEC Treaty that they cannot all be taken in, and so it is appropriate to mention only the most important of the programmes which are currently continuing.

In the field of information technology, the most significant is the ESPRIT programme, the second phase of which was the subject of a Council decision of 11 April 1988.[76] For that five-year phase, which commenced retroactively on 1 December 1987,[77] a total of 1,600 million ECU has been made available from Community funds,[78] thus making ESPRIT the EC's biggest single programme.[79] In the context of the implementation of the third framework programme, the Council adopted as early as 8 July 1991 a specific programme in the field of information technology,[80] constituting, according to the description given in Annex I, a further stage in the ESPRIT programme. According to Article 2(1),

---

71 OJ 1990 L 117, see Annex I to the decision.
72 OJ 1983 C 208, p. 1, Annex III to the resolution.
73 See n. 70, above.
74 See in that regard Damiani, p. 369, writing about the second framework programme.
75 As to the reasons for this, see the eighth recital in the preamble to the second framework programme, op. cit., n. 68.
76 OJ 1988 L 118, p. 32.
77 ibid., Art. 1 of the decision.
78 ibid., Art. 5 of the decision.
79 See the First Report on the State of Science and Technology in Europe, COM(88) 647.
80 OJ 1991 L 218, p. 22.

approximately 1.3 billion ECU, thus nearly one-quarter of the total funds allocated to the third framework programme, has been allocated to this programme, which is to continue until the end of 1994.

For the RACE programme,[81] relating to telecommunications technologies, finance has been provided in the sum of 550 million ECU.[82] On 7 July 1991 the Council adopted, on the basis of the third framework programme, a specific research and development programme in the field of communication technologies,[83] to which 484 million ECU has been made available pursuant to Article 2(1) of the decision.

Research and technological development in the fields of industrial manufacturing technologies and advanced materials applications is covered by the BRITE/EURAM programme,[84] combining the BRITE[85] and EURAM[86] programmes. BRITE/EURAM, with financing of just under 500 million ECU, may be reckoned one of the larger Community programmes.

To the field of improvement in the quality of life belongs what is now the fourth programme in the field of medical and health research,[87] the specific research and technological development programme in the field of health: human genome analysis,[88] the STEP and EPOCH environmental programmes[89] and the specific programme in the field of the environment[90] already adopted on the basis of the third framework programme.

Two further specific programmes concern not research but research scientists themselves: the SCIENCE programme,[91] which is restricted to 'the exact and natural sciences',[92] is intended to stimulate international cooperation and interchange of research scientists in that branch of science[93]; the SPES programme[94] is intended to achieve the same objective in the field of economics.[95] Both stimulation plans are intended to create a 'Researchers' Europe'.[96]

The MONITOR programme,[97] adopted on 20 June 1989, plays a significant role in the long-term planning of Community research.

Based on the FAST programme,[98] MONITOR is primarily intended, by means of research in the fields of analysis, forecasting and evaluation, 'to be instrumental

---

81   OJ 1988 L 16, p. 35.
82   *ibid.*, Art. 5 of the decision.
83   OJ 1991 L 192, p. 8.
84   OJ 1989 L 98, p. 18.
85   OJ 1985 L 83, p. 8.
86   OJ 1986 L 159, p. 36.
87   OJ 1987 L 334, p. 20.
88   OJ 1990 L 196, p. 8.
89   OJ 1989 L 359, p. 9; both programmes are combined in a single piece of legislation.
90   OJ 1991 L 192, p. 29.
91   OJ 1988 L 206, p. 34.
92   *ibid.*, see the Annex to the decision.
93   *ibid.*, see Art. 1 of the decision.
94   OJ 1989 L 44, p. 43.
95   *ibid.*, see Art. 1 of the decision.
96   See the sixth recital in the preamble to the SCIENCE decision, op. cit., n. 91; fifth recital in the preamble to the SPES decision, op. cit., n. 94.
97   OJ 1989 L 200, p. 40.
98   Phase 1, OJ 1978 L 225, p. 38; Phase 2, OJ 1983 L 293, p. 20.

in identifying new directions and priorities for Community research and technological development policy'.[99]

Finally, mention should be made of the Council Decisions of 14 October 1988 adopting specific research programmes to be implemented by the Joint Research Centre for the EEC and the EAEC between 1988 and 1991,[100] which represent a special case of the implementation of the framework programmes. Those decisions specify in summary form the contribution to research to be made by the Joint Research Centre in the implementation of the second framework programme, and concern, as regards the EEC Treaty, the action to be taken in respect of 'Quality of life' and 'Modernization of industrial sectors'[101] and, as regards the EAEC Treaty, that relating to 'Quality of life', 'Modernization of industrial sectors' and 'Energy'.[102]

(c) Cooperation with non-Member States

In the field of science, the Council has concerned itself not only with research within the Community but also with research carried out in collaboration with non-Member States. On 20 June 1989 it adopted a resolution on the relationship between 'European cooperation in the field of scientific and technical research' (COST) and the EC.[103] It singled out, as specific advantages of COST, its flexibility and its informality,[104] and placed emphasis on COST's complementary role in relation to Community research and development policy.[105]

2. THE COMMISSION

During the 1980s, the Commission also promoted, through the issue of communications and reports, the impending consolidation and change in Community policy in the field of science.[106] Thus, in 1981, it proposed, in a document entitled 'Towards new Community policies',[107] a qualitative alteration to the previously sectoral approach of research policy.[108] The 'new phase in the advancement of European research and development'[109] was to be characterized

---

99 See OJ 1989 L 200, p. 40, Annex I to the decision.

100 OJ 1988 L 286, pp. 29 and 33.

101 *ibid.*, Annex A to the first decision.

102 *ibid.*, Annex A to the second decision.

103 OJ 1989 C 171, p. 1.

104 See in that regard Glaesner, *Gemeinschaftspolitik*, p. 71.

105 The agreements concluded within the framework of COST are regularly published by the COST Secretariat, which is established within the Secretariat-General of the Council; e.g. see *Compilation of COST Agreements - Volume 5, 1987–1988* (Office for Official Publications of the EC, 1989).

106 In addition to the general communications dealt with here, the Commission has produced reports on individual programmes, e.g. ESPRIT, COM(86) 687 and COM(86) 269, and FAST, COM(86) 10; it has also devoted greater attention to the Joint Research Centre; e.g. see the communication entitled 'A New Outlook for the Joint Research Centre', COM(87) 491/2/Rev.; communication concerning the Joint Research Centre, COM(91) 281.

107 *EC Bulletin* Supplement 4/81.

108 *ibid.*, p. 27.

109 *ibid.*

above all by the definition of a global strategy and the exploitation of the advantages inherent in the European dimension.[110] In the Commission's view, the attainment of that objective required the formulation of a general framework programme for joint research and development.[111]

The first manifestation of a 'qualitative leap forward'[112] in Community research and technology policy may be regarded as having occurred with the publication by the Commission in mid-1985 of its memorandum on a 'Technology Community'.[113] This was followed soon afterwards by a communication on the implementation of the memorandum[114] and in March 1986 by a further communication on 'The Science and Technology Community'.[115] In that communication, the Commission put forward guidelines for the second Community framework programme, but emphasized at the same time that the European Science and Technology Community should not be restricted to the EC Member States. Instead, what was needed was the definition of a technological research and development strategy on a continental scale.[116] Consequently, there would in the future need to be symbiosis between Community programmes, COST initiatives[117] and EUREKA[118] projects.[119]

Towards the end of 1988 the Commission submitted a comprehensive analysis of the situation in respect of research and technological development in Europe,[120] in which it concluded that European efforts were lagging behind those of its major competitors, the USA and Japan,[121] but that Europe could afford, in the circumstances then prevailing, to invest more in research and development.[122]

In mid-1989 the Commission produced, on the basis *inter alia* of the findings made in that report, its considerations on the 'framework for Community action in the fields of research and development during the 1990s'.[123] It clarified the concept of subsidiarity, which it described as constituting, in the scientific field, a 'working principle' and guideline, and which was characterized by the rule that tasks should invariably be performed at the level at which they may most effectively be carried out, regardless of whether it is a higher or lower level.[124]

---

110 *EC Bulletin* Supplement 4/81, p. 28.

111 *ibid.*, p. 30.

112 See Stremmel, p. 133.

113 COM(85) 350.

114 COM(85) 530.

115 COM(86) 129.

116 *ibid.*, p. 2.

117 See in that regard the Commission communication entitled 'COST and the European Technology Community', COM(88) 191.

118 EUREKA (European Research Coordination Agency) was set up on 17 July 1985 at the first EUREKA Ministerial Conference in Paris; see the final communiqué, EA 1986, D 33 *et seq.*; see also the Commission's communications entitled 'Reinforcing cooperation between EUREKA and the European Community', COM(88) 291 and 'EUREKA and the European Technology Community', COM(86) 664.

119 See COM(86) 129, p. 29; for an overview, see the communication entitled 'Cooperation in Science and Technology with Third Countries', COM(90) 256.

120 First Report on the State of Science and Technology in Europe, COM(88) 647.

121 *ibid.*, p. 2.

122 *ibid.*

123 SEC(89) 675.

124 *ibid.*, p. 7.

Further specific and general guidelines developed by the Commission in that document were intended to indicate how the 'challenges of 1992 and the ensuing period in a changed international and scientific environment'[125] could be managed. With a view to facilitating the exchange of information needed for that purpose, on 6 May 1991 the Commission recommended to the Member States the harmonization of databases in the field of research and technological development.[126]

3. The European Parliament

From as early as the beginning of the 1980s, the European Parliament had been calling for the 'establishment of a European scientific area'[127] and for a 'fundamental restructuring of research policy in Europe'.[128] Consequently, it considered that the Treaty needed to be amended, in order to anchor Community research policy firmly in the EEC Treaty,[129] such policy being an 'important potential means of adapting to the transformation of society brought about by technological change'.[130] In a resolution of 13 June 1985, the Parliament drew attention once again to the advantages of a 'European scientific technology space'[131] and welcomed in that regard the participation of non-Community European States in that initiative.[132] The Parliament put forward details of its conception of a European research area at its sitting on 9 October 1985.[133] Its general aim was the avoidance of duplication of work and the more rational use of research funds;[134] in particular, a common research area could also 'help to narrow the gap between the technologically highly developed and less developed Member States'.[135]

In the context of discussions on the second framework programme for research and technological development, the European Parliament adopted on 10 July 1986 three resolutions on European research policy,[136] the first of which calls upon the Community 'to implement without delay a genuine and adequately funded research policy, which will enable it to meet present and future technological challenges'.[137]

---

125 SEC(89) 675, p. 1.
126 OJ 1991 L 189, p. 1.
127 Point 20 of the Resolution of 18 November 1982 on the common research policy: problems and prospects (OJ 1982 C 334, p. 96).
128 *ibid.*, point 8.
129 *ibid.*, point 49.
130 *ibid.*, point 7.
131 Point C of the Resolution on European initiatives in the research and development sphere (OJ 1985 C 175, p. 212).
132 *ibid.*, point 4.
133 Resolution on the creation of a European research area (OJ 1985 C 288, p. 59).
134 *ibid.*, point 2.
135 *ibid.*, point 6.
136 OJ 1986 C 227, pp. 101, 102, 103.
137 *ibid.*, point 1 of the first resolution.

Chapter 3

THE CULTURAL SPHERE IN THE NARROWER SENSE

I. INTRODUCTION

The fields of education and science can be defined relatively precisely; however, the field of culture is more extensive in its scope, and the matters falling within its ambit do not lend themselves to any fixed definition. The application of a more precise definition depends on what is meant by 'culture' in any given case. If 'culture' is taken to mean (as Werner Thieme wrote in 1960) the 'values of beauty, goodness and truth, values which cannot be expressed in terms of money, even though they may ... of necessity have a price expressible in money',[1] that is a relatively narrow conception of culture. If, on the other hand, one applies more modern definitions, one arrives at a broad concept of culture, the contours of which are scarcely susceptible of delineation. Thus the Brockhaus Encyclopaedia describes culture as 'the typical lifestyles of a people taken as a whole, including the spiritual characteristics, and especially the system of values, underlying them',[2] and a still wider definition of culture is given by UNESCO, according to which it is 'the combined spiritual, material, intellectual and emotional characteristics of a society or social group'. In addition to literature and the arts, it encompasses lifestyle, fundamental human rights, values, traditions and beliefs.[3]

This work does not set out to lay down any particular definition of culture, since any attempt to do so could result in the exclusion of individual measures

---

1   Thieme, *Kulturordnung*, p. 59.
2   Brockhaus Enzyklopädie (17th ed., Wiesbaden, 1970), vol. 10, under: *'Kultur'*.
3   See point 2.2. of the Opinion of the Economic and Social Committee on the communication from the Commission on a fresh boost for culture in the European Community (OJ 1988 C 175, p. 40).

classed by the Community institutions as falling within the ambit of culture.[4] Thus, for pragmatic reasons, what is dealt with here is 'the narrower cultural sphere', in contradistinction to the fields of education and science. Accordingly, the narrower cultural sphere encompasses, as a residual concept, all cultural matters which cannot be ascribed to the fields of education or science. This raises the question as to which provisions of the Community Treaties are directly concerned with the cultural sphere outside the ambit of education and science.

It is only in the EEC Treaty that the concept is mentioned; it features twice in the German version, in different contexts. According to Article 36 of the EEC Treaty, the provisions regarding the elimination of quantitative restrictions do not preclude restrictions on imports, exports or goods in transit which are 'justified on grounds of ... the protection of national treasures [in the German text: 'nationales Kulturgut'] possessing artistic, historic or archaeological value'. The third paragraph of Article 131 of the EEC Treaty states that the purpose of the association of overseas countries and territories is to further the interests of the inhabitants of those countries and territories, 'in order to lead them to the economic, social and *cultural* development to which they aspire'. Thus the Community treaties scarcely mention culture at all; they are 'extrêmement discret'[5] in that regard. The Single European Act has not altered the situation, although proposals had been put forward for Treaty amendments in that respect.[6] Yet the development and intensification of Community activities in the cultural field should not be ignored.

II. THE BEGINNINGS OF COMMUNITY ACTION IN THE NARROWER CULTURAL SPHERE

1. THE COUNCIL

As long ago as 15 October 1963, the Council adopted a directive on the abolition of restrictions on freedom to provide services in the film industry;[7] and approximately one-and-a-half years later it adopted a second, supplementary directive in that regard.[8] Steps were taken to secure the attainment of freedom of establishment in respect of activities of self-employed persons in film distribution and the attainment of freedom of establishment and freedom to provide services in respect of activities of self-employed persons in film production by means of two

---

4   A similar approach is adopted by Köstlin, p. 21, in justifying the use of moderation in any attempt to hit upon a definition.

5   Wägenbaur, *L'Europe des citoyens*, p. 447.

6   See de Zwaan, p. 759.

7   OJ, English Special Edition 1963-1964, p. 52 (OJ 1963 No. 159, p. 2661, in other language versions).

8   Directive of 13 May 1965 (OJ, English Special Edition 1965-1966, p. 62; OJ 1965 No. 85, p. 1437, in other language versions).

directives dated 15 October 1968[9] and 29 September 1970[10] respectively.[11] Finally, reference should be made to the directive of 12 January 1967 concerning the attainment of freedom of establishment and freedom to provide services in respect of activities of self-employed persons in certain specified activities,[12] Article 3(2)(g) of which provides that it is also to apply to literary and artistic activities.

Although the directives referred to above are intended to facilitate the pursuit of activities relating to culture within the Community, and thus fall within the ambit of culture in the narrower sense, they cannot be regarded as constituting the beginnings of any 'policy' in the cultural sphere. They are each restricted to a narrow sector of occupational activity in the field of culture and do not fit into any more extensive strategy in that field, but instead form part of the comprehensive efforts made at Community level to achieve freedom of establishment and freedom to provide services for various different occupations.[13]

2. The Commission

The first half of the 1970s saw efforts by the Commission to develop a Community policy in the narrower cultural sphere; these took the form of a working document on Community action in the cultural sector which was submitted by the Commission to the European Parliament in January 1976.[14] Nearly two years later, it also submitted to the Council a communication on 'Community action in the cultural sector',[15] which focused on the 'application of the Treaty in the cultural sector',[16] but also dealt with 'other measures'.[17] The first part concerned, for example, free trade in cultural goods, vocational training of a practical nature for young persons engaged in the cultural sector, the harmonization of taxation in the cultural field and the harmonization of copyright. The measures referred to in the second part included, in particular, the maintenance of architectural monuments[18] and the promotion of cultural exchanges.

The Commission derives the legitimacy of its involvement in the cultural sector from the definition of that sector, which it describes as 'the socio-economic framework of persons and undertakings producing and distributing cultural goods'.[19] It logically concentrates on solving the economic and social problems

---

9 OJ, English Special Edition 1968 (II), p. 520 (OJ 1968 L 260, p. 22, in other language versions).

10 OJ, English Special Edition 1970 (II), p. 620 (OJ 1970 L 218, p. 37, in other language versions).

11 For further details regarding these four directives, see Keßler, pp. 58 et seq.

12 OJ, English Special Edition 1967, p. 3 (OJ 1967 No. 10, p. 140, in other language versions).

13 See EEC General Report 7/1964, points 41 et seq.

14 See EC General Report 10/1976, point 406.

15 EC Bulletin Supplement 6/77.

16 ibid., pp. 7 et seq.

17 ibid., pp. 20 et seq.

18 See in that regard the Commission Recommendation of 20 December 1974 to Member States concerning the protection of the architectural and natural heritage (OJ 1975 L 21, p. 22).

19 See EC Bulletin Supplement 6/77, p. 5.

arising in that sector, as in every other field.[20] What is involved in that regard is not cultural policy, any more than culture *per se* can be said to constitute the cultural sphere.[21]

Whilst the Commission thus derives competence for its activities in the cultural sphere primarily from the EEC Treaty,[22] it also relies in part, by way of justification, on matters falling outside the ambit of the Treaty. For example, it justifies the need for action at Community level to counter the theft of cultural goods by stating that such thefts have become a 'real plague', and that measures at Community level are more likely to meet with success, since black marketeers would otherwise have only to get their haul across the border.[23] The communication concludes with what may, in the light of subsequent developments, be described as a bold proposal, in the form of a draft resolution, to be adopted by the Council alone, for the implementation of action in the cultural sphere.[24]

3. THE EUROPEAN PARLIAMENT

The activities of the Commission described above may ultimately be traced back to the European Parliament's resolution of 13 May 1974[25] on measures to protect the European cultural heritage.[26] That resolution is far more extensive in its scope than its title suggests. In addition to the preservation of works of art and cultural monuments,[27] it concerns *inter alia* the defence and promotion of works of culture,[28] the harmonization of copyright[29] and the harmonization of tax arrangements in the cultural sector.[30] Of decisive significance, however, is the expression by the Parliament of its hope 'that the problem of protecting the European cultural heritage and a number of other cultural problems, for which Community action is possible and desirable, will be included in the agenda for meetings of the Council of Ministers of the European Communities'[31] and the request made to the Commission 'to propose to the Council a series of concrete measures to be adopted in application of the provisions of the EEC Treaty'.[32]

By way of reaction to the measures subsequently taken by the Commission, the Parliament adopted on 8 March 1976[33] and on 18 January 1979[34] two further

---

20 *EC Bulletin* Supplement 6/77, pp. 5 and 6.
21 *ibid.*, p. 6.
22 *ibid.*, p. 7.
23 *ibid.*
24 *ibid.*, p. 28.
25 OJ 1974 C 62, p. 5.
26 In its communication on Community action in the cultural sector, the Commission describes this resolution as the 'foundation stone' of such action; see *EC Bulletin*, Supplement 6/77, p. 5.
27 See OJ 1974 C 62, p. 5, points 12 and 13 of the resolution.
28 *ibid.*, point 4.
29 *ibid.*, point 11.
30 *ibid.*, point 10.
31 *ibid.*, point 8.
32 *ibid.*, point 9.
33 OJ 1976 C 79, p. 6.
34 OJ 1979 C 39, p. 50.

resolutions, in which it deplored the absence of a timetable[35] and again called upon the Commission to submit formal proposals to the Council.[36]

In addition to the formulation of a general policy in the cultural sphere, the European Parliament has also dealt with individual aspects of a cultural dimension, such as the formation of a European Community youth orchestra[37] and the possibility of designating 1985 'European Music Year',[38] as well as the social situation of cultural workers.[39]

All in all, it will be seen that the activities of the European Parliament in the narrower cultural sphere have promoted, even more strongly than in the fields of education and science, the emergence of a Community policy.

III. THE INTENSIFICATION OF COMMUNITY ACTIVITY IN THE NARROWER CULTURAL SPHERE

1. The Council and the Representatives of the Governments of the Member States

(a) The representatives of the Governments of the Member States

The adoption of resolutions by the 'representatives of the Governments of the Member States' signifies, in formal terms, that, of all the conceivable steps which are capable of being taken at Council level, it is those with the most tenuous connection with the Community which have been chosen for adoption: the ministers are not even 'meeting within the Council'. Nevertheless, they act as the representatives of the 'Member States', and thus in a capacity which distinguishes them from representatives of other States and lends special legitimacy to their meetings.

Such resolutions of the representatives of the Governments of the Member States are rare. However, the initial activities at Council level in the narrower cultural sphere were characterized by that form of action. They took the form of three resolutions of 24 July 1984,[40] one of which concerned measures to combat audio-visual pirating,[41] another the rational distribution of films through all the audio-visual communication media,[42] and the third measures to ensure that an appropriate place is given to audio-visual programmes of European origin.[43]

---

35 See OJ 1976 C 79, p. 6, point 2 of the resolution.

36 *ibid.*, point 4 of the resolution; OJ 1979 C 39, p. 50, point 10 of the resolution.

37 Resolution of 8 March 1976 (OJ 1976 C 79, p. 8).

38 Resolution of 18 November 1980 (OJ 1980 C 327, p. 13).

39 Resolution of 16 January 1981 (OJ 1981 C 28, p. 82).

40 However, the ministers responsible for cultural matters have been meeting regularly ever since 1982; see Beutler et al., *3rd ed.*, p. 487.

41 OJ 1984 C 204, p. 1.

42 OJ 1984 C 204, p. 2.

43 *ibid.*

(b) The representatives of the Governments of the Member States meeting within the Council

Between June 1985 and November 1986 the ministers of the Member States responsible for cultural affairs adopted a greater number of resolutions with reference to their meetings within the Council. A great many of those resolutions concerned the field of art; the rest were devoted to other individual cultural activities.

The first category included the resolution concerning a European sculpture competition of 13 June 1985[44] and the resolution on special conditions of admission for young people to museums and cultural events of 20 December 1985,[45] as well as three resolutions dated 13 November 1986 on the protection of Europe's architectural heritage,[46] the conservation of works of art and artefacts[47] and business sponsorship of cultural activities.[48]

The second group comprised the resolutions of 13 June 1985 concerning the annual event 'European City of Culture'[49] and on events including European audio-visual productions in third countries,[50] and the resolution of 17 February 1986 on the establishment of transnational cultural itineraries.[51]

Those measures appeared to herald the end of the adoption of resolutions by the ministers meeting within the Council. It is only more recently that decisions have once again been adopted by the ministers meeting within the Council, acting alone. On 18 May 1990, the ministers adopted conclusions on future eligibility for the 'European City of Culture' and on a special European Cultural Month event;[52] and on 7 June 1991 they passed a series of resolutions and conclusions concerning the temporary access of artists of EC origin to the territory of the USA,[53] the development of the theatre in Europe[54] and copyright and neighbouring rights.[55]

(c) The Council and the governmental representatives acting jointly

Following the adoption of the aforementioned resolution of 17 February 1986 of the ministers meeting within the Council,[56] resolutions have increasingly been adopted by ministers acting in their dual capacity as the Council and as the

---

44 OJ 1985 C 153, p. 3.
45 OJ 1985 C 348, p. 2.
46 OJ 1986 C 320, p. 1.
47 *ibid.*, p. 3.
48 *ibid.*, p. 2.
49 OJ 1985 C 153, p. 2.
50 *ibid.*
51 OJ 1986 C 44, p. 2.
52 OJ 1990 C 162, p. 1.
53 OJ 1991 C 188, p. 2.
54 *ibid.*, p. 3.
55 *ibid.*, p. 4.
56 OJ 1986 C 44, p. 2.

ministers with responsibility for cultural affairs, meeting within the Council.[57] The 'mixed' formula has led to the establishment of a further form of decision-making in the narrower cultural sphere, without giving rise to any general change in the contents of resolutions accounting for the new form of decision-making. As before, the resolutions and conclusions concern a very wide variety of cultural areas, for instance the European Year of Cinema and Television (1988),[58] the promotion of books and reading,[59] the protection of the national heritage with regard to Article 36 of the EEC Treaty,[60] the training of arts administrators[61] and the promotion of translation of important works of European culture;[62] the latter resolution has the particular characteristic that – alone, apparently, amongst measures adopted in the narrower cultural sphere – it is expressly based on the EEC Treaty, albeit not on any specific provision thereof.

The frequency with which measures have been adopted in 'mixed form' at Council level appears to represent a trend towards greater involvement of the Council in the narrower cultural sphere. This is substantiated by, for example, the conclusions of the Council and of the ministers meeting within the Council of 6 October 1989 on the youth card in Europe.[63] Those conclusions concern privileges to be granted to young people in the fields of culture, sport, travel and *mobility* accommodation, in order to contribute to their mobility. They are thus aimed at the same objectives as the abovementioned resolution adopted in 1985 on special conditions of admission for young people to museums and cultural events,[64] with which, however, the Council has not yet been involved.

The growing intensification of Community activity in the narrower cultural sphere during the 1980s is apparent not only from resolutions on individual subjects within the field of culture but also, and above all, from two resolutions of a general nature dated 27 May 1988. First of all, the Council and the ministers responsible for cultural affairs adopted a resolution on the future organization of their work,[65] in which they set up a committee on cultural affairs consisting of the representatives of the Member States and of the Commission and instructed the Commission to implement, in cooperation with that committee, actions decided on at Council level.

Secondly, they adopted conclusions on future priority actions in the cultural field,[66] giving priority to promotion of the audio-visual sector, the book sector, training in the cultural sector, and business sponsorship. On that latter point, a resolution had previously been adopted on 13 November 1986 without the

---

57 Prior to that date, the only resolutions adopted by the Council and the ministers responsible for cultural affairs, meeting within the Council, concerned greater recourse to the European Social Fund in respect of cultural workers (OJ 1985 C 2, p. 2) and collaboration between libraries in the field of data processing (OJ 1985 C 271, p. 1).

58 Resolution of 13 November 1986 (OJ 1986 C 320, p. 4).

59 Resolution of 18 May 1989 (OJ 1989 C 183, p. 1).

60 Conclusions of 19 November 1990, *EC Bulletin* 11/1990, point 1.3.187.

61 Resolution of 7 June 1991 (OJ 1991 C 188, p. 1).

62 Resolution of 9 November 1987 (OJ 1987 C 309, p. 3).

63 OJ 1989 C 277, p. 7.

64 OJ 1985 C 348, p. 2.

65 OJ 1988 C 197, p. 1.

66 *ibid.*, p. 2.

participation of the Council.[67] This illustrates once again the increased involvement of the Council in the narrower cultural sphere.

In the conclusions of 27 May 1988,[68] the Council and the ministers also expressed their agreement 'on the desirability of fully implementing the resolutions adopted since 1984 in the cultural sector'. No distinction is drawn between the originators of the various resolutions, the result being a clear intention henceforth to attribute to the Council even those resolutions in the original adoption of which it had taken no part.

(d) The Council

The activities of the Council acting alone in the narrower cultural sphere can be summed up under the headings 'youth exchanges', 'tourism', 'television in Europe' and 'copyright protection'.

Youth exchanges are promoted at Community level by the 'Youth for Europe' programme, the first phase of which, lasting until 31 December 1991, was the subject of a Council decision of 16 June 1988.[69] The second phase, following on immediately from the first and lasting until the end of 1994, was adopted by the Council on 29 July 1991.[70] According to Article 2 of the decision on the first phase, the programme, based on Article 235 of the EEC Treaty, applies to groups of young people between the ages of 15 and 25 years wishing to arrange exchanges of at least one week's duration. According to Article 2 of that decision, such exchanges should enable young people to develop skills for active and working life as young people and adults in the Community by gaining a better understanding of the economic, social and cultural life of other Member States, by exchanging ideas with other young people and by strengthening their awareness of belonging to Europe. Whilst the programme thus has certain connections with the field of vocational training, it is nevertheless characterized by an objective relating to culture in the narrower sense of the term. The second phase is essentially based on the same ideas as the first,[71] but according to the first paragraph of Article 2 it involves, by comparison with the first phase, a budget which is nominally 60 per cent larger in relation to the same time-span.

In the field of tourism, the Council adopted on 22 December 1986 four specific measures. In adopting its decision establishing a consultation and cooperation procedure in the field of tourism,[72] it set up an advisory committee on tourism, the task of which, according to Article 2, is 'to facilitate exchanges of information, consultation and, where appropriate, cooperation on tourism, and, in particular, on the provision of services for tourists'. In addition, it addressed to the Member States a recommendation on standardized information in hotels[73] and a further

---

67 OJ 1986 C 320, p. 2.
68 OJ 1988 C 197, p. 2.
69 OJ 1988 L 158, p. 42.
70 OJ 1991 L 217, p. 25.
71 *ibid.*, see the annex thereto.
72 OJ 1986 L 384, p. 52; see in that regard the decision of 17 December 1990 on the implementation of a two-year programme (1991-1992) for developing Community tourism statistics (OJ 1990 L 358, p. 89).
73 OJ 1986 L 384, p. 54.

recommendation on fire safety in existing hotels,[74] both of which, like the aforementioned decision, are based on Article 235 of the EEC Treaty. Finally, it adopted on the same day a resolution on a better seasonal and geographical distribution of tourism.[75] In the second recital in the preamble to that resolution, it emphasizes the importance of tourism, not only for the economies of the Member States, but also for drawing the peoples of Europe closer together, and states in the following recital that tourism depends to a large extent on using the natural and cultural resources of a country to attract visitors.

The connection between the economic and cultural aspects of tourism is also expressed in the decision of 21 December 1988 on an action programme for the European Year of Tourism.[76] Article 1 of the decision designates 1990 as European Year of Tourism; and, according to Article 2, its objectives are not only to 'prepare for the establishment of the large area without frontiers, turning the integrating role of tourism to account in the creation of a people's Europe', thereby emphasizing the cultural aspects of tourism, but also to 'stress the economic and social importance of the tourism sector'.

The heading 'television in Europe' covers two different areas of regulation. First, it involves the field of standardization of technical norms. In that regard, the Council adopted on 3 November 1986 a directive on the adoption of common technical specifications for direct satellite television broadcasting,[77] with a view to simplifying the broadcasting of television programmes in all countries of the Community.[78] In addition, it adopted on 27 April 1989 a decision on high-definition television (HDTV),[79] in which it developed a comprehensive strategy for the introduction of HDTV in Europe and declared as its objective in that connection the acceptance throughout the world of the European HDTV standard.[80]

The second area of regulation concerns the setting up of the common market in television broadcasts. On 3 October 1989, the Council adopted, on the basis of Articles 57(2) and 66 of the EEC Treaty, a directive on the coordination of certain provisions laid down by law, regulation or administrative action in Member States concerning the pursuit of television broadcasting activities,[81] hereinafter referred to as 'the television directive'. Action by the Council in the field of television is made possible by acceptance of the assertion that television broadcasting 'constitutes, in normal circumstances, a service within the meaning of the Treaty'.[82] The Treaty is stated to provide for 'free movement of all services

---

74 OJ 1986 L 384, p. 60.
75 OJ 1986 C 340, p. 1.
76 OJ 1989 L 17, p. 53.
77 OJ 1986 L 311, p. 28.
78 *ibid.*, third recital in the preamble.
79 OJ 1989 L 142, p. 1.
80 See in that regard the Council decision of 7 December 1989 on the common action to be taken by the Member States with respect to the adoption of a single world-wide high-definition television production standard by the Plenary Assembly of the International Radio Consultative Committee (CCIR) in 1990 (OJ 1989 L 363, p. 30).
81 OJ 1989 L 298, p. 23.
82 *ibid.*, sixth recital in the preamble.

normally provided against payment, without exclusion on grounds of their cultural or other content'.[83]

The directive contains rules, regarded by the Council as the minimum measures needed to guarantee freedom of transmission in broadcasting,[84] on the right of reply, the protection of minors, television advertising and sponsorship and the promotion of the distribution and production of television programmes. The latter area of regulation requires the Member States, pursuant to Article 4 of the directive, to 'ensure, where practicable and by appropriate means, that broadcasters reserve for European works, within the meaning of Article 6, a majority proportion of their transmission time, excluding the time appointed to news, sports events, games, advertising and teletext services'. European works were to have been given preferential treatment pursuant to the original proposals of the Commission for the fixing of specific quotas.[85] The legally binding effect of the considerably weakened text ultimately adopted was the subject of a number of statements in the minutes[86] calling it into question.[87] The Commission itself stated that the compromise adopted entailed only a political obligation, and not a legal one.[88]

On 21 December 1990 the Council adopted, as a further measure to promote the European audio-visual industry, the MEDIA programme.[89] Two Commission proposals, one of which, based on Article 235 of the EEC Treaty, proposes the implementation of an action programme to promote the development of the European audio-visual industry,[90] and the other of which, based on Article 128 of the EEC Treaty, concerns the implementation of a Community vocational training measure in the audio-visual sector,[91] are comprised in the programme.[92] It is based overall on Article 235 of the EEC Treaty, because 'it appears necessary to promote the European audio-visual programme-making industry as part of the operation of the single market; [but] ... the Treaty has not provided the necessary powers [for that purpose]'.[93] This gives rise to the question whether, if the so-called quota rule had acquired legal significance,[94] the television directive would not also have had to be based on Article 235 of the EEC Treaty.

Until recently, the Council had not adopted any measures in the field of

---

83 OJ 1989 L 298, p23, seventh recital in the preamble.

84 *ibid.*, thirteenth recital in the preamble.

85 Art. 2 of the Commission proposal (OJ 1986 C 179, p. 4).

86 See Europe-Agence Internationale No. 5103 of 4.10.1989, p. 7.

87 See the criticism of this 'secret legislation' in Written Question No. 758/89 to the Commission (OJ 1990 C 97, p. 21).

88 See n. 86, above.

89 OJ 1990 L 380, p. 37.

90 OJ 1990 C 127, p. 5.

91 *ibid.*, p. 13.

92 See Schwartz, *ZUM 1991*, pp. 156 *et seq.* The measures contained in the MEDIA programme for the promotion of vocational training in the audio-visual sector are dealt with in the final indent of Art. 2, which refers to the improvement of the management and marketing abilities of professionals in the audio-visual industry in the Community, and in point 4 of Annex I (see n. 89, above).

93 Penultimate recital in the preamble to the MEDIA decision (see n. 89, above).

94 For further details in that regard, see 'The binding force and legality of the quota rules', pp. 163 *et seq.*, below.

copyright. In particular, the television directive,[95] contrary to the Commission's proposal,[96] contains no rules relating to copyright. On 14 May 1991 the Council adopted its first piece of legislation in that field, the directive on the legal protection of computer programs.[97] According to Article 1(1) of that directive, which is based on Article 100a of the EEC Treaty, 'Member States shall protect computer programs, by copyright, as literary works within the meaning of the Berne Convention for the Protection of Literary and Artistic Works'. The directive essentially contains provisions relating to the authorship of computer programs, acts requiring authorization and the term of protection of copyright, which basically amounts, according to Article 8(1) of the directive, to a period of 50 years after the death of the author.

[handwritten: Software Directive]

[handwritten: life of 50.]

2. THE COMMISSION

(a) Principal characteristics of action in the cultural sphere

During the 1980s, the Commission engaged in numerous activities in the narrower cultural sphere, which may be classified within a framework of Community policy by means of two basic communications dating from 1982 and 1987. The first of those communications was linked by its title, 'Intensification of Community action in the cultural sector',[98] to the above-mentioned[99] communication dating from 1977. It was chiefly concerned with improving the quality of life and working conditions of cultural workers, but also contained, *inter alia*, proposals relating to the free exchange of cultural goods and conservation of the architectural heritage. In the foreword to the communication, the then President of the Commission, Gaston Thorn, stressed that, in seeking to promote the field of culture, there was no need for the Community to involve itself in areas of alien competence; tangible powers had been conferred on it, and there was no cause for concern in that regard.[100] It is once again affirmed, a few pages later in the communication, that Community action is not intended to bring about the coordination of the cultural policies of the Member States; that remains in each case a matter for the individual States, regions and municipalities concerned.[101]

In the 1987 communication on 'A fresh boost for culture in the European Community',[102] on the other hand, Commissioner Carlo Ripa di Meana referred only in passing to the need for compliance with the Treaty, and ultimately justified action in the cultural sphere by stating that it was dictated by 'political necessity and socio-economic demands with regard to the completion of the extended internal market'.[103] The communication is chiefly devoted to setting

---

95 OJ 1989 L 298, p. 23.
96 OJ 1986 C 179, p. 4.
97 OJ 1991 L 122, p. 42.
98 *EC Bulletin* Supplement 6/82.
99 See 'The Commission', pp. 65 *et seq.*, above.
100 *EC Bulletin* Supplement 6/82, p. 5.
101 *ibid.*, p. 8.
102 *EC Bulletin* Supplement 4/87.
103 *ibid.*, p. 5.

out a framework programme for 1988-1992, for which the Commission proposes five action areas, namely the creation of a European cultural area, the promotion of the European audio-visual industry, access to cultural resources, training in the cultural sector, and cultural dialogue with the rest of the world.

With a view to the future development of action in the cultural sphere, the Commission set up an advisory committee on cultural affairs, which was constituted on 8 November 1988 and submitted, a good year later, a final report entitled 'Culture for the European Citizen in the Year 2000'.[104]

(b) Individual measures

Amongst the numerous specific measures taken by the Commission, particular mention should be made, first, of those relating to the field of cinema and television. In mid-1983 the Commission submitted to the European Parliament an interim report on 'Realities and tendencies in European television: perspectives and options',[105] which chiefly concerned the possible introduction of a European television channel, but which also called more ambitiously for a Community policy in the field of cinema and television.[106]

In 1984 the Commission proceeded to submit its Green Paper on 'Television Without Frontiers'[107] which sought to provoke public debate about its concept for the setting up of a common market for broadcasting.[108] According to the Commission, broadcasting clearly could not be regarded in exclusively technical and economic terms, 'even though its economic dimension must necessarily form the starting point for the development of any policy in an economic community'.[109]

Following the aforementioned adoption by the Council of the television directive on 3 October 1989,[110] the Commission intensified its efforts towards the development of a policy in the audio-visual sector, submitting to the Council and to the European Parliament in February 1990 a communication on that subject,[111] in which it set forth a framework for the promotion of the European programme-making industry. As has previously been noted in other areas, the Commission emphasized in this regard that Community action must be based on the principle of subsidiarity,[112] but without going into detail on the point. Shortly afterwards, the Commission presented concrete proposals, which have since been accepted by the Council, in a further communication concerning an action programme for the promotion of the audio-visual industry in Europe.[113]

Finally, in the field of harmonization of technical standards, the Commission

---

104 See *EC General Report* 23/1989, point 714; Written Question No. 2005/88 to the Commission (OJ 1989 C 157, p. 35).

105 COM(83) 229.

106 *ibid.*, p. 5.

107 COM(84) 300.

108 See *EC Bulletin* 5/1984, point 1.3.1.

109 *ibid.*, point 1.3.5.

110 See 'The Council', pp. 70 *et seq.*, above.

111 COM(90) 78.

112 *ibid.*, p. 14.

113 COM(90) 132.

submitted to the Council on 15 July 1991 a proposal for a directive on the adoption of standards for satellite broadcasting of television signals,[114] which was intended to replace the Council directive of 3 November 1986,[115] which by Article 3 was due to expire at the end of 1991, and which sought to achieve increased standardization.

Within the context of cultural action, books are becoming increasingly important as a cultural medium. The submission by the Commission at the end of 1985 of a communication on measures in the field of books[116] was followed some four years later by a further communication, the title of which is a programme in itself: 'Books and reading: a cultural challenge for Europe'.[117] The Commission explained its new initiative by stating that books constituted cultural and economic objects and consequently occupied a position of prime importance with regard to the completion of the internal market.[118]

The communication deals with the various aspects of the book sector, including the economic and social situation of authors, publishing, translation, the book trade and libraries, as well as book prices; but it also ends with a section on 'promoting books and reading'. The Commission considers that such promotion is necessary, since 'in the face of the growth in the audio-visual media, reading is no longer the favourite leisure activity'; this is described as 'a dangerous trend from both the educational and cultural points of view'.[119] It is observed without comment that, as has previously been seen, the Commission itself persistently promotes the development of the audio-visual sector.

In more recent times, the measures taken by the Commission in favour of tourism have been chiefly concerned with the promotion of rural tourism;[120] in addition, the Commission has submitted a general action plan for to assist tourism[121] and has reported in detail on the European Year of Tourism.[122]

As regards the economic situation of cultural workers, considerable importance attaches to copyright, the numerous problems relating to which are addressed by the Commission in its Green Paper on 'Copyright and the Challenge of Technology'.[123] According to its findings, the new dissemination and reproduction technologies have brought about a *de facto* abolition of national frontiers and have increasingly made the territorial application of national copyright law obsolete.[124] Above all, those new technologies are said to foster 'piracy', i.e. the unauthorized reproduction, copying or use of works protected by copyright – a field which is also comprehensively dealt with in the Green Paper.[125]

The considerations expressed in the Green Paper are all developed further in the

---

114 OJ 1991 C 194, p. 20.
115 OJ 1986 L 311, p. 28.
116 COM(85) 681.
117 COM(89) 258.
118 *ibid.*, p. 1.
119 *ibid.*, pp. 18 and 19.
120 COM(90) 438.
121 COM(91) 97.
122 COM(91) 95.
123 COM(88) 172.
124 *ibid.*, p. 5.
125 *ibid.*, pp. 19–98a.

Commission's communication entitled 'Follow-up to the Green Paper',[126] which the Commission describes as a 'general policy programme' encompassing the initiatives necessary, in its view, to be implemented in the field of copyright up until completion of the internal market.[127] By way of initial measures for the implementation of that programme, the Commission submitted to the Council on 11 December 1990 a proposal for a decision concerning the accession of the Member States to the Berne Convention for the Protection of Literary and Artistic Works,[128] on 13 December 1990 a proposal for a directive on rental right, lending right, and on certain rights related to copyright[129] and on 22 July 1991 a proposal for a directive on the coordination of certain rules concerning copyright and neighbouring rights applicable to satellite broadcasting and cable retransmission.[130]

Further measures taken by the Commission in the narrower cultural field concern the problems envisaged, following the planned abolition of internal frontiers, in relation to the protection of national treasures possessing artistic, historic or archaeological value, as referred to in Article 36 of the EEC Treaty,[131] vocational training in the arts field,[132] library cooperation based on the application of new information technologies[133] and the introduction of a European over-sixties' card.[134]

In addition, the Commission has devoted its attention to the financial promotion of individual cultural activities, such as the conservation of architectural monuments[135] and of Europe's architectural heritage,[136] sporting activities,[137] the translation of contemporary literary works[138] and the Eurovision Song Contest.[139] In addition, it has endowed prizes to those engaged in the literary field, such as the European Literary Prize[140] and the Stendhal Prize for young journalists,[141] and has bestowed awards, such as those covered by the 'Platform Europe' scheme, which is intended *inter alia* 'to invigorate local, regional and national cultural life by promoting ambitious cultural events with a European profile' and 'to raise and consolidate consciousness of common cultural roots and achievements in Europe'.[142]

---

126 COM(90) 584.

127 *ibid.*, p. 1; as to the procedure followed by the Commission in the field of copyright, seen from the Commission's standpoint, see Verstrynge, pp. 66 *et seq.*

128 OJ 1991 C 24, p. 5.

129 OJ 1991 C 53, p. 35.

130 OJ 1991 C 255, p. 3.

131 COM(89) 594.

132 COM(90) 472.

133 COM(89) 234.

134 Commission recommendation of 10 May 1989 (OJ 1989 L 144, p. 59).

135 OJ 1984 C 145, p. 4; OJ 1987 C 98, p. 16; OJ 1988 C 308, p. 3.

136 Written Question No. 1577/87 (OJ 1988 C 303, p. 9); Written Question No. 2440/90 (OJ 1991 C 90, p. 51); Written Question No. 2443/90 (OJ 1991 C 90, p. 52).

137 Written Question No. 912/88 (OJ 1989 C 111, p. 28).

138 OJ 1990 C 89, p. 4; OJ 1991 C 86, p. 3.

139 Written Question No. 2911/90 (OJ 1991 C 98, p. 42).

140 OJ 1990 C 35, p. 7.

141 Europe-Agence Internationale No. 5205 of 2.3.1990, p. 15.

142 OJ 1990 C 167, p. 2; see also the 'Kaleidoscope' programme launched within the framework of the 'Platform Europe' scheme (OJ 1991 C 205, p. 19).

3. The European Parliament

The European Parliament has continued to fulfil the role played by it during the early stages of Community activity in the cultural sphere, by promoting the consolidation of that policy during the 1980s. It has adopted a wealth of resolutions, concerning not only all individual aspects of cultural action but also their general development. In that regard, the Parliament stressed in a resolution of 18 November 1983[143] that the Community's purpose is to act on behalf of culture rather than on culture, and that action in the cultural sector must fully respect the principles of freedom of expression, pluralism and national values.[144] According to a resolution adopted on 17 February 1989,[145] however, the diversity of individual national cultures is such that Community action must turn European culture into a 'culture of cultures'.[146] It is stated in that regard that cultural action must preserve the institutional balance within the Community's field of competence.[147]

The resolutions of the Parliament on the individual aspects of the narrower cultural sphere are concerned to a significant extent with the audio-visual media,[148] but also with the field of books,[149] the conservation of the Community's architectural and archaeological heritage,[150] sport,[151] music,[152] youth exchanges,[153] tourism,[154] town-twinning schemes,[155] the founding of a centre for European culture and civilization[156] and, finally, the development of a European leisure policy.[157] The last of those resolutions illustrates once again the European Parliament's role in the vanguard of the development of new areas of Community policy.

---

143 Resolution on stronger Community action in the cultural sector (OJ 1983 C 342, p. 127).

144 *ibid.*, point 1.

145 Resolution on a fresh boost for Community action in the cultural sector: 'Education, culture, société - le chantier est immense' (OJ 1989 C 69, p. 180).

146 *ibid.*, point C.

147 *ibid.*, point E.

148 e.g. see the resolutions of 12 March 1982 (OJ 1982 C 87, p. 110); 30 March 1984 (OJ 1984 C 117, pp. 198 and 201); 13 April 1984 (OJ 1984 C 127, p. 147); 10 October 1985 (OJ 1985 C 288, pp. 113 and 119); 16 February 1989 (OJ 1989 C 69, p. 138).

149 Resolutions of 12 March 1987 (OJ 1987 C 99, p. 172) and 10 July 1987 (OJ 1987 C 246, p. 136).

150 Resolution of 28 October 1988 (OJ 1988 C 309, p. 423).

151 Resolutions of 16 September 1988 (OJ 1988 C 262, p. 208) and 17 February 1989 (OJ 1989 C 69, p. 234).

152 Resolutions of 10 February 1988 (OJ 1988 C 68, p. 46) and 20 May 1988 (OJ 1988 C 167, p. 461).

153 Resolution of 7 June 1983 (OJ 1983 C 184, p. 22).

154 Resolution of 13 December 1990 (OJ 1991 C 19, p. 238).

155 Resolution of 15 April 1988 (OJ 1988 C 122, p. 376).

156 Resolution of 16 September 1988 (OJ 1988 C 262, p. 206).

157 Resolution of 17 February 1989 (OJ 1989 C 69, p. 231).

Part 3

INDIVIDUAL ASPECTS
OF COMMUNITY LAW
IN THE FIELD OF
CULTURE

Chapter 1

THE FIELD OF EDUCATION

I. FREEDOM OF MOVEMENT IN THE FIELD OF EDUCATION

1. INTRODUCTION

Title III of Part 2 of the EEC Treaty relates – as is apparent from its heading – to the concept of freedom of movement of workers and the right of establishment. Both forms of freedom of movement are characterized by the fact that nationals of one Member State of the European Community[1] move to another Member State in order to pursue a gainful occupation in that latter State, either as employees or in a self-employed capacity. As regards freedom of movement in the field of education, therefore, the question arises whether, and subject to what conditions, nationals of the Member States are authorized to take up employment as teachers in another Member State or to establish themselves there with a view to providing educational services as self-employed persons. In the field of freedom of movement for workers, the case-law of the Court of Justice has been chiefly concerned with issues relating to the public education system; as to the right of establishment in the field of education, there has hitherto, apparently, been only one decision by the Court.

2. FREEDOM OF MOVEMENT FOR WORKERS IN THE PUBLIC EDUCATION SYSTEM

(a) Teaching staff as workers

The application of Articles 48-51 of the EEC Treaty to teachers in the public education system presupposes their being classed as workers within the meaning of the provisions referred to. The Court of Justice has dealt with this question in three cases to date. In its judgment of 3 July 1986 in Case 66/85

---

1   The chapter on the right of establishment applies not only to natural persons but also, according to Art. 58 of the EEC Treaty, to legal persons operating on a profit-making basis.

Lawrie-Blum,[2] it held that a trainee teacher must be regarded, under German law, as a worker.[3] It stated that the term 'worker' must be interpreted broadly as a concept of Community law. The criteria for the existence of an employment relationship, the essential feature of which is that for a certain period of time a person performs services for and under the direction of another person for which he receives remuneration, were fulfilled in that case. The amounts received were held to represent remuneration for the services provided in giving lessons, which were of some economic value, and for the duties involved in completing the period of preparatory service.[4] The Court rejected the view that the activities of a trainee teacher are not economic activities within the meaning of Article 2 of the EEC Treaty but are governed instead by the education policy of the Member States. The sphere in which an employed person performs services in return for remuneration was immaterial.[5] The legal nature of the employment relationship between employer and employee was likewise of no consequence as regards the application of Article 48 of the EEC Treaty.[6]

One cannot but concur, in the final result, with the classification of a trainee teacher as an employee within the meaning of Community law, even though the judgment does not make clear what is meant in this connection by the 'economic value' of teaching.[7] Consequently, Forch suggests that attention should be focused solely on the 'training service', or even that the characteristic feature of the services performed be dispensed with altogether.[8] The advantage of that view is that it gets round the problem of how to measure the 'economic value' of the teaching services actually provided by a trainee teacher. The decisive factor for the purposes of classification as an employment relationship would in those circumstances consist solely of the employer's interest in the training of the trainee teacher, the economic value of which will perhaps generally manifest itself not immediately but in the future.

The argument rejected by the Court, concerning the absence of any connection with economic activities within the meaning of Article 2 of the EEC Treaty, is in any event erroneous because Article 2 does not limit the subsequent provisions, but is instead given concrete form by them.[9] Consequently, it is only by interpreting what is meant by, for example, a 'worker' that one is able to ascertain

---

2   [1986] ECR 2121.
3   *ibid.,* at p. 2145. That finding by the Court of Justice accords with the view taken by the European Parliament; see the resolution of 24 October 1986 on encouraging teacher mobility in the European Community (OJ 1986 C 297, p. 158). Accordingly, the Court has not needed to express a view on the question whether any right to equal treatment may be inferred from the nature of teacher training as vocational training within the meaning of Art. 128 of the EEC Treaty; see in that regard 'The general prohibition of discrimination', pp. 115 *et seq.,* below.
4   [1986] ECR 2121 (at p. 2144).
5   *ibid.,* at p. 2145.
6   *ibid.* Thus the Court rejected the view expressed in the reference for a preliminary ruling made by the Bundesverwaltungsgericht (Federal Administrative Court) (DVBl. 1985, p. 742) that the corresponding finding in the Court's judgment of 12 February 1974 in Case 152/73 *Sotgiu* [1974] ECR 153 related only to Art. 48(4) of the EEC Treaty and not to Art. 48 *simpliciter.*
7   That wording has led to the Court's reasoning being described as 'artificial'; see Oppermann, *EG-Freizügigkeit,* p. 14; Forch, p. 28.
8   Forch, *ibid.*
9   For a concurring view, see Steindorff, *NJW 1982,* p. 1904.

what ranks as economic activities within the meaning of that provision. Were this not the case, the rule contained in Article 48(4) of the EEC Treaty, which excepts from the provisions on freedom of movement an area not defined in a fairly narrow economic sense, would be superfluous.[10]

A further judgment of the Court of Justice concerned two foreign language assistants working in an Italian university. In its judgment of 30 May 1989 in Case 33/88 *Allué and Coonan*,[11] the Court, whilst not ruling expressly on their employment relationship,[12] nevertheless based its decision on Article 48 of the EEC Treaty. It follows from that judgment that foreign language assistants in State universities are also to be regarded, in principle,[13] as employees.

Lastly, the Court, in its judgment of 28 November 1989 in Case 379/87 *Groener*,[14] concerning an art teacher at a public college in Ireland, based its findings without hesitation on the assumption that the provisions on freedom of movement were applicable.

The question of the status as employees of teachers working (as civil servants)[15] in the public education sector had not yet been the subject of proceedings before the Court of Justice. However, in its judgment in Case 33/88 *Allué and Coonan*, the Court took the view that it had tackled the question of 'teaching posts' in its judgment in Case 66/85 *Lawrie-Blum*.[16] Although that view may be regarded as too far-reaching,[17] it may nevertheless be concluded, by virtue of the application of the criteria established in Case 66/85 *Lawrie-Blum*, that teachers are to be classified as workers within the meaning of Article 48 of the EEC Treaty.[18] In particular, it cannot be concluded from the principle that civil servants are paid a stipend ('alimentation')[19] that they do not receive 'remuneration'.[20] This is because that principle is part and parcel of being a civil servant,[21] and thus of the legal configuration of the relationship, and that, according to the above-mentioned case-law of the Court, that relationship has no bearing on whether

---

10 See also Hochbaum & Eiselstein, p. 25; Steindorff, op. cit.

11 [1989] ECR 1591.

12 However, this question, which had been raised during the proceedings, albeit not on the grounds referred to in Case 66/85 *Lawrie-Blum*, was considered by Advocate-General Lenz. It was not absolutely certain whether foreign language assistants were employed or self-employed.

13 Provided that the foreign language assistants are not to be regarded as self-employed persons by reason of the specific terms of their contracts.

14 [1989] ECR 3967.

15 In at least seven Member States of the European Community, teachers working in the public education sector normally have the status of civil servants; see Commission of the European Communities, *Conditions of Service of Teachers*, p. 37. The study did not cover Portugal or Spain.

16 [1989] ECR 1591 (at p. 1609). The French text of the judgment refers to 'les emplois d'enseignant', the German to 'Lehrerstellen'.

17 See Everling, *DVBl. 1990*, p. 229; for an opposing view, see Dörr, *EuZW 1990*, p. 569, who wrongly ascribes to the Court itself, however, observations made by Advocate-General Lenz ([1986] ECR 2135 *et seq.*).

18 See also, in support of this view, Forch, p. 30; for an opposing view, see Gallwas, p. 11, who casts doubt on its validity.

19 See in that regard Goerlich & Bräth, *DÖV 1987*, p. 1044.

20 For a concurring view, see Advocate-General Mayras in Case 149/79 *Commission* v. *Belgium* [1980] ECR 3881 (at p. 3916).

21 Goerlich & Bräth, op. cit., n. 19.

there exists an employment relationship within the meaning of Community law.[22]

(b) Employment in the public service

Teachers working in the public education service cannot, however, rely on the rights of freedom of movement laid down in Article 48 of the EEC Treaty if their activities constitute 'employment in the public service' under Article 48(4). The Court of Justice has interpreted that provision in a number of its judgments.

(i) Basic features of the relevant case-law

Whether the Court of Justice has jurisdiction to interpret the expression 'employment in the public service' depends on whether it is a concept of Community law or constitutes a reference to the relevant national law. Although the Court stated in that regard, in its interim judgment of 17 December 1980 in Case 149/79 *Commission* v. *Belgium*,[23] that the demarcation of that concept cannot be left to the *total* discretion of the Member States,[24] it clarified its view by stating that the term requires uniform interpretation and application throughout the Community[25] and that recourse to domestic law would impair the unity and efficacy of Community law.[26] It follows that, whilst the concept of the public service, as referred to in Article 48(4) of the EEC Treaty, cannot be said to be wholly distinct from the conceptions prevailing in the Member States,[27] a uniform meaning must nevertheless be applied to the term in each case throughout the Community.[28] The isolated reservations expressed in opposition to that view[29] are not convincing. If the concept of a worker within the meaning of Article 48(1) of the EEC Treaty is a concept of Community law,[30] a rule *restricting* the class of persons entitled to benefit under the provision cannot be effectuated by rules of national law of varying scope. Moreover, the terms used in the EEC Treaty lend support to the view that they are to be given a meaning under Community law.[31]

As the Court of Justice held in its judgment of 16 June 1987 in Case 225/85 *Commission* v. *Italy*,[32] Article 48(4) of the EEC Treaty, as a derogation from the

---

22 See also, in the final result, Goerlich & Bräth, op. cit., n. 19.

23 [1980] ECR 3881.

24 *ibid.*, at p. 3903.

25 *ibid.*, at p. 3901.

26 *ibid.*, at p. 3903.

27 For a concurring view, see Hochbaum, ZBR 1989, p. 40.

28 See also Hochbaum, *Der Staat 1990*, p. 583; Dörr, *EuZW 1990*, p. 568.

29 See, in particular, Lecheler, *DV 1989*, p. 139; by the same author, *Nationaler öffentlicher Dienst*, p. 130.

30 This is conceded even by Lecheler, *Nationaler öffentlicher Dienst*, p. 129, who goes so far as to state, as the reason for his conclusion, that it would 'indeed be unacceptable if the scope of application of Community law were to vary by reason of subsequent divergences (in domestic law)'.

31 See Everling, *DVBl. 1990*, p. 227; Beutler et al., *3rd ed.*, p. 223.

32 [1987] ECR 2625.

principle of freedom of movement, must be construed in such a way as to limit its scope to 'what is strictly necessary for safeguarding the interests which that provision allows the Member States to protect'.[33] In that regard, the term 'public service' should be considered not from an institutional standpoint but from a functional angle. In its interim judgment in Case 149/79 *Commission* v. *Belgium*, the Court rejected the Belgian Government's view that, in contradistinction to Article 55 of the EEC Treaty, which expressly uses a functional concept in relation to the right of establishment, the concept of the public service in Article 48(4) of the EEC Treaty must be given an institutional interpretation.[34]

Instead, it held that Article 48(4) of the EEC Treaty removes from the ambit of Article 48 only those posts 'which involve direct or indirect participation in the exercise of powers conferred by public law and duties designed to safeguard the general interests of the State or of other public authorities'. The Court stated that such posts in fact presume on the part of those occupying them the existence of a special relationship of allegiance to the State and reciprocity of rights and duties which form the foundation of the bond of nationality. The issue was held principally to involve distinguishing the typical functions of the public service from the economic and social responsibilities which have been assumed by those exercising powers conferred by public law in the Member States.[35]

The functional description applied by the Court of Justice to posts falling within the ambit of Article 48(4) of the EEC Treaty has prompted the question whether the criteria of direct or indirect 'participation in the exercise of powers conferred by public law' and 'duties designed to safeguard the general interests of the State' are cumulative or alternative. In Case 307/84 *Commission* v. *France*, Advocate-General Mancini expressly advanced the view that both criteria must be fulfilled,[36] whilst in Case 66/85 *Lawrie-Blum* the Bundesverwaltungsgericht (Federal Administrative Court) making the reference and the defendant *Land* took the opposite view.[37] Lastly, Dörr advances the view that it is 'not always' necessary for both requirements to be fulfilled cumulatively.[38] In its judgment in Case 225/85 *Commission* v. *Italy*, the Court of Justice then appeared to accept that the criteria are to be applied in the alternative.[39] In that judgment, it stated that the

---

33 [1987] ECR 2625 at p. 2638; see also, in a similar vein, the judgment of 3 July 1986 in Case 66/85 *Lawrie-Blum* [1986] ECR 2121 (at p. 2146); for a view opposing a narrow interpretation, see Meyer, p. 97, n. 1.

34 [1980] ECR 3881 (at p. 3888).

35 *ibid.*, at p. 3900. The Commission provided an illuminating explanation for the difference in wording between Arts 48(4) and 55 of the EEC Treaty by arguing that an employee can only participate in the exercise of official authority when he occupies a public post whereas the position is fundamentally different in the case of self-employed occupations (at p. 3890); see also Bleckmann, *EuR 1987*, p. 45.

36 [1986] ECR 1725 (at p. 1730); see, to the same effect, Advocate-General Lenz in Case 66/85 *Lawrie-Blum* [1986] ECR 2121 (at p. 2135) and in Case 225/85 *Commission* v. *Italy* [1987] ECR 2625 (at p. 2634).

37 [1986] ECR 2121 (at pp. 2125 and 2133).

38 Dörr, *EuZW 1990*, p. 569.

39 This is overwhelmingly the interpretation applied to the judgment by academic legal writers; see Hochbaum, *Der Staat 1990*, p. 589; Sedemund & Montag, p. 607; Handoll, *Foreign Teachers*, p. 38; *idem*, *ELR 1988*, p. 230; for an opposing view, see Goerlich & Bräth, *NVwZ 1989*, p. 330; Lecheler, *ZBR 1991*, p. 100.

nature of the activities in question did not in itself establish 'that the researchers are responsible for exercising powers conferred by public law *or* for safeguarding the general interests of the State'.[40]

In fact, the use of the conjunction 'or' in the grounds of the judgment does not take us very much further, because the relevant phrase comes after a negative formulation, and thus merely states that in that particular case neither of the criteria was fulfilled.[41] Admittedly, if a cumulative test had been applied, the non-fulfilment of either of the criteria would have sufficed; however, it cannot be inferred generally from the fact that both criteria were applied and found not to have been satisfied that that test was used, since the fulfilment of either criterion would have been enough to bring the exception contained in Article 48(4) of the EEC Treaty into play.[42] Consequently, it is not possible to infer with sufficient clarity from the actual grounds of the judgment that the alternative test is applicable. However, stronger support for such a test is to be found in the second paragraph of the summary of the judgment, where it is stated, in positive terms, that Community law does not prohibit a Member State from reserving for its own nationals those posts within a career bracket in the public sector which involve 'participation in the exercise of powers conferred by public law *or* the safeguarding of the general interests of the State'.[43] It should be added that the use of the conjunction 'and' in the earlier judgments should not necessarily be interpreted as requiring the application of a cumulative test – with the result that the judgment of 30 May 1989 in Case 33/88 *Allué and Coonan*, in which the conjunction 'and' was again used,[44] does not necessarily have to be interpreted as meaning that the test must be cumulative.[45]

However, as Everling has convincingly shown, this debate, 'conducted with religious zeal',[46] does not go to the root of the question.[47] The relatively widely formulated requirements attaching even to only indirect participation in the exercise of powers conferred by public law or the safeguarding of the general interests of the State are such that the two criteria overlap in numerous respects,[48] the result being that they will often be fulfilled cumulatively in any case. However, this cannot be regarded as a condition governing the application of Article 48(4) of the EEC Treaty.[49] Instead, what should be regarded as the decisive factor is the requirement, apparent behind the two criteria and clearly thought by the Court of Justice to be explanatory, that the posts in question must form the basis of 'a special relationship of allegiance to the State on the part of persons occupying them and reciprocity of rights and duties which form the foundation of

---

40 [1987] ECR 2625 (at p. 2639); emphasis added.
41 For a concurring view, see Lecheler, *Interpretation*, p. 35; Wölker in: GTE, *Kommentar zum EWGV*, Art. 48, n. 112.
42 See also B. Lenz, p. 100.
43 [1987] ECR 2625 (at p. 2626).
44 [1989] ECR 1591 (at p. 1609).
45 This is, however, the view expressed in Wölker, op. cit., n. 41.
46 See Everling, *Rechtsprechung*, p. 39.
47 *ibid.*
48 See in that regard *ibid.*, p. 40; Goerlich & Bräth, *NVwZ 1989*, pp. 330 *et seq.*
49 For a concurring view, see Everling, *Rechtsprechung*, p. 40; Battis, p. 54.

the bond of nationality'.[50] In a concurring view, this formulation has been described as the 'guiding principle *for* application'.[51] By means of this guiding principle, the Court of Justice has kept its options open as regards developing its case-law further, in order to be able to adapt it to the requirements of continuing integration.[52]

The interpretation applied here is confirmed by the fact that the Court has specifically classified certain posts as falling within the ambit of the public service. In its final judgment of 26 May 1982 in Case 149/79 *Commission* v. *Belgium*,[53] the Court held that such posts included, *inter alia*, certain specified supervisory activities as well as the post of municipal night watchman.[54] However, the work of a night watchman, at the very least, can hardly be described as involving the safeguarding of the general interests of the State.[55] In Case 225/85 *Commission* v. *Italy*, the Court found that, within the Italian National Research Council, only the duties of management or of advising the State fell within the exception laid down by Article 48(4) of the EEC Treaty.[56] Even advisory duties could hardly be regarded as constituting indirect participation in the exercise of powers conferred by public law.[57]

(ii) Teaching as employment in the public service

Only in two cases has the Court of Justice decided the question whether Article 48(4) of the EEC Treaty can be applied to teaching in the public education sector. In its judgment in Case 66/85 *Lawrie-Blum*, it summarily held that the 'very strict conditions' of Article 48(4) were not fulfilled in the case of a trainee teacher, 'even if he does in fact take the decisions described by (the defendant in the proceedings before the national court)'.[58] In the last half of that sentence, the Court was referring to the participation by the trainee teacher, as submitted by the defendant Land, in measures taken in daily school life which constituted administrative acts.[59] One can only speculate on the grounds for that decision.[60]

The statements made in the Court's judgment in Case 33/88 *Allué and Coonan* are still more surprising. In that case, it held that foreign language assistants at a university were not covered by Article 48(4) of the EEC Treaty, on the ground that it had previously stated, in Case 66/85 *Lawrie-Blum*, that *teaching posts* did not fulfil the criteria laid down by it.[61] In paragraph 1 of the summary of the case, it is

---

50　e.g. see [1980] ECR 3881 (at p. 3900). In the judgment in Case 33/88 *Allué and Coonan* this formulation is apparently applied as an independent third criterion; see Case 33/88 [1989] ECR 1591 (at p. 1609).

51　Handoll, *ELR 1988*, p. 231; see also B. Lenz, pp. 98 *et seq.*

52　Handoll, *ibid.*

53　[1982] ECR 1845.

54　*ibid.*, at p. 1851.

55　According to Everling, *Rechtsprechung*, p. 40.

56　[1987] ECR 2625 (at p. 2639).

57　For a concurring view, see Handoll, *ELR 1988*, p. 230; for an opposing view, see Wölker in: GTE, *Kommentar zum EWGV*, Art. 48, n. 112.

58　[1986] ECR 2121 (at p. 2147).

59　*ibid.*, at pp. 2133 *et seq.*

60　For further details in that regard, see Forch, p. 29.

61　[1989] ECR 1591 (at p. 1609).

even stated *expressis verbis* that 'employment as a teacher, in general, and as a foreign-language assistant at a university, in particular', does not fulfil the conditions laid down by Article 48(4) of the EEC Treaty. In so finding, the Court attached to its judgment in Case 66/85 *Lawrie-Blum* a meaning which no-one had previously attributed to it.[62] However, since the Court relied, as described above, on its judgment in Case 66/85 *Lawrie-Blum*, it is reasonable to assume that the classification of teaching posts as 'employment in the public service' may be precluded on the same grounds as were applied in the previous case for the exclusion therefrom of the activities of trainee teachers. In the final analysis, the case-law appears broadly to reflect the view advanced by Advocate-General Lenz in Case 66/85 *Lawrie-Blum*, to the effect that Article 48(4) covers, in the public education sector, only activities concerned 'with the basic pedagogical direction of teaching or its general structure', and not individual measures taken by teachers in daily school life.[63]

It follows, therefore, that teaching staff in the public education sector basically enjoy the right of freedom of movement. Support for this view is to be found in the document entitled 'Commission action in respect of the application of Article 48(4) of the EEC Treaty', in which the Commission advances the view that teaching in State educational establishments would 'only very rarely' be covered by the exception in Article 48(4) of the Treaty.[64]

(iii) Conclusions

It may generally be concluded that teachers from other Member States may not, by reason of their nationality, be treated differently from nationals of the host State, on the basis of Article 48(2) of the EEC Treaty, as regards employment, remuneration and other working conditions. The same applies in respect of indirect discrimination.[65] In applying those principles, the Court of Justice held in Case 33/88 *Allué and Coonan* that the imposition of a limit on the duration of the employment of foreign-language assistants constituted indirect discrimination based on nationality, where there was in principle no such limit for other workers and (only) 25 per cent of foreign-language assistants working in Italian universities were Italian nationals. The factual reasons advanced could not justify limiting the contracts of other nationals.[66]

On the other hand, the plaintiff in the main proceedings in Case 379/87 *Groener* was unsuccessful. The Court of Justice considered that knowledge of the Irish language as a condition of employment as an art teacher in a college was covered by

---

62 See the views expressed by Everling, *DVBl. 1990*, p. 229; Weberling, p. 134.

63 [1986] ECR 2121 (at p. 2135).

64 OJ 1988 C 72, p. 2; for a critique of the action, see Hochbaum, *ZBR 1989*, pp. 33 *et seq.*; BR-Drs. 80/88 (decision) of 18 March 1988; BR-Drs. 178/88 (decision) of 10 March 1989; for an opposing view, see Schmidhuber, p. 109.

65 Rules in respect of access to employment are expressly laid down in the second indent of Art. 3(1) of Regulation 1612/68 (OJ, English Special Edition 1968 (II), p. 475; OJ 1968 L 257, p. 2, in other language versions); apart from that, see the judgment of the Court of Justice in Case 33/88 *Allué and Coonan* [1989] ECR 1591 (at pp. 1610).

66 [1989] ECR 1591 (at pp. 1610 *et seq.*).

the second subparagraph of Article 3(1) of Regulation 1612/68, and that it was thus permissible provided that the requirement in question was 'imposed as part of a policy for the promotion of the national language which is, at the same time, the first official language and provided that that requirement is applied in a proportionate and non-discriminatory manner'.[67]

However, the Court of Justice has not clarified the question whether it is permissible in the Federal Republic of Germany to continue to apply the nationality requirement in relation to appointments to posts having civil service status.[68] The answer depends on whether the Court would be prepared to find that the engagement of foreign teachers on the basis of a contract of employment sufficed with regard to Article 48(2) of the EEC Treaty.[69] Certain indications can be derived in that regard, however, from the judgments of the Court in Cases 307/84 *Commission* v. *France* and 225/85 *Commission* v. *Italy*. In the first of those judgments, the Court held that engagement as an employee was enough, provided that it was subject to rules by which the employee enjoyed 'advantages and safeguards which were in every respect equivalent to those deriving from the status of members of the established staff, which is reserved to French nationals'.[70] A similar view was expressed in the second of those judgments.[71] The Court's rulings are thus based on the actual comparability of legal relationships. Consequently, the difference between employees and civil servants under constitutional law cannot be the sole deciding factor.[72]

3. The Right of Establishment for Teachers and Educational Agencies

(a) Applicability of the provisions concerning the right of establishment

The second paragraph of Article 52 of the EEC Treaty restricts the right of establishment for nationals of the Member States to take up and pursue activities as self-employed persons. Consequently, it excludes those activities which are not conducted for gain.[73] By analogy, Article 58 provides that the rules relating to freedom of establishment do not apply to companies or firms governed by public or private law which do not carry on business on a commercial basis. The concept of carrying on business on a commercial basis is subject to a wide interpretation

---

67 [1989] ECR 3967 (at p. 3995); as to the (limited) significance of that judgment, see the review of it by McMahon, p. 129.

68 See § 4(1)(1) of the BRRG (framework law on the civil service).

69 For a sceptical view, see Magiera, *DÖV 1987*, p. 227; Everling, *Rechtsprechung*, p. 42; for a dissenting view, see Lecheler, *ZBR 1991*, p. 101; Dörr, *EuZW 1990*, p. 571; see also in that regard the reference for a preliminary ruling made by order of the Elmshorn Labour Court of 28 September 1990 in Case C-332/90 *Steen* (OJ 1990 C 310, p. 13), concerning the question whether it constitutes reverse discrimination, contrary to Community law, for a German national to be offered a post carrying only civil servant status where that post would have had to be offered to a national of another Member State on the basis of a contract of employment.

70 [1986] ECR 1725 (at p. 1739).

71 [1987] ECR 2625 (at p. 2640).

72 Battis points this out as a possibility on p. 57.

73 Randelzhofer in: Grabitz, *Kommentar zum EWGV*, Art. 52, n. 13.

and does not necessarily entail any profit-making intention.[74] All that is required is the payment of consideration for the service provided.[75] Nor should Article 60 of the EEC Treaty be overlooked; this confirms that economic activities, within the meaning of Article 2 of the Treaty, are to include activities of the professions which are primarily carried on not with a view to profit but by virtue of a 'commitment to the performance of professional functions'.[76] Consequently, the provisions of Articles 52 et seq. of the Treaty are also applicable to self-employed activities in the field of education which constitute activities of the professions.[77] This was confirmed by the Court of Justice in its judgment of 15 March 1988 in Case 147/86 *Commission* v. *Greece*,[78] since it applied the rules on freedom of establishment to the setting up of private educational establishments and to the giving of private lessons at home.

However, the Court held that it would not be contrary to Community law to prohibit the setting up of private schools generally, even by nationals of the Member State in question.[79] This clearly shows that Article 52 of the Treaty requires only that nationals of other Member States be treated in the same way as nationals of the home State; it does not – unlike the rules on the free movement of goods and freedom to provide services[80] – contain any general prohibition against the imposition of restrictions.[81] It is true that Article 52 of the Treaty prohibits not only formal (i.e. overt) discrimination but also substantive (i.e. covert or indirect) discrimination.[82] However, where there is a total prohibition against the carrying on of the activity in question by the State's own nationals and by nationals of other States alike, no discrimination can be said to exist either formally or substantively. Such restrictions based on constitutional or, as the case may be, ordinary law must therefore be accepted or, if need be, removed by way of harmonization.[83]

(b) Restriction of freedom of establishment pursuant to Article 55 of the EEC Treaty

Article 55 of the EEC Treaty precludes the application of the chapter on freedom of establishment to activities 'which in [a Member State] are connected, even

---

74   Everling, *Niederlassungsrecht*, p. 15.

75   Randelzhofer, op. cit., n. 73, Art. 52, n. 15; Skouris, p. 25.

76   Randelzhofer, *ibid.*

77   See Scherer, p. 159; de Crayencour, p. 140.

78   [1988] ECR 1637.

79   *ibid.*, at p. 1655.

80   See in that regard 'Principles', pp. 139 et seq., and 'Permissible restrictions on the free movement of television broadcasts', pp 157 et seq., below.

81   See Troberg in: GTE, *Kommentar zum EWGV*, Art. 52, n. 38; for a critical view, see Steindorff, *EuR 1988*, pp. 19 et seq.

82   e.g. see the judgment of the Court of Justice of 7 May 1991 in Case C-340/89 *Vlassopoulou* [1991] ECR I-2357, in which it stated that a Member State to which an application for admission to a regulated profession is made by a national of another Member State is required to examine to what extent the knowledge and qualifications attested by the diploma obtained by the person concerned in his country of origin correspond to those required by the rules of the host State; see also the judgment of 28 April 1977 in Case 71/76 *Thieffry* [1977] ECR 765.

83   See Skouris, p. 24.

occasionally, with the exercise of official authority'. In Case 147/86 *Commission* v. *Greece*, the Hellenic Republic relied upon that provision in seeking to justify restrictions on freedom of establishment in the field of education. It contended that it was for the Member States to define which activities were connected with the exercise of official authority. In Greece's view, education was a fundamental duty of the State. If private persons carried on activities in that sphere, they did so as repositories of State authority.[84]

The Court accepted the basic point underlying that line of argument and concurred with Greece inasmuch as 'it is for each Member State to determine the role of, and the responsibilities attaching to, official authority with regard to instruction'. It went on to find, however, that the setting up of schools of the type at issue and the giving of private lessons at home were not connected with the exercise of official authority within the meaning of Article 55 of the Treaty.[85] In the ultimate analysis, the Court thereby confirmed the interpretation of Article 55 of the Treaty adopted in the judgment of 21 June 1974 in Case 2/74 *Reyners*,[86] in which it had held that the exceptions allowed by Article 55 could not be given a scope which would exceed the objective for which they were inserted. It stated that Article 55 concerned only those activities 'which, taken on their own, constitute a direct and specific connexion with the exercise of official authority'.[87] It added, however, that possible recourse to Article 55 must be considered separately in connection with each Member State, having regard to the national provisions applicable to the organization and exercise of the profession in question.[88]

That latter *dictum* was relied upon by Greece in Case 147/86 *Commission* v. *Greece* in support of its argument that the criteria inherent in the concept of official authority may not be the same in all the Member States.[89] This is based on a misunderstanding.[90] In its judgment in Case 2/74 *Reyners*, the Court of Justice referred only to the various rules governing professions which have not yet been harmonized. Only in so far as those rules *actually* provide that specific activities[91] are connected with the exercise of official authority can Article 55 apply. It is not enough merely to rely on a constitutional provision of the type described – or merely to *maintain*, so to speak, that an activity falls within the exercise of official authority.

Consequently, each Member State is free to specify which activities it wishes to link to the exercise of official authority; but Member States are not free to determine what is to be regarded as official authority.[92] The Court of Justice has held that the concept of official authority in the first paragraph of Article 55 of the

---

84 [1988] ECR 1637 (at p. 1654).
85 *ibid.*
86 [1974] ECR 631.
87 *ibid.*, at p. 654.
88 *ibid.*, at p. 655.
89 [1988] ECR 1637 (at p. 1642).
90 Tomuschat, *ZaöRV 1967*, pp. 67 *et seq.*, demonstrates that the notion of 'official authority' in Art. 55 of the EEC Treaty is a concept of Community law, not a reference to the understanding applied to the term by the Member States.
91 Art. 55 of the EEC Treaty refers to individual activities, not professions; see Scheuing, *JZ 1975*, p. 154; for an opposing view, see Tomuschat, *op. cit.*, pp. 70 *et seq.*
92 See also, to that effect, Troberg in: GTE, *Kommentar zum EWGV*, Art. 55, n. 3.

Treaty must be limited in scope to those restrictions on freedom of establishment which are strictly necessary in order to safeguard the interests which it allows the Member States to protect.[93] In Case 147/86 *Commission* v. *Greece*, it did not consider that that criterion was satisfied, since the Greek State had at its disposal appropriate means for ensuring, by means of supervision of the private activities at issue, the protection of its interests.[94]

II. EDUCATION RIGHTS DERIVING FROM THE EXERCISE OF FREEDOM OF MOVEMENT

1. INTRODUCTION

(a) The problem

The exercise of the two forms of freedom of movement laid down by the Treaty[95] is intended primarily to lead to the integration of the nationals of the Member States concerned into the economic life of the host State. However, such integration of workers could in practice render the right to freedom of movement nugatory if a person working in one Member State had to leave his family behind in his home State. Consequently, Article 10(1) of Council Regulation No. 1612/68 of 15 October 1968 on freedom of movement for workers within the Community[96] provides that the spouse of a worker and their descendants aged under 21 are to have the right to install themselves with that worker, as well as children aged over 21 and other relatives of the worker or of his spouse to whom he provides accommodation. A similar rule is laid down by the Council directive of 21 May 1973 on the abolition of restrictions on movement and residence within the Community for nationals of Member States with regard to establishment and the provision of services,[97] Article 1(1)(c) and (d) of which applies to relatives of self-employed persons.

If, therefore, migrant workers and self-employed persons, together with members of their families, have the right to establish themselves permanently in another Member State of the Community, the question arises as to what further rights they have as regards integration in the host State in a capacity going beyond the purely economic sphere. This is discussed below in the light of the rights to education enjoyed by migrant workers and those entitled to freedom of establishment, together with members of their families.

---

93 [1988] ECR 1637 (at p. 1654).
94 *ibid.*, at p. 1655.
95 See in that regard 'Introduction', p. 81, above.
96 OJ, English Special Edition 1968 (II), p. 475 (OJ 1968 L 257, p. 2, in other language versions).
97 OJ 1973 L 172, p. 14.

(b) Rules laid down by Community secondary legislation

Freedom of movement for workers is governed by several regulations and directives which exhibit links with the educational rights of migrant workers and members of their families. Central to these is Regulation No. 1612/68, cited above,[98] Article 7 of which, dealing with equal treatment for any worker employed in another Member State, provides in paragraphs (2) and (3) as follows:

'2. He shall enjoy the same social and tax advantages as national workers.
3. He shall also, by virtue of the same right and under the same conditions as national workers, have access to training in vocational schools and retraining centres'.

Article 12 lays down the following rules in favour of the children of migrant workers:

'The children of a national of a Member State who is or has been employed in the territory of another Member State shall be admitted to that State's general educational, apprenticeship and vocational training courses under the same conditions as the nationals of that State, if such children are residing in its territory. Member States shall encourage all efforts to enable such children to attend these courses under the best possible conditions'.

Mention should also be made of Commission Regulation No. 1251/70 of 29 June 1970 on the right of workers to remain in the territory of a Member State after having been employed in that State.[99] Article 7 of that regulation is of particular significance:

'The right to equality of treatment, established by Council Regulation (EEC) No. 1612/68, shall apply also to persons coming under the provisions of this Regulation.'

Finally, attention is drawn to the Council directive of 25 July 1977 on the education of the children of migrant workers.[100]
In the field of the right of establishment there exist, it is true, a Council directive on the abolition of restrictions on movement and residence for nationals of Member States[101] and a further Council directive concerning the right of nationals of a Member State to remain in the territory of another Member State after having pursued therein an activity in a self-employed capacity.[102] However, those measures contain no provisions comparable with those adopted in the field

---

98   At n. 96; see also the Commission's proposal for an amendment of 11 January 1989 (OJ 1989 C 100, p. 6), as modified on 11 April 1990 (OJ 1990 C 119, p. 10); see in that regard Gesser, pp. 435 *et seq.*
99   OJ, English Special Edition 1970 (II), p. 402 (OJ 1970 L 142, p. 24, in other language versions).
100 OJ 1977 L 199, p. 32.
101 Directive of 21 May 1973 (OJ 1973 L 172, p. 14).
102 Directive of 17 December 1974 (OJ 1975 L 14, p. 10).

of freedom of movement for workers. Mention need only be made of Article 7 of the latter directive:

'Member States shall apply to persons having the right to remain in their territory the right of equality of treatment recognized by the Council Directives on the abolition of restrictions on freedom of establishment pursuant to Title III of the General Programme which provides for such abolition.'

In so stating, that provision refers to the General Programme for the abolition of restrictions on freedom of establishment of 18 December 1961,[103] which provides in Title III *inter alia*:

'Such restrictive provisions and practices are in particular those which, in respect of foreign nationals only ... prohibit or hinder access to any vocational training which is necessary or useful for the pursuit of an activity as a self-employed person'.

It is apparent, therefore, that secondary Community legislation, at least in the field of freedom of movement for workers, is not restricted to the abolition of legal barriers to the taking up of an occupation, but is also aimed at the removal of more extensive *de facto* barriers in the social and cultural fields.[104]

2. THE RIGHTS OF MIGRANT WORKERS AND OF MEMBERS OF THEIR FAMILIES

(a) Migrant workers

The nature and scope of migrant workers' educational rights are apparent from Article 7(2) and (3) of Regulation No. 1612/68, cited above, as interpreted, in particular, by the Court of Justice. It is appropriate to begin with an examination of Article 7(3), since that provision is, by its very wording, more closely connected with the field of education.

(i) Article 7(3) of Regulation No. 1612/68

This Article, which enables migrant workers, by virtue of the same right and under the same conditions as national workers, to have access to training in vocational schools and retraining centres, gives rise, first, to the question as to what is meant by the term 'access'. The English version suggests that what is meant is merely an equal right to attend courses at the establishments concerned, and not, for example, training grants as well. This point was mentioned by Advocate-General Sir Gordon Slynn in Case 39/86 *Lair*;[105] he concluded that Article 7(3) of Regulation No. 1612/68 was not limited merely to the right to attend a course, but related also to measures to facilitate participation in training

---

103 OJ, English Special Edition, Second Series IX, p. 7 (OJ 1962 No. 2, p. 36, in other language versions).
104 See de Witte, *Educational Equality*, p. 71.
105 Judgment of 21 June 1988 ([1988] ECR 3161).

itself.[106] He pointed out that in other language versions, including the German and French, the term 'access' does not appear.[107] In addition, it was necessary, he said, to give a similar interpretation to the expression 'under the same conditions', which is used in Article 7(3) and in Article 12 of Regulation No. 1612/68. The Advocate-General pointed out that according to the case-law of the Court of Justice, however, Article 12 also covers training grants.[108] That view was also expressed by the Commission.[109]

The Court was not called upon to express an opinion on that question in its judgment. Nevertheless, it is appropriate to concur with the view taken by the Advocate-General and by the Commission.[110] First, the other paragraphs of Article 7 of Regulation No. 1612/68 are aimed at the achievement of equal treatment for foreign workers; to restrict paragraph (3) to access to the educational establishments concerned, as is suggested only by the English text, would run counter to the system of the article. Secondly, it would not be logical for Article 7(3) to grant foreign workers equal access to training in vocational schools and retraining centres, not only 'by virtue of the same right' but also 'under the same conditions' as national workers, but then to preclude migrant workers from enjoying what may in the event be equal conditions of a much more significant kind during the training itself.

A further problem of interpretation is posed by the term 'vocational schools' appearing in Article 7(3) of Regulation No. 1612/68. The German text refers to the term 'Berufsschulen'. That term is defined unequivocally and restrictively in the educational laws of the German *Länder*. Article 8 of the Rhineland-Palatinate educational law, for example, provides that vocational schools are to lead, 'in equal partnership with industrial training, by means of progressive basic and technical training, to the final attainment of professional qualifications'. The question which arises is whether that definition can be applied outright to Article 7(3) of Regulation No. 1612/68. The notion of a vocational school, within the meaning of that provision, is a concept of Community law and is, as such, subject to the 'principle of uniformity of interpretation'.[111] For that reason, it should not without circumspection be defined on the basis of the contents of concepts of national law.[112]

In Cases 39/86 *Lair*[113] and 197/86 *Brown*,[114] the question at issue was whether university studies constituted training in a 'vocational school' within the meaning of Article 7(3) of Regulation No. 1612/68. That question was prompted by the judgment of the Court of Justice of 13 February 1985 in Case 293/83 *Gravier*,[115] in which the Court had applied a wide construction to the concept of vocational training

---

106 [1988] ECR 3161 (p. 3185).

107 *ibid.*, at p. 3184; the German text refers to 'Inanspruchnahme' and the Italian text refers to '*fruisce* ... dell'insegnamento', thus also going further than the English text of the regulation.

108 *ibid.*, at p. 3186.

109 *ibid.*, at p. 3173.

110 As do de Witte, *Educational Equality*, p. 73; Avenarius, p. 390.

111 According to Streil, p. 97.

112 Beutler et al., *3rd ed.*, p. 223.

113 [1988] ECR 3161.

114 Judgment of 21 June 1988 ([1988] ECR 3205).

115 [1985] ECR 593.

in Article 128 of the EEC Treaty.[116] The United Kingdom, in its observations in Case 197/86 *Brown*, took the view that no distinction could be drawn between the term 'vocational training' in Article 128 of the Treaty and the phrase 'training in vocational schools' appearing in Article 7(3) of Regulation No. 1612/68.[117] Advocate-General Sir Gordon Slynn concurred with that interpretation.[118]

The Court, however, decided that the term 'vocational school' has a narrower meaning and refers solely to establishments which provide only instruction interposed between periods of employment or else closely connected with employment, particularly during apprenticeship. That was not the case as far as universities were concerned.[119] Consequently, the concept of vocational schools under Community law approximates to that applied under German law. However, the judgment does not explain the reason for such a narrow interpretation of the term 'vocational school'.

(ii) Article 7(2) of Regulation No. 1612/68

Under this Article, migrant workers are to enjoy in the host State the same social and tax advantages as those afforded to national workers. The bearing which that provision has on the educational rights of migrant workers is not immediately apparent and is only made clear by the case-law of the Court of Justice. Of central importance in that regard is the concept of social advantages. The Court has defined these, in a consistent line of case-law, as meaning all advantages 'which, whether or not linked to a contract of employment, are generally granted to national workers primarily because of their status as workers or by virtue of the mere fact of their residence on the national territory and whose extension to workers who are nationals of other Member States therefore seems likely to facilitate the mobility of such workers within the Community'.[120]

In Cases 39/86 *Lair* and 197/86 *Brown*, the question at issue was whether that definition was capable of covering financial grants made for a student's maintenance and to enable him to complete a course of university study. The United Kingdom argued that that question should be answered in the negative in Case 197/86 *Brown*, on the ground that Article 7(3) of Regulation No. 1612/68 must be regarded as a *lex specialis* restricting the rights of workers to the fields of training and associated social benefits.[121] A similar view was expressed by the German Government in Case 39/86 *Lair*.[122] The English and French versions of the regulation support that view. They respectively state, in Article 7(3): 'He shall *also*, by virtue of the same right ...' and 'Il bénéficie *également*, au même titre ...'. It

---

116 For further details in that regard, see 'The concept of vocational training', pp. 118 *et seq.*, below.

117 [1988] ECR 3205 (at pp. 3213 *et seq.*).

118 *ibid.*, at p. 3228.

119 *ibid.*, at p. 3242.

120 e.g. see the judgment of 21 June 1988 in Case 39/86 *Lair* [1988] ECR 3161 (at pp. 3196 *et seq.*); the judgment of 17 April 1986 in Case 59/85 *Reed* [1986] ECR 1283 (at p. 1303); the judgment of 20 June 1985 in Case 94/84 *Deak* [1985] ECR 1873 (at p. 1886); as to the evolution of the concept generally, see Magiera, *DÖV 1987*, pp. 225 *et seq.*; O'Keeffe, pp. 93 *et seq.*

121 [1988] ECR 3205 (at p. 3216); for a concurring view, see Avenarius, p. 390.

122 [1988] ECR 3161 (at p. 3166).

could be concluded from such wording that Article 7(3) covers something different from Article 7(2). The Advocate-General did not accept that argument, contending that the legislative purpose behind Article 7(3) was to prevent the social advantages to which it refers from being by interpretation excluded from Article 7(2).[123]

This view is convincing, since the rights granted by Article 7 of Regulation No. 1612/68 are basically linked to a person's status as an employee.[124] Consequently, there was a particular need for clarification to the effect that the person concerned need not invariably be in existing employment. Concurring with the Advocate-General, the Court ultimately held that, while it was true that Article 7(3) of the regulation provides for a specific social advantage, a training grant not falling within that provision could still be covered by Article 7(2).[125] The Court considered that that was the position in the cases before it. Grants awarded for a student's maintenance and training were 'particularly appropriate from a worker's point of view for improving his professional qualifications and promoting his social advancement'.[126]

The Court referred to its classification of training grants as a social advantage in Case 39/86 *Lair* when delivering its judgment of 27 September 1988 in Case 235/87 *Matteucci*,[127] involving the special case of scholarships which, by virtue of the Cultural Agreement between Germany and Belgium, were reserved for nationals of the contracting parties for the purposes of study courses in the other State. Mrs Matteucci, an Italian national, maintained that, as a migrant worker, she should also be capable of qualifying for such a scholarship on the basis of Article 7(2) of Regulation No. 1612/68. That claim, although surprising at first sight, was found on closer inspection to be entirely consistent with Regulation No. 1612/68, which by its very nature confers a right to equal treatment in areas reserved to nationals of individual Member States. Consequently, the Court of Justice held that such scholarships should also be open to nationals of other Member States, even where they relate to training in another Member State.[128]

It has been inferred from that judgment that all bilateral cultural agreements entered into by EC Member States, including those concluded with non-member countries, must henceforth be open to nationals of other EC Member States.[129] However, that fear is as a whole unfounded. Nationals of other EC Member States only derive rights from such agreements in so far as they contain social advantages as defined by the case-law of the Court of Justice. Furthermore, it should be noted, with regard to cultural agreements with non-member countries, that although the Member State concerned will be obliged to nominate nationals of other Member States as well as its own nationals for the scholarships awarded under such an agreement, the non-member country, which is not subject to the obligations

---

123 [1988] ECR 3161 (at p. 3187).
124 See the judgment of 18 June 1987 in Case 316/85 *Lebon* [1987] ECR 2811 (at p. 2839).
125 [1988] ECR 3161 (at p. 3198).
126 *ibid.*, at p. 3197.
127 [1988] ECR 5589.
128 *ibid.*, at p. 5613.
129 See Hochbaum, *DUZ 20/1987*, p. 20.

imposed by Community law, would not be bound to accept as scholarship holders the nationals of any country other than the contracting State.[130]

(iii) The concept of a worker

The rights deriving from Article 7 of Regulation No. 1612/68 can be asserted only by a 'worker'. Article 48 of the EEC Treaty also refers to 'workers', even in subparagraphs (a) and (b) of paragraph (3) of that article in relation to the question of *access* to employment. However, the Court of Justice has made it clear that Article 7 of Regulation No. 1612/68 does not apply to persons who move in search of employment.[131] Consequently, such persons at least cannot be regarded as workers within the meaning of Regulation No. 1612/68.[132] This interpretation is in line with the scheme of Regulation No. 1612/68, which invariably refers in Title I of Part I (Eligibility for employment) to 'a national of a Member State' but uses in Title II (Employment and equality of treatment) the term 'worker'.

The concept of a worker, which falls to be determined under Community law,[133] necessarily involves *inter alia*,[134] according to the case-law of the Court of Justice, the 'pursuit of effective and genuine activities' the scale of which is not so small as be regarded as purely marginal and ancillary.[135]

Cases 39/86 *Lair*[136] and 197/86 *Brown*[137] prompted an occasion for the application and specific definition of these principles. Mrs Lair had been working in Germany for several years and enrolled, during a period of unemployment, for a master's degree course at the University of Hanover. She based her claim for a training grant pursuant to the BAföG (Bundesausbildungsförderungsgesetz, or Federal Law on Training Grants) *inter alia* on Article 7(2) of Regulation No. 1612/68. In the proceedings before the Court of Justice, the German Government submitted that, by undertaking a course of study, Mrs Lair had abandoned her status as a worker and thus waived her rights of free movement.[138]

That argument was not accepted by the Court. It demonstrated, by means of various provisions of primary and secondary Community law, that 'migrant workers are guaranteed certain rights linked to the status of worker even where they are no longer in an employment relationship'.[139] In the field of grants for university education, there must be some continuity between the previous

---

130 In Case 235/87 *Matteucci*, the Court of Justice inferred Germany's obligation to accept the selection of a non-Belgian national from Art. 5 of the EEC Treaty; see [1988] ECR 5589 (at pp. 5611 *et seq.*).

131 [1987] ECR 2811 (at p. 2839).

132 See also Everling, *Rechtsprechung*, p. 30, with reference to Art. 48 of the EEC Treaty.

133 For an early judgment, see that of 19 March 1964 in Case 75/63 *Unger* [1964] ECR 379 (at p. 400); see also the judgment of 23 March 1982 in Case 53/81 *Levin* [1982] ECR 1035 (at p. 1049).

134 For further details as to the concept of a worker, see 'Teaching staff as workers', pp. 81 *et seq.*, above.

135 [1982] ECR 1035 (at p. 1050); judgment of 3 June 1986 in Case 139/85 *Kempf* [1986] ECR 1741 (at p. 1750); as to the concept of a worker, see also Hailbronner, *ZAR 1990*, pp. 109 *et seq.*

136 Judgment of 21 June 1988 ([1988] ECR 3161).

137 Judgment of 21 June 1988 ([1988] ECR 3205).

138 [1988] ECR 3161 (at p. 3166).

139 *ibid.*, at p. 3200.

occupational activity and the course of study, that is to say, there must be an objective link between the two, save in the case of involuntary unemployment.[140]

Thus the Court did not extend the concept of a worker but merely determined, subject to the criterion as to continuity between the occupational activity and the course of study, the consequential effect of rights conferred by Article 7(2) of the regulation. The Court also stated in that judgment that it was contrary to Community law for a Member State to make the grant of workers' rights pursuant to Article 7 of Regulation No. 1612/68 conditional on the completion by the claimant of a minimum period of occupational activity within its territory. The concept of a worker under Community law could not depend on national criteria. However, abuses of the rights in question, for example where a student grant is claimed after what is deliberately planned as a very short period of occupational activity, were not covered by Community law.[141]

Case 197/86 *Brown* also involved a student grant applied for *inter alia* as a social advantage pursuant to Article 7(2) of Regulation No. 1612/68. The plaintiff in the main proceedings had completed an eight-month period of industrial training and subsequently commenced university studies in the same field. On the one hand, his engagement by the undertaking as a trainee was conditional on his having obtained his university place; on the other, the university required students to have completed a period of industrial training by the end of their second year. Having regard to the judgment in Case 39/86 *Lair*, it might be thought that Brown qualified for the student grant for which he had applied, since he not only satisfied the concept of a worker under Community law was but also able to show a link between his previous occupational activity and his subsequent course of study.[142]

The Court of Justice also considered that the criteria governing status as a worker were fulfilled by the period of industrial training, but was unable to accept Brown's submission that he had retained his rights as a worker, since he had acquired his status as a worker exclusively as a result of his being accepted for the course of study; in such circumstances, the employment relationship is merely ancillary to the course of study concerned.[143]

That decision has on occasion been regarded as an application of the 'abuse rule' developed in Case 39/86 *Lair*.[144] It is not evident, however, that Brown was in a position to abuse his position as a worker, or that he intended to do so. As far as he was concerned, his period of industrial training was not merely a pretext to enable him to acquire workers' rights but a necessary condition attaching to his training. In addition, the Court based its decision solely on the ancillary nature of the occupational activity and not on the existence of any abuse.[145]

The decision has been criticized on the grounds that it appears first of all to define status as a worker on an objective basis but then proceeds to lay down subjective exceptions to the definition.[146] If a person is a 'real' worker, it is said,

140 [1988] ECR 3161 (at p. 3200).
141 *ibid.*, at p. 3201.
142 See Hartley, p. 340.
143 [1988] ECR 3205 (at p. 3245).
144 See Hartley, p. 340; also, evidently, Lichtenberg, p. 1282.
145 See also Flynn, *YEL 1988*, p. 74.
146 See Lonbay, p. 379.

then he should be able to claim all the rights enjoyed by workers.[147] However, that criticism, although plausible at first sight, does not hold water. It is true that a link may be assumed to have existed between Brown's activities as a worker and his studies, with the result that he apparently fulfilled the criterion governing the retention of workers' rights laid down in the judgment in Case 39/86 *Lair*.[148]

However, it is impossible to accept the argument that, according to that decision, it is enough that *any* given link should exist. On the contrary, there must be a presumption that the subsequent course of study necessarily represents a further step in the implementation of a previously adopted occupational decision. Case 39/86 *Lair* involved only a link falling within the precise scope of that definition. It follows that the law excludes *ab initio* cases in which the type of occupational activity is not in fact based on any occupational decision but results from the requirements imposed by a system of study.[149] In graphic terms, the link must develop one-dimensionally from the occupational activity to the course of study; conversely, it cannot arise from a previously adopted decision to pursue a given course of study.[150]

The question of continuity between employment and study in the case of voluntary abandonment of occupational activity was addressed by Advocate-General Van Gerven in his Opinion in Case C-3/90 *Bernini*,[151] in which he expressed the view that the continuity requirement is satisfied only if a worker has given up his occupational activity with the intention of taking up studies. The fact that a relatively long time elapses between the cessation of employment and the commencement of the studies may indicate the absence of such an intention.[152]

On the other hand, in his Opinion in Case C-357/89 *Raulin*,[153] he took a wide view with regard to involuntary unemployment, in relation to which the case-law of the Court does not require there to be an objective link between the occupational activity and the studies pursued: the phrase 'involuntarily becoming unemployed' had been used in the judgment in *Lair* merely by way of example, in order to explain the subsequent wording in that decision.[154] In that subsequent wording, the Court was concerned with the question whether the worker is obliged by conditions on the job market to undertake occupational retraining in another field of activity.[155]

On the whole, the requirement of continuity appears to be of little practical utility, since it can be expected to give rise to considerable problems of interpretation. Furthermore, the criterion is doubtful from a legal point of view. If the aim of Article 7 of Regulation No. 1612/68 is to secure for workers from other Member States complete equality of treatment with national workers, then it must be contrary to that aim to impose on migrant workers who wish to take up studies requirements regarding continuity between their occupational activities

---

147 See Lonbay, p. 379.
148 [1988] ECR 3161 (at p. 3200).
149 See also Lichtenberg, p. 1282.
150 For a similar view, see Lichtenberg, *ibid*.
151 Opinion of 11 July 1991 ([1992] ECR I-1085).
152 *ibid.*, para. 15.
153 Opinion of 11 July 1991 ([1992] ECR I-1040).
154 *ibid.*, para. 14.
155 [1988] ECR 3161 (at p. 3200).

and their studies which do not have to be satisfied by national workers in a similar situation.[156] However, regard should be had in that connection to the limitations laid down by the Court in Case 197/86 *Brown*, discussed above.

(b) The children of migrant workers

(i) Article 12 of Regulation No. 1612/68

This Article entitles the children of migrant workers to be admitted to the host State's general educational, apprenticeship and vocational training courses under the same conditions as its own nationals, if they are residing in the host State. The rule laid down by Article 12 has on occasion formed the subject-matter of decisions of the Court of Justice, and has been interpreted by the Court from a number of different standpoints. Case 9/74 *Casagrande*[157] involved the question whether that provision also concerned equal treatment in the award of educational grants for school attendance. It was submitted in the course of the proceedings that Article 12 of Regulation No. 1612/68 provides only a right to be admitted to the educational establishments in question under the same conditions as nationals, but not to receive individual educational grants.[158]

The Court held, contrary to that argument, that Article 12 'refers not only to rules relating to admission, but also to general measures intended to facilitate educational attendance'.[159] That decision was confirmed by the Court in its judgment of 29 January 1975 in Case 68/74 *Alaimo*,[160] in which it ruled even more clearly that Article 12 of Regulation No. 1612/68 must be interpreted as ensuring an equal position with regard to all the rights arising from admission to educational courses.[161] It has been observed in relation to that case-law that the Court has interpreted Article 12 teleologically and has read into it a greater significance than it in fact possesses, the argument being that, according to its wording, the provision relates only to formal admission.[162]

That view is clearly based on the English text of the regulation, which indeed states: 'The children of a national of a Member State ... *shall be admitted* to that State's general educational, apprenticeship and vocational training courses ...'.[163] The wording of other language versions likewise emphasizes the admission factor, as, for example, in the Italian text, which uses the phrase '*ammessi* a frequentare i corsi d'insegnamento generale'; the French text, where the words '*admis* aux cours d'enseignement général' appear; and the Dutch text, which contains the formulation '*toegelaten* tot het algemeene onderwijs'.[164] The German text, on

---

156 See also Flynn, *YEL 1988*, p. 76.
157 Judgment of 3 July 1974 ([1974] ECR 773).
158 According to the Public Prosecutor's Office, as the representative of the public interest ('Vertreter des öffentlichen Interesses'); *ibid.*, at p. 776.
159 *ibid.*, at p. 779.
160 [1975] ECR 109.
161 *ibid.*, at p. 114.
162 According to de Witte, *Educational Equality*, p. 72.
163 Emphasis added.
164 Emphasis added.

the other hand, refers to *'Teilnahme* unter den gleichen Bedingungen',[165] and thus focuses in its wording on the education itself, rather than on admission to such education. Thus at least the German text of the regulation, which, like all the other language versions, has binding effect,[166] cannot be held up as running counter to the Court's interpretation.

As regards the type of education covered by Article 12 of Regulation No. 1612/68, the Court of Justice clearly ruled in its judgment of 15 March 1989 in Joined Cases 389 and 390/87 *Echternach and Moritz*[167] that the principle of equal treatment 'extends ... to all forms of education, whether vocational or general'[168] and that, consequently, the children of migrant workers are to be afforded equal treatment as regards all conceivable educational matters.[169]

In those proceedings the Court was also called upon to decide the particular question whether a child of a migrant worker is entitled to rely on Article 12 of Regulation No. 1612/68 and claim a study grant in the host State if he initially accompanied his parents when they returned to live in their Member State of origin but was unable to continue the studies commenced by him there and returned to the host State in order to do so. In response to that question, the Court held that the child in that case retained his status as a child of a migrant worker within the meaning of Article 12 of Regulation No. 1612/68. It ruled that, in order for integration to come about, a child of a Community worker must have the possibility of pursuing a course of study in the host State and, as the case may be, of returning to the host State in order to complete his studies if, because of a lack of coordination of school diplomas, he has no choice but to do so.[170]

That ruling relates primarily not to the integration of the child of a migrant worker but to the worker himself. In the Court's view, the social integration of migrant workers in the host State is conditional upon their having the right to the same treatment as national workers in relation to the benefits granted to members of their families.[171] Thus the Court's interpretation of Article 12 of Regulation No. 1612/68 is aimed at eliminating all inequalities of treatment which might prevent a worker, in the interests of his children, from availing himself of his right to freedom of movement.

The Court's judgment of 13 November 1990 in Case C-308/89 *di Leo*[172] is on similar lines. It concerned the question whether the child of a migrant worker is entitled to claim a grant from the State pursuant to Article 12 of Regulation No. 1612/68 for education which takes place in a State other than the host State, in particular in the State of which the child is a national, if the nationals of that State are so entitled. The Court ruled that in such circumstances Article 12 requires equal treatment which is exactly the same as that afforded to nationals. The fact that the education does not take place within the territory of the host State is not

---

165 Emphasis added.

166 See Schweitzer in: Grabitz, *Kommentar zum EWGV*, Art. 248, n. 5.

167 [1989] ECR 723.

168 *ibid.*, at p. 763.

169 For confirmation of this view, see Oppermann, *EG-Recht und Deutsche Bildungsordnung*, p. 45.

170 [1989] ECR 723 (at p. 761).

171 *ibid.*

172 [1990] ECR I-4185.

inconsistent with the condition of residence laid down by Article 12 of the regulation, because although that condition is designed to restrict equal treatment to children residing within their parents' host State, that does not mean that the right to equal treatment depends on the place in which the child concerned pursues his studies.[173] The Court, considering Article 12 in conjunction with Article 7(2) of Regulation No. 1612/68, inferred therefrom a general rule requiring each Member State, in matters of education, to ensure comprehensive equal treatment between its own nationals and the children of migrant workers.[174] It was essential, the Court held, to secure the creation of the best possible conditions for the integration of the Community worker's family in the society of the host State.[175]

Certain commentators have levelled at that judgment the criticism that it is difficult to see how study abroad can be said to promote integration in the host State,[176] particularly where it takes place in the home State of the child of a migrant worker.[177] It is argued that unequal treatment in the promotion of education in the State of which the student is a national may in fact be based not on questions of nationality but on the fact that a State, whilst wishing to promote mobility in the higher education of its own students, may not wish to have to contribute to the financing of grants for studies pursued in other Member States by nationals of those States.[178]

It is apparent from the very words used that such assessments are inimical to integration. For example, the State of which the migrant worker's child is a national is designated without qualification as the 'home State'; furthermore, that child is classed, as regards mobility in higher education, simply in terms of the State of which he is a national. Any integration which may already have been achieved in the host State is ignored. Consequently, the reservations expressed in relation to the Court's decision should be rejected.

In actual fact, the judgment may be regarded as correct, from two points of view. First, the Court has removed a legal obstacle existing under domestic law which could otherwise have prevented nationals of the Member States from exercising their right of freedom of movement. Secondly, the judgment also serves to promote the integration of the children of migrant workers in the host State. Advocate-General Darmon demonstrated conclusively in his opinion that inequality of treatment between the children of nationals and those of migrant workers as regards grants for studies abroad may operate to restrict integration, particularly since they have previously been treated in exactly the same way in the host State.[179] It is moreover evident that the child's connection with the host State, and thus its integration within that State, can also be strengthened by the award of a grant for the pursuit of studies abroad.

---

173 [1990] ECR I-4185 (at p. 4208).
174 *ibid.*, at pp. 4208 *et seq.*
175 *ibid.*, at p. 4208.
176 See Weberling, pp. 135 *et seq.*
177 See Teske, p. 55; see also, to the same effect, Hailbronner, *JuS 1991*, p. 13.
178 See Hailbronner, *EuZW 1991*, p. 175.
179 [1990] ECR I-4185 (at p. 4195).

However, the Court has declined in two cases to apply Article 12 of Regulation No. 1612/68. In its judgment of 27 September 1988 in Case 263/86 *Humbel*,[180] it adhered to the residence requirement laid down in that provision and rejected the reliance by a French pupil living in Luxembourg and studying in Belgium on the fact that pupils of Luxembourg nationality studying in Belgium were exempt from having to pay an enrolment fee. It held that Article 12 of Regulation No. 1612/68 imposes obligations only on the Member State in which the migrant worker resides.[181] In its judgment of 21 June 1988 in Case 197/86 *Brown*,[182] it ruled that a child of a migrant worker may not claim the benefit of that provision in a Member State in which his parent last resided prior to his birth.[183]

(ii) The directive on the education of the children of migrant workers

The directive on the education of the children of migrant workers[184] differs from the provisions hitherto considered, in that it not only lays down rules as to the treatment of migrant workers as nationals but also requires the Member States to adopt positive measures to teach the children of migrant workers the official language of the host State, their mother tongue and the culture of their country of origin, i.e. measures the benefit of which is not enjoyed by the host State's own nationals.[185]

Doubts have been expressed as to whether Article 49 of the EEC Treaty constitutes the appropriate basis for this directive. It is argued that the object of that provision is merely to eliminate restrictions on freedom of movement, not to promote positive action in order to create specific incentives to mobility. Furthermore, according to the case-law of the Court of Justice, the conferment of competence by virtue of the material context ('Kompetenz kraft Sachzusam-menhangs') such as that involved here is apparently subject to the condition that the express powers given by the Treaty can be applied judiciously and appropriately only if such competence has been extended by effective judicial interpretation. That may be the case as regards the rights of family members to reside and remain with a migrant worker, but not in relation to the measures provided for by the directive in question.[186]

In opposition to that argument, it should be pointed out, first, that there is nothing in Article 49 of the EEC Treaty which suggests that it is restricted to measures to eliminate obstacles to freedom of movement.[187] The concept (in the German text) of 'Herstellung' of freedom of movement has a wider meaning in Article 49 of the Treaty than in Article 48. This is apparent from a comparison of

---

180 [1988] ECR 5365.
181 *ibid.*, at p. 5389.
182 [1988] ECR 3205.
183 *ibid.*, at p. 3246.
184 OJ 1977 L 199, p. 32.
185 See de Witte & Post, p. 147.
186 See Hiermaier, pp. 95 *et seq.*; as to the problem of reverse discrimination against the children of national workers, see de Witte, *Educational Equality*, p. 75.
187 Even though the directive has been described as 'a piece of legislation which nobody might have dreamt to read in Articles 48–49 at the time of drafting the Treaty'; see de Witte, *Scope of Community Powers*, p. 267.

the German text with the English and French versions. The English and French wording used in Article 48 is respectively 'shall be secured' and 'est assurée', whilst that appearing in Article 49 is respectively 'to bring about ... freedom of movement' and 'en vue de réaliser ... la libre circulation'. Furthermore, the characteristic of *requirement* in Article 49 ('measures *required* to bring about') has resulted in the conferment on the Council of very wide discretionary powers,[188] encompassing *inter alia* measures to make freedom of movement 'more attractive'.[189] Consequently, what is involved in the case of the directive on the education of the children of migrant workers is a problem not of implicit competence existing by virtue of the material context but of the interpretation of express competence.

(c) The spouse of a migrant worker

No express rights in the field of education are granted to the spouse of a migrant worker by secondary Community law. Article 11 of Regulation No. 1612/68 merely entitles the spouse to take up any activity as an employed person throughout the territory of the host State, even if he or she is not a national of any Member State.[190] The children of a migrant worker, on the other hand, enjoy – as we have seen – comprehensive rights in the field of education by virtue of Article 12 of Regulation No. 1612/68. This gives rise to the question whether the failure to take the spouses of migrant workers into account reflects the wishes of the Community legislature and is thus to be accepted as such, or whether what is involved here is a *lacuna* in Community law which needs to be filled.

The answer to that question must lie in the latter interpretation.[191] First, reference should be made to Regulation No. 1251/70, which extends to the members of a migrant worker's family to whom the right to remain applies the 'right to equality of treatment established by Council Regulation (EEC) No. 1612/68'. This involves an independent rule against discrimination, i.e. reference is not simply made to the factual criteria laid down by Regulation No. 1612/68.[192] It follows that a spouse of a migrant worker enjoying the right to remain can claim all the advantages and privileges to which the spouse of a national worker whose employment has ceased is entitled. The principle underlying this rule is expressly stated in the last recital in the preamble to Regulation No. 1251/70, according to which persons to whom the right to remain in the

---

188 See Wölker in: GTE, *Kommentar zum EWGV*, Art. 49, n. 7.

189 Karpenstein in: GBTE, *Kommentar zum EWGV*, Art. 49, n. 3.

190 As regards spouses who are nationals of a Member State, the significance of Art. 11 of Regulation No. 1612/68 is merely declaratory, since their right to carry on an activity as an employed person already derives directly from Art. 48 of the EEC Treaty. This is the case even where they were already residing in the host State for other reasons; see also Advocate-General Sir Gordon Slynn in Case 235/87 *Matteucci* [1988] ECR 5589 (at p. 5599), as regards children of a migrant worker who take up employment in the host State.

191 This is the view unanimously held by legal writers; e.g. see Traversa, p. 49; Avenarius, pp. 390 *et seq.*; Steiner, p. 348; Steindorff, *NJW 1983*, p. 1231.

192 See Karpenstein in: GBTE, *Kommentar zum EWGV*, Art. 48, n. 35; for a concurring view, see Wölker in: GTE, *Kommentar zum EWGV*, Art. 48, n. 83.

country of employment applies must enjoy equality of treatment with national workers who have ceased their working lives.

If, therefore, the spouse of a migrant worker whose employment has ceased enjoys the same rights in the field of education as the spouse of a national worker whose employment has ceased, then the spouse of a migrant worker who is still in employment must be able *a fortiori* to claim those rights.[193] To this somewhat formal conclusion deriving from Article 7 of Regulation No. 1251/70 must be added a line of argument advanced by the Commission in Case 152/82 *Forcheri*:[194] conditions for access to education which discriminate against the spouse of a migrant worker in another Member State may constitute an obstacle to the safeguarding of that worker's freedom of movement. Integration in the host country depends on non-discriminatory opportunities in education being available not only for the children of a migrant worker but also for his or her spouse.[195]

It follows from the whole of the foregoing that the spouse of a migrant worker must also be able to claim the rights granted to the children. From a technical legal point of view, it is possible to apply Article 7(2) of Regulation No. 1612/68 if the educational rights claimed by the spouse of a migrant worker are taken to constitute a social advantage in favour of the migrant worker himself.[196] Where this is not the case, the application by analogy of Article 12 of Regulation No. 1612/68[197] in conjunction with the first paragraph of Article 7 of the EEC Treaty is to be preferred to just such an application of Article 7(2) of Regulation No. 1612/68,[198] since the situation of the spouse of a migrant worker is comparable with that of his children rather than with that of the migrant worker himself.[199]

The Court of Justice has not hitherto given an express ruling on this question. However, in its judgment in Case 152/82 *Forcheri*,[200] the Court indirectly confirmed the conclusion arrived at above.[201] In that case, the wife of an official of

---

193 See also Avenarius, pp. 390 *et seq.*; Oppermann, *EG-Recht und Deutsche Bildungsordnung*, p. 45.

194 Judgment of 13 July 1983, [1983] ECR 2323.

195 *ibid.*, at p. 2330; Oppermann, op. cit., p. 45, also regards it as inadmissible, from the standpoint of the protection of the human rights of the family, to differentiate between children and spouses.

196 This is clearly what is meant by Wölker in: GTE, *Kommentar zum EWGV*, Art. 48, n. 74, when he states that Art. 7(2) of Regulation No. 1612/68 is in his view applicable. By virtue of that provision, the members of a migrant worker's family are only indirectly entitled to claim benefits. The relevant question is whether there exists a social advantage in favour of the worker himself; see the judgment of the Court of Justice of 18 June 1987 in Case 316/85 *Lebon* [1987] ECR 2811 (at p. 2836).

197 Hartley, p. 328, clearly regards this as a possibility.

198 de Witte, in *Educational Equality*, p. 73, favours the application of this provision.

199 See also the Commission proposal for the amendment of Regulation No. 1612/68, OJ 1990 C 119, p. 10, in which the Commission proposes the extension of Art. 12 of the regulation to cover all members of a migrant worker's family.

200 [1983] ECR 2323.

201 Concurring views are thus expressed by Traversa, p. 49: '... la Cour a ainsi, par le biais de l'interprétation, comblé la lacune ... de l'article 12'; Lonbay, p. 375: 'In *Forcheri* this was extended to spouses'; Magiera, *DÖV 1987*, p. 226: 'As regards spouses ... the Court reached the same conclusion in its 1983 judgment in *Forcheri*': the spouses of migrant workers, like their children, are, he argues, entitled to equality of treatment in the field of education and training.

the EC Commission working in Brussels objected to having had to pay a fee for enrolment in a non-university further education establishment from which Belgian students were exempt. The Court merely examined whether this constituted an infringement of the first paragraph of Article 7 of the EEC Treaty[202] and debated whether the legal position of an EC official fell within the 'scope of application of the Treaty'. It answered that question in the affirmative, first, by reference to the employment relationship of Community officials and, secondly, on the basis of the consideration that EC officials must 'enjoy all the benefits flowing ... for the nationals of Member States in relation to freedom of movement, freedom of establishment and social security'.

That finding as to the applicability *ratione personae*[203] of the EEC Treaty was followed by the affirmation of its applicability *ratione materiae*: access to such kinds of instruction was held to fall within the scope of the Treaty.[204] Thus, although the Court expressly found that the rules on freedom of movement apply to EC officials (without, however, designating such officials as workers within the meaning of Community law), it clearly did not regard the application of Regulation No. 1612/68 as admissible. However, no arguments can be inferred from this against the solution suggested above in relation to Article 12 of Regulation No. 1612/68. The fact is that the Court actually *refrained* from designating EC officials as *workers*.[205] This may have prevented it from applying any of the provisions of Regulation No. 1612/68.[206] The decisive point, however, is that the Court, in reaching its judgment within the framework of the first paragraph of Article 7 of the EEC Treaty, examined not a right which was personal to Mrs Forcheri but a right which, in so far as the personal applicability of Article 7 of the Treaty arose only from the legal position of her husband, derived from Mr Forcheri.[207]

The Court's *dicta* on the legal position of spouses cannot be explained in any other way. In its judgment, the Court invariably refers to Mrs Forcheri as the spouse of an official of the Community, and makes particular reference to the fifth recital in the preamble to Regulation No. 1612/68, primarily to the right of a

---

202 Oliver, in *YEL 1985*, p. 72, found, with reference to Art. 7(2) of Regulation No. 1612/68, that it was 'somewhat surprising that the Court did not base its judgment in *Forcheri* on this provision'.

203 As it is described by C.O. Lenz in *Zuständigkeiten und Initiativen*, p. 191.

204 [1983] ECR 2323 (at p. 2336).

205 For a concurring view, see Oppermann, *EG-Recht und Deutsche Bildungsordnung*, p. 44; see also Advocate-General Rozès, [1983] ECR 2341, who considered in her opinion in Case 152/82 *Forcheri* that the position of EC officials, although comparable with that of migrant workers, did not constitute an adequate ground for granting the spouse of such an official any rights to equality of treatment.

206 This was ultimately held to be correct by Starkle, pp. 685 and 688 *et seq.* He based his view, first, on the wording of Art. 48(3)(c) of the EEC Treaty, which in his submission excludes from classification as 'workers' persons whose employment relationship is determined by the staff regulations of an international organization, and, secondly, on the fact that EC officials do not fall within the ambit of a social security system, as is invariably the case with 'workers'.

207 Thus, in the case of Mrs Forcheri, what was involved was an educational right deriving 'from the exercise of freedom of movement' (see the heading of section II, p. 92, above). For that reason, it is also appropriate to speak of a 'middle way' between the application of special rules on freedom of movement and the general prohibition of discrimination; see de Moor, p. 452; for a different view, see Starkle, p. 693, who reasons that the rights to which Mrs Forcheri was found to be entitled were not dependent on her status as the wife of a Community servant.

worker, mentioned therein, to be joined by his family and the conditions for the integration of that family into the host country.[208] Later on, the Court abandoned its efforts to examine the scope of application *ratione personae* in the context of the first paragraph of Article 7 of the EEC Treaty.[209] At all events, the *Forcheri* judgment was of only limited significance as regards the question of the general educational rights of spouses of migrant workers, since it related only to access to education and not to any rights going beyond that, such as student grants.

3. THE RIGHTS OF SELF-EMPLOYED PERSONS AND MEMBERS OF THEIR FAMILIES

In the field of establishment, the rules relating to the educational rights of those entitled to freedom of movement and members of their families are, as has been shown above,[210] appreciably 'sparser'[211] than in the field of freedom of movement for workers. As in the case of spouses of migrant workers, this raises the question as to what conclusions are to be drawn; and as in that case, one is bound ultimately to assume that there exists a *lacuna* in the rules which needs to be filled.[212] The right of establishment constitutes, like freedom of movement for workers, a branch of the concept of the free movement of persons. The difference between the two types of freedom of movement lies merely in the nature of the occupation which is carried on. The reasons for having separate rules in relation to the two types of freedom were purely practical: it was assumed that freedom of movement for workers could be secured more quickly than that accorded to self-employed persons.[213] The need for parallel treatment of the two matters is reflected in various measures of the Community legislature.

Thus the Council, in adopting Directive 75/34/EEC on the right of self-employed persons to remain,[214] did so on the basis that such persons clearly have an interest in enjoying the same right to remain as that granted to workers.[215] By Regulation No. 1390/81,[216] the Council extended to self-employed persons and members of their families Regulation No. 1408/71 on the application of social security schemes to employed persons and their families moving within the Community. In so doing, it declared that 'for reasons of equity, it would be appropriate to apply, to the largest possible extent, the same rules to self-employed persons as are laid down for employed persons'.[217]

A concurring view is to be found in the case-law of the Court of Justice, which is based on the assumption that rights to freedom of movement should be

---

208 [1983] ECR 2323 (at pp. 2334 *et seq.*).
209 For further details, see 'The scope of the EEC Treaty', pp. 115 *et seq.*, below.
210 See 'Rules laid down by Community secondary legislation', pp. 93 *et seq.*, above.
211 As Oppermann puts it in *EG-Recht und Deutsche Bildungsordnung*, p. 45.
212 For a concurring view, see Oppermann, *ibid.*, pp. 45 *et seq.*; Avenarius, p. 391; Hochbaum & Eiselstein, p. 40.
213 Troberg in: GTE, *Kommentar zum EWGV*, preliminary remark regarding Arts 52–58, n. 3; Randelzhofer in: Grabitz, *Kommentar zum EWGV*, preliminary remark regarding Art. 52, nn. 8 *et seq.*
214 Directive of 17 December 1974, OJ 1975 L 14, p. 10.
215 *ibid.*, third recital in the preamble.
216 Regulation of 12 May 1981, OJ 1981 L 143, p. 1.
217 *ibid.*, sixth recital in the preamble.

fundamentally comparable.[218] It follows that the right to equal treatment in the field of education extends in equal measure to self-employed persons and members of their families – whether directly, by virtue of Article 52 of the EEC Treaty, or by way of application of the rules concerning migrant workers in conjunction with the first paragraph of Article 7 of the Treaty[219] – as it does to employed persons and their families.

III. EDUCATION RIGHTS FOR ALL COMMUNITY CITIZENS

1. INTRODUCTION

The preceding two sections have been concerned with rights in the field of education which are connected, directly or indirectly, with the pursuit of economic activities in another Member State. There now follows an analysis of the question whether, and on what basis, citizens of EC Member States can claim entitlement to educational rights in other Member States irrespective of such activities. It is appropriate to consider, as a starting point, the rules on freedom to provide services and the general prohibition of discrimination.

2. FREEDOM TO RECEIVE SERVICES FOR PUPILS AND STUDENTS IN THE PUBLIC EDUCATION SECTOR IN OTHER MEMBER STATES

The obligation incumbent on EC Member States to open up their public education systems to nationals of other Member States might arise from the rules laid down in the EEC Treaty on freedom to provide services. There are, in that regard, two essential questions which need to be answered:

(1) do Articles 59 *et seq.* of the EEC Treaty entitle a person to whom a service is provided to go to the country of origin of the supplier of the service in order to receive the service?;[220] and

(2) can education opportunities provided by the State be regarded, in accordance with Article 60 of the EEC Treaty, as services, i.e. as services which are 'normally provided for remuneration'?

(a) Recipients of services as persons enjoying the benefit of freedom to provide services

The chapter of the EEC Treaty on services appears to be framed solely for the benefit of persons providing services. The first paragraph of Article 59 of the

---

218 e.g. see the judgment of 8 April 1976 in Case 48/75 *Royer* [1976] ECR 497 (at pp. 509 *et seq.*) and the judgment of 7 July 1976 in Case 118/75 *Watson and Belmann* [1976] ECR 1185 (at p. 1197).

219 See de Witte & Post, p. 144.

220 In such circumstances, it is appropriate to speak of 'passive freedom to provide services' ('passive Dienstleistungsfreiheit'); see Oppermann, *EG-Freizügigkeit*, p. 25; Völker, p. 61.

Treaty expressly provides merely for the abolition of restrictions 'in respect of nationals of Member States who are established in a State of the Community other than that of the person for whom the services are intended' – in other words, suppliers of services. The third paragraph of Article 60 confers on the persons providing a service the right, in order to do so, temporarily to pursue his activity in the State where the service is provided. Lastly, Article 65 of the EEC Treaty imposes on the Member States the obligation to apply any restrictions which have not yet been abolished 'without distinction on grounds of nationality or residence to all persons providing services within the meaning of the first paragraph of Article 59'.[221] Accordingly, Advocate-General Trabucchi concluded in Case 118/75 *Watson and Belmann*[222] that there could in principle be no question of including the recipients of services amongst those entitled to the freedom in question, since to do so would have the practical effect of extending the right of freedom of movement to all nationals of the Member States. 'The most that can be done', he stated, 'is to recognize freedom of movement for recipients of services ... but only in so far as it appears to be indissolubly linked with the right to movement of those who have to provide those services'.[223] Advocate-General Capotorti likewise expressed the view in Case 66/77 *Kuyken*[224] that the rules on freedom to provide services are designed to remove obstacles to the free movement only of suppliers of services and not of those who receive them.[225]

However, the Commission had already expressed a contrary view in Case 118/75 *Watson and Belmann*,[226] relying on certain legal measures adopted by the Council. Thus Article 1 of the Directive of 25 February 1964 on the coordination of special measures concerning the movement and residence of foreign nationals which are justified on grounds of public policy, public security or public health includes, amongst those persons to whom the directive applies, any national of a Member State who travels to another Member State 'as a recipient of services'.[227] Article 1 of the Directive of 21 May 1973 on the abolition of restrictions on movement and residence with regard to establishment and the provision of services, which obliges the Member States to abolish restrictions *inter alia* for Community nationals 'wishing to go to other Member States as recipients of services', is even more explicit.[228] However, the significance of the legislation referred to is at best circumstantial, since it cannot in principle, as secondary Community legislation, affect the interpretation of primary Community law.

The issue was not clarified by the Court of Justice until it delivered its judgment of 31 January 1984 in Joined Cases 286/82 and 26/83 *Luisi and*

---

221 The significance of Art. 65 of the EEC Treaty has not been diminished by the expiry of the transitional period or by the direct applicability of Arts 59 *et seq.* of the Treaty established by the case-law of the Court of Justice; see Randelzhofer in: Grabitz, *Kommentar zum EWGV*, Art. 65, n. 4.

222 [1976] ECR 1185.

223 *ibid.*, at p. 1204; for a similar view, see Riegel, *NJW 1978*, p. 469.

224 [1977] ECR 2311.

225 *ibid.*, at p. 2325; see also Steindorff, *NJW 1983*, p. 1231.

226 [1976] ECR 1185 (at p. 1193).

227 OJ, English Special Edition 1963-1964, p. 117 (OJ 1964 No. 56, p. 850, in other language versions).

228 OJ 1973 L 172, p. 14.

Carbone.[229] The Court held that the freedom of a recipient of services to go to the State in which the person providing them is established is the necessary corollary of the corresponding freedom enjoyed by the supplier of the service, which fulfils the objective of 'liberalizing all gainful activity not covered by the free movement of goods, persons and capital'.[230] The freedom to provide services includes the freedom, for recipients of services, to go to another Member State in order to receive a service there, without being obstructed by restrictions.[231]

Those findings cannot be taken to mean – as suggested by Advocate-General Trabucchi in Case 118/75 *Watson and Belmann* – that a recipient of services is protected by the rules on freedom to provide services only in so far as a restriction affecting him personally is at the same time to be regarded as involving a restriction on the freedom enjoyed by the person providing the services. The recipient of the services is himself directly included within the ambit of freedom to provide services. Otherwise, it would be impossible to understand on what basis – as in Joined Cases 286/82 and 26/83 *Luisi and Carbone* – recipients of services could themselves be capable of relying on the freedom to provide services.

Clearly, the point which the Court was seeking to make in the findings referred to above was that what is involved is the liberalization of all gainful activity. The central issue is the liberalization of the provision of the service itself, not the person providing it. However, that liberalization would remain incomplete if areas of economic activity in which services are typically provided on the basis that the recipient goes to the supplier of the service were to remain excluded.[232] That interpretation was confirmed in general terms in the Court's judgment of 30 May 1991 in Case C-68/89 *Commission* v. *Netherlands*.[233] In that case, the Court stated that it was 'now settled case-law' that the freedom to provide services is enjoyed both by providers and by recipients of services.[234]

(b) State education facilities as services

Having established that nationals of Member States are entitled to go to another Member State in order to receive services there, we now turn to the question whether Article 59 of the EEC Treaty requires the abolition, as regards the enjoyment of educational facilities provided by the State, of restrictions existing in relation to non-residents. According to the first paragraph of Article 60 of the Treaty, this is conditional on the provision of State education facilities constituting 'services ... normally provided for remuneration'. The first point to be made in this regard is that the concept of services is to be understood in the widest possible sense and relates to all activities which are not covered by the other freedoms.[235]

---

229 [1984] ECR 377; discussed by Louis, *CML Rev. 1984*, pp. 625 *et seq.*
230 [1984] ECR 377 (at p. 401).
231 *ibid.*, at p. 403.
232 For a concurring view, see Advocate-General Mancini in Joined Cases 286/82 and 26/83, *Luisi and Carbone* [1984] ECR 377 (at p. 415).
233 [1991] ECR I-2637.
234 *ibid.*, para. 10 of the judgment.
235 See Bleckmann, *EuR 1987*, p. 32; see also, to the same effect, Magiera, *DÖV 1987*, p. 224.

Consequently, the provision of education must clearly be regarded as constituting such a service.[236]

However, problems arise from the use of the phrase 'normally provided for remuneration'. It is necessary, first, to examine the question of remuneration, since the qualification imposed on the remuneration requirement by the expression '*normally* provided for remuneration' does not take effect unless and until it is established that there is an absence of consideration. The phrase cannot have been intended to have the effect of excluding from the scope of the EEC Treaty services which are in fact provided for remuneration merely because they are *not normally* provided for remuneration.

The concept of remuneration in the field of the provision of services is intended, like that of commercial objectives in the context of freedom of establishment,[237] to restrict the applicable rules to circumstances constituting 'economic activities' within the meaning of Article 2 of the Treaty.[238] Consequently, both concepts must be given an equally wide interpretation.[239] It follows that no requirement may be imposed necessitating the existence on the part of the supplier of the service of an intention to make a profit.[240] However, it is easier to define what is not covered by the concept of remuneration than to establish what it means in positive terms. In its judgment of 27 September 1988 in Case 263/86 *Humbel*,[241] the Court of Justice stated, apparently for the first time, its views on this point.

In that judgment, it held that teaching provided under a national education system was not provided in return for consideration, on the ground that the essential characteristic of remuneration lies in the fact that it constitutes commercial consideration for the service in question and is normally agreed upon between the provider and the recipient of the service. That characteristic was absent, since the State, in establishing such a national education system, was not seeking to engage in gainful activity but was fulfilling its duties towards its own population in the social, cultural and educational fields. Furthermore, the education system is, as a general rule, funded from the public purse and not by pupils or their parents. That position was not altered by the fact that pupils or their parents must sometimes pay fees in order to make a certain contribution to the operating expenses of the system.[242] Ultimately, therefore, the Court upheld the view expressed by Advocate-General Sir Gordon Slynn in Case 293/83 *Gravier.*[243]

The reference in the German text of the Court's judgment to the absence of any intention to engage in a 'gewinnbringende' activity may give rise to misunder-

---

236 See also Advocate-General Sir Gordon Slynn in Case 293/83 *Gravier* [1985] ECR 593 (at p. 602); Oppermann, *EG-Recht und Deutsche Bildungsordnung*, p. 48.

237 Randelzhofer in: Grabitz, *Kommentar zum EWGV*, Art. 60, n. 8; see in that regard 'The right of establishment for teachers and education agencies', pp. 89 *et seq.*, above.

238 von Wilmowsky, p. 237.

239 Thus an excessively narrow view is expressed by Börner, at pp. 578 *et seq.*, who contends that there must exist a contractual link – normally based on private law – between the person providing the service and the person receiving it.

240 von Wilmowsky, 1990, p. 236; Völker, p. 97.

241 [1988] ECR 5365.

242 *ibid.*, at p. 5388.

243 [1985] ECR 593 (at pp. 602 *et seq.*).

standing. The French text of the judgment is clearer, French being the language of the case; that version states that the State 'n'entend pas s'engager dans des *activités rémunérées*'.[244] Similarly, in the other language versions of the judgment, emphasis is placed not on the element of commercial gain but on that of payment and remuneration.[245] Consequently, the Court cannot be deemed to have held it necessary for there to exist, as an essential characteristic of remuneration for a service within the meaning of the first paragraph of Article 60 of the EEC Treaty, the intention to make a profit.

One is bound to concur with the specific definition applied by the Court to the concept of services.[246] First, the view that there is no remuneration where the education system is funded *wholly* from the public purse would appear to be correct. It is true to say that the requisite remuneration may be paid not only by the recipient of the service but by a third party.[247] It is equally correct that that third party may be the State.[248] However, it cannot be argued that, for that reason alone, all funding from the public purse in the context of the administration of services is to be regarded as remuneration. The concept of remuneration cannot be reduced to the argument that it is enough that a service is 'paid for'.[249] Otherwise, the concept would scarcely have any independent meaning of its own,[250] since ultimately all services have to be 'paid for' by somebody.[251]

Not even the examples of the existence of remuneration given by the Commission in its Green Paper on 'Television without frontiers' go so far as to include funding from State taxes. The Green Paper expressly refers only to 'levies assimilated to a tax' and 'transfers from public funds corresponding to the levies or fees raised on the recipients of the service'.[252] Similarly, the use of taxes in order to finance the discharge of public functions can hardly be regarded as remuneration, since it is impossible to determine in such circumstances who is to make payment to whom. The levying of taxes must also be eliminated as a possibility.[253]

What is the position, however, where pupils or their parents are called upon to pay fees? Clearly, a satisfactory answer cannot be provided by concentrating on the

244 Emphasis added.
245 See the Danish text: 'virksomhed *mod betaling*'; and the Dutch text: 'bedoeling *tegen vergoeding*'. Moreover, the English text of the judgment refers to *'gainful* activity', not, for example, to *'profitable* activity'; emphasis added.
246 For a contrary view, however, see von Wilmowsky, p. 262.
247 See the Court's judgment of 26 April 1988 in Case 352/85 *Bond van Adverteerders* [1988] ECR 2085 (at p. 2131); see also Advocate-General Warner in Case 52/79 *Debauve* [1980] ECR 833 (at p. 876).
248 See von Wilmowsky, p. 262.
249 As contended by the EC Commission in COM(84) 300, p. 107.
250 See Advocate-General Sir Gordon Slynn in Case 263/86 *Humbel* [1988] ECR 5365 (at p. 5379): '[That is] a criterion which I do not think can be simply ignored'.
251 For a concurring view, see Magiera, *DÖV 1987*, p. 224, who points out that, as is generally acknowledged, few services are provided for no remuneration.
252 See EC Commission, COM(84) 300, p. 107.
253 The argument that it is possible to found remuneration on the fact that teachers have to be paid and that running expenses have to be met was decisively rebutted by Advocate-General Sir Gordon Slynn in Case 263/86 *Humbel* [1988] ECR 5365 (at p. 5379).

extent of the funds needed to cover expenses,[254] since there is inherent in such an approach the risk that arbitrary decisions may be made. Were the mere fact that something is payable, regardless of the amount concerned and irrespective of the reasons for the payment,[255] to be regarded as sufficient to establish the existence of remuneration, the paradoxical result, in the event of such a fee being payable only by foreign nationals, would be that the fee, the legitimacy of which was contested by those having to pay it, would produce a form of consideration, with the result that Articles 59 *et seq.* of the EEC Treaty would be applicable.[256] In that case too, therefore, the question of remuneration falls to be determined according to the same criteria as in the case of funding provided entirely from tax revenues, i.e. it depends whether the State is pursuing a gainful objective as regards the establishment concerned or whether it is seeking to fulfil a socio-political duty *vis-à-vis* its citizens. This follows from the above-mentioned finding by the Court that the 'nature of the activity' is not affected by the fact that pupils or their parents must sometimes pay teaching or enrolment fees in order to contribute to the maintenance of the system. Where, however, the State is fulfilling a socio-political duty *in the form* of commercial activities, the existence of remuneration cannot be denied.

Once it is established that teaching provided under a national education system cannot be regarded as a service provided for remuneration within the meaning of the first paragraph of Article 60 of the EEC Treaty,[257] it becomes necessary to consider whether the services in question are not 'normally' provided for remuneration. The answer to that question must be in the negative from the outset. In the Court's view, the *nature* of teaching provided under a national education system must be such that it is directed towards the fulfilment of a socio-political objective for the benefit of the population. Accordingly, any gainful activity is diametrically opposed to the achievement of that objective. On examining the essential characteristic of services 'normally provided for remuneration', therefore, there can be no question of the 'norm' being found to include educational services which are provided within the Community in the context of gainful activity, that is to say, in return for remuneration.[258]

The position is in no way altered if the rule as to remuneration is considered not in terms of a type of activity to be defined in the abstract as existing throughout

---

254 As is contended by von Wilmowsky, p. 236, who rightly contests the view expressed by Steindorff in *RIW 1983*, p. 837, that it depends whether the consideration given constitutes a 'significant contribution towards the meeting of expenses'.

255 It is clearly this possibility which von Wilmowsky had in mind when he wrote at p. 237, that the Court of Justice had held in *Sacchi* that a broadcasting organization provides a service to its viewers which falls, *irrespective of the funding system applied*, within the scope of the provisions of the Treaty relating to services. Thus not only television systems financed by licence fees but also those funded by advertising revenues would be covered.

256 Only, however, if one follows the trend of regarding teaching funded from budgetary resources as something other than a service.

257 The Court's *dictum* is expressed in terms of general application and is not limited to the 'underlying teaching facilities available in the circumstances'; this restrictive view is shared by Müller-Graff, *FS für Rudolf Lukes*, p. 473; and is rightly contested by Lichtenberg, p. 1281.

258 As to that starting-point for establishing the provision of regular consideration for a service, see Advocate-General Sir Gordon Slynn in Case 293/83 *Gravier* [1985] ECR 593 (at p. 603).

the Community but in terms of the specific person providing the service, and if one poses the question whether *that person* normally provides the service in question for remuneration.[259] This explains why the Court, in giving its judgment in Case 263/86 *Humbel*, did not set out any observations concerning the requirement for the normal payment of remuneration.

3. The General Prohibition of Discrimination

(a) Equality of access to education in other Member States

(i) The scope of the EEC Treaty

The first paragraph of Article 7 of the EEC Treaty provides that, within the scope of application of the Treaty, and without prejudice to any special provisions contained therein, any discrimination on grounds of nationality is prohibited. The 'general prohibition of discrimination'[260] thereby laid down is directly effective,[261] that is to say, individuals may rely on that rule before national courts in asserting that domestic law infringes Community law.[262] The Court of Justice confirmed this for the first time[263] in its judgment of 13 July 1983 in Case 152/82 *Forcheri*.[264] It established in that case that the charging of a fee not payable by nationals for the participation by the wife of an EC official in a course of non-university higher education fell within the scope of the EEC Treaty and thus infringed the first paragraph of Article 7 of the Treaty.

The Court substantiated this finding, *ratione personae*,[265] by referring to the employment relationship between EC officials and the Community and to the need for them to be able to enjoy the right to freedom of movement laid down by the Treaty. As regards the scope *ratione materiae* of the Treaty, it concluded from Article 128 of the Treaty and the Decision of the Council of 2 April 1963 laying down general principles for implementing a common vocational training policy[266] that 'although it is true that educational and vocational training policy is not as such part of the areas which the Treaty has allotted to the competence of the Community institutions, the opportunity for such kinds of instruction falls within the scope of the Treaty'.[267]

Although there existed in that case a reference, *ratione personae*, to Community

---

259 For a concurring view, see Völker, p. 98.

260 Grabitz in: *idem, Kommentar zum EWGV*, Art. 7, n. 1.

261 Ipsen, *Europäisches Gemeinschaftsrecht*, p. 639; Grabitz in: *idem, Kommentar zum EWGV*, Art. 7, n. 23.

262 de Moor, p. 458.

263 The judgments referred to by Oppermann in *EG-Recht und Deutsche Bildungsordnung*, p. 19, n. 33, namely those in Case 36/74 *Walrave and Koch* [1974] ECR 1405 and Case 13/76 *Donà* v. *Mantero* [1976] ECR 1333, cannot be regarded as confirming the direct effect of the first para. of Art. 7 of the Treaty, since they deal only with the effect of Art. 48, the first para. of Art. 59 and the third para. of Art. 60.

264 [1983] ECR 2323.

265 See in that regard 'The spouse of a migrant worker', pp. 105 *et seq.*, above.

266 OJ, English Special Edition 1963-1964, p. 25 (OJ 1963, p. 1338, in other language versions).

267 [1983] ECR 2323 (at p. 2336).

law, there was none whatever in Case 293/83 *Gravier*.[268] The plaintiff in the main proceedings, a French woman, had travelled to Belgium solely in order to take up a course of art studies. She contested before the Belgian courts the imposition of an enrolment fee not payable by Belgian nationals, relying on the first paragraph of Article 7 of the EEC Treaty. The Court of Justice found, first, that 'access to and participation in courses of instruction and apprenticeship, in particular vocational training, are not unconnected with Community law'.

However, that observation left open the question of determining when the scope of application of the Treaty is positively affected. The Court concluded, with reference to Articles 7 and 12 of Regulation No. 1612/68, Article 128 of the EEC Treaty and the above-mentioned decision of 2 April 1963, as well as statements made by the Council and by the Ministers for Education meeting within the Council, that the common vocational training policy referred to in Article 128 of the Treaty was gradually being established. It laid emphasis on the significance of this as regards freedom of movement, which was likely in particular to be promoted by access to vocational training in another Member State. It was thus held that the conditions of access to vocational training fell within the scope of the Treaty.[269]

There are two striking differences between that case and the judgment in Case 152/82 *Forcheri*. The first is that the Court construed the scope of the Treaty more narrowly, in that it made express reference in the latter case only to vocational training.[270] However, the really significant difference[271] lies in the fact that the Court refrained from examining the question whether the scope of application of the EEC Treaty was also affected *ratione personae*. Accordingly, Article 7 of the Treaty is no longer applicable merely to persons falling within the scope of the Treaty by virtue of special provisions contained therein, but to all Community citizens.[272] The only requirement is that there must be discrimination on grounds of nationality such as to fall *ratione materiae* within the scope of the Treaty. As we have seen, the Court accepted this with regard to the conditions of *access*. The absence of any reference to *participation* in courses of instruction, previously described unwaveringly by the Court as 'not unconnected with Community law', cannot be taken to signify that it is not covered by the first paragraph of Article 7 of the Treaty. Otherwise, the right to equality of access would be robbed of (practically) all significance.[273]

The decision in Case 293/83 *Gravier* has been criticized, not on account of the extension of the scope *ratione personae* of the first paragraph of Article 7 of the

---

268 Judgment of 13 February 1985, [1985] ECR 593.

269 [1985] ECR 593 (at pp. 612 *et seq*.).

270 Flynn suggests, in *Gravier: Suite de Feuilleton*, p. 98, that the Court was seeking to distance itself from the decision in Case 152/82 *Forcheri*.

271 Oppermann, in *EG-Freizügigkeit*, p. 21, sees this as 'the decisive "qualitative leap", in the sense that it involves a change from the established interpretation to the conscious laying down of judge-made law'.

272 For a concurring view, see Streil, p. 114; C.O. Lenz, in *Zuständigkeiten und Initiativen*, p. 191, refers in that regard to the possibility of 'direct reliance' on the prohibition against discrimination, which is not to be confused with the 'direct effect' which the first para. of Art. 7 of the Treaty has been established as possessing.

273 See also, in the final analysis, Hochbaum, *WissR 1986*, p. 213.

Treaty, but because of the way it determines the scope of the EEC Treaty *ratione materiae*.[274] According to Oppermann, it is true that the question is not whether specific obligations were already imposed on the Member States; but if it is expressly provided – as in the field of vocational training – that an issue must first be transposed into secondary Community legislation, then Article 7 of the Treaty cannot become effective until such transposition has taken place. No transposition of that kind can be ascertained in the legal measures of the Council cited by the Court.[275]

It should be noted in that regard, first, that the question of competence to legislate on a particular subject falls in principle to be distinguished from the question of the scope of Community law. Whilst the first of those points involves the powers or obligations of the organs of the Community to adopt legislation, the second concerns the ability of Member States to maintain discrimination on grounds of nationality.[276]

Exceptionally, however, the decision whether a particular subject is included within the scope of the Treaty may be entrusted to the Community organs. In such circumstances, the scope of the Treaty prior to such decision remains unaffected.[277] It is true that Article 128 of the Treaty may be regarded as an instance of this; however, it would appear to be going too far to contend that vocational training can only be included within the scope of the Treaty if 'the differences between the systems are offset by Community action'.[278] In adopting the above-mentioned decision of 2 April 1963,[279] the Council made use of the power conferred by Article 128 of the Treaty and took, at the very least,[280] a decision, in conjunction with the other legal measures referred to by the Court of Justice, in favour of the inclusion of access to vocational training.

It has further been contended that it would 'definitely be going too far' to attribute legislative force to the decisions of the Council referred to in the judgment.[281] In opposition to this, it should be pointed out that the 'legislative force' derives not from the decisions themselves but from the first paragraph of Article 7 in conjunction with Article 128 of the Treaty. The aforementioned legal measures of the Council and of the Education Ministers meeting within it, from which it is at least partly apparent 'that even the Council accepts that the actual

---

274 Oppermann, in *EG-Freizügigkeit*, p. 23, sees this as the 'crucial weakness of the *"Gravier* school of thought"'; see also the critical observations made by Streinz in *Auswirkungen des EG-Rechts*, p. 41.

275 Oppermann, *EG-Recht und Deutsche Bildungsordnung*, pp. 72 et seq.

276 See Starkle, p. 682.

277 Bleckmann in: GBTE, *Kommentar zum EWGV*, Art. 7, n. 28.

278 See Oppermann, *EG-Recht und Deutsche Bildungsordnung*, p. 73.

279 OJ, English Special Edition 1963-1964, p. 25 (OJ 1963, p. 1338, in other language versions).

280 According to the findings of the Court in Case 293/83 *Gravier*, the particular attention given by the Community institutions concerned not only access to vocational training but also 'its improvement throughout the Community'; see [1985] ECR 593 (at p. 612). Advocate-General Sir Gordon Slynn expressed the view that, for the purposes of Art. 7 of the EEC Treaty, vocational training falls generally within the scope of the Treaty; see [1985] ECR 593 (at p. 601).

281 See Streinz, *Auswirkungen des EG-Rechts*, p. 41; for a similar but more declaratory view, see Hochbaum, *BayVBl. 1987*, p. 486; for a view concurring with the Court's approach, however, see Schulz, p. 76.

competence of the EC in the educational field is very limited',[282] constitute only evidence of the gradual development of the common vocational training policy.[283] The application of such decisions is in line with the idea, accepted by the Court, that 'the task of implementing the general principles of the common vocational training policy is one for the Member States and the Community institutions working in cooperation'.[284]

Thus the decisions referred to constitute merely the actual expression of cooperation between the Community and the Member States in the field of education, the level of development of which justifies, in the Court's view, accepting that access to vocational training already falls within the scope of the Treaty. The Court thereby respects, in the final analysis, the discretion conferred on the Council by Article 128 of the EEC Treaty in defining the common vocational training policy.[285]

(ii) The concept of vocational training

Having established that access to vocational training falls within the scope of the Treaty, the Court of Justice was still faced with the task, in Case 293/83 *Gravier*, of clarifying what is meant by the concept of vocational training. It defined this as including 'any form of education which prepares for a qualification for a particular profession, trade or employment or which provides the necessary training and skills for such a profession, trade or employment ..., whatever the age and the level of training of the pupils or students, and even if the training programme includes an element of general education'.[286] Consequently, the Court decided on a 'functional' interpretation[287] of the concept of vocational training, focusing on the nature of the teaching rather than on the establishment providing it.[288]

It has been inferred from that definition of the concept that the Court extended the notion of vocational training to general education.[289] Lest reliance be placed on the passage quoted in support of the contention that it makes no difference if the syllabus also includes an element of general education, it should be said that

---

282 Wägenbaur, *EuR 1990*, p. 140.

283 For further details, see 'Effects of Council resolutions by virtue of their being legally relevant facts in connection with the first paragraph of Article 7 of the EEC Treaty', pp. 266 *et seq.*, below.

284 Judgment of the Court of 30 May 1989 in Case 242/87 *Commission* v. *Council ('ERASMUS')* [1989] ECR 1425 (at p. 1453).

285 See, in particular, the wording of the judgment in Case 242/87, [1989] ECR 1425 (at p. 1453): 'From an interpretation of Article 128 based on that conception [i.e. that underlying the Council Decision of 2 April 1963] it follows that the Council is entitled to ...'. By reason of the wide discretion in matters of policy conferred on the Council in the context of Art. 128 of the Treaty, the Court is exceptionally obliged in this instance to have recourse to secondary Community law in order to interpret a Treaty provision.

286 [1985] ECR 593 (at p. 614).

287 Traversa, p. 58, draws a parallel with the interpretation by the Court of the provisions of Art. 48(4) of the EEC Treaty; see in that regard 'Employment in the public service', pp. 84 *et seq.*, above.

288 For a concurring view, see Advocate-General Sir Gordon Slynn in Case 309/85 *Barra* [1988] ECR 355 (at p. 367): 'attention has to be directed to the course rather than the institution'.

289 See Streinz, *Auswirkungen des EG-Rechts*, p. 41; Hochbaum, *BayVBl. 1987*, p. 486.

this appears to be a misinterpretation. The reference must be understood as constituting no more than a self-evident indication of the fact that there can be hardly any prospect of putting together a meaningful syllabus without the inclusion of general subjects. However, in so far as the reference in Case 293/83 *Gravier* to the apparent inclusion of general education is taken to indicate that even teaching in general educational institutions established under national law may fall within the ambit of vocational training, such a conclusion must, at the very least, be misleading, since it is not made clear that the Community law concept differs from the national concept.

In its judgment of 2 February 1988 in Case 24/86 *Blaizot*,[290] the Court of Justice applied the concept of vocational training developed by it in Case 293/83 *Gravier* to university studies. It held that, in general, university studies fulfil those criteria. The only exceptions are certain courses of study primarily constituting general education.[291] In view of the 'functional' definition of the concept, this is consistent. However, the Court limited the retroactive effect of the judgment. This was the first time that it had dealt with the question of university studies. A little later on in the judgment, the Court stated the real reason for the limit placed on its temporal effect: the repayment claims in respect of past periods would 'retroactively throw the financing of university education into confusion' and 'have unforeseeable consequences for the proper functioning of universities'.[292]

The significance of that decision is not exhausted, however, by the fact that it includes university studies within the concept of vocational training. The Court also stated its view on the question whether a stage in a course of study which is not in itself of a vocational nature, but completion of which is a condition of access to and completion of a further – vocational – stage, falls outside the scope of the Treaty. It answered that question in the negative: the two stages together must be regarded as a single unit of vocational training.[293] That finding was subsequently applied by the Court in its judgment of 27 September 1988 in Case 263/86 *Humbel*. In that case, the facts were such that it was an open question whether it was the general element or the vocational element which predominated. Consequently, the Court was unable to state its view as unequivocally as it had done in Case 24/86 *Blaizot*, but it held that the various years of a study programme cannot be assessed individually but must be considered within the framework of the programme as a whole, provided that the programme forms a coherent single entity.[294]

There is thus a limit to the extent to which general education can be linked to vocational training. Whilst it may be desirable to 'apply the prohibition of discrimination to the initial stages of general education',[295] it cannot be

---

290 [1988] ECR 379.

291 *ibid.*, at p. 404. This finding was confirmed by the Court in its judgments of 27 September 1988 in Case 39/86 *Lair* [1988] ECR 3161 (at p. 3194) and Case 197/86 *Brown* [1988] ECR 3205 (at pp. 3241 *et seq.*).

292 [1988] ECR 379 (at pp. 406 *et seq.*).

293 *ibid.*, at p. 404.

294 [1988] ECR 5365 (at p. 5387).

295 Tomuschat, *F.I.D.E. Reports*, p. 26; for a critical view, however, see Berggreen, *Diskussionsbeitrag*.

maintained that these stages and a subsequent course of vocational training, taken together, can be regarded as a single educational unit.[296]

(b) Equal treatment in the award of educational grants

The obligation incumbent on the Member States to afford the same treatment, as regards access to vocational training, as that given to their own nationals raises the question whether the same applies in relation to the award of educational grants. That question arises in particular if educational grants are classified not as falling within the ambit of social law but as forming part of the educational system and as constituting an 'educational subsidy'.[297] In its judgments of 21 June 1988 in Case 39/86 *Lair*[298] and Case 197/86 *Brown*,[299] the Court of Justice took a differentiated view.[300] It held that, in so far as financial assistance is granted to cover fees charged for access to education, it falls within the scope of the Treaty.[301] In so stating, the Court was expressing a view consistent with the judgment in Case 293/83 *Gravier*. It went on to state, however, that, under Community law as it then stood, assistance given for maintenance and for training fell in principle outside the scope of the EEC Treaty. It was, on the one hand, a matter of educational policy, which was not as such included in the spheres entrusted to the Community institutions, and, on the other, a matter of social policy, which fell only within certain areas of specific competence conferred on the Community.[302]

In so saying, the Court confirmed a view which had previously been expressed on a number of occasions.[303] Even though it must ultimately be regarded as correct, it is nevertheless unclear from the aforementioned judgments why the Court excludes grants from the scope of the Treaty.[304] The reference to 'the present stage of development of Community law' is of no assistance, since that stage of development is not explained. Furthermore, the reference to the apportionment of competence in the field of educational and social policy casts no light on the point. The Court cannot have intended this to constitute a reason for its view that the scope of the Treaty remained unaffected.[305] That would amount to a virtually inexplicable dogmatic innovation having great implications. For in its judgment of 2 February 1989 in Case 186/87 *Cowan*,[306] the Court rejected, for example, the objection that because a rule falls within the law of criminal procedure, it cannot be included within the scope of the Treaty. It held that although in principle such

---

296 Flynn, in *Gravier: Suite de Feuilleton*, p. 102, considers that 'any attempt to reduce "vocational training" to a pleonasm and interpret that distinction away cannot succeed'.

297 See Thieme, GS *Wilhelm Karl Geck*, pp. 907 *et seq.*

298 [1988] ECR 3161.

299 [1988] ECR 3205.

300 The wording of the relevant passages is identical in the two judgments; consequently, the references appearing hereinafter relate only to the judgment in Case 39/86 *Lair*.

301 [1988] ECR 3161 (at pp. 3194 *et seq.*).

302 *ibid.*, at p. 3195.

303 e.g. see Magiera, *DÖV* 1987, p. 228: Tomuschat, *F.I.D.E. Reports*, p. 27; Hochbaum, *BayVBl.* 1987, p. 486, n. 48; Avenarius, p. 389.

304 See also Lonbay, p. 373.

305 For a critical view of the reasons given, see also von Wilmowsky, pp. 243 *et seq.*

306 [1989] ECR 195.

rules are a matter for which the Member States are responsible, Community law sets certain limits to their power.[307]Consequently, the reference to the division of competence between the EC and the Member States in the field of educational and social policy can only be understood as constituting a conclusion drawn from the previously established lack of Community competence in the field of educational grants.[308]

An examination of the Court's finding that an award of a maintenance grant by the State falls outside the scope of the Treaty must be based on two fundamental questions: first, whether access to vocational training is dependent on the award of such a grant, and secondly, whether, irrespective of this, such an award falls outside the scope of the Treaty on other grounds. The first question can without hesitation be answered in the negative. Admittedly, as Advocate-General Sir Gordon Slynn correctly points out in Case 197/86 *Brown*,[309] 'if a student cannot eat or have a bed he cannot study'. However, the concept of access to vocational training has a narrower meaning and covers only what is needed to enable the student to attend the course in the first place.[310]

The second question gives rise, however, to greater difficulty. It may be argued, in opposition to the inclusion within the scope of the Treaty of maintenance grants awarded by the State, that Case 293/83 *Gravier* concerned the elimination of 'negative' measures preventing or impeding access, whereas the award of a grant involves equal treatment with regard to 'positive' State benefits which facilitate and promote such access. According to such an argument, only the first of those cases is covered, in the light of the judgment in Case 293/83 *Gravier*, by the prohibition of discrimination contained in the first paragraph of Article 7 of the EEC Treaty.[311]According to this argument, it should be borne in mind, moreover, that the various national grant systems have not yet been approximated throughout the Community.[312]

This line of argument is clearly based on the difference between negative and positive integration.[313] It is questionable, however, whether such differentiation is of any importance in the context of the first paragraph of Article 7 of the EEC Treaty. It is not possible to draw from the first paragraph of Article 7 the inference that the scope of that provision is limited, as a matter of principle, to the elimination of barriers, to the exclusion of rights of participation.[314] This follows from the Court's finding, in Cases 39/86 *Lair* and 197/86 *Brown*, that study grants awarded to cover enrolment fees fall within the scope of the Treaty. According to

---

307 [1989] ECR 195 (at pp. 221 *et seq.*); for the basis of this *dictum*, see the judgment of 3 July 1974 in Case 9/74 *Casagrande* [1974] ECR 773 (at p. 779).

308 This is indicated by the French text of the judgment, the relevant passage in which reads: '*En effet*, elle relève, d'une part, de la politique de l'enseignement ...' (emphasis added).

309 [1988] ECR 3205 (at p. 3230).

310 See also, in the same vein, Advocate-General Sir Gordon Slynn, *ibid.*; Avenarius, p. 389.

311 Avenarius, *ibid.*; Oppermann contends, in *EG-Recht und Deutsche Bildungsordnung*, p. 73, that Case 293/83 *Gravier* was concerned merely with an 'act of liberalization'.

312 Oppermann, *EG-Recht und Deutsche Bildungsordnung*, p. 32.

313 As to those concepts, see Bieber, *Educational aspects*, p. 83; Scherer, p. 163; de Witte, *Scope of Community Powers*, p. 266; Scheuing, *JZ 1975*, p. 155.

314 See also Bleckmann in: GBTE, *Kommentar zum EWGV*, Art. 7, n. 22; if the Member States were to grant a benefit, they would be prohibited by the first para. of Art. 7 of the Treaty from exercising any discrimination.

those judgments, the position ultimately depends solely on the stage of development of Community law.[315]

Consequently, the view advanced by legal writers that it is difficult to see on what logical grounds nationals from other EC countries could be refused the award of a grant for vocational training courses[316] carries less weight, since the determination of a given stage of development of Community law does not merely depend on legal criteria but is subject instead to the assessment of priority made by the Court of Justice. That assessment allows scope for policy considerations and may explain the failure to give reasons for the exclusion of maintenance grants from the scope of the Treaty. The Council Directive of 28 June 1990 on the right of residence for students[317] does not preclude the further development of Community law and the future inclusion of maintenance grants within the scope of the Treaty pursuant to the first paragraph of Article 7 of the EEC Treaty, since Article 3 merely states that the directive does not establish any entitlement to the payment of maintenance grants by the host Member State.

(c) The right of residence for educational purposes

If there exist 'education rights for all Community citizens', then a right of residence is of decisive importance for securing those rights. The recognition of this by the Council led to the adoption by it of the directive of 28 June 1990 on the right of residence for students.[318] That directive might appear to render superfluous the question whether the right to equal access to vocational training institutions establishes an independent right of residence under Community law. On closer inspection, however, that assumption may be seen to be erroneous. If it were found to be the case that the directive establishes the right of residence for students not only on a declaratory basis but on a constitutive basis, when that right in fact derives from primary Community law, namely from the requirement of equal treatment as regards access to vocational training, then the directive would have to be assumed to be unlawful. In those circumstances, it would have been necessary to base the directive not (as it in fact was) on Article 235 of the EEC Treaty but (as the Commission proposed[319]) on paragraph 2 of Article 7 of the Treaty, because Article 235 takes effect only where no other powers are provided for in the EEC Treaty, and is thus applicable only on a subsidiary basis.[320] The second paragraph of Article 7 of the Treaty provides for just such a power, since it authorizes the Council to adopt rules designed to prohibit discrimination on grounds of nationality.

---

315 Magiera contends, in *DÖV 1987*, p. 228, that, under the law as it presently stands, it is the Member State in which the student was resident prior to the commencement of the course which is responsible for providing financial support.

316 See Steiner, p. 352; for a similar view, see Hartley, p. 341; von Wilmowsky, p. 243; Lonbay, p. 373.

317 OJ 1990 L 180, p. 30.

318 *ibid.*

319 Proposal of 26 June 1989, OJ 1989 C 191, p. 2; amended proposal of 21 December 1989, OJ 1990 C 26, p. 15.

320 e.g. see the judgment of the Court of 30 May 1989 in Case 242/87 *Commission* v. *Council* ('ERASMUS') [1989] ECR 1425 (at p. 1452).

The Council clearly proceeded on the basis of a constitutive recognition of the right of residence for students. According to Article 1 of the directive, Member States are obliged, 'in order to facilitate access to vocational training, (to) *grant* the right of residence' to students.[321] Article 1 of the Commission's proposal, on the other hand, provided merely for Member Sates to take measures to facilitate the exercise of the right of residence. Furthermore, the Council declined to adopt a recital proposed by the Commission, according to which equal access to vocational training presupposes the possibility of residence on the territory of the Member State concerned.[322] It is also logical to have based the directive on Article 235, since there appears to be no other legal basis for the constitutive recognition of the right of residence. Consequently, it is necessary to examine whether the premise underlying the directive, to the effect that the right of residence for students does not derive from the first paragraph of Article 7 of the Treaty in conjunction with Article 128, and that the directive cannot therefore have been based on the second paragraph of Article 7, is correct.

The overwhelming majority of legal writers take the view that the right to be treated in the same way as nationals as regards access to vocational training automatically entails a right of residence.[323] Thus Oppermann describes a refusal to grant a place on a study course on the ground that the student has no residence permit as a 'blatantly crude circumvention of the ban on discrimination'.[324] However, the judgment of the Court in Case 152/82 *Forcheri* could be said to run counter to that view. The operative part of that judgment states that, if a Member State organizes educational courses, 'to require of a national of another Member State *lawfully established* in the first Member State an enrolment fee which is not required of its own nationals in order to take part in such courses constitutes discrimination by reason of nationality, which is prohibited ...'.[325]

There are in fact a number of isolated cases in which the view has been advanced that, rather than entailing a right of residence, the right to equal access to education presupposes the existence of such a right.[326] According to that view, the conditions governing access to education are different from those applying to the right of residence. It is said that the effect of the judgment in Case 293/83 *Gravier* is such as to make the freedom of movement which is to be promoted (i.e. presumably, the right of residence) conditional[327] on the 'enumerative and

321 Emphasis added.

322 See the amended proposal (op. cit. n. 319), fourth recital in the preamble.

323 See Traversa, p. 66; Wägenbaur, *MittHV 1989*, p. 139; Hochbaum & Eiselstein, p. 39; Avenarius, p. 387; Magiera, *DÖV 1987*, p. 228; Oppermann, *EG-Recht und Deutsche Bildungsordnung*, pp. 17 and 33; Zuleeg, *NJW 1987*, p. 2196; Sieveking, p. 118; Steiner, p. 352; Völker, p. 116; Reich, *Förderung und Schutz*, p. 82; Kampf, p. 401; Hailbronner, *JuS 1991*, p. 11; para. 18 of the opinion of Advocate-General Van Gerven of 11 July 1991 in Case 357/89 *Raulin* [1992] ECR I-1027. Following delivery of the judgment in Case 293/83 *Gravier*, the Commission excepted from the scope of the directive on the right of residence, as originally proposed, 'nationals of a Member State who go to another Member State for the sole purpose of vocational training at a university or an institute of higher learning'; see OJ 1985 C 171, p. 8.

324 Oppermann, *EG-Recht und Deutsche Bildungsordnung*, p. 33.

325 [1983] ECR 2323 (at p. 2337); emphasis added.

326 See Beutler, p. 154; B. Huber, p. 3060; Forch, pp. 30 *et seq.*

327 See Beutler, *ibid*. It is not easy to understand the qualification applied by him in his contention that 'the grounds given in that specific case for denying the residence necessary for that purpose [i.e. for access to education] would scarcely be justifiable' (p. 15).

conclusive' determination, by primary Community law and by the rules of secondary Community law implementing the Treaty provisions, of the class of persons entitled to such freedom of movement.[328]

That line of argument underestimates the particular significance of the judgment in Case 293/83 *Gravier*. Whilst it may have been possible to assume, on the basis of the judgment in Case 152/82 *Forcheri* that a lawful[329] right of residence was a necessary precondition of equal access to education,[330] it was no longer possible to make that assumption following delivery of the judgment in Case 293/83 *Gravier*. As is demonstrated above,[331] the decisive innovation introduced by that judgment lay in the fact that the Court refrained from examining the scope *ratione personae* of the Treaty within the framework of the first paragraph of Article 7.[332] There was simply no longer any need for a pre-existing right of residence on the basis of the Treaty provisions relating to freedom of movement.[333]

However, it would be wrong to interpret the idea of an independent right of residence as an *unconditional* right. Like the residence rights of persons entitled to freedom of movement by virtue of special measures, the right of residence of students is subject, in the context of the directive on the coordination of special measures concerning the movement and residence of foreign nationals,[334] to restrictions which are justified on grounds of public policy, public security or public health, since the extension by the judgment in Case 293/83 *Gravier* of the class of persons entitled to a right of residence must necessarily entail an extension of the scope of that directive. In the third subparagraph of Article 2(2) of the directive on the right of residence for students, the Council logically extended the scope of application of the 1964 directive to students enjoying a right of residence.

In the light of all the foregoing, it may be concluded that the right to equal access to vocational training in another Member State vests not only in persons already resident in that State but in all Community citizens. It follows that there exists a right of residence which is independent of the provisions of the EEC Treaty relating to freedom of movement, the purpose of which is to safeguard that right of

---

328 See B. Huber, p. 3060.

329 This would raise the question whether the lawfulness of the right of residence must necessarily derive from Community law or whether it would be enough for it to ensue from the general law on aliens; see in that regard Hartley, p. 329, n. 11; Starkle, pp. 692 *et seq.*

330 Doubt has already been cast on the justification given for this frequently cited conclusion; see Advocate-General Sir Gordon Slynn in Case 293/83 *Gravier* [1985] ECR 593 (at p. 599): 'I do not, however, read the judgment [in Case 152/82 *Forcheri*] as laying down that a necessary precondition of the right to undertake a particular vocational course depends on a pre-existing right of residence. As a matter of description, Mrs Forcheri clearly was lawfully established, and there would be no justification for granting a right to a course to someone who was unlawfully in a country.'

331 See 'The scope of the EEC Treaty', pp. 115 *et seq.*, above.

332 For a similar view, see Kampf, p. 401: the Court *extended* the scope of application to persons.

333 See Magiera, *DÖV 1987*, p. 227: 'Thus the Court expressed itself in favour of a special freedom of education, as compared with the special freedoms laid down in the Treaty ...'.

334 Council Directive of 25 February 1964 on the coordination of special measures concerning the movement and residence of foreign nationals which are justified on grounds of public policy, public security or public health, OJ, English Special Edition 1963-1964, p. 117 (OJ 1964 No. 56, p. 850, in other language versions).

access. The directive on the right of residence for students can only serve as confirmation, and as a more detailed formulation, of that right of residence;[335] accordingly, it should have been based on the second paragraph of Article 7 of the EEC Treaty.

The European Parliament, which shares this view, consequently brought an action on 28 September 1990 before the Court of Justice for the annulment of the directive on the right of residence for students.[336] In particular, it complained that, as a result of the choice of legal basis, its prerogatives in the Community legislative process had been curtailed, since the second paragraph of Article 7 of the EEC Treaty provides for cooperation with the Parliament, whereas Article 235 provides merely for the Parliament to be consulted. Not only that case, but also Case C-357/89 *Raulin*, provides an opportunity for the Court to clarify the question of the right of residence for students.[337]

IV. PROGRAMMES IN THE FIELD OF EDUCATION

1. Overview

In the mid-1980s the Community began to adopt programmes in the field of education, the number of which is now substantial.[338] These programmes relate to the educational field in a number of different ways, the overwhelming majority concerning vocational training. These include the COMETT[339] and ERAS-MUS[340] programmes, the action programme for the vocational training of young people[341] and the LINGUA,[342] EUROTECNET[343] and FORCE[344] programmes. It is more appropriate to classify within the field of general education, on the other hand, the third general programme to encourage the exchange of young

---

335 Wägenbaur, *MittHV 1989*, p. 139, has advanced the view that the adoption of the directive was necessary on grounds of legal certainty.

336 Case C-295/90, OJ 1990 C 285, p. 13.

337 See question 6 posed by the court making the reference, [1992] ECR I-1027 (at p. 1058).

338 Thus the Commission has recently had occasion to submit a 'Memorandum on the rationalization and coordination of vocational training programmes at Community level'; see COM(90) 334.

339 Programme on cooperation between universities and enterprises regarding training in the field of technology; Phase 1: Council Decision of 24 July 1986 OJ 1986 L 222, p. 17; Phase 2: Decision of 16 December 1988, OJ 1989 L 13, p. 28.

340 European Community action scheme for the mobility of university students, Council Decision of 15 June 1987, OJ 1987 L 166, p. 20; extended and amended by Decision of 14 December 1989, OJ 1989 L 395, p. 23.

341 Council Decision of 1 December 1987, OJ 1987 L 346, p. 31; amended by Decision of 22 July 1991, OJ 1991 L 214, p. 69.

342 Action programme to promote foreign language competence; Council Decision of 28 July 1989, OJ 1989 L 239, p. 24. That programme also contains references to general education.

343 Action programme to promote innovation in the field of vocational training resulting from technological change; Council Decision of 18 December 1989, OJ 1989 L 393, p. 29.

344 European Community action programme for the development of continuing vocational training; Council Decision of 29 May 1990, OJ 1990 L 156, p. 1.

workers,[345] which is due to expire no later than the end of 1991, and the 'Youth for Europe' action programme.[346]

It is principally the programmes in the field of vocational training which give rise to legal problems; accordingly, the following remarks are limited to those programmes. Despite the differences in their content, the programmes in question have a number of features in common:

(1) they were all adopted by the Council in the form of decisions;

(2) their legal basis is invariably Article 128 of the EEC Treaty[347] and, in most cases, the Council Decision of 2 April 1963 laying down general principles for implementing a common vocational training policy;[348]

(3) all of the programmes provide for measures to be taken at Community level by the Commission;

(4) the vocational training programmes are intended in principle to support and complement measures taken by the Member States in the area in question,[349] although the COMETT and ERASMUS programmes incorporate new measures for which no parallel exists at national level;

(5) all of the programmes provide for financing by the Community; and

(6) lastly, and most importantly, all of the programmes impose duties of cooperation on the Member States. This point will be examined in greater detail below.

It will be noted generally that a committee composed of representatives of the Member States, whose powers differ from case to case, is normally assigned to assist the Commission. There is no indication that the Member States have any option as to the delegation of representatives to the committees. Furthermore, a duty of active cooperation is imposed on the Member States in order to enable the Community programmes to achieve their objective of supporting and complementing the measures taken by the Member States. The ERASMUS programme may be cited as a specific example of the potentially far-reaching obligations on the Member States within the framework of such programmes. The establishment of a European university network provided for by that programme[350] obliges the

---

345 Council Decision of 13 December 1984, OJ 1984 L 331, p. 36, extended by Decision of 29 May 1990, OJ 1990 L 156, p. 8; as to the integration of this programme in the action programme for the vocational training of young people, see 'Vocational training', pp. 40 et seq., above.

346 Programme for the promotion of youth exchanges in the Community; Phase 1: Council Decision of 16 June 1988, OJ 1988 L 158, p. 42; Phase 2: Council Decision of 29 July 1991, OJ 1991 L 217, p. 25.

347 The current versions of the programmes – apart from the LINGUA programme – are based solely on Art. 128 of the EEC Treaty. The LINGUA programme was additionally based on Art. 235 of the Treaty.

348 OJ, English Special Edition 1963-1964, p. 25 (OJ 1963, p. 1338, in other language versions); it is only the decision amending the ERASMUS programme (see n. 340) and the decision adopting the FORCE programme (see n. 344) which are not based on that decision.

349 e.g. see Art. 1(2) of the FORCE programme, op. cit., n. 344: 'The aim of the Force programme is to support and complement the policies and activities developed by and in the Member States in the area of continuing vocational training'.

350 Action 1; see the Annex to the decision (n. 340).

Member States to create the statutory outline conditions for participation by the universities concerned.[351] The contrary view that they are under no such obligation[352] cannot be accepted. Admittedly, participation by universities is voluntary;[353] but this is not a characteristic peculiar to programmes in the field of vocational training.[354] It is necessary to draw a distinction between this question and that of the obligations of Member States, the answer to which lies in the interpretation of the relevant legal instrument.[355]

2. ARTICLE 128 OF THE EEC TREATY AS THE LEGAL BASIS

(a) The problem

Article 128 of the EEC Treaty empowers the Council to 'lay down general principles for implementing a common vocational training policy capable of contributing to the harmonious development both of the national economies and of the common market'. On the basis of that provision, the Council adopted on 2 April 1963 a decision 'laying down general principles for implementing a common vocational training policy'.[356] The question which arises is whether those provisions are capable of covering Community programmes in the field of vocational training which possess the characteristics referred to above.[357] This depends primarily on the question whether the Community institutions are able, pursuant to Article 128 of the Treaty, to take specific measures which are effective in budgetary terms and whether, and to what extent, they are capable of imposing obligations on the Member States.

The Court of Justice has to date expressed a view on this question in three judgments. The proceedings in Case 242/87 *Commission* v. *Council*[358] were prompted by the Commission's application for the annulment of the ERASMUS decision. The Commission contended that the reference to Article 235 of the Treaty as the legal basis of the decision, in addition to Article 128, was wrong on the ground that the latter provision alone was sufficient to confer on the Community the power to adopt the programme. Case 56/88 *United Kingdom* v.

---

351 See, generally, Classen, *EuR 1990*, p. 14; Hochbaum, *DUZ 8/1989*, p. 11; Zilioli, p. 67; for a detailed analysis, see Lenaerts, *ERASMUS*, pp. 122 *et seq.*; as to further obligations incumbent on the Member States within the framework of the ERASMUS programme, see the opinion of Advocate-General Mischo in Case 242/87 *Commission* v. *Council ('ERASMUS')* [1989] ECR 1425 (at p. 1443).

352 See, for this view, Frowein, *Bundesrat*, p. 300; also Gölter, p. 136. The Commission advanced the view in Case 242/87 that, whilst the Member States might need to amend their internal rules, this would apply only to Member States voluntarily taking part in the scheme; see [1989] ECR 1425 (at p. 1431).

353 This point is contested by Frowein, *Bundesrat*, p. 300.

354 For a concurring view, see Advocate-General Mischo in Case 242/87 *Commission* v. *Council* [1989] ECR 1425 (at p. 1443).

355 See Lenaerts, *ERASMUS*, p. 113: '... the Decision is binding upon the Member States where it contains precise obligations to be fulfilled by the latter'.

356 OJ, English Special Edition 1963-1964, p. 25 (OJ 1963, p. 1338, in other language versions).

357 See 'Overview', pp. 125 *et seq.*, above.

358 Judgment of 30 May 1989, [1989] ECR 1425.

Council[359] concerned, to some extent, the reverse situation.[360] The United
Kingdom applied for the annulment of the decision concerning an action
programme for the vocational training of young people, because it took the view
that that programme should have been based not only on Article 128 of the Treaty
but also on Article 235. The same objection was raised in the proceedings in
Joined Cases C-51, C-90 and C-94/89 *United Kingdom and Others* v. *Council*,[361] in
which the United Kingdom, Germany and France contested the decision
concerning the second phase of the COMETT programme.

The scope of the dispute was wide-ranging, since the question of the correct
legal basis has implications for the method of voting: Article 128 of the EEC
Treaty is one of the few Treaty provisions permitting the adoption of decisions by a
simple majority[362] (see Article 148(1) of the Treaty), whereas Article 235 of the
Treaty requires a unanimous vote. Furthermore, in the context of Article 128, the
participation of the European Parliament is merely optional, whereas in the case of
Article 235 it is mandatory, in that the Parliament must be consulted. However,
the wording of Article 235 is such that it takes effect only where Article 128 does
not already confer the requisite powers for the adoption of vocational training
programmes of the type in question. This point is considered further below. There
is no need for any further consideration of the development, discussed above,[363] of
the concept of vocational training.[364]

(b) Powers of the Community in the field of vocational training

(i) Principles underlying the powers of action of the Community institutions

Depending on how it is read, the provision contained in Article 128 of the EEC
Treaty exhibits either one or two approaches to the powers of action of the
Community institutions in the field of vocational training. If emphasis is placed
on the question of power to lay down general principles, and if the phrase 'for
implementing a common ... policy capable of contributing to the harmonious
development' is regarded merely as the substantive precondition for laying down
such principles, the scope of the provision must be limited to the conferment of
power to lay down those general principles alone, and the adoption of specific
programmes on that basis would appear to be excluded from the outset, since –
without there being any need to examine the point in any greater depth – such
programmes can under no circumstances be regarded as 'general principles'. If, on

---

359 Judgment of 30 May 1989, [1989] ECR 1615.
360 See Advocate-General Mischo's opinion in Case 56/88 *United Kingdom* v. *Council* [1989]
ECR 1615 (at p. 1617).
361 Judgment of 11 June 1991, [1991] ECR I-2757.
362 For a more detailed examination, see Lenaerts, *ERASMUS*, p. 116.
363 See 'The concept of vocational training', pp. 118 *et seq.*, above.
364 It is interesting to note in this connection, however, that the Court of Justice held, in its
judgment in Case 242/87, that it was legitimate to include within the programme university
courses which (exceptionally) do *not* constitute vocational training (see [1989] ECR 1425 (at p.
1453)), thereby disappointing the expectation of Lenaerts, *ERASMUS*, at p. 120, that this point
would be decisive as regards the question of the legal basis. Consequently, Flynn considers, in
YEL 1988, at p. 85, that 'the Court took a *de minimis* approach to competence'.

the other hand, independent significance is attached, as regards the question of Community powers of action, to the passage concerning the implementation of a common policy, different conclusions may be drawn.

Article 128 of the Treaty has often been interpreted in accordance with the first of those viewpoints, that is to say, as relating to the division of powers between the Community and the Member States: the Community has the power, it is argued, to lay down general principles, and the Member States are responsible for the implementation of the common vocational training policy.[365] In the context of Article 128 of the Treaty, it is claimed, the Community's powers are limited to the establishment of general principles.[366]

The argument is frequently advanced in this connection that Article 128 refers to a 'common policy' and not to a 'Community policy'.[367] It is first of all necessary, therefore, to examine in greater detail the meaning of the term 'common policy'. There are three other references in the EEC Treaty, apart from that contained in Article 128, to the implementation of a 'common policy', namely in the provisions relating to agriculture (Articles 38 et seq.), transport (Articles 74 et seq.) and commercial policy (Articles 110 et seq.).[368] The introduction of a common policy is predominantly regarded as the most extensive way of bringing an area under the umbrella of the Community.[369]

That view is correct. The recognition of a policy as 'common' cannot be taken to indicate any power of action on the part of the Member States themselves. The situation is in fact the opposite. This is clear from the following considerations: the establishment of the European Economic Community was based on the intention of the Member States henceforth to act, no longer separately but 'in common', in the fields laid down by the Treaty. This is evidenced by the resolution expressed by the Member States in the preamble to the EEC Treaty 'to ensure the economic and social progress of their countries by *common* action'.[370] They further state their desire 'to contribute, by means of a *common* commercial policy, to the progressive abolition of restrictions on international trade'.[371] The designation of the union of the Member States as an economic *community* has no other meaning. The EEC Treaty vests the Member States' notions of common action with legal

---

365 e.g. see the view advanced by the Council in Case 242/87 *Commission* v. *Council* [1989] ECR 1425 (at p. 1432); Hochbaum, *WissR 1986*, pp. 214 et seq.; Knolle, p. 379; Sprung in: WEGS, *Die EWG*, Art. 128: ' in order to prompt the Member States to implement a common policy in that area'.

366 See C.O. Lenz, *Zuständigkeiten und Initiativen*, p. 204; Classen, *EuR 1990*, p. 16.

367 e.g. see Fiedler, p. 167; Hochbaum, *Federal Structure*, p. 153; Konow, *RdJB 1989*, p. 125.

368 See also the reference in Art. 40 of the EEC Treaty to the possible introduction, in the context of the Common Agricultural Policy, of a common price policy and the somewhat casual acknowledgement as common policies, in Art. 130f(3) of the Treaty, of the rules on competition and trade.

369 See Classen, *EuR 1990*, p. 15; C.O. Lenz, *Zuständigkeiten und Initiativen*, p. 203; *idem, Die Rechtsordnung der EG*, p. 86; Levi Sandri, p. 26; Vedder in: Grabitz, *Kommentar zum EWGV*, Art. 113, n. 3: 'In the field of commercial policy pursuant to Article 113, the EC possesses an exclusive competence according to its nature as a common policy'; see also Opinion 1/76 of the Court of Justice of 26 April 1977 [1977] ECR 741.

370 Emphasis added.

371 Emphasis added.

form; in other words, the Member States use the EEC as a vehicle for the pursuit by them of their *common* interests. Where the Treaty intends that there should not be 'communautarization' but merely coordination of the policies of individual States, it makes it completely clear.[372]

As regards the Common Vocational Training Policy referred to in Article 128 of the Treaty, it has been objected that, although Article 3 of the Treaty mentions the other common policies, it does not refer to that mentioned in Article 128.[373] In his Opinion in Case 242/87 *Commission* v. *Council*, Advocate-General Mischo advanced the view that it was 'difficult to deny that if the common policy in the sphere of vocational training had the same scope and the same degree of Community involvement as the common policies in the spheres of agriculture, transport or external trade it would have been mentioned in Article 3, which lists the major objectives of the Community'.[374]

There is no intention to suggest that the Common Vocational Training Policy forms one of the 'major objectives' of the Community, nor that it has the same weight under Community law as the other common policies, although that view appears, in the light of the developments which have taken place in Community law, to be not wholly unarguable. Nor is it sought to be denied that the other common policies contain substantive preconditions and procedures for their implementation which are considerably more precise than those contained in Article 128.[375]

However, all those arguments fail in their aim of segregating the common vocational training policy from the other common policies laid down by the Treaty and of assigning responsibility for its implementation to the Member States. The fact is that there is no apparent reason why the notion of the common policy referred to in Article 128 of the Treaty should have any different meaning from that found elsewhere in the Treaty.[376] As has already been shown, the very use of the word 'common' cannot be made to accord with any power on the part of the Member States. For the same reason, it is not possible to base the purported 'special role' of the common policy in the sphere of vocational training on the argument that Article 128 of the Treaty merely provides that that policy – as laid down in the German text – 'beitragen *kann*' to the harmonious development of the national economies and of the Common Market, rather than that it should *necessarily* do so.[377] On the contrary, what is involved here is a commitment to an objective, as is clear from the English text of the Treaty, which uses the term 'capable of contributing'. Were the position otherwise, the relevant passage would be superfluous.

It follows from all this that Article 128 of the Treaty empowers the Community institutions not only to lay down general principles but equally to implement a

---

372 e.g. see Art. 103 of the EEC Treaty, concerning conjunctural policy: 'Member States shall regard their conjunctural policies as a matter of common concern'.

373 Classen, *EuR 1990*, p. 16; Hochbaum, *BayVBl. 1987*, p. 487.

374 [1989] ECR 1425 (at p. 1438).

375 This is emphasized by Advocate-General Mischo in Case 242/87 *Commission* v. *Council* [1989] ECR 1425 (at pp. 1439 *et seq.*).

376 For a concurring view, see Levi Sandri, p. 26.

377 Although that argument is advanced by Hochbaum, *BayVBl. 1987*, p. 487; emphasis added.

common policy in the sphere of vocational training.[378] That view was confirmed by the Court of Justice in its judgment in Case 242/87 *Commission* v. *Council* (*'ERASMUS'*), in which it stated that the Community cannot be denied the means of action necessary to carry out the Common Vocational Training Policy effectively.[379] It is impossible to concur with the view that Article 128 of the Treaty did not contemplate the pursuit of that common policy 'until a point in time far in the future'[380] or that it allowed for the development of that policy at an embryonic stage only.[381] No such limitations can be inferred from the wording or meaning of the provision.

(ii) Individual powers

The conclusion reached immediately above, to the effect that the Community institutions are empowered in principle to adopt measures for the implementation of the Common Vocational Training Policy, leaves open the question of which individual powers are vested in the Community institutions.

It is necessary first of all to examine whether they can adopt, on the basis of Article 128 of the EEC Treaty, specific programmes of the type in question. Article 128 lays down the form which the Common Vocational Training Policy is permitted to take only to the extent of requiring it to comply with the general objective, previously mentioned in Article 2 of the Treaty, of contributing to 'the harmonious development both of the national economies and of the common market'. By contrast with the other common policies provided for by the Treaty,[382] Article 128 prescribes no further requirements of a formal or substantive kind. However, the authors of the Treaty compensated for this deficiency by imposing on the Council, in Article 128, the obligation to lay down general principles for implementing the Common Vocational Training Policy.[383] From a technical legal standpoint, that approach may be described as *'contractum ad contrahendum'*.[384] The form which the common policy is to take is left to the

---

378 That power goes hand in hand with the obligation to pursue the common policy; see Boulouis, p. 58; Fastenrath, p. 494: following the expiry of the transitional period, the Community institutions are under a duty 'to formulate themselves the essence of the substantive law'; an opposing view is apparently held, however, by Grabitz, *Integration 1985*, p. 106.

379 [1989] ECR 1425 (at p. 1453).

380 That is the view expressed, however, by Oppermann, *EG-Recht und Deutsche Bildungsordnung*, p. 36.

381 According to the Council in Case 242/87 *Commission* v. *Council* (*'ERASMUS'*) [1989] ECR 1425 (at p. 1452).

382 See in particular the detailed rules governing the Common Agricultural Policy, contained in Arts 38 *et seq.* of the EEC Treaty.

383 Their designation as 'general principles' does not limit their binding effect, but merely affects the degree to which their obligatory nature is defined in concrete terms; for arguments in support of their binding effect, see, for example, C.O. Lenz, *Zuständigkeiten und Initiativen*, p. 204; Ipsen, *Europäisches Gemeinschaftsrecht*, p. 943; Levi Sandri, p. 28; Knolle, p. 379; for a contrary view, see, for example, Hailbronner, *JuS 1991*, p. 18; Konow, *RdJB 1989*, p. 125; Hochbaum, *BayVBl. 1987*, p. 483; Sprung in: WEGS, *Die EWG*, Art. 128; Schlotfeld, pp. 54 *et seq.*

384 See Lochner, p. 37. Advocate-General Lenz refers in his Opinion in Case 13/83 *European Parliament* v. *Council* (*'Common transport policy'*) to a *'pactum de contrahendo'*; see [1985] ECR 1537.

Council, which has in that regard a discretion recognized by the Court of Justice[385] as being wide.[386]

The Common Vocational Training Policy was first given concrete form by the adoption by the Council of its decision of 2 April 1963 laying down general principles for that common policy.[387] As the Court of Justice stated in its judgment in Case 242/87 *Commission* v. *Council ('ERASMUS')*, that decision constitutes the point of departure for the gradual development of the Common Vocational Training Policy and is based on the idea that the task of its implementation is one for the Member States and the Community working in cooperation.[388] What this means, clearly, is cooperation between the Community and the Member States, not cooperation between the Member States themselves.[389]

That finding by the Court is not inconsistent with the view expressed above that it is the Community institutions alone which are empowered to define the Common Vocation Training Policy. As we have seen, Article 128 of the EEC Treaty itself does not lay down the form which the Common Vocation Training Policy is to take; the Council, in the exercise of its discretion, has given concrete form to that policy in the manner described by the Court. A characteristic feature of a *'contractum ad contrahendum'* is to be found in the fact that the Court is obliged to respect the concrete form given by the Council, in accordance with the Treaty, to the Common Vocational Training Policy. The Court has logically based its interpretation of Article 128 of the Treaty on the idea, expressed in the above-mentioned decision of 2 April 1963, of cooperation between the Member States and the Community institutions; it follows from this that the Court has acknowledged the power of the Council to adopt measures providing for Community action in the sphere of vocational training and imposing corresponding obligations of cooperation on the Member States. According to the Court, such an interpretation ensures the practical effectiveness of Article 128 of the EEC Treaty.[390]

The principle of the *'effet utile'* is therefore such as to entitle the Council to translate the notion of cooperation between the Community institutions and the Member States into concrete measures. The argument against this, to the effect that there is no apparent reason 'why the adoption of specific promotional programmes should be necessary in order to perform the task of "laying down general principles" ',[391] does not hold water. The *'effet utile'* relates not only to the establishment of general principles but also to the implementation of the Common Vocational Training Policy provided for in Article 128 of the Treaty.

---

385 See the judgment of 22 May 1985 in Case 13/83 *European Parliament* v. *Council ('Common transport policy')* [1985] ECR 1513 (at p. 1596).

386 See Frohnmeyer in: Grabitz, *Kommentar zum EWGV*, n. 5 preceding Art. 74; Grabitz, *Integration 1985*, p. 106.

387 OJ, English Special Edition 1963-1964, p. 25.

388 [1989] ECR 1425 (at p. 1453). Concurring with this, Pertek points out, at p. 135, that the concept of cooperation marks the furthest limit to which the Community institutions are prepared to go in their actions.

389 See, however, Pertek, p. 135: 'Le Conseil ... peut créer le cadre de la coopération entre les Etats membres'.

390 [1989] ECR 1425 (at p. 1453).

391 See Classen, *EuR 1990*, p. 18.

Whilst it may thus be concluded that the Community institutions possess, in principle, the power to adopt action programmes of the type referred to, there remains the question whether those programmes can also legitimately provide for expenditure by the Community. This touches upon fundamental questions concerning the financing of Community activities. Some writers have expressed the view in this regard that financial measures by the Community are invariably conditional on express authorization being laid down in the Treaty; were the situation otherwise, it is argued, it would be necessary to apply Article 235.[392] That view cannot be accepted: the Community cannot be prevented from exercising its powers under the Treaty simply because that would require the application of financial resources, and no such limitation can be inferred from the EEC Treaty.

Consequently, it is necessary to show only that the requisite competence exists to perform the task in question, not to show that there is a specific power to finance it.[393] That view was shared by the Court of Justice in Case 242/87 *Commission* v. *Council* (*'ERASMUS'*), in which it dismissed the objection that the EEC Treaty subjects budgetary decisions to more onerous procedural requirements than those laid down in Article 128: different rules govern the legislative procedure, on the one hand, and the budgetary procedure, on the other.[394]

To classify this line of argument as one which is merely technically correct but unconvincing in practical terms[395] is to misunderstand the significance of the split between legislative and budgetary procedures.[396] It may be concluded, therefore, that the Community is empowered, pursuant to Article 128 of the EEC Treaty, to adopt concrete programmes which may also provide for expenditure on the part of the Community.

---

392 See Heck in: GBTE, *Kommentar zum EWGV*, Art. 199, nn. 9 *et seq.*; for a similar, albeit vaguely expressed, view, see Fiedler, p. 172.
393 See Magiera in: Grabitz, *Kommentar zum EWGV*, Art. 199, n. 10; Bieber, *EuR 1982*, p. 118.
394 [1989] ECR 1425 (at p. 1454).
395 See Schmidt-Räntsch, p. 3072.
396 For further details in this regard, see Läufer, pp. 52 *et seq.*; Magiera, *FS Hans-Jürgen Schlochauer*, pp. 829 *et seq.*

Chapter 2

THE FIELD OF CULTURE
IN THE NARROWER SENSE

I. FREE MOVEMENT OF GOODS IN THE CULTURAL FIELD

1. INTRODUCTION

Culture in the narrower sense exhibits two distinct points of contact with the free movement of goods: first, there is the potential question of the free movement of cultural goods, and secondly, that of the influence of the free movement of goods on Member States' decisions with regard to cultural policy matters.

The concept of cultural goods is to be construed in a comprehensive sense: it encompasses not only individual items, such as works of art consisting of sculptures, pictures and the like, but also products with cultural connotations[1] which are, to a greater or lesser extent, mass-produced, such as records, video cassettes, films and books. The latter category covers not only products with a cultural or artistic *content* but those products *in themselves*, as an expression of cultural movements in society, in the broadest sense of the term.[2]

There is a significant economic dimension to trade in cultural goods.[3] For example, paintings are frequently collected purely for the purposes of financial investment.[4] It is worth mentionig the pre-tax turnover of book publishers in the Federal Republic of Germany, which amounted in 1988 to around DM 8.4 billion.[5] The economic importance of trade in cultural goods raises the question

---

1   As to the problem of defining the concept of culture, see 'Introduction', pp. 63 *et seq.*, above.

2   By way of example, books *in themselves* are the subject-matter of the communication of the Commission entitled: 'Books and Reading: A Cultural Challenge for Europe', COM(89) 258. Ipsen, in *GS Wilhelm Karl Geck*, p. 341, writes that, essentially, books and periodicals belong indisputably to the cultural sphere.

3   This is undisputed; see, amongst many others, Ipsen, op. cit., p. 346, refers to the 'economic relevance of trade in cultural products and their manufacture'.

4   See in that regard, with examples, Frey & Serna, pp. 109 *et seq.*

5   Including address books; see *Buch und Buchhandel in Zahlen* (published by the German Federal Book Trade Association), p. 56.

whether, and to what extent, the Court of Justice has rendered the rules on the free movement of goods beneficial to activities of this kind. Regard should also be had to the second point of contact between the cultural field and the free movement of goods to which reference was made at the beginning of this section.

2. The Concept of Goods Within the Meaning of the EEC Treaty

The application of the Treaty provisions on the free movement of goods is conditional on the cultural goods referred to in the introduction qualifying as goods. The EEC Treaty does not define the concept of goods. Although Article 9(1) of the EEC Treaty provides that the customs union is to cover *all* trade in goods, this does not clarify what is meant by the term 'goods'. In Case 7/68 *Commission* v. *Italy*,[6] the problems to which this question gives rise were addressed – apparently for the first time – from a fundamental standpoint.[7] Italy sought in those proceedings to plead that a national law impeding, by means of taxes, the export of articles of an artistic nature was justified on the ground that such objects were not subject to the rules laid down by the EEC Treaty, since they could not be equated with consumer goods or articles of general use.[8] It argued that the EEC Treaty was concluded in order to create an economic community and not a community in articles of artistic, historic or ethnographic interest.[9] Advocate-General Gand, whilst conceding that 'works of art are more than mere common-place merchandise', nevertheless considered that they did not fall outside the general framework of the EEC Treaty, since they can be traded in.[10]

The Court of Justice accepted that view and held that the term 'goods', within the meaning of Article 9 of the Treaty, covered products which can be valued in money and were capable, as such, of forming the subject of commercial transactions. That conclusion was not affected by the characteristics which distinguished the articles covered by the Italian law from other types of merchandise. The rules of the Common Market applied to those goods subject only to the exceptions expressly provided by the Treaty.[11] Although that judgment made it quite clear that cultural goods were subject to the Treaty provisions on the movement of goods, it was subsequently submitted by France at the pre-litigation stage in Case 269/83 *Commission* v. *France*,[12] with regard to newspapers and periodicals, that it was questionable whether Article 30 of the EEC Treaty applied to products which served as vehicles for political, social and cultural information.[13] However, France did not persist in that view in the proceedings before the Court.

---

6   Judgment of 10 December 1968 ([1968] ECR 423); see also the subsequent judgment of 13 July 1972 in Case 48/71 *Commission* v. *Italy* [1972] ECR 527, which was concerned with the enforcement of the judgment of 10 December 1968.
7   See Roth, *ZUM 1989*, p. 101.
8   [1968] ECR 423 (at p. 428).
9   *ibid.*, at p. 433.
10   *ibid.*
11   *ibid*, at p. 429; for a concurring view, see Pescatore, *RTDE 1985*, pp. 451 *et seq.*, who refers in that connection to an 'affirmation banale, mais de grande portée pratique'.
12   Judgment of 14 March 1985 in Case 269/83 *Commission* v. *France* [1985] ECR 837.
13   *ibid.*, at p. 838.

Following its judgment in Case 7/68 *Commission* v. *Italy*,[14] the Court has applied the rules on the free movement of goods to a variety of cultural goods. To the extent to which, in those proceedings, it expressly stated its views on the concept of goods, it did so not in order to reinforce the solution arrived at in its earlier judgment,[15] but merely for the more particular purpose of demarcating the rules on the free movement of goods and the other provisions of the Treaty, especially those on freedom to provide services.[16]

3. THE CUSTOMS UNION

(a) The elimination of customs duties and charges having equivalent effect

Article 16 of the EEC Treaty obliged the Member States to abolish between themselves customs duties on exports and charges having equivalent effect by the end of the first stage, that is to say, according to Article 8(1), by the end of 1961 at the latest. That provision, which has had direct effect since 1 January 1962,[17] formed the subject of the judgment in Case 7/68 *Commission* v. *Italy*.[18] In the opinion of the Commission, the tax provided for in the contested Italian legislation, which was fixed in accordance with the value of the artistic objects to be exported, constituted a tax having equivalent effect to a customs duty. Italy argued for its part that Article 16 of the Treaty was not applicable, and that the relevant provisions were instead those of Articles 30 *et seq.* of the Treaty. It contended that the quantitative restrictions on exports laid down by the Italian law were justified under Article 36 of the Treaty, since they related to the protection of national treasures possessing artistic, historical and archaeological value.[19]

The Court was unwilling to accept this, and held that the question whether export trade was hindered by a pecuniary burden imposed on the price of the exported articles fell within the ambit of Article 16 of the Treaty.[20] This being the

---

14 [1968] ECR 423.

15 Only in the judgment of 20 January 1981 in Joined Cases 55 and 57/80 *Musik-Vertrieb membran* [1981] ECR 147 does the position appear to have been otherwise. In that judgment, the Court held that sound recordings, even if incorporating protected musical works, are products to which the system of free movement of goods provided for by the Treaty applies (at p. 161).

16 e.g. see the judgment of 30 April 1974 in Case 155/73 *Sacchi* [1974] ECR 409, in which the Court held that the transmission of television signals constituted the provision of services, but classified trade in material, sound recordings, films, apparatus and other products used for the diffusion of television signals as falling within the rules on the movement of goods; for a critical view of that judgment, see Schwarze, *Rundfunk und Fernsehen*, p. 34; Ipsen, *Rundfunk im EG-Recht*, pp. 86 *et seq.*; see also the judgment of 7 May 1985 in Case 18/84 *Commission* v. *France* [1985] ECR 1339, in which the Court considered that the printing work needed in order to produce a newspaper constituted not an independent service but preparatory work relating to, and necessary for, the production of the newspaper (at p. 1347).

17 See the judgment of the Court of Justice of 26 October 1971 in Case 18/71 *Eunomia* [1971] ECR 811 (at p. 817).

18 [1968] ECR 423.

19 *ibid.*, at pp. 427 *et seq.*

20 The situation is different, however, where the tax constitutes payment for a service provided by the State on crossing the border and is fair and reasonable; see Beutler et al., *3rd ed.*, p. 280.

case, there could be no question of applying Articles 30 *et seq.* of the Treaty.[21] It follows from this that the rules on the customs union constitute *leges speciales vis-à-vis* the rules on quantitative restrictions.[22] Article 36 of the Treaty was held by the Court to be inapplicable within the framework of the rules on the customs union. It stated that that provision must be strictly construed and was not applicable to measures falling outside the scope of the chapter on the elimination of quantitative restrictions.[23] This is because customs duties and charges having equivalent effect merely make the export in question more expensive, without achieving the objective of Article 36, which is to protect the artistic, historical or archaeological heritage.[24]

(b) The Common Customs Tariff

According to Article 9 of the EEC Treaty, the customs union involves not only the prohibition between Member States of customs duties on imports and exports and of all charges having equivalent effect but also the adoption of a common customs tariff in their relations with third countries. Since 10 September 1987, Council Regulation (EEC) No. 2658/87 of 23 July 1987 'on the tariff and statistical nomenclature and on the Common Customs Tariff'[25] has been applicable. The scope of the regulation includes cultural goods. Thus, like its predecessor,[26] it contains, for example, a chapter on 'works of art, collectors' pieces and antiques',[27] which are exempt from duty, and also a chapter on 'printed books, newspapers, pictures and other products of the printing industry; manuscripts, typescripts and plans'.[28]

The exemption from duty applying to the objects listed in the chapter on 'works of art, collectors' pieces and antiques' has led to a series of references for preliminary rulings in which the importer regarded the above-mentioned chapter as pertinent, whilst the competent customs authorities relied on a different classification and demanded payment of customs duties. That was the position, for example, with regard to the classification of colour screen prints,[29] a wall relief,[30] a

---

21 [1968] ECR 423 (at pp. 429 *et seq.*).
22 Grabitz in: *idem, Kommentar zum EWGV*, Art. 12, n. 18.
23 Subsequently, however, the Court did apply Art. 36 of the Treaty analogously in the field of freedom to provide services; see the judgment of 6 October 1982 in Case 262/81 *Coditel II* [1982] ECR 3381 (at p. 3401).
24 [1968] ECR 423 (at p. 430).
25 OJ 1987 L 256, p. 1; as to the date of its entry into force, see Art. 17 of the regulation; Annex I was amended by Commission Regulation of 31 July 1990, OJ 1990 L 247, p. 1.
26 Regulation (EEC) No. 950/68 of the Council of 28 June 1968 on the common customs tariff, OJ, English Special Edition 1968 (I), p. 275.
27 OJ 1987 L 256, p.1, Annex I, Chapter 97; Chapter 99 in the superseded regulation (see Regulation (EEC) No. 950/68).
28 OJ 1987 L 256, p. 1, Annex I, Chapter 49.
29 Judgment of 27 October 1977 in Case 23/77 *Westfälischer Kunstverein* [1977] ECR 1985.
30 Judgment of 15 May 1985 in Case 155/84 *Onnasch* [1985] ECR 1449.

vintage car,[31] lithographs,[32] art photographs,[33] glass paperweights,[34] and an enamel picture.[35]

In its judgment in Case 23/77 *Westfälischer Kunstverein*, the Court of Justice addressed the fundamental problem of the distinction between headings; it held that it could not be based on the possible artistic merit of the objects in question but must be founded on objective criteria adopted on grounds of practicability and legal certainty.[36] Accordingly, the concept of 'works of art' referred to in the heading of the aforementioned chapter is not meant in the sense of a value judgment. As is apparent from the tariff headings in that chapter, the decisive criterion is originality, which is mentioned in greater detail in the notes to the chapter and is characterized primarily by the personal participation of the artist in the production of the work.[37] In the Court's view, the intention of the exemption from duty of works of art is to give 'favourable treatment to artistic production'.[38] It may therefore be concluded that the Common Customs Tariff is not only applicable to cultural goods but also takes into account, by virtue of different tariff classifications, their cultural significance.

4. The Elimination of Quantitative Restrictions and Measures Having Equivalent Effect

(a) Article 30 of the EEC Treaty

(i) Principles

Article 30 of the EEC Treaty prohibits in principle quantitative restrictions on imports and all measures having equivalent effect. In its judgment of 11 July 1974 in Case 8/74 *Dassonville*,[39] the Court of Justice explained that all trading rules enacted by Member States which are capable of 'hindering, directly or indirectly, actually or potentially, intra-Community trade' were to be regarded as measures having an effect equivalent to quantitative restrictions on imports.[40] This very wide formula, covering not only overtly discriminatory rules but also those which do not differentiate between domestic and imported goods, needed to be revised[41] in relation to provisions applicable without distinction in fields in which no rules of Community law yet existed and legislative competence in respect of the production and distribution of goods remained vested in the Member States.[42] That revision was undertaken by the Court in its judgment of 20 February 1979 in

---

31 Judgment of 10 October 1985 in Case 200/84 *Daiber* [1985] ECR 3363.
32 Judgment of 14 December 1988 in Case 291/87 *Huber* [1988] ECR 6449.
33 Judgment of 13 December 1989 in Case 1/89 *Raab* [1989] ECR 4423.
34 Judgment of 18 September 1990 in Case 228/89 *Farfalla Flemming* [1990] ECR I-3387.
35 Judgment of 8 November 1990 in Case C-231/89 *Gmurzynska-Bscher* [1990] ECR I-4003.
36 [1977] ECR 1985 (at p. 1990).
37 See also Pieroth & Kampmann, p. 1390.
38 Case 291/87 *Huber* [1988] ECR 6449 (at p. 6466).
39 [1974] ECR 837.
40 *ibid.*, at p. 852.
41 See also, to that effect, Langbein, p. 229.
42 See Beutler et al., *3rd ed.*, p. 284.

Case 120/78 (*'Cassis de Dijon'*),[43] in which it held that rules impeding trade which are applicable without distinction[44] must be accepted in so far as they are necessary to satisfy mandatory requirements relating in particular to the effectiveness of fiscal supervision, the protection of public health, the fairness of commercial transactions and consumer protection.[45]

(ii) Application to cultural goods

The above principles relating to Article 30 of the Treaty have been applied frequently by the Court of Justice to national rules relating to the free movement of cultural goods. In its judgment of 10 January 1985 in Case 229/83 *Leclerc*,[46] the Court was concerned with French rules concerning the fixing of book prices. Those rules required all publishers or importers to fix a retail price from which retailers could deviate only to a minimal extent. In the case of reimported books, the price fixed by the importer was required to correspond to a price no lower than that originally fixed by the domestic publisher. The principal distributor of the books was deemed to be the importer.

The Court drew a distinction, first of all, between the importation of books published abroad and the re-importation of books published in France. It held that the rules were discriminatory with regard to the importation of foreign books, since the person responsible for fixing the price, i.e. the principal distributor, operated at a different stage in the commercial process than the domestic publisher. The rules made it impossible for any other importer to charge the retail price that he considered adequate. They were therefore liable to impede trade in books.[47] Contrary to the Commission's contentions,[48] the Court held that the rules regarding the fixing of prices on the re-importation of books published in France were applicable without distinction to domestic and imported books; nevertheless, it held that they constituted a measure having equivalent effect within the meaning of Article 30 of the Treaty, since they prevented the importer from passing on an advantage resulting from a lower price obtained in the exporting State. However, where the sole purpose of the re-importation was to circumvent the price-fixing legislation, the provision in question did not infringe Article 30 of the Treaty.[49]

Although, as we have seen, the Court held that the legislation referred to was applicable without distinction, it did not examine whether there existed any 'mandatory requirements', in particular from the point of view of consumer protection in the form of the protection of books as cultural media.[50] Without

---

43   *Rewe-Zentral AG* v. *Bundesmonopolverwaltung für Branntwein* [1979] ECR 649.

44   It was not until later that the Court stated its view in quite such express terms; e.g. see the judgment of 14 July 1988 in Case 90/86 *Zoni* [1988] ECR 4285 (at p. 4303).

45   [1979] ECR 649 (at p. 662).

46   [1985] ECR 1.

47   *ibid.*, at pp. 34 *et seq.*

48   *ibid.*, at pp. 22 *et seq.*

49   *ibid.*, at p. 35; this limitation is criticized by Müller-Graff, *EuR* 1985, p. 307.

50   This has not been fully appreciated by certain authors; see Müller-Graff, op. cit., p. 306; Kuyper, p. 801.

giving any further reasons, it held that the legislation in question fell to be assessed solely in the light of Article 36 of the Treaty.[51]

The judgment in Case 229/83 *Leclerc* was followed by two further decisions on the same issue, neither of which resulted in any fresh determinations.[52] However, after the French rules had been adapted to bring them into line with the judgment in Case 229/83 *Leclerc* and reimported books ceased, save in cases of abuse, to be tied to the price fixed by the French publisher, the Court had to decide whether the resulting discrimination between French and foreign traders infringed Article 30 of the EEC Treaty. The Court held in that regard that Article 30 concerned only the importation of goods and did not preclude differences in the treatment of domestic goods.[53]

Two further judgments of the Court were concerned, respectively, with preferential postal tariffs and tax advantages in respect of newspapers and periodicals. The first case concerned French legislation providing that publications produced in France, or the editor of which was of French nationality and resident in France, qualified for a preferential postal tariff, whereas publications printed wholly or partly abroad were to be treated as normal printed matter. France denied that its legislation could possibly constitute an obstacle to the free movement of goods, principally on the grounds that the price of a publication did not determine its sales and that the choice of a publication was guided by matters of taste and cultural or political affinity. The Court disagreed, holding that France had infringed Article 30 of the EEC Treaty. It was unable to accept the argument that a reduction of subscription costs due to a preferential postal tariff had no influence on the decision to buy a publication, even if that choice was guided primarily by non-economic considerations.[54]

The second case[55] again concerned French legislation, this time measures affording certain tax advantages to specific newspaper publishers, but not in respect of publications which such publishers printed abroad. France submitted that it was of no consequence to the reader where a publication was produced, and that the place where it was produced did not, consequently, influence his decision to buy it. It argued that the legislation did not, therefore, encourage the purchase of domestic products only.[56]

In its judgment, however, the Court concentrated not on the influence exerted by the legislation on the final consumer's decision to buy the publication but on the effect which the tax rules might have on French newspaper publishers, which would be encouraged to have printing work done in France rather than in another Member State. This might have the result of restricting imports of publications from other Member States.[57] That finding is to be interpreted as meaning that

---

51   See in that regard 'Article 36 of the EEC Treaty', pp 144 *et seq.*, below.

52   Judgment of 11 July 1985 in Case 229/83 *Leclerc* v. *Syndicat des librairies de Loire-Océan* [1985] ECR 2515; judgment of 10 July 1986 in Case 95/84 *Boriello* [1986] ECR 2253.

53   Judgment of 23 October 1986 in Case 355/85 *Cognet* [1986] ECR 3231.

54   Judgment of 14 March 1985 in Case 269/83 *Commission* v. *France* [1985] ECR 837 (at p. 846).

55   Judgment of 7 May 1985 in Case 18/84 *Commission* v. *France* [1985] ECR 1339.

56   *ibid.*, at p. 1347.

57   *ibid.*, at p. 1348.

Article 30 of the EEC Treaty prohibits not only restrictions on the importation of products which already exist but also rules which impede production.

Lastly, mention should be made of a further judgment of the Court, concerning the free movement of video-cassettes. Joined Cases 60 and 61/84 *Cinéthèque*[58] concerned French legislation prohibiting the marketing in video cassette form, prior to the expiration of a given period, of films on release in cinemas. The Commission regarded that provision, which applied without distinction to domestic and foreign films, as permissible; films, it submitted, formed a part of contemporary culture, and it was legitimate, for the purposes of assisting cultural activities, to introduce restrictions on the free movement of goods taking precedence over Article 30 of the Treaty. The Commission evidently regarded support for specific cultural activities as a further 'mandatory requirement' within the meaning of the judgment of 20 February 1979 in Case 120/78 ('*Cassis de Dijon*').[59]

It is not clear from the Court's judgment whether it shared the Commission's view.[60] In the result, it regarded the exploitation rules as compatible with Article 30 of the Treaty. The central argument appears to be that the rules protected not *domestic* film production, but film production *generally*. In the Court's view, there could be no objection under Community law to any restrictions on trade arising from the legislation at issue.[61] Thus it may be concluded, at the very least, that the unilateral protection of national cultural products is inconsistent with Article 30 of the EEC Treaty.[62]

(iii) Influence on Member States' decisions regarding cultural policy

The second point of contact between the free movement of goods and the narrower cultural field to which reference has been made in the introduction to this section concerns the possible effects of such free movement on Member States' decisions regarding cultural policy. Mention should be made in this regard to the judgment of the Court of Justice of 23 November 1989 in Case C-145/88 *Torfaen Borough Council*.[63] The subject-matter of the proceedings giving rise to the reference for a preliminary ruling was the United Kingdom Sunday-trading legislation, which in principle prohibited the sale of goods on Sundays. Detailed justification for considering that that legislation was, at least partly, motivated by considerations of cultural policy will not be provided here, particularly since the concept of cultural policy gives rise to the same problems of definition as the concept of culture itself. It is enough, for the present purposes, simply to draw attention to the Joint Declaration of the German Bishops' Conference and the Council of the

---

58 Judgment of 11 July 1985 in Joined Cases 60 and 61/84 *Cinéthèque and Others* v. *Fédération nationale des cinémas françaises* [1985] ECR 2605.

59 [1979] ECR 649.

60 Oliver, *CML Rev.* 1986, p. 347, has consequently described the statements made by the Court as a 'cryptic pronouncement'.

61 [1985] ECR 2605 (at p. 2626).

62 This view is also taken by Gormley, *ELR 1985*, p. 445; Roth, *ZUM 1989*, p. 109.

63 [1989] ECR 3851.

Protestant Church in Germany, which states *inter alia*: 'Sunday rest is a key value in our culture'.[64]

According to the findings of the national court, the legislation at issue, which was applicable without distinction, resulted in a fall in total sales and thus a corresponding fall in sales of goods stocked from other Member States. The conventional approach would have necessitated considering whether there were any 'mandatory requirements' within the meaning of the *Cassis de Dijon* case-law. However, Advocate-General Van Gerven proposed that the decisive point was whether the legislation operated to partition the market.[65]

The Court did not accept that suggestion, but referred instead to its judgment in Joined Cases 60 and 61/84 *Cinéthèque* and examined whether the legislation was justified by an approved objective of Community law. It held that it was, on the basis that rules controlling hours of work, delivery and sale are consistent with the objectives of the EEC Treaty;[66] they reflected political and economic choices taken in accordance with regional and cultural characteristics which were, in the current state of Community law, a matter for the Member States.[67] That decision was confirmed by the Court in its judgments of 28 February 1991 in Case C-312/89 *Conforama and Others* and C-332/89 *André Marchandise and Others*,[68] which concerned a ban not on Sunday trading but on Sunday working.

The judgment in Case C-145/88 *Torfaen Borough Council* has not only been criticized by academics for its brevity and for creating legal uncertainties[69] but has also prompted further proceedings.[70] In Case C-304/90 *Payless DIY Ltd*, the national court expressly requested an interpretation of the judgment in Case C-145/88 *Torfaen Borough Council*.[71] It is not possible here to remove the confusion to which the judgment has given rise; however, various ways in which it might be clarified may be indicated.

The simplest explanation, but also the least probable in view of the absence of any express indication to that effect in the judgment, is that the Court merely applied the *Cassis de Dijon* formula.[72] On that basis, a ban on Sunday trading or working would represent a rule corresponding to the 'mandatory requirement' of working and trading hours arranged in accordance with the relevant regional and cultural characteristics.

Another, somewhat more plausible interpretation, linked to the *purpose* of the

---

64 Printed in FR No. 27 of 13 February 1988, p. 10; see also Häberle, *Sonn- und Feiertagsrecht*, p. 53: 'Sunday touches and concerns people in their cultural existence'; Kunig, p. 7: the prohibition against Sunday working constitutes, in the final analysis, a cultural policy decision.

65 [1989] ECR 3851 (at pp. 3876 *et seq.*); this approach has been criticized by Gormley, *CML Rev. 1990*, p. 148.

66 The Court referred in that regard to its judgment of 14 July 1981 in Case 155/80 *Oebel* [1981] ECR 1993, which concerned rules governing working hours in bakeries.

67 [1989] ECR 3851 (at p. 3889).

68 [1991] ECR I-997 and [1991] ECR I-1027.

69 e.g. see Gormley, *CML Rev. 1990*, p. 149: '... the reasoning appears to be unclear to say the least'; Arnull, p. 112: 'terse and unhelpful judgment'; see also, generally, Schweitzer, *Rechtsetzung*, p. 21, who states that, to a researcher seeking to find a dogmatic structure, the quest to derive any systematic answers from an analysis of the Court's *dicta* will be 'a labour in vain'.

70 e.g. see the judgments of the Court referred to at n. 68, above.

71 [1992] ECR I-6493; see the first question referred for a preliminary ruling.

72 See Arnull, p. 115.

rule, is to be found in the subdivision of national measures into product-related and market-related measures.[73] On that basis, market-related rules such as those at issue in Case C-145/88 *Torfaen Borough Council*, unlike product-related rules, are to be classed as measures having equivalent effect only where specific circumstances exist.[74] The reference by the Court in *Torfaen Borough Council* to the judgment in Joined Cases 60 and 61/84 *Cinéthèque* appears to support that view. That judgment also concerned rules which were market related and not product related.

A final explanation, related to the preceding one but concentrating on the *consequence* of the rule, is to be found in the distinction between, on the one hand, national rules of a discriminatory nature, imposing a more onerous burden upon some than on others, and, on the other hand, national rules which are equally onerous for everyone: discriminatory measures may unquestionably be regarded as measures having equivalent effect within the meaning of Article 30 of the Treaty, and may only be justified under Article 36. Amongst national rules applicable without distinction it is possible, first of all, to discern those which disadvantage foreign products by virtue of the fact that it is more difficult for foreign producers to comply with them than it is for domestic producers. Product-related rules fall into that category. It is to those rules which the *Cassis de Dijon* decision applies. On the other hand, rules which are applicable without distinction also include provisions which place an equally onerous burden on domestic and foreign producers, and it is within that group that market-related rules fall. According to the case-law of the Court, rules of the latter type are least subject to the requirements of Community law.

(b) Article 36 of the EEC Treaty

(i) Principles

Article 36 of the Treaty sets out a series of grounds entitling Member States, where there are no Community rules governing the area concerned,[75] to establish import prohibitions and restrictions by way of derogation from the provisions of Article 30. Those grounds are exclusive and cover neither the safeguarding of consumers' interests[76] nor 'the protection of creativity and cultural diversity in the realm of publishing', as the Court held in its judgment of 10 January 1985 in Case 229/83 *Leclerc*.[77] According to the case-law of the Court, moreover, a Member State may not invoke Article 36 of the Treaty for purposes of an economic nature.[78] This is confirmed by the second sentence of Article 36, which precludes *inter alia* reliance

---

73 See Mortelmans, pp. 115 *et seq.*

74 See Fezer & Grosshardt, p. 143.

75 Matthies in: Grabitz, *Kommentar zum EWGV*, Art. 36, n. 2.

76 However, consumer protection may be regarded as being a 'mandatory requirement' within the context of Art. 30 of the Treaty; see 'Principles', pp. 139 *et seq.*, above.

77 [1985] ECR 1 (at p. 35).

78 e.g. see the judgment of 9 June 1982 in Case 95/81 *Commission* v. *Italy* [1982] ECR 2187 (at p. 2204) and the judgment of 7 February 1984 in Case 238/82 *Duphar* [1984] ECR 523 (at p. 542).

on Article 36 in the case of a disguised restriction on trade between Member States.

Of the grounds set out in Article 36 of the Treaty, the following are of particular significance in the field of culture: (1) the protection of national treasures possessing artistic, historic or archaeological value,[79] and (2) the protection of industrial and commercial property.

Above all, the latter ground has acquired practical relevance because it has been regarded as justifying import restrictions which have been made possible by virtue of national rules on copyright. This point is dealt with below.

(ii) Copyright protection

Although the Court of Justice initially left open the question whether protective rights in the nature of copyright fell within the concept of industrial and commercial property,[80] it subsequently expressly included copyright – contrary to its tendency to interpret Article 36 of the Treaty narrowly[81] – within the ambit of that provision.[82] The Court held that, having regard to the economic aspect of copyright, as opposed to its nature as a right of personality, there was no reason to make a distinction between copyright and other industrial and commercial property rights.[83]

Having set this basic precedent, the Court has subsequently had frequent occasion to rule on the effect on the free movement of goods of national copyright legislation.[84] The Court basically draws a distinction between the *existence* of the right, which is not affected by the EEC Treaty, and its *exploitation*, which may fall within the prohibitions laid down by the Treaty.[85] It has held in that regard that Article 36 of the EEC Treaty allows restrictions on free trade only to the extent to which they safeguard rights constituting the specific subject-matter of the copyright.[86] As regards the specific subject-matter of the copyright, the Court starts with the possible forms of exploitation, i.e. the right of reproduction and the

---

79 See in that regard the Commission communication 'on the protection of national treasures possessing artistic, historic or archaeological value: needs arising from the abolition of frontiers in 1992', COM (89) 594. Oliver refers in *Free Movement of Goods in the EEC*, p. 203, to the fact that this ground of justification is primarily of significance on relation to *export* restrictions.

80 e.g. see the judgment of 8 June 1971 in Case 78/70 *Deutsche Grammophon* [1971] ECR 487 (at p. 499). That case concerned the right of distribution of sound recordings.

81 See de Witte, *FS Werner Maihofer*, p. 658.

82 Judgment of 20 January 1981 in Joined Cases 55 and 57/80 *Musik-Vertrieb membran* [1981] ECR 147 (at p. 161). Copyright was not included simply by analogy, as Dietz, *Urheberrecht*, p. 42, claimed that it should.

83 [1981] ECR 147 (at p. 162).

84 For an overview, see Reischl, *Europäisches Urheberrecht*.

85 As to the derivation of that distinction from Article 222 of the EEC Treaty, see the judgment of the Court of Justice of 13 July 1966 in Joined Cases 56 and 58/64 *Consten and Grundig* v. *Commission* [1966] ECR 299 (at p. 345); for a critical view of the distinction drawn between the existence and the exploitation of a right, see Reich, *Förderung und Schutz*, p. 141; for a view rejecting that split, see Riegel, *RIW 1979*, pp. 745 *et seq.*; Börner, p. 577, indicates that the existence of a right is defined by the right to exploit it, and that distinction is apparent only (p. 585); for a more positive view, see the assessment by Friden, p. 193.

86 Judgment of 8 June 1971 in Case 78/80 *Deutsche Grammophon* [1971] ECR 487 (at p. 500).

right of public performance.[87] A copyright is said to be 'exhausted'[88] when a work has been reproduced, that is to say, distributed as a *product*, for example as a video cassette or record, on the market in another Member State by the proprietor of the right or with his consent.[89] In such circumstances, the proprietor of the right may no longer oppose the importation of the work or demand royalties in that regard. Were the position otherwise, the partitioning of national markets would be maintained solely on the ground that distribution did not occur within the territory of the domestic market.[90] A different situation applies where distribution in another Member State has taken place lawfully, following the expiration of the protection period provided for in that State, but without the consent of the proprietor of the right.[91]

However, the other aspect of the right of exploitation, namely the right of public performance, is not exhausted by the marketing of a product in another Member State, and it may thus be asserted against a person who is in possession of such a product and who wishes to give a public performance of the work, for example in the form of demands for the payment of royalties.[92] The Court has also held that the right to hire out the products concerned is not exhausted by the fact of their having already been marketed in another Member State,[93] since it forms an essential part of the copyright if the legislation of a Member State provides for a specific right of hiring-out.[94]

II. FREEDOM TO PROVIDE SERVICES IN THE CULTURAL FIELD

1. INTRODUCTION

The provision of services within the Community may in principle be effected in three ways. From a commercial point of view, the basic form of provision (1) may be regarded as covering cases in which services are rendered across an internal Community border, without being dependent on the person supplying the service or the person receiving it crossing any border.[95] The service, as an economic product, is 'despatched', like an item of merchandise. From this basic form there derive the two other variants, the characteristic feature of which lies in the fact that

---

87   Those forms of exploitation are recognized in all Member States; see the Opinion of Advocate-General Lenz in Case 402/85 *Basset* [1987] ECR 1747 (at p. 1759).

88   This term was used by the Court in its judgment of 22 January 1981 in Case 58/80 *Dansk Supermarked* [1981] ECR 181 (at p. 193), in connection with a trade mark.

89   [1981] ECR 147 (at p. 163).

90   [1971] ECR 487 (at p. 500); Dietz refers in this connection, in *Urheberrecht*, p. 136, to the 'Europeanization of the principle of exhaustion'.

91   See the judgment of 24 January 1989 in Case 341/87 *EMI Electrola* v. *Patricia* [1989] ECR 79 (at p. 97).

92   See the judgment of 9 April 1987 in Case 402/85 *Basset* [1987] ECR 1747; the judgment of 13 July 1989 in Case 395/87 *Tournier* [1989] ECR 2521 (at p. 2571); and the judgment of 12 December 1990 in Case C-270/86 *Cholay* [1990] ECR I-4607.

93   See the judgment of 17 May 1988 in Case 158/86 *Warner Brothers* v. *Christiansen* [1988] ECR 2605.

94   *ibid*, at p. 2630.

95   For a critical view of the 'basic form' proposition, see Müller-Graff, *FS für Rudolf Lukes*, pp. 476 *et seq.*

the 'transportation' of the service across the border requires the crossing of that border either (2) by the person providing the service or (3) by the person receiving it.[96] The case-law of the Court of Justice contains examples of the provision of services in each of those three ways as regards the narrower cultural field.[97] The topics of 'tourism' and 'cross-border television' will be used as vehicles for a closer examination of those three forms of cross-border provision of services. For the purposes of such examination, the second form of provision will be discussed in the light of freedom of movement for tourist guides, and the third in that of freedom of movement for tourists. Lastly, the first form of provision, described as the basic form, will be illustrated using the example of cross-border television.

2. FREEDOM OF MOVEMENT FOR TOURIST GUIDES

The freedom of tourist guides to provide services has formed the subject-matter of three judgments of the Court of Justice, delivered on 26 February 1991. Each of the three cases – Case C-154/89 *Commission* v. *France*, Case C-180/89 *Commission* v. *Italy* and Case C-198/89 *Commission* v. *Greece*[98] – concerned national legislation requiring tourist guides accompanying groups of tourists from other Member States, as a condition of the provision of their services, to hold a licence or permit allowing them to exercise their profession. As a result of the similarity in the subject-matter of the three actions, the wording of the Court's judgments broadly coincided in each case; consequently, the following remarks may be restricted to the judgment in Case C-154/89.[99]

The application of the rules on freedom to provide services gave rise, first of all, to a problem in connection with the requirement that they be provided on a cross-border basis. Advocate-General Lenz rightly concluded that the services in question were 'not provided on a purely national basis' and were undeniably supplied in a different Member State from the one in which the provider resided.[100] However, the problem lay in the fact that the recipients of the services did not normally reside in the Member State in which the service was provided and that they were in fact normally resident in the same Member State as that from which the supplier of the service originated, thus giving rise to circumstances which did not appear to be covered by Article 59 of the EEC Treaty.[101]

---

96 See M. Seidel, *Dienstleistungsfreiheit*, p. 120; Opinion of Advocate-General Lenz in Case 186/87 *Cowan* [1989] ECR 205; as to the three variants, see also Bleckmann, *Europarecht*, n. 1161; see also the submissions of the Commission in Joined Cases 110 and 111/78 *van Wesemael* [1979] ECR 35 (at p. 44).

97 As to the second form, see, for example, the judgment of 14 July 1976 in Case 13/76 *Donà* v. *Mantero* [1976] ECR 1333 (professional football); the judgment of 15 October 1986 in Case 168/85 *Commission* v. *Italy* [1986] ECR 2945 (activities in the fields of tourism and journalism); and the judgment of 14 July 1988 in Case 38/87 *Commission* v. *Greece* [1988] ECR 4415 (activities as an architect).

98 Respectively [1991] ECR I-659, [1991] ECR I-709 and [1991] ECR I-727.

99 Advocate-General Lenz delivered a single Opinion, dated 5 December 1990, covering the three cases together; see [1991] ECR I-666.

100 *ibid.*, point 13.

101 See Advocate-General Lenz, *ibid.*, point 15.

Advocate-General Lenz considered in that regard that the matter should best be approached on an a *maiore ad minus* basis: in the case at issue, the interests of the host State in restricting the activities of the providers of the service, that is to say, the tourist guides, were lesser than those at stake in circumstances clearly falling within Article 59 of the Treaty where the service is provided to nationals of that Member State. The objective underlying freedom to provide services was such that the national measures at issue must necessarily be regarded as restrictions on that freedom.[102]

The Court chose as the starting point for its reasoning the judgment of 18 March 1980 in Case 52/79 *Debauve*.[103] In that case it had held that 'the provisions of the Treaty on freedom to provide services cannot apply to activities whose relevant elements are confined within a single Member State'.[104] In its judgment in Case C-154/89 *Commission* v. *France*, however, the Court held that it was only in such circumstances that the Treaty provisions on freedom to provide services were inapplicable;[105] and it proceeded in the following paragraph to state that Article 59 of the Treaty must consequently apply in all cases where a person providing services supplies them in another Member State, regardless of where the recipient may be established.[106]

A further problem arose in relation to the question whether there could be any justification for the national rules at issue. The Court examined whether they might be justified by the mandatory requirement of safeguarding the general interest. The French Government had contended that that general interest consisted in the proper appreciation of places and things of historical interest and the widest possible dissemination of knowledge of the artistic and cultural heritage of the country.[107] The Court held in that regard that such an interest could constitute a mandatory requirement justifying a restriction on freedom to provide services, but added that the national measures should not go beyond what was necessary to ensure the protection of that interest.[108] In the Court's view, this was not the case. The effect of the national rules was to reduce the number of tourist guides qualified to accompany tourists from other Member States and to entail disproportionate drawbacks for tourists, in that the local guides were not familiar with their language, their interests and their specific expectations.[109]

Thus it is clear that the Court is prepared to recognize the validity of restrictions on freedom to provide services which are founded on cultural considerations. As regards the proportionality of such restrictions, however, the Court applies a strict test involving, in the final analysis, a review of the plausibility of the general interest pleaded: only where the restrictions are proportionate can it be assumed that the actual reasons behind the legislation coincide with those on which it purports to be based.

---

102 [1991] ECR I-666, points 18 *et seq.*
103 [1980] ECR 833.
104 *ibid.*, at p. 855.
105 See n. 98, above (para. 9 of the judgment).
106 *ibid.*, para. 10.
107 *ibid.*, para. 16.
108 *ibid.*, para. 17.
109 *ibid.*, paras 19 and 21.

3. Freedom of Movement for Tourists

(a) The problem

The Treaty provisions on freedom to provide services confer on a recipient of services – as has been established above[110] – an independent right to go to the country of origin of the person providing the services in order to receive them, and to stay there for that purpose. This raises the question whether, and to what extent, a national of a Member State who travels to another Member State solely for the purposes of tourism enjoys the protection afforded by the freedom to provide services. The answer seems to be clear, since tourists regularly receive services of one kind or another for consideration during their stay in the host country.[111] However, closer examination reveals certain problems which have not hitherto been unequivocally clarified by the case-law of the Court.[112] In its judgment of 31 January 1984 in Joined Cases 286/82 and 26/83 *Luisi and Carbone*,[113] the Court had merely held that tourists, amongst others, were to be regarded as recipients of services;[114] that finding was confirmed in the judgment of 2 February 1989 in Case 186/87 *Cowan*.[115] The Court did not expressly state, however, who is to be regarded as a tourist within the meaning of those judgments, nor the manner in which his right of residence is constituted.[116] Both questions are dealt with below.

(b) The concept of a tourist

The Court's finding that tourists are to be regarded as recipients of services might be seen as indicating that the touristic nature of their cross-border movement is decisive in bringing them within the protection afforded by the rules on freedom to provide services. That view would be incorrect if it were impliedly based, for example, on the intention of the traveller concerned to seek recreation or cultural enrichment, because those are merely motives for crossing the border which have no relevance in Community law.[117] The position is different, however, if the touristic nature of a trans-frontier movement is regarded not from the standpoint of the multifarious motives prompting travellers to make their journeys but in the light of the fact that tourists typically receive services for consideration in the host country. Only from that standpoint does a tourist have any interest for Community law. From the point of view of Community law, the *purpose* of the journey is to be found in the receipt of services in the course of the visit to the host

---

110 See 'Recipients of services as persons enjoying the benefit of freedom to provide service', pp. 109 *et seq.*, above.

111 Bogdan, p. 471, mentions the use of hotels, restaurants, taxis, public telephone booths and theatre visits.

112 For a different approach, see Steindorff, *RIW 1983*, p. 833.

113 [1984] ECR 377.

114 *ibid.*, at p. 403.

115 [1989] ECR 195 (at pp. 220 *et seq.*).

116 This is regretted by Hackspiel, p. 2169.

117 For a concurring view, see Bogdan, p. 473.

country.[118] That view is also shown to be correct by the consideration that it is not based solely upon the frequently somewhat incidental interest of the recipient of the service in its provision,[119] but also takes into account the generally more pronounced interest of the supplier of the service in providing it.

The special characteristic of visits by tourists to other Member States lies in the fact that – in contrast, for example, to cases of medical treatment – the relationship of supplier and recipient of services has not necessarily already been planned as between the traveller and the provider of the services at the time when the border is crossed.[120] The Italian Government concentrated on this factor in Joined Cases 286/82 and 26/83 *Luisi and Carbone* in arguing that Articles 59 *et seq.* of the EEC Treaty should not apply to tourists. It contended that the essential components of the service relationship had to be present and that Article 60 was intended to cover *actual* services. A tourist was merely a *potential* user of as yet unspecified services.[121]

That demarcation of the class of persons eligible to benefit under the Treaty had previously been discussed by academics, but had been rejected on grounds of impracticability and undesirability.[122] In fact, such a restriction would not meet the requirements laid down in the Court's judgment in *Luisi and Carbone*, in which it unreservedly[123] applied Articles 59 *et seq.* of the Treaty to tourists. The Court cannot possibly have intended to exclude a form of tourism which, albeit untypical, is nevertheless so widespread. It may also be observed, from a systematic point of view, that even in the field of freedom of movement for workers no employment relationship necessarily has to exist prior to the time when the border crossing takes place.[124]

It is further necessary to examine whether the application to tourists of the principle of freedom to provide services is ultimately intended to benefit only those who *actually* avail themselves of the services offered in the host country or whether it covers, independently of any such finding, all those who travel to another Member State for the purposes of tourism. In his Opinion in Case 186/87 *Cowan*, Advocate-General Lenz suggested in that regard the possible adoption of a specific *ex post* approach to the matter, or alternatively the application of generalizing *ex ante* reasoning, and expressed a preference for the latter.[125] The Advocate-General's remarks are clearly based on the assumption that the Court's

---

118 The Court's judgment of 31 January 1984 in Joined Cases 286/82 and 26/83 *Luisi and Carbone* [1984] ECR 377 refers to the fact that a recipient of services may go to another Member State *in order to receive* a service there (at p. 403).

119 See van der Woude & Mead, p. 117: 'Tourism implies the travelling of individuals who do not have any intention of exercising economic activities during their stay abroad'.

120 Séché, p. 708; the position is different where, for example, an advance hotel reservation has been made.

121 [1984] ECR 377 (at p. 388).

122 Tomuschat, *CDE 1977*, p. 107; Demaret & Ernst de la Graete, p. 267, n. 28.

123 This is also expressly stated by Louis, *CML Rev. 1984*, p. 630.

124 See Art. 48(3)(a) and (b) of the EEC Treaty; see in that regard Magiera, *DÖV 1987*, p. 223. The Court of Justice held in its judgment of 26 February 1991 in Case C-292/89 *Antonissen* [1991] ECR I-745 that the right of residence laid down by Art. 48(3) of the Treaty is not even conditional on the actual advertisement of a job: Art. 48(3) is not conclusive (para. 13 of the judgment).

125 [1989] ECR 195 (at p. 209); for a critical view in that regard, see Völker, p. 170.

case-law provided no guidance on this question.[126] However, as is explained above, the use of the term 'tourist' is already based on a typifying, and thus - in the words of the Advocate-General - a generalizing *ex ante* approach. To adopt an *ex post* approach would place an unjustifiable restriction on the scope of the judgment in Joined Cases 286/82 and 26/83 *Luisi and Carbone.*

It follows that tourists are also protected as potential recipients of services by the rules on freedom to provide services. That view accords with the objective of the rules on services, which is to liberalize '*all* gainful activity not covered by the free movement of goods, persons and capital',[127] i.e. to formulate the criteria governing recourse to services in the most favourable terms possible. From the point of view of Community law, the risk of abuse created by the *ex ante* approach is of no concern. The Court has held in a different connection that 'such abuses are not covered by the Community provisions in question'.[128]

(c) Tourists' right of residence

It follows from the application of a generalizing *ex ante* approach that all nationals of Member States who travel to another Member State for the purposes of tourism have a right to stay there which is accorded and guaranteed by primary Community law through the medium of the principle of freedom to provide services. That is the position, notwithstanding that, according to secondary Community law, a Member State is not automatically entitled to ask questions of persons arriving at the frontier concerning the purpose of their stay in order to determine whether they have a right of residence under primary Community law.[129]

An attempt could, of course, be made to challenge that conclusion by reference to the first subparagraph of Article 4(2) of the directive on the abolition of restrictions on movement and residence with regard to establishment and the provision of services,[130] which provides that the right of residence for persons providing and receiving services 'shall be of equal duration with the period during which the services are provided'. Quite apart from the fact that that provision cannot, as a rule of secondary Community law, restrict the scope of a right of residence secured by the Treaty, a literal application of the provision in question would mean that persons involved in the provision or receipt of services would never be assured, under Community law, of being able to cross the frontier, since a right of residence would not be granted for the purposes of the journey to visit the

---

126 The starting-point for the relevant observations by the Advocate-General is his conclusion that 'it is not made clear who is to be regarded as a "tourist" or to what extent a tourist is entitled to rely on the prohibition of discrimination under Community law'; see [1989] ECR 195 (at p. 208).

127 [1984] ECR 377 (at p. 401); emphasis added.

128 Judgment of 21 June 1988 in Case 39/86 *Lair* [1988] ECR 3161 (at p. 3201). The risk of abuse was seen as lying in the possibility that a person might enter a Member State as a worker and then, after a short period in employment, claim the benefit of a student grant pursuant to Art. 7(2) of Regulation No. 1612/68.

129 See the judgment of the Court of Justice of 30 May 1991 in Case C-68/89 *Commission* v. *Netherlands* [1991] ECR I-2637.

130 Council Directive of 21 May 1973 (OJ 1973 L 172, p. 14).

provider or recipient of the services, as the case may be. If according to that provision, however, a tourist must necessarily be entitled to stay in the host country for the purposes of travelling from the border to visit the provider of the services, the same must apply in respect of periods of time *between* the provision of individual services. This was implicitly confirmed by the Court in its judgment in Case 186/87 *Cowan*, in which it described a tourist, without reference to any particular provision of services,[131] as a person 'in a situation covered by Community law'.[132]

It should not be forgotten that practically every Community citizen now has the right to go to another Member State. This has been the subject of systematic critical analysis by Oppermann, according to whom the Treaties of Rome plainly did not provide for general freedom of movement.[133] As against this, it may be argued that a *permanent* establishment in another Member State is not permitted by Articles 59 *et seq.* of the EEC Treaty.[134] It follows that there are no grounds for impugning the justification for the existence of the latest directive adopted by the Council on the right of residence,[135] Article 1(1) of which is expressed to apply only to persons 'who do not enjoy [the right of residence] under other provisions of Community law'.

4. TRANS-FRONTIER TELEVISION

(a) The case-law of the Court of Justice

(i) The EEC Treaty and television

The relationship of television as a medium with the EEC Treaty was first dealt with by the Court of Justice in its judgment of 30 April 1974 in Case 155/73 *Sacchi*.[136] In its decision, it held that, in the absence of any express provisions to the contrary in the Treaty, television signals must, by reason of their nature, be regarded as a provision of services, and that the transmission of television signals, including those in the nature of advertisements, comes, as such, within the rules of the Treaty relating to services. On the other hand, trade in all products used for the diffusion of television signals is subject to the rules relating to the free movement of goods.[137]

In so stating, the Court was giving its views on the questions of interpretation referred by the national court for a preliminary ruling, which were based on the proposition that the restriction by the State of private television broadcasting fell to be assessed in the light of the rules on the free movement of goods. Although the

---

131 See Everling, *EuR 1990, Beiheft 1*, pp. 94 *et seq.*
132 [1989] ECR 195 (at p. 219).
133 Oppermann, *EG-Recht und Deutsche Bildungsordnung*, p. 47; the same reasons were given by Advocate-General Trabucchi as long ago as Case 118/75 *Watson and Belmann* [1976] ECR 1185 (at p. 1203).
134 See the judgment of the Court of Justice of 5 October 1988 in Case 196/87 *Steymann* [1988] ECR 6159 (at p. 6173).
135 Directive of 28 June 1990 (OJ 1990 L 180, p. 26).
136 [1974] ECR 409.
137 *ibid.*, at p. 427.

Court's *dicta* were primarily concerned with the mutual demarcation of the basic freedoms referred to, its remarks were necessarily based on the view that television broadcasts did not 'as such' fall outside the ambit of the EEC Treaty.[138] This tends to be overlooked by the criticisms of certain academics to the effect that 'mention should have been made of the salient question whether broadcasting as a subject was covered by the EEC Treaty at all'.[139]

That statement assumes that the Court approached the matter the wrong way round – erroneously, from the standpoint of legal theory – in other words, that it left a step out. However, such criticism fails to take account of the fundamental approach adopted by the Court in applying the Treaty provisions to cultural matters. That approach is clearly expressed in the judgment of 10 December 1968 in Case 7/68 *Commission* v. *Italy*. The Court held in connection with the free movement of goods that, *subject only to the exceptions expressly provided by the Treaty,* the rules of the Common Market apply to goods, including those of a cultural nature.[140] Accordingly, there was no need for any specific justification for applying Community law to television broadcasts, since the EEC Treaty contains no express exceptions in that regard.

(ii) Television broadcasts as services provided for remuneration across national borders

In its judgment in Case 155/73 *Sacchi*, the Court had described the transmission of television broadcasts as constituting, in principle, a service; it expanded that *dictum* in its judgment of 18 March 1980 in Case 52/79 *Debauve*[141] to cover the relaying of television broadcasts by cable. However, in its judgment in Case 155/73 it had left open the questions of provision for remuneration and the crossing of borders. There was no occasion in the proceedings for any discussion of those points, since that case was concerned merely with the demarcation of the scope of the principle of free movement of goods as compared with that of freedom to provide services.[142]

The Court did not have an opportunity to deal more extensively with this issue until Case 352/85 *Bond van Adverteerders*.[143] The proceedings giving rise to the reference for a preliminary ruling by the Court concerned the Netherlands 'Kabelregeling', a ministerial decree governing *inter alia* the diffusion of television programmes via cable networks. That decree restricted the importation

---

138 See to this effect Schwarze, *Rundfunk und Fernsehen*, p. 26; Mestmäcker et al., p. 36; Reinert, p. 174, is unclear on the point.

139 Ossenbühl, p. 21; in a similar vein, Koszuszeck, pp. 545 *et seq.*; Delbrück, *Rundfunkhoheit*, p. 40.

140 [1968] ECR 423 (at p. 429); for further details in that regard, see 'The concept of goods within the meaning of the EEC Treaty', pp. 136 *et seq.*, above.

141 [1980] ECR 833.

142 See Steindorff, *Grenzen*, p. 40; also Roth, ZHR 1985, p. 686, who argues that the Court found that the diffusion of television broadcasts fell within the provisions of the Treaty on freedom to provide services, without going in detail into the problem of provision for remuneration; for a different view, see Gulich, *Grenzen*, p. 298, who states that the Court confirmed, without discussing the point, that broadcasts are in principle provided for remuneration.

143 Judgment of 26 April 1988, [1988] ECR 2085.

of foreign television programmes which could not be received over the air but were beamed from telecommunications satellites[144] by stipulating that such transmissions were not permitted to contain any advertising aimed especially at the public in the Netherlands. That prohibition was bolstered by the additional rule that other advertising could not contain subtitles in Dutch.

The Netherlands Government denied that the rules had any Community dimension. It submitted that, in relaying signals received via telecommunications satellites, the cable operators acted not merely as intermediaries engaged in the retransmission of signals already broadcast but as broadcasters offering the programme for the first time. Without the cable operator, the programme could not be received.[145]

The Court did not accept those arguments, finding instead that 'at least two separate services'[146] were involved, both of which were of a trans-frontier nature and provided for remuneration:

(1) the operator of the cable network provided a service[147] to the foreign broadcasters by relaying to domestic viewers the programmes transmitted by those broadcasters. That service was a trans-frontier service, because the provider was established in a Member State other than that of the persons for whom it was intended. Remuneration was received by the cable network operators from their subscribers; and

(2) the foreign broadcasters provided a service to domestic advertisers, by transmitting advertisements specially intended for the domestic public. That service was also held to be a trans-frontier service, and the remuneration was received by the foreign broadcasters from the advertisers.

In the light of those findings, the three elements mentioned by the Court, namely, the service relationship, the crossing of frontiers and provision for remuneration, are discussed in further detail below.

Criticism has been levelled at the construction placed by the Court on the service relationship. The services found to have been provided have been described as 'perhaps too far removed from the *broadcast* itself';[148] and it has been argued that the provision of services is 'remote from the actual technical process of broadcasting whereby the broadcast is transported along the chain linking the broadcaster with the person receiving it via the cable operator'.[149]

That criticism patently overlooks an unequivocal statement by the Court on the nature of the broadcasting of a programme and its retransmission.[150] In so

---

144 As to the technical details, see Advocate-General Mancini's Opinion in Case 352/85 *Bond van Adverteerders* [1988] ECR 2085 (at p. 2105).

145 See the summary given by Advocate-General Mancini, *ibid.*, at pp. 2109 *et seq.*

146 [1988] ECR 2085 (at p. 2131).

147 The concept of 'service' is used here by the Court in a non-technical sense; having regard to the first para. of Art. 60 of the EEC Treaty, a 'provision' must have been involved.

148 Bueckling, p. 290.

149 See Koszuszeck, p. 546, on the relationship between the broadcaster and the advertiser.

150 The proceedings in Case 352/85 *Bond van Adverteerders* involved a dispute as to whether both processes were to be regarded as a single service or as two different ones; see the Opinion of Advocate-General Mancini, [1988] ECR 2085 (at pp. 2108 *et seq.*).

doing, it fails to do justice to the Court's decision. The Court expressly held that 'the *transmission of programmes* at issue' involved at least two services.[151] Thus its statements related entirely to the transmissions in themselves. Moreover, the Court, whilst not excluding the possible existence of other services, based its decision solely on what it considered to be an undoubted provision of services. On grounds of procedural economy, that approach cannot be criticized.

It is clear from the judgment in Case 352/85 *Bond van Adverteerders* that the trans-frontier element relates only to the provision of services and not to the remuneration, since the fee-paying relationship between the cable network operator and its subscribers does not involve the crossing of borders and yet may form the basis of the remunerative nature of the service relationship between the former and the foreign broadcasting organization.[152] In those circumstances, the remuneration is paid by a third party, i.e. the mere fact of payment does not mean that the person making the payment is necessarily to be regarded as the actual recipient of the service. In the words of the Court, the recipients of services are those for whom the specific services are performed.[153]

By focusing on the two service relationships referred to, the Court avoided tackling the problems relating to the crossing of frontiers, particularly as regards the relationship between the cable network operator and its subscribers, which the Netherlands Government regarded as decisive and of no relevance from the standpoint of Community law. Nor does the judgment in Case 52/79 *Debauve*[154] appear to provide any answer to the question whether a trans-frontier provision of services can even be said to exist where the provider of a service is established in the same State as the recipient, that is to say, the person for whom the service *is performed*, but the substance of the service *itself* is trans-frontier in nature.[155] That case concerned the retransmission of foreign programmes which were received by a domestic cable company over the air and relayed by it to its domestic subscribers.

The Court of Justice's determinations were based on the national court's view that a trans-frontier service existed, although it did not itself make any such finding.[156] It merely formulated the general rule that the provisions on freedom to provide services did not apply to activities 'whose relevant elements are confined within a single Member State'.[157] That finding begs the question what it is that constitutes the relevant elements of an activity. It must be assumed, however, that at least the substance of the service is to be regarded as a relevant element of the provision of services. Consequently, the rules on the provision of services – contrary to the wording of the first paragraph of Article 59 of the EEC Treaty, and by way of

---

151 [1988] ECR 2085 (at p. 2131), emphasis added

152 For this view, see, for example, Mestmäcker, *Wege zur Rundfunkfreiheit*, pp. 25 *et seq.*; Deringer, p. 636; for a different view, see Jarass, p. 80; Börner, p. 578, with whom Koszuszeck, p. 546, concurs.

153 [1988] ECR 2085 (at p. 2131).

154 [1980] ECR 833.

155 That question was expressly posed by the national court in Case 62/79 *Coditel* [1980] ECR 881 (at p. 901); however, on the facts, the Court of Justice considered it unnecessary to answer it.

156 For a concurring view, see Börner, p. 581.

157 [1980] ECR 833 (at p. 855). That formulation gives the widest conceivable concrete expression to the characteristic element of the crossing of frontiers. It is incorrect, therefore, to assume that the Court thereby restricted its views on the categorization of trans-national broadcasts, although that is the contention put forward by Pracht, p. 64.

teleological extension thereof – also cover cases in which it is only the service which crosses frontiers, even where the provider of the service and its recipient are not established in different Member States.[158]

As to the question of remuneration, the answer lies in the express finding reiterated by the Court in Case 352/85 *Bond van Adverteerders*, as referred to in the foregoing remarks on the trans-frontier element: Article 60 of the EEC Treaty does not require the service to be paid for by those for whom it is performed.[159] The remuneration relationship and the service relationship may thus exist between different parties.

In that case, the Court had no difficulty in attributing clear remuneration connections to the service relationships established. It did not express a view, therefore, on the question of the criteria needing to be fulfilled in order for remuneration to exist. In its judgment of 27 September 1988 in Case 263/86 *Humbel*,[160] the Court considered that the essential characteristic of remuneration lay in the fact that it constitutes commercial consideration for the service in question, and is normally agreed upon between the provider and the recipient of the service.[161]

That finding appears to confirm Börner's theory of the synallagmatic link between the provision of a service and remuneration.[162] However, the Court did not regard such reciprocity as necessary; it merely considered it – in the context, clearly, of a factual finding – to be something which exists as a general rule. Nor is it possible to infer from the Court's delineation of the essential characteristic of remuneration any indication that it is restricted to relationships under private law.[163] It follows that fees paid in the sphere of public law may in principle also constitute remuneration within the meaning of the first paragraph of Article 60 of the EEC Treaty.[164]

It is not possible, on the other hand, to concur with the view that remuneration may be said to exist where television is financed from general tax revenues.[165] It is contended, as a supposedly conclusive argument, that there is hardly any compelling reason for denying television broadcasts financed in that way the protection afforded by freedom to provide services. It is argued that, in his Opinion in Cases 52/79 *Debauve* and 62/79 *Coditel*, Advocate-General Warner did not regard the method of financing as a decisive factor.[166] The objection to that argument is that the criterion of remuneration is an entirely appropriate means of

---

158 That is the view ultimately arrived at by Mestmäcker, *Wege zur Rundfunkfreiheit*, pp. 25 *et seq.*; Deringer, p. 636.

159 [1988] ECR 2085 (at p. 2131).

160 [1988] ECR 5365.

161 *ibid.*, at p. 5388; for further details, see 'State education facilities as services', pp. 111 *et seq.*, above.

162 See Börner, p. 578, with whom Koszuszeck, p. 546, concurs.

163 Although that, in principle, is the view advanced by Börner, p. 579.

164 Gulich, in *Rechtsfragen grenzüberschreitender Rundfunksendungen*, pp. 43 *et seq.*, concurs in principle with that view, but denies that it holds true in the specific case of the organization of the German licence-fee system; for an extensive interpretation of the concept of remuneration, see also Müller, p. 126.

165 Although that is the view expressed by von Wilmowsky, p. 237; it is opposed, as here, by Steindorff, in *Grenzen*, p. 41, and by Scharf, p. 157; see also in that regard the remarks contained in 'State education facilities as services', pp. 111 *et seq.*, above.

166 von Wilmowsky, *ibid.*, n. 21.

subjecting to, or exempting from, the rules laid down by the EEC Treaty situations which are outwardly wholly identical. Moreover, the financing methods mentioned by Advocate-General Warner constituted without exception methods the remunerative nature of which was not in doubt.[167]

(iii) Permissible restrictions on the free movement of television broadcasts

It can be assumed from the case-law of the Court of Justice that the rules on freedom to provide services prohibit not only formal but also substantive discrimination in respect of the provision of trans-frontier services, and, furthermore, that they require – as in the case of the free movement of goods – the elimination of other restrictions on freedom to provide services.[168] Thus the Court held in its judgment of 3 December 1974 in Case 33/74 *van Binsbergen*[169] that the restrictions to be abolished pursuant to Article 59 of the EEC Treaty include all requirements connected with the nationality of the person providing the service, or the fact that he does not habitually reside in the State where the service is provided, which do not also apply to persons established within the national territory,[170] or which 'may prevent or otherwise obstruct the activities of the person providing the service'.[171]

This was confirmed by the Court, with regard to the prohibition of overt and covert discrimination, in its judgment of 4 December 1986 in Case 205/84 *Commission* v. *Germany*, in which it again held that Articles 59 and 60 of the EEC Treaty require the removal not only of all discrimination against a provider of a service on the grounds of his nationality but also all restrictions on his freedom to provide services imposed by reason of the fact that he is established in a Member State other than that in which the service is to be provided.[172] In its judgment of 25 July 1991 in Case C-76/90 *Säger*, the Court also reinforced the basic prohibition of other restrictions on freedom to provide services, ruling that Article 59 of the Treaty requires the abolition of any restriction, even if it applies without distinction to national providers of services and to those of other Member States, when it is liable to prohibit or otherwise impede the activities of a provider of services established in another Member State where he lawfully provides similar services.[173]

This raises the question of the extent to which the Court regards restrictions on

---

167 For a concurring view, see the Opinion of Advocate-General Slynn in Case 293/83 *Gravier* [1985] ECR 593 (at p. 603).

168 This is the view taken by the great majority of academic legal authors; see Roth, *Niederlassungs- und Dienstleistungsfreiheit*, p. 46; Mestmäcker et al., p. 46; Müller, p. 137; Ipsen, *Rundfunk im EG-Recht*, p. 87; EC Commission, Green Paper entitled 'Television Without Frontiers', COM(84) 300, p. 140; for a different view, see M. Seidel, *Dienstleistungsfreiheit*, pp. 126 *et seq.*; Börner, p. 582; see also, apparently, Reinert, p. 160.

169 [1974] ECR 1299.

170 This covers cases of overt and covert discrimination on grounds of nationality.

171 [1974] ECR 1299 (at p. 1309); this concerns the prohibition of restrictions going beyond the ban on discrimination.

172 [1986] ECR 3755 (at p. 3802); as to this formulation, and the distinction between overt and covert discrimination, see the Court's judgment of 3 February 1982 in Joined Cases 62 and 63/81 *Seco* v. *Evi* [1982] ECR 223 (at p. 235).

173 [1991] ECR I-4221 (at p. 4243); see in that regard Speyer, pp. 588 *et seq.*

the free movement of television broadcasts as permissible. Three points of reference fall to be considered in relation to such restrictions: Article 56 of the EEC Treaty; Article 36 of the Treaty; and the requirements of the general interest.

Article 56 of the EEC Treaty permits, in conjunction with Article 66, the imposition, in the field of freedom to provide services, of special rules for foreign nationals which are justified on grounds of public policy, public security or public health, and, *a fortiori*,[174] of provisions of that sort which are applicable without distinction. In Case 352/85 *Bond van Adverteerders*, the Court regarded the rules on advertising mentioned above as special rules, and considered the question of justification only with regard to Article 56(1) of the Treaty. It held, first, that economic aims cannot constitute grounds of public policy within Article 56. The Court did not consider further the objection of the Netherlands Government that the contested rules were designed to preserve the non-commercial nature of the Netherlands broadcasting system, but merely held that the rules were in any event disproportionate. This leaves open the question whether special national characteristics relating to the organization of broadcasting may in principle be taken into account within the framework of Article 56 of the Treaty.[175]

As regards Article 36 of the EEC Treaty, the leading judgment of the Court is that delivered on 18 March 1980 in Case 62/79 *Coditel*.[176] In that decision, the Court was concerned with the lawfulness of national rules on copyright which permitted the grant, restricted to the territory of a Member State, of the proprietary rights in a film. On the basis of those provisions, the retransmission through the cable network of a film received from abroad had been declared impermissible, although the copyright owner had authorized the broadcasting of it abroad. The Court held that the situation in relation to films, made available to the public by performances which may be infinitely repeated, was not the same as that in respect of works such as books or records, which are put into circulation in physical form. It stated that the owner of the copyright had a legitimate interest in calculating the fees due in return for the grant of performance rights on the basis of the actual or probable number of performances. This formed part of the *essential function* of copyright in a film, and was not covered, in principle, by Article 59 of the Treaty.[177]

In so stating, the Court was by implication applying Article 36 of the Treaty within the context of the rules on the provision of services;[178] however, it ruled with good reason – thereby departing from its case-law on copyright in the context of the free movement of goods[179] – against the exhaustion of copyright.

In its judgment of 6 October 1982 in Case 262/81 *Coditel II*,[180] it went on expressly to state that the distinction, implicit in Article 36, between the existence of a copyright, which cannot be affected by the EEC Treaty, and the

---

174 See Reinert, p. 210; Advocate-General Warner's Opinion in Case 52/79 *Debauve* and Case 62/79 *Coditel* [1980] ECR 833 (at p. 877).

175 For a concurring view, see Magiera, *Rechtliche Grundfragen*, p. 73; Koszuszeck, p. 547, expresses optimism in this regard.

176 [1980] ECR 881.

177 *ibid.*, at pp. 902 *et seq.*

178 For a concurring view, see Sturm, pp. 193.

179 See in that regard, 'Copyright protection', pp. 145 *et seq.*, above.

180 [1982] ECR 3381.

exercise of that right, which might constitute a disguised restriction on trade, also applies where that right is exercised in the context of the free movement of services.[181] In so far, therefore, as the manner in which copyright is asserted is linked to its existence in such a way that a prohibition of the form taken by its assertion renders the right worthless in practice, the matter lies outside the ambit of the EEC Treaty, so that the right can be enforced against the free circulation of television broadcasts.

Having discussed Articles 56 and 36 of the EEC Treaty, it remains to mention the restrictions on the free movement of television programmes which are justified in the general interest. In its judgment in Case 52/79 *Debauve*,[182] the Court held that, in view of the particular nature of certain services such as the broadcasting and transmission of television signals, specific requirements imposed on providers of services which are founded on the application of rules regulating certain types of activity and (1) are justified by the general interest and (2) apply to all persons and undertakings established within the territory of the Member State concerned cannot be said to be incompatible with the EEC Treaty, but only to the extent to which (3) a provider of services established in another Member State is not subject to similar regulations there. Consequently, there can be no objection under Community law to a total prohibition on television advertising imposed in a Member State which also extends to the domestic retransmission of foreign programmes via the cable network, in the absence of any harmonization of the relevant rules at Community level.[183]

That judgment confirmed a line of reasoning previously developed[184] and subsequently reinforced by the Court.[185] The question whether that case-law falls to be interpreted as restricting or extending freedom to provide services depends on the construction applied to the concept of the restrictions to be eliminated. If Articles 59 *et seq.* of the EEC Treaty are interpreted as imposing in essence merely a requirement in relation to national treatment, the case-law referred to must be regarded as extending the bounds of the freedom provided for under the Treaty.[186] Since – as indicated above[187] – that view is not shared, it is consequently necessary to assume a restriction of that freedom.[188]

Clearly, the requisite general interest, which cannot be equated with the grounds of justification contained in Article 56 of the Treaty,[189] since it is more

---

181 [1982] ECR 3381 (at 3401); for a more detailed analysis, see Reischl, *Rechtsprechung des Gerichtshofs*, pp. 48 *et seq.*

182 [1980] ECR 833.

183 *ibid.*, at pp. 856 *et seq.*

184 e.g. see the judgment of 3 December 1974 in Case 33/74 *van Binsbergen* [1974] ECR 1299. In that case, the Court focused not on the particular nature of certain services but on that of the services in general (at p. 1309); see in that regard Gulich's analysis of the case-law in *Rechtsfragen grenzüberschreitender Rundfunksendungen*, pp. 82 *et seq.*

185 e.g. see the judgment of 4 December 1986 in Case 205/84 *Commission* v. *Germany* [1986] ECR 3755 (at p. 3803).

186 This is the logical conclusion drawn by M. Seidel, *Dienstleistungsfreiheit*, p. 129.

187 See the beginning of this chapter, above.

188 For a concurring view, see Schwartz, *Liberalisierung*, p. 158, n. 17, who refers to the introduction of an exception not envisaged by the Treaty.

189 For a concurring view, see Schwarze, *Rundfunk und Fernsehen*, p. 32, who argues that the case-law of the Court of Justice lends no support to that contention; likewise, for example, Reich, *Rundfunkrecht und Wettbewerbsrecht*, p. 227; for a different view, see Pracht, p. 102.

extensive in scope, falls to be defined primarily from the standpoint of the Member State concerned.[190] In its judgment in Case 52/79 *Debauve*, the Court of Justice did not express a view on the permissibility of the advertising ban in its entirety, focusing instead only on the decision by the Member State concerned to apply such a ban. That does not conflict with the fact that the rules in question must also fulfil requirements of Community law.[191]

The view advanced here was confirmed by the Court in its judgment of 25 July 1991 in the '*Mediawet*' case, Case C-288/89.[192] In those proceedings, the Court examined the compatibility of the Netherlands 'Mediawet' (Law on the Media) of 21 April 1987 with the rules on freedom to provide services. It was primarily concerned to consider whether it was possible to justify in the general interest requirements imposed on broadcasting organizations by that law whereby (1) any advertisements transmitted had to be produced by a legal person separate from the broadcasting body; (2) the entire revenue earned from advertising had to be used for the production of programmes; and (3) bodies which had obtained air time could not be used to enable a third party to make a profit.[193]

The essence of the Netherlands Government's submissions was that the rules were required in order to guarantee the non-commercial nature of broadcasting.[194] It claimed that they were justified by the imperatives relating to the cultural policy implemented by it in the audio-visual sector, the aim of which was to safeguard the freedom of expression of the various social, cultural, religious and philosophical groups in the Netherlands.[195]

The Court first of all confirmed in general terms the point of view of the Netherlands Government: a cultural policy understood in that sense could indeed constitute an mandatory requirement relating to the general interest such as to justify a restriction on the freedom to provide services, particularly since the fundamental right of freedom of expression formed an integral part of the Community legal order.[196] In the result, however, the Court was unwilling to find that the rules laid down by the Mediawet were justified. It held that there was no necessary connection between such a cultural policy and the conditions relating to the structure of foreign broadcasting bodies. In order to ensure pluralism in the Netherlands, the Government could confine itself to formulating the statutes of its own broadcasting bodies. Consequently, the rules in question were not objectively necessary in order to secure the pluralism aimed for.[197]

---

190 For a concurring view, see Bueckling, p. 289.

191 In its judgment in Case 205/84 *Commission* v. *Germany* [1986] ECR 3755, the Court held that the national rules in question had to be objectively justified having regard to the attainment of the objective pursued; Reich, op. cit., n. 189, refers somewhat unclearly to a 'general interest defined by Community law'.

192 *Stichting Collectieve Antennevoorziening Gouda* v. *Commissariaat voor de Media* [1991] ECR I-4007; see also the judgment of 25 July 1991 in Case C-353/89 *Commission* v. *Netherlands* [1991] ECR I-4069, the wording of which corresponds in part.

193 For a more detailed analysis of the requirements laid down by the Mediawet, see Schwartz, *ZUM 1991*, p. 163.

194 See n. 192, above (para. 21 of the judgment).

195 *ibid.*, para. 22.

196 *ibid.*, para. 23.

197 *ibid.*, paras 24 *et seq.*

Accordingly – as has already been established[198] – restrictions on freedom to provide services which are motivated by considerations of cultural policy and applicable without distinction can be justified by mandatory requirements relating to the general interest. It is not enough, however, merely to assert that a national measure constitutes the expression of a cultural policy which is being pursued. The Court of Justice first of all determines the *concrete* objective of the national approach described as the cultural policy of the individual State and then examines whether the national measure in question is appropriate and necessary in order to accomplish that objective.

(b) The television directive

(i) The need for coordination of national rules

The statements set out above show that the free movement of television broadcasts may be restricted by virtue of the application *mutatis mutandis* of Article 36 of the EEC Treaty and, on grounds of the 'general interest', by rules which are applicable without distinction. From a legal standpoint, this situation made the harmonization of such rules – in the fields of copyright and television advertising, for example – appear 'urgently necessary in order to establish freedom for cross-border broadcasting'.[199] But a need for harmonization also emerged from a practical standpoint. The technical possibilities relating to the transmission of programmes, especially in the form of satellite broadcasting,[200] began 'in practical terms to go beyond the artificial boundaries of national jurisdiction'.[201] Ultimately,[202] the recognition of that factual situation resulted in the adoption on 3 October 1989 of the television directive based on Articles 57(2) and 66 of the EEC Treaty.[203]

On the one hand, the coordination of national provisions undertaken by that directive fails to satisfy in terms of its subject-matter the case-law of the Court of Justice, since it does not relate to copyright provisions;[204] on the other hand, it

---

198 See 'Freedom of movement of tourist guides', pp. 147 *et seq.*, above.

199 See Schwarze, *Rundfunk und Fernsehen*, p. 38; for a critical view of the rules on television advertising, see Bullinger, *AfP 1985*, p. 263, who maintains that harmonization is not permissible in so far as advertising rules conclusively determine the nature and financing of broadcasting relating to a given area. In such circumstances, the advertising rules fall, by virtue of their democratic function, outside the ambit of Community competence.

200 See in that regard Kreile, p. 408.

201 Dicke, p. 194; for further details, see Magiera, *Rechtliche Grundfragen*, pp. 52 *et seq.*

202 The resolution of the European Parliament of 12 March 1982 on radio and television broadcasting in the European Community (OJ 1982 C 87, p. 110) may be regarded as the starting-point for this development; in that resolution, the Parliament called for outline rules to be drawn up on European radio and television broadcasting, *inter alia* 'with a view to protecting young people and establishing a code of practice for advertising at Community level' (para. 7); as to the background to the television directive, see Magiera, *Rechtliche Grundfragen*, pp. 66 *et seq.*; Wallace & Goldberg, pp. 175 *et seq.*

203 OJ 1989 L 298, p. 23.

204 EC Commissioner Dondelinger has since announced a fresh initiative with regard to copyright in films; see Europe-Agence Internationale No. 5340 of 1-2 October 1990, p. 10; see also the Commission communication entitled 'Follow-up to the Green Paper' (COM(90) 584, pp. 36 *et seq.*). The Commission had already provided for rules in that regard in Chapter V of its proposal for the television directive; see OJ 1986 C 179, p. 4.

goes beyond it, since it contains, in addition to rules on advertising, provisions in respect of areas – such as the protection of minors[205] and the right of reply[206] – which have not to date been considered by the Court of Justice. Consequently, rules have been laid down in respect of further areas which, in the view of the Council, could have led, in terms of Community law, to unobjectionable restrictions on the free movement of television broadcasts.[207]

(ii) Permissibility and significance of national rules on programmes

German law, at least, lays down certain requirements with regard to the content of broadcasts. Thus Article 8(1) of the Rundfunkstaatsvertrag (Broadcasting Treaty, concluded between the German *Länder*) of 1–3 April 1987 provides that, in principle, the content of private radio programmes must essentially reflect the plurality of views and that significant political, ideological and social movements and groups must be given a reasonable opportunity to express themselves in complete programmes. According to Article 9(1) of the Rundfunkstaatsvertrag, broadcast programmes must have regard to human dignity and to the moral, religious and ideological convictions of others.

The question of the permissibility of such national programme requirements is clearly answered by the television directive. As emerges from the thirteenth recital in the preamble, it lays down only the minimum rules needed to guarantee freedom of transmission in broadcasting. For the rest, it does not affect the competence of the Member States 'with regard to the organization, ... financing and the content of programmes'.

This gives rise to the 'explosive'[208] question of the extent to which foreign television transmissions must satisfy such programme requirements. Prior to the adoption of the television directive the question was discussed whether such rules, applicable without distinction, could be justified by the 'general interest'.[209] The television directive solved that problem by introducing the principle of the State of transmission, according to which it is enough, for the purposes of the diffusion of television programmes within the Community, if a foreign television programme fulfils the requirements of the directive and complies with the laws of the State from which it is transmitted.

It is true that this appears to be contradicted by Article 2(2) of the directive, which prohibits the restriction by Member States of reception and retransmission for reasons which fall within 'the fields coordinated by this Directive'. That

---

205 As to the need for harmonization in that regard, see Kreile, pp. 408 *et seq.*

206 See in that regard Damm, pp. 175 *et seq.*, who provides examples showing the need for rules in that field.

207 This is apparent from the thirteenth recital in the preamble, which states that the directive 'lays down the minimum rules needed to guarantee freedom of transmission in broadcasting'.

208 See Roth, *ZHR 1985*, p. 689.

209 That view is rejected by Mestmäcker in *Wege zur Rundfunkfreiheit*, p. 29; Deringer, p. 632; Schwartz, *Fernsehen ohne Grenzen*, pp. 134 *et seq.*; EC Commission, Green Paper entitled 'Television Without Frontiers', COM(84) 300, p. 177; for a view which differs according to whether or not the foreign organization deliberately transmits to domestic viewers, see Jarass, p. 88, who contends that where the organization does not deliberately broadcast to domestic viewers there is an absence of proportionality.

wording may be taken to mean that restrictions continue to be permissible for *other* reasons, namely reasons falling within uncoordinated areas. Roth considers, for example, that the directive does not prevent control of a programme by the recipient State, since the requirements relating to programming have not been harmonized.[210]

However, that view runs counter to the twelfth recital in the preamble to the directive, which succinctly provides that it is 'necessary and sufficient that all broadcasts comply with the law of the Member State from which they emanate'. The fourteenth recital reinforces this by stating that all broadcasts emanating from and intended for reception within the Community, 'and in particular those intended for reception in another Member State, should respect the law of the originating Member State applicable to broadcasts intended for reception by the public in that Member State and the provisions of this Directive'. In this way, steps have been taken towards the mutual recognition of national rules, in fields beyond those harmonized by the directive.[211]

(iii) The binding force and legality of the quota rules

The rules contained in Article 4(1) of the television directive are customarily referred to as the 'quota rules', although unlike the Commission proposal[212] they do not provide for any specific quota. According to Article 4(1), the Member States are to ensure, 'where practicable and by appropriate means, that broadcasters reserve for European works, within the meaning of Article 6, a majority proportion of their transmission time, excluding the time appointed to news, sports events, games, advertising and teletext services'. This provision is central to Chapter III of the directive, which is intended, according to its somewhat misleading title, to ensure the 'Promotion of distribution and production of television programmes'. It is in fact designed 'to promote markets of sufficient size for television productions in the Member States to recover necessary investments'.[213]

It is questionable whether that provision is lawful under Community law.[214]

---

210 Roth, *AfP 1991*, p. 505, n. 22; see also Gulich, *Rechtsfragen grenzüberschreitender Rundfunksendungen*, p. 81; Bullinger, *Werbung und Quotenregelung*, p. 100, who expresses the view that the quota rules, which are not in his opinion legally binding, have brought about – doubtless by virtue of the recognition of their binding political force (author's comment) – adequate coordination within the meaning of Art. 2(2) of the television directive, with the result that national quotas may henceforth no longer constitute a bar to foreign television transmissions within the EC.

211 As to the alternative concepts of 'harmonization' and 'mutual recognition', see M. Seidel, *Europäische Rundfunkzone*, p. 140; Hoffmann-Riem contends somewhat unclearly in *Rundfunkrecht neben Wettbewerbsrecht*, p. 194, that the television directive created only partial harmonization.

212 OJ 1986 C 179, p. 4; as to the background to the quota rules, see Maggiore, pp. 37 *et seq.*

213 See the twentieth recital in the preamble to the television directive (OJ 1989 L 298, p. 23).

214 On the other hand, the question whether quota rules are meaningful is not dealt with; see in that regard, *inter alia*, Wiesand, pp. 161 *et seq.*; Frohne, pp. 390 *et seq.*; Späth, p. 227; Wenger, pp. 548 *et seq.*; Bullinger, in *Werbung und Quotenregelung*, pp. 98 *et seq.*, regards the quota rules as inappropriate and thus unnecessary, and for that reason contends that the criteria of Art. 57(2) of the EEC Treaty are not fulfilled.

First of all, however, it is necessary to determine whether the quota rules are capable of producing any legal effects, that is to say, whether they are binding. The starting-point in that regard is the third paragraph of Article 189 of the EEC Treaty, which provides that a directive is to be binding, as to the result to be achieved, upon each Member State to which it is addressed, but shall leave to the national authorities the choice of form and methods. According to Article 27, the television directive is addressed to all of the Member States.

Doubts as to the binding nature of the directive arise, however, from the 'soft' wording of Article 4(1). In Everling's view, the wording used is not such as to impose any binding legal obligation; instead, Article 4(1) constitutes merely a 'best endeavours' provision. Whilst acknowledging that its wording is not unequivocal, he submits that, if the Council had intended to impose a legal obligation, it would have used a stricter formulation.[215]

In the first place, that view cannot be countered by relying on the third paragraph of Article 189 of the EEC Treaty, since the legal nature of a piece of legislation depends not on its designation (e.g. as a 'directive') but on its substantive content.[216] In the final analysis, however, Everling's view must be rejected. Even though the Member States are required only to 'ensure where practicable' that the purported objective is achieved, and whilst it is thus possible to speak of a 'best endeavours' provision, nevertheless there is no apparent reason why the Member States should not, at the very least, be under a legal obligation to use their 'best endeavours' to that end. Support for that view is to be found in Article 4(2), which provides that the proportion laid down in paragraph 1 must not in any event be 'lower than the average for 1988 in the Member State concerned', and in the third subparagraph of Article 4(3), according to which the Commission is to 'ensure the application of this Article ... in accordance with the provisions of the Treaty'.[217]

A significant factor in determining the binding nature of the television directive is therefore whether recourse may be had, for the purposes of interpretation, to the declarations contained in the minutes annexed to the directive. The relevant declaration in this connection is primarily the fifteenth declaration in the minutes, in which the Council and the Commission concur in stating that 'the Member States agree, from a political standpoint, to be bound by Articles 4 and 5 as regards the achievement of the objectives stipulated therein'.[218] It has to some extent been accepted that regard should be had to that declaration and that, in consequence, the quota rules do not have binding legal force.[219]

However, that view cannot be reconciled with the case-law of the Court of Justice. The Court declines to have regard to declarations recorded in minutes, at

---

215 Everling, *EuR 1990*, pp. 218 *et seq.*; see, ultimately to the same effect, L. Seidel, p. 121.

216 For a concurring view, see Pechstein, *EuR 1990*, p. 264; for a more detailed discussion of the point, see 'Criteria for distinguishing between legal and non-legal acts', pp. 252 *et seq.*, below.

217 The objection raised against this by Bullinger in *Werbung und Quotenregelung*, pp. 99 *et seq.*, to the effect that the constitutional and administrative laws of the Member States include provisions which have been interpreted as non-binding in their effects, is not convincing.

218 See *Media Perspektiven Dokumentation* II/89, pp. 115 *et seq.*; unofficial German version.

219 See Everling, *EuR 1990*, pp. 218 *et seq.*; Pechstein, *EuR 1990*, pp. 265 *et seq.*; without any detailed explanation, Möwes & Schmitt-Vockenhausen, p. 123.

least[220] in cases where to do so would lead to an interpretation different from that suggested by the wording of the provision falling to be interpreted.[221] This is acknowledged even by Pechstein, who states that a declaration may not conflict with the content of the legal act which is to be interpreted, and that only specification, clarification and explanation are admissible.[222] He consequently attempts to derive support for his view that regard may be had to declarations recorded in minutes by differentiating between declarations relating (a) to rules of law which are already in existence and (b) to those which are brought into existence in the course of the legislative process. If, however, a legal act brought into existence in that way may be interpreted *only* by reference to the contents of the relevant declaration, then those contents should have been included in the legal act. A declaration recorded in minutes does not form part of a legal act, even though its contents could unquestionably have been incorporated in it.[223] According to the judgment of the Court of Justice of 26 February 1991 in Case C-229/89 *Antonissen*,[224] however, that is a condition which must be fulfilled if declarations contained in minutes are to be taken into consideration;[225] in such circumstances, their nature is merely interpretative.

It follows that it is invariably the wording and the sense of the provision in question which constitute the starting-point for its interpretation. As has been explained above, the quota rules contain a legal obligation to use 'best endeavours'. Accordingly, the declarations in the minutes which are inconsistent with that duty can have no legal effect. It is true that this may possibly result in an 'ineffective illusory solution', contrary to the intentions of the institutions which made the declarations.[226] However, the fact that the unanimity required for an amendment of the text could not be established[227] shows that the contents of the provision of the directive and those of the declaration in the minutes are contradictory.[228] In the final analysis, the declaration in the minutes is not intended, as Karl submits in relation to declarations in minutes generally, to remove remaining 'doubts about the content and scope of a provision ... by means of clarifications or amplifications falling outside the actual legislative act, in order thereby to create a provision acceptable to all concerned'.[229] On the contrary, the position is precisely the reverse: the ambiguities in the act which were deliberately not removed from it were used in order to enable the act to be adopted. The risk inherent in the omission of such clarification is borne by the assenting Member State.

---

220 Mestmäcker et al., p. 34, consider that the Court of Justice is inclined generally to refrain from drawing inferences from declarations contained in minutes for the purposes of interpreting secondary Community legislation.

221 e.g. see the judgment of 23 February 1988 in Case 429/85 *Commission v. Italy* [1988] ECR 843 (at p. 852); judgment of 18 February 1970 in Case 38/69 *Commission v. Italy* [1970] ECR 47 (at p. 57); see also Karl, p. 597.

222 Pechstein, *EuR 1990*, p. 256.

223 See also, to the same effect, Karl, p. 598.

224 [1991] ECR 745.

225 *ibid.*, para. 18.

226 That argument is advanced by Pechstein in *EuR 1990*, p. 263.

227 This is pointed out by Pechstein, *ibid.*

228 That is the conclusion reached in the result by Wallace & Goldberg, pp. 192 *et seq.*

229 Karl, p. 594.

The lawfulness of the quota rules depends *inter alia*[230] on whether they operate, in accordance with Article 57(2) read in conjunction with Article 57(1) of the EEC Treaty, 'to make it easier for persons to take up and pursue activities as self-employed persons'. That question appears to be answered by the eighteenth recital in the preamble to the television directive, which states that 'coordination is ... needed to make it easier for persons and industries producing programmes having a cultural objective to take up and pursue their activities'. That view is also expressed by Schwartz, who states that, by favouring existing undertakings and the establishment of new undertakings, the quota rules *make it easier* for persons to take up and pursue their activities.[231]

That view is based on a misunderstanding of the meaning of the phrase 'make it easier' used in Article 57 of the EEC Treaty. That concept relates not to the formulation in more favourable terms of the *actual* conditions in which an activity is taken up or pursued but to the recognition or harmonization of the various rules of national law which are applicable without distinction and the greater ease with which an activity as a self-employed person may *consequently* be pursued.[232] In terms of Community law, the quota rules cannot, on that construction of Article 57 of the EEC Treaty, be justified on the grounds mentioned.[233]

A different position could only validly apply if the situation involved coordination of the quota rules existing under *national* law in favour of domestic production. It may be argued in opposition to that, however, that national quota rules are incompatible with Community law and that, according to the first paragraph of Article 59 of the EEC Treaty, they could not be relied on against television broadcasts by Member States, so that the justification for coordination would then cease to exist.[234] It must nonetheless be acknowledged that measures for the approximation of legislation may be taken not only with regard to national provisions which are justified under Community law but also – on grounds of legal certainty, for example, or the ponderousness of Treaty infringement proceedings –

---

230 No mention is made here of the problems arising from the infringement of the basic right, enshrined at Community level, to broadcasting freedom and freedom of information. However, such an infringement suggests itself; see Mestmäcker et al., at pp. 75 *et seq.*, who examine and confirm the existence of an infringement of Art. 10 of the European Convention on Human Rights. They contend that the connection with Community law results from the fact that the ECHR constitutes 'at the present time the most important guide to the protection of human rights in the Community' (p. 99); see, to the same effect, Magiera, *Ansätze*, p. 23; for an opposing view, see Jacqué, pp. 341 *et seq.*

231 Schwartz, *ZUM 1989*, p. 387.

232 Troberg in: GTE, *Kommentar zum EWGV*, Art. 57, n. 1; for a view basically in the same vein, see Everling in: WEGS, Art. 57 (p. 185). His view must, however, be rejected, inasmuch as it favours only adjustment in line with the most liberal rules in each case (p. 186).

233 For a similar view, see Frohne, pp. 394 *et seq.*; Delbrück, *Rundfunkhoheit*, p. 54; Stoiber, *ZUM 1986*, p. 673; M. Seidel, *Europäische Rundfunkzone*, p. 145.

234 This is the view advanced by Everling, *EuR 1990*, p. 218, who contends that a national provision restricting freedom to provide services may only be justified on non-economic grounds in the 'general interest'. However, since programme quota rules favouring domestic production constitute rules which are at least covertly discriminatory, it is clear from the outset that there can be no question of their being justified in the 'general interest'. Art. 56 of the EEC Treaty, which is the only provision applicable, is likewise incapable, however, of being asserted for economic purposes. On 25 September 1985, the Commission of the EC brought proceedings under Art. 169 of the EEC Treaty against France in relation to the French quota rules; see Schwartz, *Debatte*, p. 114.

in relation to national rules which are prohibited under primary Community law itself.[235] The illegality of national quota rules does not, therefore, necessarily conflict with coordination at Community level.

However, support for the objective of coordinating national quota rules by means of the quota rules contained in the television directive cannot in the final analysis be inferred from Article 57(2) of the EEC Treaty, since it would only be possible to coordinate existing national provisions on programme quotas which favour national production by *eliminating* national quotas. The introduction of a European quota represents, by contrast, a different matter. Such a measure could at best be based only on Article 235 of the EEC Treaty.[236]

III. FREEDOM OF MOVEMENT IN THE CULTURAL FIELD

1. INTRODUCTION

According to Commission data, in 1984 approximately 3–4 per cent of the working population of the Member States of the EC were employed in the cultural field.[237] Although the message to be gleaned from such figures is limited, given the necessarily arbitrary nature of the demarcation of the cultural field,[238] they nevertheless point to the appreciable significance which that field has with regard to employment and self-employment.[239]

The Community institutions have as a matter of course made persons working in the cultural field subject to the rules of the EEC Treaty. For example, in Article 3(2) of the Council Directive of 12 January 1967 concerning the attainment of freedom of establishment and freedom to provide services in respect of specified activities of self-employed persons,[240] the Council included literary and artistic activities amongst the 'business services not elsewhere classified' in respect of which restrictions on freedom of establishment and freedom to provide services were to be eliminated. A further example is to be found in the Directive of 10 June 1985 on the mutual recognition of qualifications in architecture,[241] which not only governs the recognition of diplomas awarded on completion of higher-

---

235 See Langeheine in: Grabitz, *Kommentar zum EWGV*, Art. 100, n. 76; Currall, p. 182; both of these commentaries relate to the free movement of goods.

236 For a concurring view, see Pechstein, *DÖV 1991*, p. 540.

237 EC Commission, *Europa im Wandel*, p. 10.

238 The Commission (*ibid.*) subsumes under the cultural field the following individual items: cultural goods, the creative field, products, design, advertising, cultural associations and cultural tourism.

239 See in that regard the Resolution of the Council and of the Ministers responsible for cultural affairs, meeting within the Council, of 18 December 1984 on greater recourse to the European Social Fund in respect of cultural workers (OJ 1985 C 2, p. 2); Resolution of the European Parliament of 25 May 1984 on the situation of cultural workers in the Community (OJ 1984 C 172, p. 212).

240 OJ, English Special Edition 1967, p. 3.

241 OJ 1985 L 223, p. 15. That directive is not affected by Directive 89/48/EEC of 21 December 1988 on a general system for the recognition of higher-education diplomas awarded on completion of professional education and training of at least three years' duration (OJ 1989 L 19, p. 16); see Art. 2 thereof.

education training but also concerns 'certain distinguished persons' whose work (in the words of the twelfth recital in the preamble) 'shows exceptional architectural talent'.

The Court of Justice has likewise focused its attention on the application of the Treaty provisions on freedom of movement, in both its forms,[242] to activities in the cultural field. The case-law concerns, in particular,[243] the freedom of movement of sportspersons,[244] architects and artists.

2. FREEDOM OF MOVEMENT FOR PROFESSIONAL SPORTSPERSONS

In the field of professional sport, the most significant decisions are to be found in two of the older judgments of the Court of Justice.[245] In its judgment of 12 December 1974 in Case 36/74 *Walrave and Koch*,[246] the Court held that, having regard to the objectives of the Community, the practice of sport is subject to Community law only in so far as it constitutes an economic activity within the meaning of Article 2 of the EEC Treaty. That was held to be the position where a sporting activity is in the nature of gainful employment or remunerated service.[247] That case-law was subsequently confirmed in the judgment of 14 July 1976 in Case 13/76 *Donà* v. *Mantero*.[248] The Court's declaration regarding the relationship between sporting activities and Community law is in no way surprising; instead, it reflects the basic approach adopted by the Court when applying the Treaty provisions to cultural matters.[249]

However, considerable difficulties arise from the further statements contained in the judgment in Case 36/74 *Walrave and Koch*, which has appropriately been described as 'sibylline'.[250] Having made the declaration referred to above, the Court went on to state that the prohibition against discrimination, which is expressed in, *inter alia*, Articles 48-51 of the EEC Treaty, nevertheless 'does not affect the composition of sports teams, in particular national teams, the formation of which is a question of purely sporting interest and as such has nothing to do with economic activity'.[251]

The Court appears at first sight to be assuming that sports teams, such as, for

---

242 For further details in that regard, 'Introduction', p. 135 *et seq.*, above.

243 There have in addition been decisions relating to activities in the field of religion (judgments of 23 October 1986 in Case 300/84 *van Roosmalen* [1986] ECR 3097 and 5 October 1988 in Case 196/87 *Steymann* [1988] ECR 6159), access to activities in the fields of journalism and tourism (judgment of 15 October 1986 in Case 168/85 *Commission* v. *Italy* [1986] ECR 2945) and the employment status of a music teacher (judgment of 3 June 1986 in Case 139/85 *Kempf* [1986] ECR 1741).

244 The question whether sport falls within the ambit of culture is superfluous. Tomuschat, *F.I.D.E. Reports*, p. 29, appears to take the view that both sport and culture are mutually exclusive.

245 See, in more recent times, the judgment of 15 October 1987 in Case 222/86 *Heylens* [1987] ECR 4097, which concerned the recognition of a foreign football trainer's diploma.

246 [1974] ECR 1405.

247 *ibid.*, at p. 1418.

248 [1976] ECR 1333 (at p. 1340).

249 See also, in that regard, 'The EEC Treaty and television', pp. 152 *et seq.*, above.

250 See Hilf, *NJW 1984*, p. 520.

251 [1974] ECR 1405 (at p. 1418 *et seq.*).

instance, national teams, picked for specific competitions, games or matches, have *no connection whatever* with Community law, because there are no identifiable economic interests (i.e. no remuneration relationships) at stake in the game.[252] If that were the case, however, the Court would have let the matter rest with its above-mentioned remark regarding the relationship between Community law and sport and could have left it to the national court to determine the question of remuneration.

It is accordingly impossible to accept that the Court did not perceive the economic aspect of participation in a national team. This view finds support, first, in the qualified wording of the statement that the composition of teams engaged in competitions has *as such* nothing to do with economic activity and, secondly, in the more precise statement in the judgment in Case 13/76 *Donà* v. *Mantero* that it is permissible to exclude foreign players from participation in certain matches *for reasons which are not of an economic nature.*[253] Finally, the Court concludes by saying that this restriction on the scope of the provisions in question must remain limited to the proper objective of the rules contested in the proceedings before the national court. However, a restriction on the scope of the prohibition against discrimination may apply only where that scope is affected in any way. It follows that, according to the case-law of the Court, the prohibition against discrimination will not apply where the members of a team are paid to participate but the exclusion of foreigners is based on non-economic grounds.[254]

No satisfactory answer is provided by the Commission, the Advocate-General or the Court itself to the question of the grounds on which such a restriction of the scope of the prohibition against discrimination are based. The Commission advances the view that no discrimination in fact exists, since the distinction based on nationality is unquestionably objectively justified.[255] Advocate-General Warner focuses on the test of the 'officious bystander', which is very much open to attack in methodological terms but assumes that such a bystander were to ask the signatories to the EEC Treaty, at the time of its conclusion, whether the Treaty should preclude a requirement that a national team should consist only of nationals of the country it represented. According to Advocate-General Warner, common sense dictates that the signatories would all have answered: 'Of course not'.[256] The Court, unlike the Commission, did not ultimately conclude that there was no discrimination whatever on grounds of nationality,[257] but merely declared that, in the selection of national teams, questions of 'sporting interest' in

---

252 This is apparently the opinion of Klose, p. 157, who regards the Court's view as untenable from a factual standpoint, since economic interests have played a role even in the composition of national teams.

253 [1976] ECR 1333 (at p. 1340).

254 This is the conclusion reached in the final analysis by Advocate-General Trabucchi in Case 13/76 *Donà* v. *Mantero* [1976] ECR 1333 (at p. 1344); see also Marticke, p. 58; Steindorff, *RIW* 1975, p. 254, who levels the same criticism at the Court of Justice, however, as Klose, op. cit., n. 252.

255 Case 36/74 *Walrave and Koch* [1974] ECR 1405 (at pp. 1409 *et seq.*); see, to the same effect – but without giving any reasons – Weatherill, p. 60, although he does preface his remarks as follows: 'A *strict* application of the rule against discrimination could give rise to some surprising results' (emphasis added).

256 [1974] ECR 1405 (at p. 1427).

257 However, this appears to be the view taken by Schermers & Waelbroeck, §122.

relation to the composition of the teams took precedence over the economic interests of foreign sportsmen, although it did not apply any legal categorization to those considerations.[258] As is shown below, however, that statement is likewise incapable of justifying the exception to the prohibition against discrimination which the Court was prepared to accept.

It might appear at first sight that a paramount sporting interest could override any potential economic implications in the composition of a national team and preclude the operation of the prohibition against discrimination.[259] However, doubts arise when the question is asked wherein the particular 'sporting' interest in the composition of national teams actually lies, or, more precisely, why the sporting interest in the formation of a national team should be greater than it is in the case of a club team. The answer can only be that the 'sporting' interest is paramount *because* the team consists only of nationals of the country which it represents. Thus the actual criterion – concealed by the arguments submitted – is not the existence of a 'sporting interest', however that may be described, but the fact that the team is made up exclusively of *nationals* of the country concerned. It is not a question of serving purely sporting purposes by focusing on a sportsman's nationality,[260] but, conversely, of using sport for nationality purposes.[261]

Thus the answer given by the Court of Justice to the question whether a provision centred on the nationality of the players is permissible under Community law relates, in the final analysis, to the *existence* of national teams, whose justification was the very point at issue in the proceedings before the national court. The reasoning is therefore circular.

The Court appears in the result to have been prompted to restrict the scope of the prohibition against discrimination on grounds ranking higher than Community law.[262] Consequently, the exclusion of the application of the prohibition against discrimination in the case of the composition of national teams cannot be justified in strict legal terms. If participation in such a team is remunerated, it must be open to nationals of other Member States.[263] If, on the other hand, it is in fact 'a matter of "national pride and identity" ',[264] then it does not appear to be asking too much to require a member of a national team to take part in competitions on an unremunerated basis.

3. Freedom of Movement for Architects

Architects – who have been described as 'an undoubtedly creative group'[265] –

---

258 For a concurring view, see Schroeder, p. 40.

259 Klose, p. 158, is clearly content to accept this argument.

260 Although that is the view taken by Weatherill, p. 60.

261 This is also the approach taken by Delannay, p. 214, who describes national teams as a 'bastion du nationalisme'.

262 For a concurring view, see also Steindorff, *NJW 1982*, p. 1904, who refers to 'extralegal parameters'.

263 For a concurring view, see also Schroeder, pp. 43 *et seq.*

264 As Weatherill contends, p. 60.

265 Roth, *ZUM 1989*, p. 103.

constitute what are termed 'members of the liberal professions'.[266] A typical characteristic of the practice of a liberal profession is the independence, in substantive and technical terms, with which it is carried on.[267] However, that does not exclude the possibility that the profession of architect may not also be practised in a dependent relationship. That possibility is taken into account by Article 29 of the Directive of 10 June 1985 on the mutual recognition of qualifications in architecture,[268] which provides that that directive is also to apply to nationals of Member States 'who, in accordance with Regulation (EEC) No. 1612/68, are pursuing or will pursue as employed persons the activities referred to in Article 1'.[269] As the Court of Justice confirmed in passing in its judgment of 26 May 1982 in Case 149/79 *Commission* v. *Belgium* (final judgment),[270] architects engaged in an employment relationship are to be regarded as *employees* under Community law.[271]

A further decision by the Court of Justice[272] concerned the right of establishment of architects. Its judgment of 28 June 1977 in Case 11/77 *Patrick*[273] concerned a British architect wishing to practise in France. His diploma had been recognized by a decree of the French Minister for Cultural Affairs as equivalent to a French diploma, but the second basic criterion, namely the existence of a reciprocal convention with the United Kingdom, was not fulfilled. According to the French legislation, that criterion could be dispensed with only in exceptional cases. On that ground, his application for authorization to practise in France was rejected.

By reference to its judgment of 21 June 1974 in Case 2/74 *Reyners*,[274] the Court of Justice held that the principle of equal treatment with nationals embodied in Article 52 of the EEC Treaty was directly applicable and that the absence of any recognition directive adopted pursuant to Article 57(1) of the Treaty could not preclude an application for authorization to practise as an architect where the right of establishment could be granted by virtue in particular of the provisions of the laws and regulations already in force.[275]

The Court thus made it clear that, in matters governed by Community law, the right to equal treatment may not be made conditional on the existence of a reciprocal agreement.[276] The exercise of discretion by a Member State in the

266 See de Crayencour, p. 115; see also the German Government's reply to the major inquiry into 'The position of the liberal professions in the context of the creation of the internal European market', BT-Drs. 11/6985.

267 See de Crayencour, pp. 20 *et seq.*

268 OJ 1985 L 223, p. 15.

269 This explains why the directive is based not only on Articles 57 and 66 of the EEC Treaty but also on Art. 49.

270 [1982] ECR 1845.

271 *ibid.*, at p. 1851.

272 See also, in the field of architecture, the judgment of 14 July 1988 in Case 38/87 *Commission* v. *Greece* [1988] ECR 4415, which concerned *inter alia* the special case of Greek legislation making admission to membership of the Technical Chamber, which was required in order to practise the profession of architect, conditional on the possession of Greek nationality.

273 [1977] ECR 1199.

274 [1974] ECR 631.

275 [1977] ECR 1199 (at pp. 1205 *et seq.*).

276 See also the judgment of 2 February 1989 in Case 186/87 *Cowan* [1989] ECR 195 (at p. 220).

granting of basic freedoms is incompatible with Community law. Consequently, the fact that national laws provide for the possibility of recognition cannot be decisive either. This was indicated by the Court of Justice when it held that the right of establishment had to be capable of being granted by virtue *in particular* of the provisions of the laws and regulations already in force. As the Court once again confirmed, the sole decisive question is 'the level of knowledge and qualifications which (the holder of the diploma) can be assumed to possess in the light of that diploma, having regard to the nature and duration of the studies and practical training to which the diploma relates'.[277]

The aforementioned recognition directive in respect of architectural qualifications[278] resolved the problems at the heart of the judgment discussed above, but not by means of the recognition rules themselves, since the recognition of the United Kingdom diploma was not in fact a problem in that case. Instead, the decisive factor is the obligation imposed on each Member State by Article 2 of the directive not only to recognize the diplomas in question but also to give such diplomas, 'as regards the right to take up activities referred to in Article 1 and pursue them under the professional title of architect pursuant to Article 23(1), *the same effect* in its territory as those awarded by the Member State itself'.[279]

4. Freedom of Movement for Artists

In its judgment of 18 June 1985 in Case 197/84 *Steinhauser*,[280] the Court of Justice had occasion to define what is meant by the reference in the second paragraph of Article 52 of the EEC Treaty to the 'pursuit' of an activity as a self-employed person. The proceedings before the national court concerned the refusal by the City of Biarritz to allow a German artist, on the grounds of his nationality, to participate in a tendering procedure for the letting of a former fisherman's shed, the use of which was reserved for commercial arts and crafts purposes.

The Court made no reference whatever to the application of the right of establishment to artists, and Advocate-General VerLoren van Themaat merely concluded, in relation to the scope of freedom of establishment under the second paragraph of Article 52 of the Treaty, that the occupation of artist undoubtedly fell within the ambit of Article 52.[281] The question referred to the Court of Justice for a preliminary ruling in fact concerned not that point but the national court's doubts as to whether Article 52 of the Treaty encompassed the Conditions of Tender of the City of Biarritz, which were not intended directly to govern the right to take up an activity as a self-employed person but laid down rules for the allocation, on the basis of tenders, of premises owned and made available for letting by the public authorities and made the acceptance of applications conditional on nationality.[282]

---

277 Judgment of 7 May 1991 in Case C-340/89 *Vlassopoulou* [1991] ECR I-2357, para. 17; see also the judgment of 15 October 1987 in Case 222/86 *Heylens* [1987] ECR 4097 (at p. 4117).
278 OJ 1985 L 223, p. 15.
279 Emphasis added.
280 [1985] ECR 1819.
281 *ibid.*, at p. 1821.
282 *ibid.*, at p. 1825.

The Court ruled in that regard that Article 52 of the Treaty related to the right not only to take up activities as a self-employed person 'but also to pursue them in the broad sense of the term'.[283] The renting of premises for business purposes was held to further the pursuit of an occupation.[284] That view was ultimately confirmed by the Court of Justice in its judgment of 30 May 1989 in Case 305/87 *Commission* v. *Greece*,[285] in which, by reference to Article 54(3)(e) of the EEC Treaty, it described the right to acquire immovable property as the corollary of freedom of establishment.[286] The Court did not in that case restrict the use of such property to use for business purposes, as the circumstances of Case 197/84 *Steinhauser* necessarily required; consequently, no such restriction can be imposed under national law.

IV. COMPETITION LAW IN THE CULTURAL FIELD

1. INTRODUCTION

The competition rules contained in the EEC Treaty encompass not only the rules applying to undertakings but also those in respect of dumping and State aid.[287] According to Article 3(f) of the EEC Treaty, their objective is 'the institution of a system ensuring that competition in the common market is not distorted'. This involves the establishment of competition which is not merely 'genuine' but also 'effective'.[288] The fundamental importance of the competition rules in establishing the Common Market and in thereby additionally ensuring the basic freedoms laid down by the Treaty[289] is evidenced by the fact of their being located in Part 3, Title I, of the Treaty under the heading 'Common rules' and also by the fact that, exceptionally, the power to administer them has been vested in the Community.[290]

As is apparent from the foregoing sections, the Court of Justice applies the basic freedoms established by the EEC Treaty to cases relating to cultural matters, and it has also, in corresponding fashion, made use of the competition rules in the cultural field. However, the case-law referred to below does not concern the whole spectrum of Community competition law but merely the 'Rules applying to undertakings' summarized in Section 1, or 'cartel law', the substantive provisions of which are essentially contained in Articles 85 and 86 of the EEC Treaty.[291] The decisive criterion for the demarcation of the respective competences of the Community and of the Member States in the field of cartel law lies in whether the

---

283 [1985] ECR 1819 (at p. 1827).
284 *ibid.*
285 [1989] ECR 1461.
286 *ibid.* at pp. 1478 *et seq.*
287 See Arts 85–94 of the EEC Treaty.
288 Koch in: Grabitz, *Kommentar zum EWGV*, text preceding Art. 85, n. 3.
289 Schröter in: GBTE, *Kommentar zum EWGV*, preliminary remarks on Arts 85–94, n. 4.
290 See Beutler et al., *3rd ed.*, p. 333.
291 See Schröter in: GBTE, *Kommentar zum EWGV*, preliminary remarks on Arts 85–89, n. 1.

practices of an undertaking may affect trade between Member States;[292] the concept of trade encompasses in this context services as well as goods.[293]

2. THE POSITION OF TELEVISION ORGANIZATIONS UNDER THE COMPETITION RULES

(a) The applicability of cartel law

As is apparent from the heading of the relevant section, the applicability of Community cartel law presupposes practices on the part of undertakings. In Case 155/73 *Sacchi*,[294] the question to be resolved was whether a television organization which had been granted a broadcasting monopoly by the State was to be treated as an undertaking and was thus subject to the cartel rules. The Italian Government contested this on the grounds that the television organization was not pursuing an economic activity but was operating a public service of a cultural, recreational and informative nature.[295] The German Government expressed a similar view, subject however to the important qualification that television organizations are undertakings within the meaning of the competition rules 'only as regards some of their activities'.[296] In its judgment, the Court assumed as a matter of course that Articles 85 *et seq.* of the Treaty applied and classified television organizations as undertakings for the purposes of the cartel rules.[297]

(b) The permissibility of monopolies

As regards the permissibility of monopolies in the field of television, the Court of Justice ruled in its judgment in *Sacchi*, by reference to Article 90(1) of the EEC Treaty, that nothing in the Treaty prevents Member States, for considerations of public interest, from removing radio and television transmissions from the field of competition by conferring on one or more establishments an exclusive right to conduct them. It stated, however, that for the performance of their tasks those establishments remain subject to the prohibition against discrimination and, to the extent that such performance comprises activities of an economic nature, fall under the provisions of Article 90(1) of the Treaty.[298]

This restriction of the scope of application of Article 90(1) of the EEC Treaty to 'activities of an economic nature' shows that the Community rules on cartels relate not to undertakings *per se* but only to some of their conduct – in other words, that they are applicable only from a functional standpoint.[299] In its judgment of 18 June 1991 in Case C-260/89 *Elliniki Radiophonia Tileorassi*,[300] the Court confirmed the permissibility of television monopolies and amplified its state-

---

292 Koch in: Grabitz, *Kommentar zum EWGV*, Art. 85, n. 88.
293 *ibid.*, n. 90.
294 Judgment of 30 April 1974 in Case 155/73 *Sacchi* [1974] ECR 409.
295 *ibid.*, at p. 419.
296 *ibid.*, at p. 418.
297 *ibid.*, at p. 430.
298 *ibid.*, at pp. 429 *et seq.*
299 See Reich, *Rundfunkrecht und Wettbewerbsrecht*, p. 228
300 [1991] ECR I-2925.

ments in Case 155/73 *Sacchi* by declaring that the public interest considerations on which the establishment of a monopoly is based must be 'of a non-economic nature';[301] in addition, the individual rules regarding the manner in which such a monopoly is organized and exercised 'must not infringe the provisions of the Treaty on the free movement of goods and services or the rules on competition'.[302]

The permissibility in principle of monopoly undertakings has affected the provision contained in Article 86 of the EEC Treaty. In its judgment in Case 155/73 *Sacchi*, the Court of Justice held that such undertakings were not *as such* incompatible with Article 86. The position was held necessarily to be the same as regards an extension of the monopoly following further intervention by the State, e.g. by its extension to cable television.[303] The applicability in principle of Article 86 of the Treaty to statutory monopolies, as indicated in that judgment, was confirmed by the Court in its judgment of 3 October 1985 in Case 311/84 *Télémarketing*,[304] which concerned the market behaviour of a television organization enjoying such a monopoly. The Court held that the sole decisive factor was the strength of the commercial position of an undertaking, where this 'enables it to hinder the maintenance of effective competition on the relevant market by allowing it to behave to an appreciable extent independently of its competitors and customers and ultimately of consumers'.[305] Thus the cause of the position of commercial strength is not important. In so ruling, the Court concurred with Advocate-General Lenz's view that 'a monopoly protected by law represents one of the clearest examples of a dominant position'.[306]

In its judgment in Case C-260/89 *Elliniki Radiophonia Tileorassi*, therefore, the Court of Justice made reference only to its judgment in Case 311/84 *Télémarketing* in order to substantiate its finding that 'an undertaking which has a statutory monopoly may be regarded as having a dominant position within the meaning of Article 86 of the Treaty'.[307] It held that where a Member State, by developing a monopoly position, creates a situation in which the monopoly undertaking in question is led to infringe Article 86 of the Treaty, that will be contrary to Article 90(1) of the EEC Treaty. That was held to be the case where the undertaking in question enjoys not only a broadcasting monopoly but also a monopoly over the retransmission of programmes from other States, and infringes Article 86 'by virtue of a discriminatory broadcasting policy which favours its own programmes'.[308]

---

301 [1991] ECR I-2925, para. 12. This qualifying phrase was already contained in the English version of the judgment of 30 April 1974 in Case 155/73 *Sacchi* [1974] ECR 409 (para. 14); it did not appear, however, in the German version.
302 *ibid.*
303 [1974] ECR 409 (at p. 430).
304 [1985] ECR 3261.
305 *ibid.*, at p. 3275.
306 *ibid.*, at p. 3265.
307 [1991] ECR I-2925, at p. I-2961.
308 *ibid.*, at p. I-2963.

3. The Permissibility of Book Price Maintenance

Book price maintenance systems are 'a piece of Europe's identity'.[309] Versions of
such systems exist in almost all of the Member States.[310] Whilst that may be so,
there remains the question whether book price maintenance systems are
permissible under the Community rules on competition.[311] To date, the Court
of Justice has expressed a view on this question in two judgments. The first, dated
17 January 1984, in Joined Cases 43 and 63/82 VBVB and VBBB v. Commission,[312]
concerned a transnational agreement between two national publishing and
bookselling associations providing for vertical book price maintenance within a
linguistic area extending beyond national borders. The second, dated 10 January
1985 in Case 229/83 Leclerc,[313] concerned national legislative rules providing for
vertical price maintenance in respect of books purchased in the Member State
concerned.[314]

(a) The permissibility of transnational book price maintenance agreements

The 'central issue of the proceedings'[315] in Joined Cases 43 and 63/82 VBVB and
VBBB v. Commission was the applicant associations' claim that the contested
decision of the Commission, in which it found that the agreement between the
applicants infringed Article 85(1) of the Treaty, took into account neither the
specific nature of books as a product nor the special nature and structure of the
book market, inasmuch as price competition was not a competitive factor in that
market.[316] The Court, in considering this plea, stated that the sole question before
it was 'the conformity of the transnational agreement with Article 85(1)'. Its
judgment could relate, therefore, only to the restrictive effects of that agreement
on trade between the markets concerned in the two Member States.[317] It was held
that, regardless of the special characteristics of the book market, Article 85(1)(a)
and (b) of the Treaty had been infringed. Nor was the position altered in any way

---

309 See J. Becker, p. 21.
310 See Wallenfels, pp. 72 et seq.; for a detailed analysis, see Langbein, pp. 4 –73.
311 See also, to that effect, the judgment of the Court of Justice of 17 January 1984 in Joined
Cases 43 and 63/82 VBVB and VBBB v. Commission [1984] ECR 19 (at p. 64), in which it held
that 'national legislative or judicial practices, even on the supposition that they are common to all
Member States, cannot prevail in the application of the competition rules set out in the Treaty'.
312 [1984] ECR 19.
313 [1985] ECR 1.
314 See, more recently, the judgment of the Court of First Instance of 9 July 1992 in Case
T-66/89 Publishers Association v. Commission [1992] ECR II-1995, concerning an application for
the annulment of a Commission decision (OJ 1989 L 22, p. 12) in which the Commission held a
non-transnational agreement between undertakings on uniform conditions of sale of 'net books' to
be contrary to Art. 85(1) of the EEC Treaty, to the extent that it covered the book trade between
Member States (Art. 1 of the decision); see also in that regard the order of the President of the
Court of Justice of 13 June 1989 in Case 56/89 R Publishers Association v. Commission [1989] ECR
1693, in which the enforcement of the Commission's decision was partially stayed.
315 According to the Court of Justice, [1984] ECR 19 (at p. 65).
316 ibid., at p. 64.
317 ibid., at pp. 65 et seq.

by the fact that the agreement in issue concerned a single linguistic region. Article 85, it was held, expressly refers to 'trade between Member States'.[318]

In emphasizing the transnational nature of the agreement in issue, the Court of Justice indicated that it wished to avoid having to take a view on the permissibility of purely national systems of book price maintenance; nor, indeed, did it need to do so on the basis of the contested decision of the Commission which had triggered the proceedings.[319] This point is explained in the Court's further statement ruling that the extension to intra-Community trade of the closely supervised price rules constituted a sufficiently marked[320] restriction of competition for the purposes of Article 85(1) of the Treaty.[321] That was the position even on the supposition 'that the specific nature of books as an object of trade may justify certain special conditions in the matter of distribution and price'.[322]

(b) The permissibility of price maintenance by order of the State

The second judgment of the Court of Justice on book price maintenance[323] concerned a purely national[324] system provided for by domestic law.[325] The application of the competition rules to this case gave rise to specific problems, since it is only to the practices of undertakings that Articles 85-90 of the EEC Treaty directly relate, not to State intervention in competition matters.

That finding formed the starting-point for the Court's considerations; it went on to discuss the question of an infringement of the second paragraph of Article 5 of the EEC Treaty, which requires Member States to 'abstain from any measure which could jeopardize the attainment of the objectives of this Treaty'. It held in that regard that the legislation at issue was not intended to provide for practices contrary to Article 85(1) of the Treaty; it imposed on publishers and importers an obligation to fix retail prices *unilaterally*.[326]

Unlike the Commission, however, the Court did not stop at this conclusion; it went on to consider whether the fact that the national legislation in issue rendered behaviour of the type prohibited by Article 85(1) superfluous might be contrary to the second paragraph of Article 5 of the Treaty. In the Court's view, however, in order for there to be an infringement of the second paragraph of Article 5 of the

---

318 [1984] ECR 19 (at p. 67).

319 See Reich, FS *für Ernst Steindorff*, p. 1081, who contends that the Commission drew a careful distinction between the domestic and international effects of price maintenance and criticized only the latter.

320 In so stating, the Court of Justice was clearly referring to the unwritten rule that the effects on trade and competition must be 'appreciable'; see in that regard Koch in: Grabitz, *Kommentar zum EWGV*, Art. 85, n. 97; Knecht, pp. 31 *et seq.*; Beutler et al., *3rd ed.*, p. 336.

321 [1984] ECR 19 (at p. 66).

322 *ibid.*

323 Judgment of 10 January 1985 in Case 229/83 *Leclerc* [1985] ECR 1.

324 This should not be confused with the question whether such a purely national price maintenance system can have appreciable effects on intra-Community trade. The application of the Community competition rules is invariably conditional on the determination of such effects.

325 See in that regard also 'Application to cultural goods', pp. 140 *et seq.*, above.

326 [1985] ECR 1 (at p. 32).

Treaty there must be a sufficiently specific obligation on the Member States which may be enforced on the basis of that provision. As Community law then stood, there was no such obligation in relation to purely national price maintenance systems. No competition policy yet existed in that sphere. Neither the Commission nor the Court had expressed a view on that question. Consequently, no prohibition against the enactment of legislation of the type at issue could be inferred from the second paragraph of Article 5 of the Treaty.[327]

So long, therefore, as there exists no competition policy relating to the field of national statutory price maintenance systems, the Court of Justice will not find against such systems. Consequently, it declined responsibility for developing a Community policy, and thus for specifying the obligations flowing from the second paragraph of Article 5 of the EEC Treaty, and extended to the Commission 'une invitation discrète' to exercise its powers in the future.[328] However, the Commission has to date declined to take any steps in this sphere. In its communication presented in August 1989, entitled 'Books and Reading: A Cultural Challenge for Europe',[329] it gave the reasons for its attitude. It stated that its only objection in principle was to resale price maintenance which distorts trade inside the Community, particularly within language areas.[330]

4. THE PERMISSIBILITY OF SELECTIVE PRESS DISTRIBUTION SYSTEMS

To date, the Court of Justice has given judgment in two cases concerning the permissibility under competition law of selective press distribution systems. Both judgments (dated 16 June 1981 in Case 126/80 *Salonia*[331] and 3 July 1985 in Case 243/83 *Binon*[332]) were based on references by national courts for preliminary rulings which were submitted to the Court of Justice in the context of actions by newspaper retailers against newspaper distributors for the supply of press publications. Supplies had been withheld from the retailers because they were not licensed to sell newspapers and periodicals. The requirement of a special licence was based on agreements between, on the one hand, the newspaper publishers and, on the other, the newsagents' federation or the intermediary newspaper wholesalers. It was not possible to circumvent the wholesalers by obtaining supplies direct from the publishers.

The Court addressed, first of all, two general problems relating to the applicability of Article 85 of the EEC Treaty. The first of the two cases concerned the question whether the contested newspaper distribution system was actually

---

327 For a view critical of this conclusion, see Müller-Graff, *EuR 1985*, p. 298, who contends that if no specific Community policy exists, the general Community objective of the Common Market is still present and may not be jeopardized by national measures; see also, to the same effect, Langbein, pp. 250 *et seq.* The Court confirmed its decision in its judgments of 11 July 1985 in Case 299/83 *Leclerc* v. *Syndicat des libraires de Loire-Océan* [1985] ECR 2515 and of 14 July 1988 in Case 254/87 *Syndicat des libraries de Normandie* [1988] ECR 4457.

328 See Waelbroeck, pp. 29 *et seq.*; in a similar vein, but with a different nuance, Kuyper, p. 804: '... a rap on the knuckles ... for failing to take a clear position ...'.

329 COM(89) 258.

330 *ibid.*, p. 15.

331 [1981] ECR 1563.

332 [1985] ECR 2015.

capable of restricting trade between Member States. This was debatable, since the distribution system covered only domestic press publications. However, the Court held, without giving detailed reasons for its view, that even such a closed system may have repercussions on intra-Community trade. In order for Article 85 to apply, however, it was necessary for it to have an 'appreciable' effect on trade. The question of appreciability, which it was for the national court to decide, had to be determined using stricter criteria in the case of press publications than in the case of other products.[333]

A second problem concerned what constitutes 'concerted practices'. The more recent of the two judgments involved an assessment of the conduct of the publishers, who had replaced a previous agreement held by the national courts to be anti-competitive by a series of individual agreements with wholesalers. The defendant in the proceedings before the national court pleaded that this constituted not a concerted practice but merely reasonable parallel conduct. The Court of Justice did not accept this, and ruled in addition that Article 85 of the EEC Treaty would have been applicable even if the old agreement had not been replaced by a new one. It held that the system of competition rules established by Articles 85 et seq. of the Treaty is concerned solely with the economic effects of agreements or of any comparable form of concerted practice or coordination, rather than with their legal form.[334]

Having thus established the basic applicability of Article 85 of the Treaty, the Court then turned to a specific examination of whether selective press distribution systems infringed that provision. It had been pleaded in favour of such systems that the specific character of the market and the socio-cultural role of the press required a stable and balanced distribution network;[335] in opposition to that argument, it had been contended that such systems would eliminate any competition whatever.[336] The Court ultimately considered, following its judgment of 25 October 1977 in Case 26/76 Metro,[337] that selective press distribution systems were compatible in principle with the Community competition rules.[338] In view of the special nature of the distribution of press publications, it held that such systems could be introduced in that field without infringing Article 85(1) of the Treaty. However, such systems must satisfy specific requirements. Resellers must be chosen on the basis of objective criteria of a qualitative nature relating to the technical qualifications of the reseller and his staff and the suitability of his trading premises, and those criteria must be applied uniformly and without discrimination to all potential resellers. Quantitative criteria, on the other hand, such as the limitation of the number of retail outlets by reference to a minimum number of inhabitants in the vicinity of an outlet, were held to be inapplicable.[339]

Although the Court did not expressly carry out a detailed examination of

---

333 Case 126/80 *Salonia* [1981] ECR 1563 (at p. 1579).
334 Case 243/83 *Binon* [1985] ECR 2015 (at p. 2040).
335 *ibid.*, at p. 2042.
336 *ibid.*, at p. 2043.
337 [1977] ECR 1875.
338 In its judgment in Case 243/83 *Binon*, op. cit., n. 332, the Court of Justice expressed a view only on Art. 85 of the EEC Treaty; its judgment in Case 126/80 *Salonia*, op. cit., n. 331 also extended to Art. 86.
339 Case 243/83 *Binon* [1985] ECR 2015 (at pp. 2043 *et seq.*).

Article 85(1) of the Treaty, the upshot of its decision is quite clear. The application of objective, *qualitative* criteria does not necessarily restrict competition appreciably. However, such criteria must also be appropriate and must not be so exaggerated as to limit, from the outset, the number of potential applicants for approved retail outlets.

5. EXERCISE OF COPYRIGHT

(a) The significance of the competition rules as regards copyright

In the context of the free movement of goods and of freedom to provide services, the Court of Justice has drawn a distinction, as we have seen,[340] between the existence of copyright, which is unobjectionable under Community law, and its exercise, which falls to be assessed in accordance with the provisions of the EEC Treaty. This raises the question whether, and, if so, in what way, that distinction plays a role in the field of the competition rules.

The starting-point for an examination of that question is the Court's judgment of 18 February 1971 in Case 40/70 *Sirena*.[341] In that judgment, the Court held, in connection with national trade mark law, that although Article 36 of the EEC Treaty appears in the Chapter dealing with quantitative restrictions, it is 'based on a principle equally applicable to the question of competition, in the sense that even if the rights recognized by the legislation of a Member State on the subject of industrial and commercial property are not affected, so far as their *existence* is concerned, by Articles 85 and 86 of the Treaty, their *exercise* may still fall under the prohibitions imposed by those provisions'.[342]

It follows that, in the context of competition law, copyright is treated in accordance with the same principles as those applying to the free movement of goods and freedom to provide services. That finding raises the further question as to when the exercise of copyright coming within the ambit of Community law may be incompatible with the competition rules. Once again, the answer to that question is to be found in the judgment in Case 40/70 *Sirena*. According to that judgment, the exercise of a trade mark right may be prohibited by Article 85(1) of the EEC Treaty where 'it manifests itself as the subject, the means or the result of a restrictive practice'.[343]

The same necessarily applies in relation to copyright. This was confirmed and specified by the Court in its judgment of 6 October 1982 in Case 262/81 *Coditel II*,[344] in line with its previous ruling to the same effect in its judgment of 8 June 1971 in Case 78/70 *Deutsche Grammophon*,[345] concerning a protective right in the nature of copyright. In its judgment in *Coditel II*, the Court found that certain aspects of the manner in which copyright is exercised may prove to be

---

340 See 'Copyright protection', pp. 145 *et seq.*, above, and 'Permissible restrictions on the free movement of television broadcasts', pp. 157 *et seq.*, above.
341 [1971] ECR 69.
342 *ibid.*, at p. 81 (emphasis added).
343 *ibid.*, at p. 83.
344 [1982] ECR 3381.
345 [1971] ECR 487.

incompatible with Article 85 of the Treaty if they serve to give effect to a cartel agreement which may have as its object or effect the prevention, restriction or distortion of competition within the Common Market. However, the mere granting of an exclusive right to exhibit a film in the territory of a Member State during a specified period is not sufficient to justify such a finding. There must also be other accompanying circumstances of a commercial or legal nature. In particular, the position will depend on 'whether or not the exercise of the exclusive right ... creates barriers which are artificial and unjustifiable in terms of the needs of the cinematographic industry, or (there exists) the possibility of charging fees which exceed a fair return on investment, or an exclusivity the duration of which is disproportionate to those requirements'.[346]

Consequently, the provisions of competition law are likewise applicable to copyright, although their application is subject to relatively tight limits in so far as a distinction is drawn between the existence and the exercise of the copyright in question.

(b) Questions of competition law in connection with distribution companies

Copyright distribution companies are frequently formed by publishers and copyright-holders as legal persons incorporated under private law for the purposes of safeguarding more effectively the exploitation rights of individual copyright-holders. The sum of the exploitation rights assigned to the distribution company – the total repertoire – is licensed as a complete package only; the individual exploitation right merges in the package as a whole. For that reason, it is legitimate to describe the total package, in relation to the individual rights forming part of it, as a 'new product'.[347]

The Court has addressed in a number of judgments the question of global access to the total repertoire, together with further questions of competition law in relation to copyright distributing companies, some important aspects of which are discussed below.

(i) Distribution companies as undertakings within the meaning of Article 90(2) of the EEC Treaty

The question whether copyright distribution companies are to be regarded as undertakings 'entrusted with the operation of services of general economic interest' within the meaning of Article 90(2) of the Treaty was addressed by the Court of Justice for the first time in its judgment of 27 March 1974 in Case 127/73 *BRT II*.[348] In its judgment, the Court held that Article 90(2) of the Treaty must be strictly interpreted, since it permits derogations from the rules of the Treaty. Private undertakings may only come under that provision if the particular tasks

---

346 [1982] ECR 3381 (at p. 3402).
347 See, in relation to the whole of this paragraph, Mestmäcker, *FS für Rudolf Lukes*, pp. 445–448.
348 [1974] ECR 313.

assigned to them are entrusted 'by an act of the public authority'. The mere fact that an undertaking safeguards intellectual property rights protected by law is not enough.[349]

That decision was confirmed by the Court in its judgment of 2 March 1983 in Case 7/82 *GVL* v. *Commission*.[350] In that judgment, it expressly held that the criteria of Article 90(2) of the Treaty were not satisfied as regards German law. It held that the German legislation did not confer the management of copyright and related rights on specific undertakings but defined in a general manner the rules applying to the activities of companies which intended to undertake the collective exploitation of such rights.[351]

(ii) The global assignment of all copyrights

The above-mentioned judgment in Case 127/73 *BRT II*[352] was also concerned with whether a distribution company enjoying a *de facto* monopoly in a Member State contravened Article 86 of the EEC Treaty by demanding from copyright-holders the global assignment of all their present and future copyrights and the conferment of authorization to continue exercising those rights for five years following the withdrawal of the copyright-holder. The provision at issue here was indent (a) of the second paragraph of Article 86 of the EEC Treaty, which defines as an abuse of a dominant position within the market, *inter alia*, the imposition of unfair trading conditions.

The Court weighed up the various competing interests. It recognized, first, the interest of a distribution company in achieving a position in which it can protect the rights of its members against major exploiters of musical material. However, the limit absolutely necessary for the attainment of that objective must not be exceeded. Otherwise, the interest which an individual copyright-holder may have in his freedom to dispose of his work must take precedence. It was held that a global assignment may constitute an abuse within the meaning of Article 86 of the Treaty, especially if such assignment is required for an extended period after the member's withdrawal from the company.[353]

It follows that requiring a global assignment does not *per se* constitute an infringement of Article 86 of the Treaty. Such an infringement may only be found to exist after an assessment of all the facts and circumstances of an individual case.

(iii) Global access to the total repertoire

Lastly, it is necessary to consider whether the practice of distribution companies, referred to in the introductory remarks above, of granting users only global access to the total repertoire, and of refusing access to individual categories, such as foreign music, is compatible with the Community competition rules: in this

---

349 [1974] ECR 313 (at p. 318).
350 [1983] ECR 483.
351 *ibid.*, at p. 504.
352 [1974] ECR 313.
353 *ibid.*, at p. 317.

instance, Article 85 of the EEC Treaty. For certain users, such as discotheques, access to the total repertoire is of no interest, since they cannot turn such access to account. However, they are obliged to pay royalties in respect of the total repertoire.

In addressing this problem in its judgment of 13 July 1989 in Case 395/87 *Tournier*,[354] the Court applied criteria similar to those applied with regard to the question of global assignments, referred to above. The distribution companies pursued what was, in principle, a legitimate objective. In pursuing that objective, they were not permitted to exceed the limits of what was necessary for its attainment. The Court held that it was necessary for separate access to be given to individual sub-divisions of the repertoire only where the interests of authors, composers and publishers of music could fully be protected.[355]

Thus it is likewise apparent here that a restriction on access to the total repertoire does not *per se* constitute an infringement of Article 85 of the EEC Treaty. Here too, however, the position will in the final analysis depend on an assessment of each individual case. [356]

---

354 [1989] ECR 2521.

355 *ibid.*, at p. 2575.

356 As the Court of Justice expressly stated in its judgment of 13 July 1989, *Tournier*, op. cit., p. 2576. However, Mestmäcker takes the view, in *FS Fritz Rittner*, p. 399, that an infringement should as a general rule be found not to have been committed, and that the criterion laid down by the Court is capable of general application.

Part 4

PRINCIPLES
AND POTENTIAL DEVELOPMENT
OF COMMUNITY LAW
IN THE CULTURAL FIELD

Chapter 1

COMMUNITY COMPETENCE
IN THE
CULTURAL FIELD

I. DIVISION OF POWERS IN THE CULTURAL FIELD BETWEEN THE COMMUNITY AND THE MEMBER STATES

1. INTRODUCTION

There exists, generally, considerable uncertainty as to the relationship between the scope of Community competence and that of the Member States, but especially with regard to the cultural field. Such uncertainty is reflected in a number of academic commentaries on that relationship, which, whilst frequently couched in appropriately indefinite terms, nevertheless fail to address the crux of the problem, and consequently take the matter no further. Thus we read that the Treaties establishing the EC confer 'no comprehensive competence in the cultural field',[1] that there exists no 'general EC competence in the field of culture and education',[2] that Article 3 of the EEC Treaty contains no reference to cultural policy,[3] that the Community has 'merely secondary powers, but at all events no primary competence, in cultural matters',[4] and finally – in relation to the television directive – that the EEC 'certainly has no mandate' to develop a body of European law on broadcasting and a European broadcasting system.[5]

Reasons are advanced from time to time to explain why it is that the Community's freedom of action is restricted in this way; those reasons are based on still more general considerations. With reference to Article 1 of the EEC Treaty, i.e. the official title of the Community, it is argued that the EEC is an *economic*

---

1 Fiedler, p. 153.
2 Schweitzer, *EG-Kompetenzen*, p. 147.
3 Eiselstein, *NVwZ 1989*, p. 328.
4 Tomuschat, *EuR 1990*, p. 341.
5 Rupp, p. 2.

community,[6] and thus that it is restricted to objects and matters forming the subject of commercial transactions.[7] That argument, which has not gone unchallenged,[8] illustrates – as does the frequent use of the nebulous concept of cultural policy – the fact that the competence debate is determined not predominantly by legal considerations but in equal measure, at least, by politics.[9] A symptom of this is to be found in the emotive nature of the debate,[10] which finds expression in the use of concepts such as 'faith in Europe' or 'commitment to Europe'.[11]

It is impossible for a jurist to isolate himself from the political background to the competence debate.[12] He has to be especially aware of his own political background and to relate each interpretation to it. In so doing, it should not be considered that each interpretation is arbitrary and that priority must be given to political will. The intention is merely to point out the danger in legitimizing, in legal terms, the interpretations which are politically desirable, thereby using the law to pursue a policy which is regarded as correct. It is a risk to which both the Community institutions, in their endeavours to extend the scope of their competence, and the authorities of the Member States, in their efforts to counteract them, are exposed. This finding is all the more momentous, in that the Community legal order, unlike practically any other, is dependent upon the authority of the law comprised within it:[13] the EC is a community based on the rule of law.[14]

An examination of the scope of Community competence is necessarily dependent on what is meant by the term 'competence'. The word derives from the Latin verb *competere*, meaning to be fit, proper or qualified, and its present participle *competens*, meaning appropriate, authoritative or empowered.[15] Its etymological derivation conveys an initial impression of the meaning of the concept of competence: it involves the 'responsibility', 'authority' – 'compe-

---

6   e.g. see Meyer, p. 97, n. 1; Lecheler, *Nationaler öffentlicher Dienst*, p. 130; Ossenbühl, p. 13; Scharf, p. 148; Riegel, *NJW 1978*, p. 470; L. Seidel, p. 125; and the submissions of the Italian Government in Case 7/68 *Commission* v. *Italy* [1968] ECR 423 (at p. 428), which advanced the argument that the tax at issue in that case fell wholly outside the natural framework of the Treaty and that the Treaty had been concluded for the purposes of establishing an economic community and not a community for articles of artistic, historic or ethnographic value.

7   Lecheler, op. cit., p. 130.

8   See, to cite but two examples, Magiera, *DÖV 1987*, p. 231; Schwartz, *Zur Zuständigkeit*, p. 80.

9   See Schumacher, p. 539, who points out in general terms that the characteristic nature of questions of competence is such that they are debated as much from the political as from the legal standpoint.

10   See the statement by the former United Kingdom Commissioner Lord Cockfield that criticism of the competence of the EC in the field of broadcasting was 'transparent nonsense', and the position adopted in that regard by Delbrück, *Rundfunkrecht*, p. 244.

11   See Delbrück, op. cit., p. 244.

12   This is aptly pointed out by Schumacher, p. 539.

13   See in that regard Stein, *Autorität*, p. 53.

14   See (to cite but a few examples) the judgment of the Court of Justice of 23 April 1986 in Case 294/83 *Les Verts* v. *Parliament* [1986] ECR 1339 (at p. 1365); Oppermann, *Europäische Integration*, p. 89; Everling, *FS Hans Kutscher*, p. 160; Hallstein, *Rechtsgemeinschaft*, pp. 343 et seq.

15   For the etymology of the term from a German standpoint, see the entry in Duden, *Etymologie* (1963), under: '*kompetent*'.

tence',[16] in fact – for the performance of a task. This relates first and foremost to institutional competence, since the Community acts not as a legal person in its own right but through its institutions, like all international organizations.[17] This is reflected in the first subparagraph of Article 4(1) of the EEC Treaty. According to that provision, the tasks entrusted to the Community are to be carried out by the Community institutions. As is indicated in the second subparagraph of Article 4(1), the Treaty confers on those institutions powers for the performance of the tasks of the Community.

Clearly, the powers of the Community institutions and the tasks of the Community are interdependent: the existence of power without the co-existence of a task to be performed is as futile as the existence of a task without the co-existence of institutions empowered to perform it.[18] It follows that to restrict the notion of competence to the power to perform a task whilst excluding the task itself[19] from the context of the work to be done is to rob that notion of all meaning. Nor is there anything to be gained by entering into the debate about the meaning of competence, which remains unclear from various points of view.[20] Instead, the concept of competence is defined, on the basis of the terminology used in the EEC Treaty,[21] as meaning that the tasks of the Community, taken as a whole, represent its collective competence ('Verbandskompetenz'[22]), whereas the powers conferred on the Community institutions, which necessarily relate to the tasks of the Community and are inseparable therefrom, are described as institutional competence ('Organkompetenz').

This concept of competence renders superfluous any debate on the question whether competence denotes 'ability in law'[23] or 'permissibility in law'.[24] The link with the tasks assigned limits the concept of competence *ab initio* to the idea of 'permissibility in law'. The idea of competence as a concept centred around 'ability in law', and thus as including legal acts which, whilst not void *ab initio*, are unlawful by reason of their exceeding the tasks conferred or of their being *ultra vires*, is of no informative value for the purposes of the present analysis, the aim of which is to cover acts of the Community institutions in the cultural field which are *permissible* under Community law.

---

16   Stettner, p. 47, regards the notions as synonymous.

17   Köck, *FS Ignaz Seidl-Hohenveldern*, p. 279, n. 1.

18   See also V. Constantinesco, *Compétences*, 83/295, who refers to 'compétences' (of the Community) and 'pouvoirs' (of the Community institutions).

19   That is the view expressed by Stettner, p. 40, disagreeing with Ehmke, *VVDStRL 20* (1963), pp. 89 *et seq.*

20   See in that regard – to cite but a few examples – Stettner, pp. 31 *et seq.*; Ehmke, op. cit., pp. 89 *et seq.*; Schneider, p. 523.

21   For a more detailed analysis, see Magiera, *GS Wilhelm Karl Geck*, pp. 513-520.

22   As to this term, see primarily E.R. Huber, *Wirtschaftsverwaltungsrecht*, pp. 716 *et seq.*

23   As is maintained by Grabitz, *Gemeinschaftsrecht bricht nationales Recht*, p. 61, and L.-J. Constantinesco, p. 234.

24   For a detailed analysis in that regard, see Pechstein, *Sachwalter*, pp. 38-42.

2. The Collective Competence of the Community

(a) Demarcation from the collective competence of the State

The first subparagraph of Article 4(1) of the EEC Treaty provides that the institutions referred to therein are to carry out the tasks entrusted to the Community by the Treaty. That sentence expresses in abstract terms the fact that the Community – unlike, in theory, the Member States – is *not competent in every sphere.*[25] To that extent, it is correct to speak of the 'principle of limited powers' underlying the Community legal order.[26] Consequently, it is also accurate to say that the Community is not in the nature of a State,[27] even though it may already have drawn closer, in many respects, to 'the immediate vicinity of statehood'.[28]

The absence of the universal competence of a State is, however, simply *one* aspect of the limited tasks conferred on the Community. The situation further differs from State sovereignty inasmuch as the fact that tasks are conferred on the Community likewise establishes the legal duty to carry out those tasks.[29] It is only the actual carrying out of those tasks which legitimizes the existence of the Community, whereas States do not need any particular legitimation in order to exist.[30]

Such demarcation between the collective competence of the Community and that of a State can be seen only as a basic approximation, and is not in itself very meaningful. The finding that the allocation of powers is only limited, whilst clear in theory, must be tested by means of a more detailed consideration of the nature and scope of the allocation of powers.

(b) Nature and scope of collective competence

The scope of the collective competence of the Community is defined by the sum of its tasks, as contained in the various Treaty provisions.[31] The assignment of tasks provided for in the Treaty as a whole has taken place in a pragmatic way, 'without being based on any particular conceptual model'.[32] It cannot be said, however, that the division of collective competence between the Community and the Member States does not follow a general rule – like Article 30 of the Grundgesetz (German

---

25 See, among numerous examples, Wagner, p. 258; Ipsen, *Europäisches Gemeinschaftsrecht*, p. 64.

26 See Magiera, *Jura 1989*, p. 597.

27 e.g. see Ophüls, *Planverfassungen*, p. 232, who describes universal competence as the characteristic of State sovereignty; Ipsen, *EuR 1987*, p. 196; Steinberger, p. 16.

28 See Oppermann, *Die EG als parastaatliche Superstruktur*, p. 697; for a critical view in that regard, see Ipsen, op. cit., pp. 200 *et seq.*

29 See Köck, *FS Ignaz Seidl-Hohenveldern*, p. 280; Grabitz in: *idem, Kommentar zum EWGV*, Art. 4, n.2.

30 Everling, *RabelsZ 50 (1986)*, p. 210. The tasks of the Community cannot be compared with so-called 'State objectives', which do not legitimize the existence of a State but merely lay down principles and guidelines for State acts; see Scheuner, p. 335; for a recent commentary, see Sommermann, pp. 34 *et seq.*

31 Grabitz in: *idem, Kommentar zum EWGV*, Art. 235, n. 21.

32 L.-J. Constantinesco, p. 235.

Basic Law) dealing with the relationship between the German *Länder* and the Federal Republic – but that the position is governed by the individual Treaty provisions:[33] there was no need for a rule of Community law corresponding to Article 30 of the Grundgesetz, since, where competence has not been assigned to the Community, only the Member States have jurisdiction.

Article 2 of the EEC Treaty states that the general task of the Community is 'to promote throughout the Community a harmonious development of economic activities, a continuous and balanced expansion, an increase in stability, an accelerated raising of the standard of living and closer relations between the States belonging to it'. For the purposes of realizing those tasks, which may also be described as objectives of the Community,[34] Article 2 of the EEC Treaty makes two instruments available, namely the establishment of the Common Market and the progressive approximation of the economic policies of the Member States. Those instruments need in turn to be realized, and from that point of view they also constitute, at the same time, Treaty objectives.[35] In principle, therefore, it is possible to describe as the essential characteristic of collective Community competence, that is to say, the 'substantive competence' of the Community,[36] the obligation to bring to fruition specific objectives of differing kinds.[37]

The Treaty objectives enshrined in Article 2 of the EEC Treaty are particularized in Article 3, which describes in greater detail, albeit not conclusively,[38] the activities of the Community. Upon a closer examination of the activities of the Community provided for in Article 3 of the Treaty, it is possible to divide them into two distinct groups. One group of activities concerns the pursuit of common policies in distinct fields capable of substantive demarcation,[39] for example the Common Agricultural Policy (subparagraph (d)) or the Common Transport Policy (subparagraph (e)). Article 74 of the Treaty expresses this in relation to the field of transport by stating that the objectives of the Treaty are, in *matters* governed by the relevant Title, to be pursued by the Member States within the framework of a Common Transport Policy.

The other group consists of activities dedicated to the attainment of specific objectives, without thereby being restricted to specific matters. This type of competence has been graphically described as 'transverse competence' ('Querschnittskompetenz'[40]). The EEC Treaty is said to define the competence of the

---

33   See Ipsen, *Rundfunk im EG-Recht*, p. 37; Grabitz, *GS Christoph Sasse*, p. 112.
34   See Grabitz in: *idem, Kommentar zum EWGV*, Art. 2, n.1; Magiera, *GS Wilhelm Karl Geck*, p. 514.
35   As regards this dual characteristic of the instruments referred to, see Magiera, op. cit., p. 516.
36   See Schwartz, *EuR 1976, Sonderheft*, p. 34.
37   For an analysis of the different degrees of abstractiveness of the objectives and tasks, see Magiera, op. cit., p. 514; Sattler, p. 174.
38   Grabitz in: *idem, Kommentar zum EWGV*, Art. 3, n.3.
39   This assumes, on an ideal level, that the fields in question are capable of being precisely demarcated.
40   Memminger, p. 849; Schwartz, *ZUM 1989*, p. 384; Pechstein, *DÖV 1991*, pp. 539 *et seq.*

Community in *functional*[41] terms, 'that is to say, cutting transversely across all fields'.[42] That type of competence includes, for example, 'the abolition, as between Member States, of obstacles to freedom of movement for persons, services and capital' (Article 3(c)), 'the institution of a system ensuring that competition in the common market is not distorted' (Article 3(f)) and – a particularly succinct example both of association with an objective and of the absence of a link to any particular subject-matter – 'the approximation of the laws of Member States to the extent required for the proper functioning of the common market' (Article 3(h)).[43]

It has in the meantime[44] come to be generally accepted that the division of powers described above informs *in principle* the EEC Treaty,[45] although frequently, for the sake of simplicity, on the basis only of the group of functional powers, i.e. powers relating to the achievement of objectives.[46] In so far as that group – which is undoubtedly the most significant[47] – is concerned, the way in which competence is divided up between the Community and the Member States is fundamentally different from the position as between the Federation and the German *Länder*, in which powers are basically divided up according to subject-matter.[48]

It would be inadequate to describe the collective competence of the Community in terms only of the above-mentioned subject-related powers and functional powers. It also includes a further group of Treaty rules which cannot, strictly speaking, be classified as falling within the concept of competence in the sense of 'permissibility in law': the extensive group of directly effective provisions

---

41   Everling, *EuR 1990*, p. 215, also refers to the assignment of *functions*. This concept has nothing to do with 'functional integration', which concerns not the method by which competence is allocated but the *general* approach of separating out individual, specific, national areas of competence and conferring them on the Community; see in that regard Sattler, p. 1; also Bleckmann, *ZRP 1990*, p. 265, who takes the view, however, that the finding that the Community has in practice full competence no longer fits into this picture today; for a basic analysis, see Bindschedler, pp. 62 *et seq.*

42   Schwartz, *Fernsehen ohne Grenzen*, p. 129.

43   See Taschner, p. 767, who states, with regard to Art. 100 of the EEC Treaty, that it is possible to conceive of few laws which do not directly affect the Common Market.

44   The view was previously held in some quarters that 'the demarcation lines between areas within the jurisdiction of the Member States and those within the jurisdiction of the Community had to be drawn in terms of specific fields of competence, that the jurisdiction of the Member States and that of the Community were, in principle, independent of each other, albeit intermeshing', and that the position as regards the transfer of sovereign rights defined in terms of their objective characteristics is in that respect no different from the position with regard to the transfer of sovereign rights defined in terms of territorial characteristics, that is to say, the cession of territory; see Ophüls, *FS Carl Heymanns Verlag*, p. 570.

45   e.g. see Hoffmann-Riem, *Europäisierung des Rundfunks*, p. 203; Schwartz, *Zur Zuständigkeit*, pp. 80 *et seq.*; Everling, *FS Karl Doehring*, p. 184; *idem, EuR 1987*, p. 221; de Witte, *Scope of Community Powers*, p. 262; Rambow, p. 241.

46   For a critical view on this point, see Ipsen, *GS Wilhelm Karl Geck*, p. 345.

47   Rambow, op. cit., n. 45, points out that the EEC Treaty recognizes only a limited number of express powers in respect of particular policies; see also, to the same effect, Klein, *VVDStRL 50 (1991)*, p. 62.

48   See Bleckmann, *DÖV 1986*, p. 126; Memminger, p. 849; Everling, *FS Karl Doehring*, p. 184; Renzsch, p. 33.

addressed to the Member States,[49] private persons[50] and even the Community institutions,[51] enjoining or prohibiting particular conduct.[52] Those provisions also fall within what is, in this respect, the comprehensive concept of collective Community competence.[53]

The fact that the Community has primarily been assigned tasks to achieve and objectives to attain, but is not so much allocated subject-related fields, and that Community law additionally contains directly effective imperative and prohibitive obligations, has effects on the relationship between collective Community competence and the collective competence of the Member States. In fields in which the Community has the task of attaining particular objectives or where there exist imperative and prohibitive obligations under the Treaty, subject-related competence remains principally with the Member States. The influence which the Community is permitted to exercise on those specific fields is defined and restricted by the objective to be pursued or, as the case may be, by the content of the imperative or prohibitive obligations. The Court likewise proceeds on the basis of that relationship between collective Community competence and the collective competence of the Member States. Thus it held, for example,[54] in the judgment of 2 February 1989 in Case 186/87 *Cowan*, in relation to the prohibition against discrimination laid down in the first paragraph of Article 7 of the EEC Treaty:

'Although in principle criminal legislation and the rules of criminal procedure ... are matters for which the Member States are responsible, the Court has consistently held ... that Community law sets certain limits to their power. Such legislative provisions may not discriminate against persons to whom Community law gives the right to equal treatment or restrict the fundamental freedoms guaranteed by Community law.'[55]

(c) Conclusions in relation to the cultural field

In the light of the foregoing, it is necessary to examine whether, and to what extent, the collective competence of the Community extends to the cultural field. The identification of areas of 'transverse competence' does not preclude *ab initio* the exemption of matters falling within the cultural field, the consequence of which would be that such competence could be exercised only in the remaining, non-exempt fields. However, such exemption would need to be derived, either directly or as a matter of construction, from Community law. It is not possible,

---

49   e.g. see Art. 30 of the EEC Treaty.
50   e.g. see Art. 85 of the EEC Treaty.
51   As regards Arts 30–36 of the EEC Treaty, see Oliver, *Free Movement of Goods in the EEC*, pp. 41-52.
52   As to provisions with direct effect, see Grabitz in: *idem, Kommentar zum EWGV*, Art. 189, n.13.
53   Grabitz in: *idem, Kommentar zum EWGV*, Art. 235, nn. 19-21.
54   See, in addition, the judgment of 14 January 1982 in Case 65/81 *Reina* [1982] ECR 33 (at pp. 44 *et seq.*); the judgment of 11 November 1981 in Case 203/80 *Casati* [1981] ECR 2595 (at p. 2618); and the judgment of 3 July 1974 in Case 9/74 *Casagrande* [1974] ECR 773 (at p. 779).
55   [1989] ECR 195 (at pp. 221 *et seq.*).

however, to infer such an exemption from the 'natural scope' of the Treaty.[56] The same applies with regard to the reference, appearing in the introduction to this section, to the designation of the Community as an *economic* community, because the more specific provisions of the Treaty give concrete form to the more general provisions, and are not restricted by the latter.[57] The precise meaning of the concept of an economic community is apparent from the individual Treaty provisions.

This corresponds with the view taken by the Court of Justice, notwithstanding that it has on occasion appeared to have had recourse to Article 2 of the EEC Treaty in order to clarify *succeeding* provisions of the Treaty. Thus it held, for example, in its judgment of 5 October 1988 in Case 196/87 *Steymann* that, in view of the objectives of the Community, participation in a community based on religion or another form of philosophy falls within the field of application of Community law only in so far as it can be regarded as an economic activity within the meaning of Article 2 of the Treaty.[58] It is clear from the next sentence, however, that the Court did not intend its reference to Article 2 to have a restrictive effect, since it went on to point out that it had previously held that *the pursuit of an activity as an employed person or the provision of services for remuneration* must be regarded as an economic activity.

It is clear from the EEC Treaty that it does not *expressly* provide for the exemption of the cultural field and that, by reason of the unfocused nature of the 'fickle'[59] concept of culture, it would scarcely be possible to formulate such an exemption in meaningful terms. Nor is it possible to discern any *implicit* exemption,[60] the existence of which must be rejected on systematic grounds. The EEC Treaty invariably specifies exemptions from the scope of application of Community law in express terms.[61] The only limitation on the scope of the Treaty which is of any significance to the cultural field is that contained in the first sentence of Article 36, in relation to prohibitions or restrictions on imports, exports or goods in transit imposed for the protection of national treasures possessing artistic, historic or archaeological value and for the protection of industrial or commercial property.[62] That limitation would have been superfluous if the field of culture as a whole fell outside the framework of Community law.[63]

---

56 As the Italian Government contended in Case 7/68 *Commission* v. *Italy* [1968] ECR 423 (at p. 433).

57 Steindorff, *NJW 1982*, p. 1904.

58 [1988] ECR 6159 (at p. 6172).

59 See Häberle, *Kulturstaat*, p. 27.

60 See also, in the same vein, Magiera, *Rechtliche Grundfragen*, p. 72.

61 See Schwarze, *Rundfunk und Fernsehen*, p. 25, as regards the question whether activities in the cultural field are taken outside the scope of the EEC Treaty.

62 According to the case-law of the Court of Justice, the concept of industrial and commercial property also covers copyright, and is to that extent of significance to the cultural field; see in that regard 'Copyright protection', pp. 145 *et seq.*, above, and 'Permissible restrictions on the free movement of televison broadcasts', pp. 157 *et seq.*, above.

63 For a concurring view, see Tomuschat, *F.I.D.E. Reports*, p. 25; de Witte, *Cultural policy*, p. 198, describes as paradoxical the fact that this small exception should knock the bottom out of the argument that the cultural field is exempted.

If, therefore, the idea of a general exemption of the cultural field falls to be rejected – just as, for the rest, the Community does not conversely possess general competence in the field of 'the economy'[64] – it may in principle be stated that the fact that a particular matter has a cultural connotation does not narrow the collective competence of the Community. There is thus inherent potential in the collective competence of the Community to affect the cultural field.[65] Such effects are not merely 'cultural secondary effects', as they have been described, in relation to German Federal legislation, by Oppermann.[66] What is in fact involved here are effects which are presupposed by the Treaty. In the sphere of functional powers and of Treaty provisions enjoining and prohibiting particular conduct, which do not, by their very nature, relate to any specific subject-matter or field, the inevitable consequence must necessarily amount to no more than 'effects'. That is really what the rules laid down by those provisions are designed to achieve.[67] This explains, informally, why the absence of any express allocation of tasks to the Community in the field of broadcasting, for example (as has frequently been put forward as an argument against Community competence[68]) does not in any way affect the power of the Community to take action in that field.[69]

That is not to say, however, that any and every 'effect' is covered by competence. The question thereby raised, namely whether, by reason of disproportionate effects, for example, the exercise of competence by the Community institutions in individual cases is subject to any restriction,[70] is dealt with further below.[71]

Given, therefore, the fact that the existence of Community competence is not impaired by 'effects' of the exercise of Community competence on areas of competence of the Member States, that also refutes the argument, frequently

---

64 For a concurring view, see Zuleeg, *JöR 1971*, p. 3; Wohlfahrt, *JIR 1961*, p. 19. The field of the economy is subject in principle to the same problems of definition as the field of culture; see Tomuschat in: BK, Art. 24, n.18.

65 For a similar view, see de Witte, *Scope of Community Powers*, p. 263: 'If one were to limit such Community powers by the existence of national policies, then none of the Community acts implementing free movement of workers would be lawful: they all affect policies which basically remain in the hands of national authorities (labour relations, social security etc.)'.

66 Oppermann, *Kulturverwaltungsrecht*, p. 583.

67 This view is shared by de Witte & Post, p. 140: 'In implementing those objectives the Community institutions necessarily have to cut across the boundaries between substantive policy areas which the States are used to defining for their own internal purposes.'

68 See, to cite but a couple of authors, Koszuszeck, p. 546; Delbrück, *Rundfunkhoheit*, p. 26, who wrongly relies on Ipsen, *Rundfunk im EG-Recht*, p. 40. Ipsen does not criticize the absence of competence in the field of broadcasting across the board, but observes that broadcasting, 'at any rate in its function as an instrument of communication, as a medium, is not expressly covered by Community law'.

69 This view is shared by Reich, *Rundfunkhoheit*, p. 68, who states that the conclusion that the Community lacks any express powers in the field of broadcasting, whilst correct, is unproductive for the purposes of understanding the development of Community law and national law.

70 It is not clear whether Fiedler, at pp. 165 *et seq.*, has those particular effects in mind when he criticizes the separation between the arrogation of competence and its effects, or whether he is generally calling in question the potential effect of collective Community competence on the fields remaining within areas left to the Member States. It would seem that the latter interpretation should be rejected.

71 See 'Restrictions on the exercise of competence in the cultural field', pp. 211 *et seq.*, above.

advanced, that the Community may only regulate matters the focal point of which does not lie within the cultural field, i.e. within the sphere of competence of the Member States.[72] That assumption is based on a misunderstanding of the division of powers between the Community and the Member States. Concentration on the focal point of a matter is founded on the view, already rejected, that the Community enjoys competence primarily in respect of 'the economy' and that, in principle, other fields falling within the domain of the Member States are closed to it. This understanding of the concept of competence finds concrete expression in formulations which characterize any activity on the part of the Community in areas of competence retained by the Member States as involvement in 'peripheral areas' of Community competence,[73] or even in 'areas of overlap'.[74] It is in fact meaningful to speak of 'peripheral areas', 'areas of overlap' or even 'marginal competences'[75] only in so far as the competences of two associations are demarcated according to subject-matters and policy fields, which, as we have seen,[76] is predominantly not the case with Community law.[77] Yet to concentrate on the focal point of a matter would ultimately bring about the exclusion of the cultural field, which has already been rejected above, because the focal point of regulatory competence is generally to be found, at least within the sphere of functional Community competence, in the Member States.[78]

The relationship described between collective Community competence and collective national competence is reflected in the case-law of the Court of Justice, which, as is shown in Part 2, applies Community law as a matter of course in the cultural field.

3. The Institutional Competence of the Community Institutions

(a) Nature and scope of institutional competence

Whilst collective competence represents the outer limit of institutional competence, it is nevertheless basically possible within that framework to discern two types of institutional competence: first, the institutions may be given *general* power to take all measures needed in order to carry out the tasks defined by

---

72 e.g. see Klein, *VVDStRL 50 (1991)*, p. 65; Delbrück, *Rundfunkhoheit*, p. 44; Hailbronner, *JZ 1990*, pp. 153 *et seq.*; R. Geiger, *Stellung der Bundesländer*, p. 67; Tomuschat, *EuR 1990*, p. 360; Vitzthum, p. 290, n. 28; Kaiser, *EuR 1980*, p. 106; for a particularly pointed view, see Klein & Beckmann, p. 187, who argue that 'a field (such as culture) falling outside the ambit of Community competence (should not) concern itself with a substantive context which is still so tenuous'; for a view which rightly opposes concentration on that focal point, see Schwartz, *ZUM 1989*, pp. 385 *et seq.*; Everling, *EuR 1987*, p. 221.

73 e.g. see Kaiser, op. cit., p. 105.

74 Ossenbühl, p. 48.

75 Klein & Beckmann, p. 186.

76 See 'Nature and scope of collective competence', pp. 190 *et seq.*, above.

77 This is overlooked by Ossenbühl, p. 48, and Delbrück, op. cit., pp. 42 *et seq.*

78 See also, to the same effect, Everling, op. cit., n. 72, p. 221; Schwartz, op. cit., n. 72, p. 385; de Witte, *Scope of Community Powers*, p. 263; for a differentiating view, see Tomuschat, *F.I.D.E. Reports*, p. 40, who argues that since matters of educational and cultural policy fall, depending on their main emphasis, within the responsibility of the Member States, it is those States which enjoy competence 'to make the basic public policy decisions'.

'collective competence'. Secondly, institutional competence may be defined more precisely, with the result that the framework of collective Community competence in certain circumstances may not be utilized.[79] The following paragraphs examine the question as to which of these models underlies the EEC Treaty and the way in which it is shaped by the Treaty.

Once again – as in the above analysis of collective competence – the starting-point in this connection is Article 4(1) of the EEC Treaty, the second sentence of which requires each Community institution to act 'within the limits of the powers conferred upon it by this Treaty'. If, however, the institutions are granted (as is clear from the use of the plural) individual powers, that precludes *ab initio* the first of the models referred to, comprising a general power to attain objectives.[80] Consequently, institutional competence derives from the sum of the individual powers conferred.

This second model was initially described by Lagrange, in relation to the ECSC Treaty, as a 'principe juridique', a legal principle underlying each of the Treaties and referred to by him as the 'principe de compétence d'attribution'.[81] That designation has found its way into legal writings along with other formulations intended to describe Community competence. Whilst Lagrange primarily had in mind institutional competence,[82] the literature frequently draws no distinction between collective and institutional competence.[83] Thus the view is advanced, for example, that the principle is expressed in various Treaty provisions, for instance Articles 2-5 of the EEC Treaty.[84] However, only Articles 4 and 5 of the EEC Treaty contain any express reference to the Community institutions, whereas the other articles are merely concerned with collective competence.

For the rest, there are a great many variations in terminology, which appear to bear out Wagner's statement as to the 'muddled use of words' in the legal literature on the European Communities.[85] Examples of this appear in the references to the 'principle of restricted individual competence',[86] the 'principle of restricted individual powers',[87] the 'principle of limited individual authority',[88] the

---

79   The two alternatives are also discussed by Lagrange, pp. 44 *et seq.*, in relation to the ECSC Treaty.

80   The contrary view was previously held by a few authors, but has not been advanced for many years; see Bärmann, p. 556, who focuses on Arts 145, 155 and 189 of the EEC Treaty, and – to a lesser extent – Kraushaar, p. 729.

81   Lagrange, p. 45.

82   *ibid.* It is true that, in his Opinion in Joined Cases 7/56 and 3-7/57 *Algera* v. *Common Assembly* [1957] ECR 39, he also related the principle chiefly to institutional competence: '… and the principle of limited authority (which is precisely called "conferred authority" ["compétence d'attribution"]) is expressly stated for each institution: …' (at p. 82); however, he also included in this the restriction of the Community to objectives and tasks (*ibid.*).

83   Even where it is the competence of the institutions which is at the forefront, as is rightly emphasized by Wagner, p. 258.

84   R. Böhm, p. 337; Schweitzer & Hummer, p. 108, likewise locate the principle, on the one hand, within Art. 3 of the EEC Treaty and, on the other, within Arts 145, 155 and 189 of that Treaty.

85   Wagner, p. 21.

86   Oldekop, p. 29.

87   Schwarze, *Rundfunk und Fernsehen*, p. 23; Klein & Beckmann, p. 188, n. 84; Dorn, p. 90.

88   C.O. Lenz, *DVBl.* 1990, p. 904.

'principle of enumerative individual authority',[89] the 'principle of so-called *compétence d'attribution*',[90] and, finally, the 'principle of limited competence'[91] and the 'principle of restricted authority'.[92] The numerous forms of wording relate in part only to collective competence,[93] in part only to institutional competence,[94] and in part to both types of competence.[95] The legal authors appear to agree only that the form taken by the competence provided for by the EEC Treaty is based on a 'principle' and that that principle operates in a way which is somehow 'restricted', 'limited' or 'individualized'.

Such a 'principle' is nevertheless of minor significance as regards institutional competence. It is apparent from the very fact that the principle is derived from the rules of the Treaty that it serves merely to characterize the *method* of allocating competence and that it is thus, as a formal principle,[96] of no importance for the purposes of determining the compass of institutional competence.[97]

The view is sometimes advanced, however, that the principle has *substantive* significance, with the result, it is said, that the Treaty provisions should, in the light of that principle, be restrictively interpreted.[98] That assessment has a bearing above all on the classification, within the scheme of the EEC Treaty, of Article 235, whose field of application is controversial. According to the view advanced in this work, Article 235 expresses and forms part of the principle, and thus constitutes one of the several powers conferred on the Community institutions;[99] according to the divergent view which is described above, it constitutes a provision which runs counter to, and transgresses,[100] the principle, but which, in its substantive content, amounts to a confirmatory derogating provision, which thus must be narrowly construed, designed to fill any *lacunae.*[101]

There are objections to attributing any substantive significance of the principle to 'mistrust on the part of the Member States, which have been willing to countenance only a narrowly restricted transfer of sovereignty to the Community'.[102] Even though such mistrust may in fact have played a part, it has not been *expressly* reflected in the Treaty.[103] Yet it seems methodologically wrong to infer the existence of a principle *tacitly* underlying and restricting the Treaty from a postulated mistrust on the part of the Member States when the Treaty was

---

89   C.O. Lenz, *Zuständigkeiten und Initiativen*, p. 183; Klein & Beckmann, p. 186; Streinz, *Grundrechtsprobleme*, p. 129.

90   Schwarze, *Funktionen*, p. 16.

91   Ipsen, *EuR 1987*, p. 197.

92   Grabitz in *idem*: *Kommentar zum EWGV*, Art. 235, n. 1; *idem, NJW 1989*, p. 1778.

93   e.g. see Lenz, op. cit., nn. 88 and 89.

94   See Schwarze, op. cit., n. 90; Dorn, op. cit., n. 87; Grabitz in: *idem, Kommentar zum EWGV*, Art. 235, n. 1; Oldekop, op. cit., n. 86.

95   Grabitz, *NJW 1989*, p. 1778.

96   See also, to the same effect, Köck, *FS Ignaz Seidl-Hohenveldern*, p. 294; R. Böhm, p. 338.

97   See also, to the same effect, Gericke, pp. 106 *et seq.*

98   Dorn, p. 95; Klein & Beckmann, p. 186.

99   See also, to the same effect, Schwartz, *EuR 1976, Sonderheft*, pp. 36 *et seq.*; Gericke, p. 104.

100 See Schweitzer & Hummer, p. 109; Schweitzer, *Rechtsetzung*, p. 22.

101 See Rabe, p. 70; von Meibom, p. 2166.

102 See Rabe, p. 71.

103 As is rightly pointed out by R. Böhm, p. 337.

concluded.[104] On the contrary, should such mistrust have played a decisive role, the necessary consequence must have been that only the most essential aspects were transferred to the Community, and that the danger of an extensive exploitation of competence would have been allowed for and taken into account when the Treaty was drafted.

Another line of reasoning advanced in the literature in favour of the principle's having *substantive* significance proves untenable, since it is based on a circular argument. It is argued that the formal approach does not deal with the significance of the principle of limited authority in Community law, which is also apparent from the reservation of decision-making to the Member States and from the nature of the Communities as a democratic organization subject to the rule of law.[105] This does not prove substantive significance, but assumes it. Consequently, there are no discernible grounds for attaching substantive significance to the principle. This accords with the fact that the canon of interpretation sometimes found in international law, according to which restrictions on sovereignty must be restrictively construed,[106] is *not* recognized in relation to Community law.[107]

Moreover, a formal approach is more in keeping with the position of Article 235 within the EEC Treaty. Article 235 is contained in Part 6, entitled 'General and final provisions'. Since the 'final provisions' only start at Article 247 of the EEC Treaty, Article 235 must be a 'general' provision. It seems absurd to construe a general competence-conferring provision narrowly. Moreover, although it is not possible here to deal with the point in greater detail, Article 235 itself scarcely affords reasons suggesting that it should be restrictively interpreted, but stands out from the other Treaty provisions by reason of the degree to which it is related to the objectives of the Community, that is to say, to collective competence.

The Court of Justice confirmed this view, albeit without express reference to the principle of limited authority, when it held that the limits of the powers conferred on the Commission by a specific provision of the Treaty are to be inferred 'not from a general principle, but from an interpretation of the particular wording of the provision in question'.[108] Consequently, the misleading concept of a principle should be discarded[109] or 'neutralized' in terms of its content, for example (to use Ipsen's words[110]) by terming it the 'principle that all acts of the institutions must be in conformity with the Treaty'.

---

104 Notwithstanding the fact that Rabe, at p. 71, proceeds, in *formal* terms, from the opposite standpoint and 'explains' the principle as having arisen from mistrust on the part of the Member States.

105 See Dorn, p. 92.

106 Köck, in *Vertragsinterpretation*, p. 52, points out that this is not followed in international practice. Similarly, Bernhardt, in *FS Hans Kutscher*, p. 19, states that the emphasis on State sovereignty in the interpretation of international treaties is increasingly declining.

107 See Bleckmann, *EuR 1979*, p. 247; Ophüls, *FG Alfred Müller-Armack*, p. 288.

108 Judgment in Joined Cases 188–190/80 *France, Italy and United Kingdom* v. *Commission* [1982] ECR 2545 (at p. 2573).

109 See also, to the same effect, Everling, *EuR 1976, Sonderheft*, p. 17, who contends that it is not possible to infer from a principle of limited individual powers, '*allegedly* underlying the Treaty', that Art. 235 of the EEC Treaty is capable of serving only to round off existing specific powers (emphasis added).

110 Ipsen, *EuR 1987*, p. 197.

(b) Consequences for the cultural field

The foregoing arguments do not have any particular connotations for the cultural field. In that field, as in others, the Community institutions may act only pursuant to powers which have been conferred on them. As is explained in greater detail above, Community law contains, in the fields of education and training[111] and science,[112] although not in the field of culture in the narrower sense, a number of specific provisions.

In addition, the Community institutions are authorized in principle to exercise their powers in the cultural field, as in others, and thus to realize the collective competence of the Community described above. This was described by the Court of Justice in its judgment of 3 July 1974 in Case 9/74 *Casagrande*, in what is now a *locus classicus*, in the following terms:

'... although educational and training policy is not as such included in the spheres which the Treaty has entrusted to the Community institutions, it does not follow that the exercise of powers transferred to the Community is in some way limited if it is of such a nature as to affect the measures taken in the execution of a policy such as that of education and training'.[113]

4. THE DYNAMIC OF COMMUNITY LAW

(a) The results of the EEC Treaty

The finding that there is an inherent dynamic of Community law does not, in the light of the foregoing passages on collective competence, require any further substantiation. The fact, as described above, that the EEC Treaty is directed towards the attainment of objectives means that it is bound to be invested with a dynamic potential. The dynamic nature of Community law is merely an aspect of teleology: whilst the concept of teleology emphasizes the objective which is to be achieved and hence the ultimate state of affairs, the concept of the dynamic of Community law focuses more sharply on *movement* towards the objective.[114] It would be wrong, however, to take 'dynamic' as meaning 'automatic', in the sense that the dynamic process must of necessity take its course.[115] Quite apart from the need for the Community institutions to be ready and able at all time to take action, that process requires 'regular political stimuli on the part of the Member States'.[116] Furthermore, the concept of the dynamic of Community law is

---

111 'Introduction', pp. 31 *et seq.*, above.

112 'Introduction', pp. 49 *et seq.*, above.

113 [1974] ECR 773 (at p. 779); for a more detailed analysis of the meaning of those words, see de Witte, *Scope of Community Powers*, p. 263.

114 The term 'dynamic' is defined in the *Oxford Advanced Learner's Dictionary* (4th ed., 1989) as a 'force that produces change, action or effects'.

115 This is reminiscent of the remark by Hallstein in *Probleme*, p. 6, where he speaks of an objective logic continuously driving the integration process further forward; see also von Simson, p. 58, who refers to an 'in-built dynamic, so to speak'.

116 As Kaiser aptly puts it in *FS Walter Hallstein*, p. 272.

different from that occasionally used to characterize national integration.[117] What this precisely involves is the drawing of a dividing line between what is, in principle, the dynamic force of the Community constitution and what is, in principle, the static nature of State constitutions.[118] The tendency of the Community 'towards constant further development and increasing integration'[119] is expressed in the need for completion of the EEC Treaty, which merely describes a 'comprehensively indistinct objective'.[120] The EEC Treaty has thus rightly been described as a framework treaty, a *traité cadre*,[121] and in still more graphic terms by Ipsen as a 'convertible constitution'.[122]

The form taken by the dynamic element in the EEC Treaty is analyzed in greater detail below. It is not intended to examine the dynamic content of the preamble or the individual provisions of the Treaty, as expressed, for example, in the laying down of a transitional period in Article 8, the stipulation in Article 8a of a final date for the completion of the internal market on 31 December 1992, or the imposition, in Article 155, of an obligation requiring the Commission to develop the Common Market. Instead, the aim is to illustrate the dynamic of Community law by means of the dynamic of Community law-making.

An essential feature of Community law-making powers – to the extent that they do not take the form of exclusive powers – is to be found in the fact that the Member States may exercise such powers *in priority to* their exercise by the Community itself. Reference is predominantly made in that regard to *concurrent* Community powers.[123] Whether the competence of the Community is exclusive or concurrent is a matter to be determined by interpretation.[124] In case of doubt, the assumption must be that competence is concurrent.[125]

The concept of concurrent competence is not to be confused with that of the cumulative concurrence of powers.[126] That term is used generally to characterize the relationship between the competence of the Community and

---

117 e.g. see Meyer-Cording, p. 293, according to whom the State is involved primarily in a dynamic process whereby the mental and spiritual consensus of its citizens as to its aims and significations is constantly being updated, reflected and renewed. *This* dynamic is certainly inherent in the Community, but its nature is different from that described; for a more detailed analysis, see also Kaiser, op. cit., pp. 267 *et seq.*

118 e.g. see Magiera, *Bundesstaat*, p. 18, who contrasts 'relations within a federal State, which are conceived as enduring' and the 'relations within the Community, which are structured towards development'; see also, in the same vein, Ophüls, *FG Alfred Müller-Armack*, p. 289, who diagnoses the aim not only of the 'average State constitution' but also of the 'average international treaty' as 'a quest for ultimate equilibrium'.

119 See Magiera, op. cit., p. 14.

120 von Simson, p. 58.

121 See Schwarze, *Funktionen*, p. 16; Louis, *Rechtsordnung*, p. 55.

122 Ipsen, *EuR 1987*, p. 201.

123 It is described differently, however, by Bieber, *ELR 1988*, pp. 147 *et seq.*, who refers to 'parallel powers'; for a critical view of the term 'concurrent powers', see V. Constantinesco, *Compétences*, p. 280, who contends that there could never be any competition ('concours') if the powers were exercised only by one authority or the other. Constantinesco proposes as alternatives the terms 'compétences successives' or 'compétences alternatives' (p. 279, n. 5).

124 Bieber, *Rolle der Mitgliedstaaten*, p. 294.

125 *ibid.*, p. 295; Bleckmann, *Bindungswirkung*, p. 205; Klein, *VVDStRL 50 (1991)*, p. 63; Steinberger, p. 20; see also, to the same effect, Schweitzer, *Rechtsetzung*, p. 29.

126 Although such confusion is to be found in U. Becker, pp. 38 *et seq.*

that of the Member States, the distinguishing feature of which is that the powers of the Member States - even in the field of exclusive Community competence - remain in existence and are not excluded in real terms, so to speak,[127] even if, ultimately, they are forced to yield to superior Community law.[128]

In the sphere of concurrent Community competence, the dynamic force of the Treaty is expressed in such a way that concurrent competence transforms itself, by being exercised, into an *exclusive* Community competence.[129] The division of powers is thus characterized - as Ophüls has aptly stated - by a 'descent towards the exclusive sovereignty of the Community'.[130] Only where concurrent competence is exercised at Community level is the Member States' loss of competence contemplated by the EEC Treaty actually realized. That loss of competence embraces not only the internal domain of the Community but also the Member States' right to conclude international agreements in the sphere in question.[131]

(b) The case-law of the Court of Justice

A decisive part in the realization of the dynamic force peculiar to the EEC Treaty has been played by the Court of Justice when interpreting Community law. Without there being any need here to carry out a detailed examination of the methods of interpretation applied by it in individual cases, it may be stated that the Court - proceeding, naturally, from the wording[132] - engages in an interpretative process which is oriented towards the spirit and purpose of the provision in question and the objectives of the Treaty,[133] and may be described as 'teleological interpretation'.[134] Where the Court construes a provision in terms of

---

127 See in that regard Grabitz, *Gemeinschaftsrecht bricht nationales Recht*, p. 70; Ipsen, *Europäisches Gemeinschaftsrecht*, p. 431.

128 See in that regard the leading judgment of the Court of Justice in Case 6/64 *Costa* v. *ENEL* [1964] ECR 585 (at p. 594). Ehlers, p. 608, describes the doctrine of primacy of application as prevailing; as to that doctrine, see Ipsen, *EuR 1979*, pp. 236 *et seq.*; Zuleeg, *NVwZ 1987*, p. 281.

129 This is the unanimous view taken by legal authors; e.g. see Bieber, *ELR 1988*, pp. 151 and 153; Oppermann, *Europäische Integration*, p. 100; Fastenrath, p. 494; Wohlfahrt, *JIR 1961*, pp. 29 *et seq.*; Ophüls, *FS Carl Heymanns Verlag*, p. 576; see also the judgment of 31 March 1971 of the Court of Justice, confirming this view, in Case 22/70 *Commission* v. *Council* ('*AETR*') [1971] ECR 263 (at p. 276).

130 Ophüls, *FG Alfred Müller-Armack*, p. 289.

131 See the judgments of the Court of Justice of 31 March 1971 in Case 22/70 *Commission* v. *Council* ('*AETR*') [1971] ECR 263 (at pp. 275 *et seq.*) and of 14 July 1976 in Joined Cases 3, 4 and 6/76 *Kramer* [1976] ECR 1279 (at p. 1310).

132 See Schlochauer, p. 448.

133 In its judgment of 21 February 1973 in Case 6/72 *Continental Can* [1973] ECR 215 (at p. 243), the Court emphasized that 'one has to go back to the spirit, general scheme and wording of Art. 86, as well as to the system and objectives of the Treaty'; it expressed itself in similar terms in its judgment of 5 February 1963 in Case 26/62 *Van Gend en Loos* [1963] ECR 1 (at p. 13).

134 See, to cite but two examples, Bleckmann, *EuR 1979*, pp. 242 *et seq.*; Kutscher, *Thesen*, I-31 *et seq.*

its effectiveness, that amounts to no more than a variation of that method of interpretation.[135] Such cases involve the question of '*effet utile*'.[136]

It would be not be correct, however, to assume that the teleological method of interpretation is one of several methods from which the Court may choose in a given individual case. The Court is not an objective authority placed above the law of the Community and of the Member States; it is a part of the Community, and its case-law is a component in a political process.[137] In the final analysis, its function, like that of the other Community institutions, is to promote the integration process. Consequently, the Court of Justice has a legal duty to interpret Community law in a manner geared towards the objective of integration.[138] In the process, the Court itself leaves the way open for a dynamic development of its interpretation, by frequently focusing on the 'present stage of development of Community law'[139] or the fact that a Community policy is gradually developing.[140]

The principle formulated by the Court, to the effect that the interpretation which the Court gives to a rule of Community law explains and clarifies 'the meaning and scope of that rule as it must be or ought to have been understood and applied *from the time of its coming into force*',[141] is only apparently in contradiction with the dynamic method of interpretation, indeed, the dynamic of Community law generally. That sentence tones down the dynamic force underlying the interpretation only as regards the *point in time at which the interpretation is given*; in other words, the dynamic is not only proactive but also retroactive in its effect, creating the fiction of the uniform application of the law from a temporal standpoint. Such a fiction can have serious effects on legal relationships which were established in the past and which were still effective when the interpretative judgment was delivered. On grounds of legal certainty, the Court therefore refrains from giving its judgments retroactive effect, in order to avoid 'calling in question legal relationships established in good faith'.[142] It is thus apparent that the principle of dynamic interpretation is confirmed, not contradicted, by that procedure followed by the Court.

---

135 See the judgments of 13 February 1969 in Case 14/68 *Walt Wilhelm* [1969] ECR 1 (at p. 14), of 12 July 1973 in Case 8/73 *Massey-Ferguson* [1973] ECR 897 (at p. 907), of 9 July 1987 in Joined Cases 281, 283–285 and 287/85 *Germany and Others* v. *Commission* ('*Migration policy*') [1987] ECR 3203 (at p. 3253) and of 30 May 1989 in Case 242/87 *Commission* v. *Council* ('*ERASMUS*') [1989] ECR 1425 (at p. 1453).

136 For a detailed commentary in this regard, see R. Böhm, pp. 72 *et seq.*

137 See Everling, *FS Hans Kutscher*, p. 183.

138 In the ultimate analysis, this is the conclusion arrived at by Kutscher in *Thesen*, I-17 and I-31 *et seq.*, and Nicolaysen in *Europarecht* I, p. 49; see also Siedentopf & Huber, p. 45, according to whom the objective-orientated, systematically hierarchical structure of the Treaties simply compels the adoption of a teleological approach to interpretation.

139 See, amongst the many relevant judgments, that of 21 June 1988 in Case 39/86 *Lair* [1988] ECR 3161 (at p. 3195); according to Ress & Bieber, p. 14, this is a 'key concept of the ECJ'.

140 As was stated in the judgment of 13 February 1985 in Case 293/83 *Gravier* [1985] ECR 593 (at p. 613).

141 See the judgments of 27 March 1980 in Case 61/79 *Denkavit* [1980] ECR 1205 (at p. 1223) and of 2 February 1988 in Case 24/86 *Blaizot* [1988] ECR 379 (at p. 406); emphasis added.

142 Case 24/86 *Blaizot* [1988] ECR 379 (at p. 406).

(c) The case-law of the German Federal Constitutional Court

The Federal Constitutional Court has recognized in its case-law the dynamic nature of the Community legal order and its fundamental compatibility with Article 24(1) of the German Basic Law. In an order given by the Federal Constitutional Court as long ago as 18 October 1967, it described the EEC as 'a unique community engaged in the process of progressive integration, an "international institution" within the meaning of Article 24(1) of the Basic Law'.[143] It adhered to this in its order of 29 May 1974 ('*Solange I*'), stating with regard to the admissibility of an application for judicial review in a case of alleged infringement of the fundamental rights laid down by the Basic Law by secondary Community legislation that 'the present level of integration is of decisive significance' and that the Community '*still* lacks, in particular, a codified catalogue of fundamental rights'.[144]

In its order of 23 June 1981 ('*Eurocontrol I*'), the Federal Constitutional Court gave a clear description of the integration made possible by Article 24(1) of the Basic Law. It held that the objective scope of Article 24(1) of the Basic Law fell to be determined having regard *inter alia* to the manner in which the institutions covered by that provision were set up and operated at international level. It stated that this occurred, 'typically, in the context of a *process* of integration during the course of which numerous individual executive acts (were) required in order to bring about the situation aspired to in the constituent Treaty'.[145] The actual content, form and timing of the steps towards integration were not required, according to the Federal Constitutional Court, to be laid down in the constituent Treaty; all that was necessary was for the process of future implementation to be regulated in a sufficiently determinable manner and to be reflected in the 'integration programme thereby established'.[146]

In its order of 8 April 1987, the Federal Constitutional Court expressly acknowledged that the Court of Justice also has the power to develop the law, without its thereby being permitted, however, to extend the competence of the Community at will.[147] With regard to the teleological method of interpretation, the Federal Constitutional Court stated in conclusion that it was 'nevertheless *positively imperative* to construe and give concrete form to existing powers of the Community in the light of, and in conformity with, the objectives of the Treaty'.[148]

---

143 BVerfGE 22, p. 293 (at p. 296).
144 BVerfGE 37, p. 271 (at p. 280); emphasis added.
145 BVerfGE 58, p. 1 (at p. 36) (original emphasis). See also the judgment of 18 December 1984 ('*Pershing*'), BVerfGE 68, p. 1 (at p. 98).
146 BVerfGE 58, p. 1 (at p. 37).
147 BVerfGE 75, p. 223 (at p. 243).
148 *ibid.*, p. 242; emphasis added.

II. THE MODALITIES OF THE EXERCISE OF COMMUNITY COMPETENCE IN THE CULTURAL FIELD

1. Introduction

As has been established in the preceding section, the Community institutions are empowered in principle to exercise their powers not relating specifically to the cultural field irrespective of the fact that the matters to be regulated have links with the cultural field.[149] Competence on the part of the Community institutions is regularly linked in this regard to the economic dimension of a matter, causing it to appear to form part of the 'economic activities' referred to in Article 2 of the EEC Treaty.[150] Matters having a cultural connection which are of relevance to Community law consequently have for the most part a 'dual nature' ('Doppelnatur'[151]): an economic one and a cultural one.[152] The two dimensions are inextricably linked,[153] with the result that the influence exerted on one dimension may always have effects on the other.

By reason of this connection, the Community institutions are exposed to requirements running in opposite directions. There are numerous legal authors who encourage them to take account of the cultural nature of a matter at Community level,[154] some of whom even regard this as indispensable; in so doing, they presuppose the existence of a corresponding power. Others, whilst criticizing the purely economic approach supposedly adopted at Community level - and to that extent concurring with the view just referred to - nevertheless regard that approach as consistent, given the economic nature of Community competence, and consequently regard the Community level as one at which it is inappropriate, at the very least, to regulate matters of a cultural nature.[155]

---

149 See 'Consequences for the cultural field', p. 200, above.

150 For a concordant view in that regard, see Kaiser, *EuR 1980*, p. 106.

151 This term is used by Fiedler, p. 175.

152 e.g. see Everling, *Instrumente*, p. 24, who speaks of the 'dual character' of books. The same term is used by Delbrück, *Rundfunkhoheit*, p. 41, with regard to broadcasting; see also Tomuschat, *F.I.D.E. Reports*, p. 24, who states that every cultural activity has at the same time an economic element. It should be borne in mind, however, that such a characterization ignores the possibility of the matter in question having any *further* dimension. No objection can be raised to this, as long as it is sought merely to emphasize the characteristics presently of interest. However, despite the contentions of Delbrück, *ibid.*, it is not possible to raise any fundamental objection against a Community power on the basis of such a 'dual character'.

153 See also Franzone, p. 275, in relation to broadcasting; and Rovan, p. 103, who contends that every cultural activity has an economic foundation.

154 e.g. see Dietz, *Harmonisierung*, pp. 59 *et seq.*; Stock, pp. 181 *et seq.*; Blaukopf, p. 557; J. Becker, p. 21.

155 e.g. see L. Seidel, p. 125; Betz, p. 685; Stoiber, *EA 1987*, p. 546; Scharf, p. 152; Kuch, p. 6; Dicke, p. 196; see also Hoffmann-Riem, *Rundfunk in Europa*, p. 78, who argues that the EC's powers of action are first and foremost aimed at economic liberalization, and that the specifically economic approach adopted in the Commission's procedures in the broadcasting field corresponds to 'the logic of the framework in which it operates'. Everling, *EuR 1990*, p. 207, n. 49, regards it as contradictory to criticize the allegedly purely economic orientation of the Community, whilst at the same time attacking it for encroaching upon areas of policy, such as health policy; for a similar view in relation to the sphere of broadcasting, see Schwartz, *ZUM 1991*, p. 165.

It is not proposed here to pursue any further whether the criticism of the purely economic approach adopted at Community level is justified.[156] Instead, it is proposed to examine the question whether the Community institutions, in exercising their powers in the cultural field, are in fact restricted to approaching such matters from an economic standpoint geared solely towards market perspectives, or whether, and to what extent, they may, or even must, take into account the cultural dimension of a matter.

2. Permissibility of Taking into Consideration the Cultural Aspects of a Matter which is to be Regulated

It should first be stated that there can only be any question of taking into consideration the cultural aspects of a matter if such consideration falls within the framework of the enabling provision concerned. The specific cultural features of a matter do not justify going beyond the framework of competence laid down by the Treaty. Thus it is not open to the Commission, for example, to justify the so-called 'quota rule' contained in Article 4(1) of the television directive by arguing that it has 'always sought to ensure that Community measures covering cultural products and services take account of the specific characteristics of the sector',[157] because the quota rule is not covered by the enabling provisions on which the television directive is based.[158]

There would be no possibility of there being a right, or indeed an obligation, to have regard to the specific cultural aspects of a matter in a legislative act if the Community institutions were compelled, by reason of the undoubtedly predominantly economic objectives of the EEC Treaty, invariably to approach a matter solely from an economic standpoint, and thus to ignore its cultural dimension.[159] It is clear even from a cursory examination of the EEC Treaty, however, that the Community is by no means bound to strictly economic objectives.[160] Thus Article 2 of the EEC Treaty, for example, justifies not unbridled economic growth, 'not growth at any price',[161] but merely a '*harmonic* development of economic activities' together with '*balanced* expansion'.[162] In addition, the objective of an accelerated 'raising of the standard of living' covers improvements in the quality of life which go beyond the economic sphere.[163] As Bleckmann states, the economic objective must 'take its proper place within the overall framework of all of Europe's general

---

156 Schwartz, *ZUM 1989*, p. 385, expresses the view, in relation to the television directive, for example, that it 'recognizes and treats television broadcasts, especially films, as cultural goods'.

157 See the answer given by Commission Vice-President Bangemann on 1 March 1990 in reply to Written Question No. 1101/89 (OJ 1990 C 125, p. 34).

158 For further details, see 'The binding force and legality of the quota rules', pp. 163 *et seq.*, above.

159 This is evidently the view held by Eiselstein, *NVwZ 1989*, p. 328.

160 See Magiera, *Ansätze*, p. 17, who states that the objectives of the Community indicate a perspective extending beyond the economic sphere; for further details, see 'The objectives of the Community in general', pp. 287 *et seq.*, below.

161 Zuleeg in: GTE, *Kommentar zum EWGV*, Art. 2, n.13.

162 Emphasis added.

163 Zuleeg in: GTE, op. cit., Art 2, n.15.

interests'.[164] Tomuschat appropriately states that a Community policy 'conceived solely from the perspective of *homo oeconomicus*' would be 'downright scamped'.[165] Accordingly, there can be no question of the Community institutions having, in the exercise of their powers, to pursue solely the objective of the greatest possible economic efficiency.

The effects of this may be explained by taking the example of the power to approximate legislation conferred by Articles 100 and 100a of the EEC Treaty – a power which may also cover national rules intended for the attainment of cultural policy objectives, for example in the field of copyright or the fixing of book prices. Where such rules are to be harmonized, a decision on the merits must be taken at Community level in the field to be covered by such harmonization,[166] since in the context of the approximation of laws the Community institutions must 'pursue all matters of national public interest ... at which the diverse coordinated national rules have hitherto been aimed'.[167]

However, no substantive criteria may be discerned from the 'formal purpose of harmonization',[168] since the result of the approximation of laws is already apparent where national law is *in any way* harmonized. Consequently, the Community institutions must develop an independent policy in the harmonized field, for which Community law is able to offer no standard criteria and (as has been demonstrated) in particular, not the criterion of a purely economic approach. Thus the substantive problems underlying the national rules must be reassessed at Community level.[169] Community law does not require the cultural aspects of the matter to be harmonized to be 'faded out'; it does not call for any 'cultural *non-decision*'. It is therefore permissible for the Commission, in the context of the approximation of rates of value added tax, to classify books, newspapers and periodicals as 'basic necessities', and to propose a lower rate of tax on them.[170]

Even if the Commission were to apply the standard rate of tax to the cultural goods referred to, it could in so doing be said to be taking into consideration the cultural aspects of printed products, albeit perhaps, from the standpoint of cultural policy, in a questionable way. The Community cannot, by referring to the ostensible orientation of the EEC Treaty towards purely economic objectives, be released from the task of adopting a decision involving some sort of appraisal of the cultural aspects of a matter – one may perhaps go so far as to speak of a decision on

---

164 See Bleckmann, *EuR 1979*, p. 245; see also, to the same effect, Schwartz, *ZUM 1989*, p. 384, who states, in relation to Art. 57(2) of the EEC Treaty, that that provision should in no way be considered from a one-sided economic standpoint but that it allows other interests to be taken into account, for example, the protection of savers, insured persons, the administration of justice, the improvement of training or progress in the medical field.

165 Tomuschat, *EuR 1976, Sonderheft*, p. 60.

166 See, for example, Rambow, p. 243; Roth, *EuR 1986*, p. 355; a different view is evidently taken by Steinberger, p. 20, who states that only the specific regulation of those aspects of the process which are relevant to the market should be regarded as falling within the competence of the Community, and not, for example, any extraneous organization of its content in relation to cultural policy.

167 Bleckmann, *FS Hans Kutscher*, p. 30.

168 Scheuing, *EuR 1989*, p. 162.

169 See Langeheine in: Grabitz, *Kommentar zum EWGV*, Art. 100, n.4.

170 See the answer given by Commissioner Scrivener on 29 January 1990 to Written Question No. 979/89 (OJ 1990 C 283, p. 5).

cultural policy. Jacques Delors has paraphrased this by saying that culture is not a sort of commodity, to be treated in the same way as refrigerators or cars.[171]

Nor is it evident that those aims and interests of Member States which are of a non-economic nature should for that reason alone no longer be taken into consideration, because a matter is no longer regulated by the Member States themselves but by the Community, since the substantive problems which necessitated the national rules continue to exist in the Common Market.[172] This means that the individual national interests must come together, within the Council, to create a Community interest.[173] Naturally, this statement relates only to those aims and interests the pursuit of which is not prohibited by primary Community law. It should be borne in mind in that regard, however, that the prohibitions contained in the Treaties are aimed primarily at the Member States and preclude them from taking any measures which they 'have taken with an eye towards their respective national markets'.[174] When the Community institutions take action, on the other hand, they do so 'in the general interest of the Community'.[175] It follows that the Community institutions may adopt legislation, even, for instance, in the cultural field, which may tend to restrict the basic freedoms established by the Treaties, where the measures in question only tend to serve the achievement of the Treaty objectives.[176]

That view finds support in the case-law of the Court of Justice. In its judgment of 29 February 1984 in Case 37/83 *Rewe-Zentral AG* v. *Direktor de Landwirtschaftskammer Rheinland,*[177] for example, the Court found, in relation to the directive at issue in that case, that, as well as seeking the elimination of obstacles to the free movement of goods, 'the directive seeks to strengthen, *in the general interest of the Community,* the protection of agricultural products against the substantial damage which may be caused by harmful organisms'.[178] Despite the fact that the plant inspections permitted in the directive also served, in the final analysis, an economic purpose, namely the protection of agricultural products, the reference to the general interest of the Community indicates that the Community institutions are empowered to pursue interests and aims common to the Member

---

171 Cited by Maggiore, p. 40.

172 See Matthies, p. 128.

173 According to the case-law of the Court of Justice, the Member States are entitled to assert their respective national interests in the Council, whilst it falls to the Commission to safeguard the Community interest; see the judgments of 14 March 1973 in Case 57/72 *Westzucker* [1973] ECR 321 (at p. 341) and of 7 February 1979 in Case 128/78 *Commission* v. *United Kingdom* [1979] ECR 419 (at p. 429).

174 Matthies, p. 127, with regard to the free movement of goods.

175 Judgment of the Court of Justice 25 January 1977 in Case 46/76 *Bauhuis* [1977] ECR 5 (at p. 17).

176 See, to this effect, Matthies, p. 129; see also the judgment of the Court of Justice of 29 February 1984 in Case 37/83 *Rewe-Zentrale* v. *Landwirtschaftskammer Rheinland* [1984] ECR 1229 (at p. 1249), in which it stated that the principle of the free movement of goods was not breached by the inclusion in a Council directive of a provision enabling Member States to carry out phytosanitary inspections on plants imported into their territory in the context of intra-Community trade in plants: the directive was not intended to hinder the movement of goods, but sought instead to achieve the abolition of measures which had been adopted unilaterally by the Member States and justified under Art. 36 of the EEC Treaty.

177 [1984] ECR 1229.

178 *ibid.*, at p. 1249; emphasis added.

States, even where they are not expressly mentioned in the EEC Treaty. The correctness of that interpretation was confirmed by the judgment of 23 February 1988 in Case 131/86 *United Kingdom* v. *Council*.[179] The Court held that efforts to achieve objectives of the Common Agricultural Policy cannot disregard requirements relating to the public interest such as the protection of consumers or the protection of the health and life of humans and animals, requirements which the Community institutions must take into account in exercising their powers.[180]

There is a correlative duty to the right of the Community institutions to have regard, within the framework of their powers, to the cultural aspects of a matter.[181] This follows from the consideration that the lawful exercise of a discretion presupposes knowledge of all of the aspects of a matter which fall to be considered.[182] That is not to say, however, that the cultural aspects of a matter must invariably be positively reflected in the legislation in question. As has been established above, a conscious non-ruling also represents an assessment falling within the discretion of the Community institutions. It is only an *unconscious* non-ruling which must be regarded as a failure properly to exercise discretionary powers.

3. The Cultural Aspects of a Matter as the Starting-point for a 'Policy in the Cultural Field'

The finding that the Community institutions are obliged, in the exercise of their powers, to take into consideration the cultural aspects of a matter prompts the question of the extent to which that enables the Community to pursue a 'policy in the cultural field'. The term 'policy' must be taken to mean in that regard, as Glaesner puts it, an activity of the Community 'which is relevant to the realization of the objectives of the Treaties and the object of which extends beyond the regulation of an individual case'.[183]

Tomuschat may be understood as taking the view that no policy exists in the cultural field: he criticizes the fact that action by the Community authorities has hitherto 'developed, by focusing on individual prominent problem areas, in an essentially empirical way, without any sure guidelines'.[184] Glaesner likewise regards the measures taken in the cultural field as not sufficiently coherent for it to be possible to speak of a 'policy'.[185] It is not proposed, however, to analyze here whether those statements are correct. Instead, the intention is to examine whether the Community is entitled in any way to bundle up such 'guidelines' in a cultural

---

179 [1988] ECR 905.

180 *ibid.*, at p. 930.

181 See also, to that effect, in relation to Art. 57(2) of the EEC Treaty, Schwartz, *ZUM 1989*, p. 384 *et seq.*; see, in general terms, Everling, *Instrumente*, p. 25, with whom Fiedler, p. 175, concurs, albeit evidently with a different intention, aimed at a restriction of competence.

182 See also Everling, *EuR 1976, Sonderheft*, pp. 11 *et seq.*, who states that, in so far as the Community is empowered to concern itself with individual national rules, it is 'also entitled, and even obliged ... to take into account the actual reasons (for the existence of those rules) and the matters relating to them, since it cannot otherwise adopt an appropriate regulation'.

183 Glaesner, *Einführung*, p. 31.

184 Tomuschat, *F.I.D.E. Reports*, p. 17.

185 Glaesner, *Les objectifs*, pp. 22 *et seq.*

policy package serving as the basis for individual legislative acts having a bearing on the cultural field and tracing out how the particular cultural aspects of a matter are to be taken into account.

There are no apparent legal objections to the development of a policy in the cultural field in that sense. Instead, the Community institutions must simply be called upon to 'develop ideas for rules which are reasonable and coherent for the purposes of the future integration process, which are comprehensively structured and which can form the basis of individual legislative acts'.[186] This also applies to Community measures in the cultural field.

Moreover, there are no apparent legal arguments which might preclude the Community institutions from using their powers under the Treaties *primarily* for reasons of cultural policy[187] in order to put a 'policy in the cultural field' into effect.[188] It is incorrect, therefore, to conclude that, although the Community can adopt rules for the free movement of goods which also apply to the free movement of cultural goods, it is precluded from drawing up such rules for the purposes of cultural policy or with a view to attaining cultural policy objectives.[189] This view is justified by the lack of any reference to cultural policy in the EEC Treaty. However, that argument is not convincing, since what is involved here is not proof of any *general* Community powers in relation to cultural policy – cultural policy 'as such' does not fall within the competence of the Community[190] – but the characterization of the modalities for the exercise of the powers which are in fact enjoyed by the Community in the cultural field.

It is clear that the flat denial, so frequently encountered, of the idea that the Community institutions possess any powers in respect of cultural policy[191] must be regarded, on the basis of the term 'policy' as defined in the introduction to this chapter, as too sweeping, and consequently as incorrect.[192]

---

186 See Bleckmann, *Bindungswirkung*, p. 209; as to the need for planning, that is to say, for the development of a policy, see Zuleeg, *Der Staat 1978*, pp. 35 *et seq.*

187 See Bleckmann, *Europarecht*, p. 76, who contends that the EC may incidentally, or even primarily, seek to achieve non-economic objectives, provided, at the very least, that it also pursues economic objectives.

188 See also, to the same effect, Rambow, p. 241, who states, in relation to Community consumer policy, that the absence of any express substantive powers in the field of consumer policy does not mean that the EC cannot conduct such a policy on the basis of the various other powers conferred on it by the EEC Treaty.

189 See Eiselstein, *NVwZ 1989*, p. 328; for a similar view in relation to so-called annex rules in the field of education and training (e.g. Art. 57 of the EEC Treaty), see Schweitzer, *EG-Kompetenzen*, p. 149.

190 See the judgment of the Court of Justice of 30 May 1989 in Case 242/87 *Commission* v. *Council ('ERASMUS')* [1989] ECR 1425 (at p. 1457): 'educational policy is not as such included in the spheres which the Treaty has entrusted to the Community institutions'.

191 See to that effect, for example, Roth, *Niederlassungs- und Dienstleistungsfreiheit*, p. 42; Konow, *RdJB 1989*, p. 128; Wittweiler, p. 557.

192 On the other hand, Maihofer, p. 64, rightly states that it is the European Community which possesses the competence in matters of cultural policy – inextricably linked with the competence in matters of economic policy conferred on it for the purposes of the completion of the internal market – to make the internal market possible for cultural goods and services also.

III. RESTRICTIONS ON THE EXERCISE OF COMPETENCE IN THE CULTURAL FIELD

1. INTRODUCTION

Compliance by the Community institutions with the division of powers under the Treaties is a necessary but perhaps insufficient precondition for the development of activities at Community level. This is because the exercise of Community competence may be subject to additional restrictions with which the Community institutions are obliged to comply. The first aspect to be taken into consideration in this regard is the fundamental rights of the individual, which, as 'negative rules of competence',[193] might not, it is true, limit collective Community competence in terms of its 'external scope', i.e. in its relationship to the collective competence of the Member States, but could certainly do so as regards its 'internal scope'.[194] Further restrictions on the exercise of competence might arise from a duty on the part of the Community institutions to respect the areas of competence retained by the Member States. Such 'restrictions on the exercise of competence' ('Kompetenzausübungsschranken'[195]) would affect collective Community competence as regards its 'external scope', since they would relate to the interface between Community competence and the competence of the Member States.

2. THE FUNDAMENTAL RIGHTS OF THE INDIVIDUAL

(a) The significance of fundamental rights in relation to the cultural field

Fundamental rights were originally developed as rights of defence against the State.[196] This remains today their primary function,[197] despite the fact that they have assumed additional functions over time.[198] The significance of fundamental rights in relation to the cultural field is dependent upon what 'culture' is taken to signify. If culture is taken to mean (as the German Federal Constitutional Court has suggested) 'the totality of the intellectual forces at work within a community, developing independently of the State and having their own inherent value',[199] and if independence from the State is thus taken to constitute simply a constituent element of the notion of culture,[200] the significance of fundamental rights in

---

193 See, in relation to this concept, Goerlich, pp. 43 *et seq.*; Ehmke, *Wirtschaft und Verfassung*, p. 30; similarly, Rinken in: AK-GG, n. 83 preceding Art. 93, where it is referred to as a 'negative definition of competence'.

194 The image is borrowed from Ehmke, op. cit., p. 30.

195 As regards this term, see Schröder, p. 49; Ossenbühl, p. 34; Delbrück, *Rundfunkhoheit*, p. 57; Stern, p. 703.

196 As to the development of fundamental rights, see Maunz & Zippelius, pp. 138 *et seq.*; W. Geiger, pp. 1401 *et seq.*

197 See, with regard to the Basic Law of the Federal Republic of Germany, Hesse, in: Benda et al., p. 91.

198 *ibid.*, pp. 92 *et seq.*

199 BVerfGE 10, p. 20 (at p. 36).

200 For a more detailed analysis in this regard, see E.R. Huber, *Zur Problematik des Kulturstaats*, pp. 8 *et seq.*, who describes independence from the State as one aspect of the ideal cultural State.

relation to the cultural field becomes immediately apparent. Such rights may then be seen as performing the task of ensuring the integrity of the free space essential for cultural development.[201]

The German Basic Law ensures the integrity of that cultural free space through a variety of fundamental rights relating directly or indirectly to culture,[202] by which, according to Article 1(3) of the Basic Law, the entire German State authority is bound. As regards the institutions of the European Community, the question arises as to the extent to which they are also subject, when exercising their powers in the cultural field, to constraints arising out of fundamental rights.[203] In answering that question, it will be necessary first of all to outline the characteristics of the protection of fundamental rights under Community law, and then to draw conclusions in relation to the cultural field.

(b) Characteristics of the protection of fundamental rights under Community law

(i) The development of fundamental rights

The European Community is a community based on the rule of law,[204] and as such is characterized by the principle of the rule of law,[205] an essential element of which is the protection of fundamental human rights.[206] It appears self-evident from this, and is in fact now generally acknowledged, that the Community institutions are obliged, in exercising their powers, to have regard to the fundamental rights of the individual. The binding force of those fundamental rights serves, not least, to legitimate the sovereign authority of the Community.[207]

Initially, however, the Court of Justice declined to review the legal acts of the Community institutions from the standpoint of fundamental rights. In its judgment of 4 February 1959 in Case 1/58 *Storck*,[208] it answered the applicant's complaint that the High Authority of the ECSC had failed to respect certain fundamental rights protected under almost all the constitutions of the Member States[209] by stating that the High Authority was only required to apply

201 For a more detailed analysis of the connection between culture and freedom, see Häberle, *Verfassungslehre*, pp. 60 *et seq.*

202 For a more detailed analysis, see Oppermann, *Kulturverwaltungsrecht*, pp. 578 *et seq.*; Maihofer in: Benda et al., pp. 988 *et seq.*

203 See also, in relation to this question, Classen, *Diskussionsbeitrag*, who discusses the question whether fundamental rights might possibly be used as a 'brake to restrain excessive regulation' in the cultural field.

204 See in this regard 'Introduction', pp. 187 *et seq.*, above.

205 Judgment of the Court of Justice of 13 February 1979 in Case 101/78 *Granaria* [1979] ECR 623 (at p. 637); Frowein, *FS Werner Maihofer*, p. 150; Siedentopf, *VOP 1991*, p. 13.

206 Maunz & Zippelius, pp. 91 *et seq.*

207 e.g. see Schwarze, *FS Werner Maihofer*, p. 529; Weber, p. 965; Pescatore, *Schutz der Grundrechte*, p. 68; and Sasse, p. 53, who goes so far as to express the view that it is primarily the legitimation of public authority which is involved, rather than the protection of the rights of the individual.

208 [1959] ECR 17.

209 *ibid.*, at p. 24.

Community law, and that the Court itself was not normally required to rule on provisions of national law.[210] The protection of fundamental rights was thus regarded as a matter of national law, and was held to be irrelevant from the standpoint of Community law.[211]

A change in this stance became apparent for the first time in the judgment of 12 November 1969 in Case 29/69 *Stauder*,[212] in which the Court held that the general principles of Community law which it was required to protect included fundamental human rights.[213] About a year later, in its judgment of 17 December 1970 in Case 11/79 *Internationale Handelsgesellschaft*,[214] the Court stated by way of clarification that its task was not to concern itself with fundamental rights under national constitutions, thereby confirming in that regard its judgment in Case 1/58 *Storck*.[215] To do so would, in the Court's view, run counter to the independence of the Community legal order. Whilst the protection of fundamental rights under Community law had to be inspired by the constitutional traditions common to the Member States, it must also be ensured 'within the framework of the structure and objectives of the Community'.[216]

The development – starting out from the constitutional traditions of the Member States – of fundamental rights geared to the needs of the Community rules out any detailed comparison of national solutions.[217] That view is not invalidated by the judgment of the Court of Justice of 14 May 1974 in Case 4/73 *Nold* v. *Commission*.[218] In that case, the Court stated that it could not uphold measures which were incompatible with fundamental rights recognized and protected by the constitutions of the Member States.[219] That dictum has frequently been interpreted as expressing a 'maximum standard' derived from national constitutional provisions.[220] However, no such meaning can be

---

210 [1959] ECR 17 (at p. 26).

211 See also, to the same effect, Pescatore, op. cit., n. 207, p. 64.

212 [1969] ECR 419.

213 *ibid.*, at p. 425.

214 [1970] ECR 1125.

215 [1959] ECR 17. The view that the validity of the acts of the institutions can only be judged in the light of Community law has been repeated by the Court of Justice in a consistent body of case-law; see, for example, its judgments of 17 October 1989 in Joined Cases 97-99/87 *Dow Chemical Ibérica* v. *Commission* [1989] ECR 3165 (at p. 3191), 8 October 1986 in Case 234/85 *Keller* [1986] ECR 2897 (at p. 2912), and 19 June 1980 in Joined Cases 41, 121 and 796/79 *Testa* [1980] ECR 1979 (at p. 1996).

216 [1970] ECR 1125 (at p. 1134). That wording expresses merely the need for the development of fundamental rights specific to the Community, and cannot be interpreted as a general restriction of fundamental rights under Community law; however, that is the construction placed on the point by Beutler, *Grundrechtsschutz*, p. 1477; see also *EC Bulletin* Supplement 5/76, p. 9.

217 For a concurring view, see Pernice, *JZ 1977*, p. 780.

218 [1974] ECR 491.

219 *ibid.*, at p. 507; see also the similar wording appearing in the judgment of 13 December 1979 in Case 44/79 *Hauer* [1979] ECR 3727 (at p. 3745).

220 e.g. see Rengeling, *DVBl. 1982*, p. 143; *EC Bulletin* Supplement 5/76, p. 9; and Sørensen, p. 34, who does not expressly refer to the judgment cited; further substantiated in Dauses, *JöR 1982*, p. 11.

derived from the words used.[221] In addition, it would not be a feasible proposition,[222] and further would be liable to cast doubt[223] on the independence of Community law.[224] The development of fundamental rights under Community law by means of judicial activism on the part of the Court[225] is not geared to any minimum[226] or maximum standard, but follows the methodology of 'valuative comparative law',[227] which aims to seek the solution 'which gives the greatest effect to the fundamental right in question without detracting from the structure and objectives of the Community'.[228]

In addition to drawing inspiration from the common constitutional traditions of the Member States, the Court of Justice derives guidance from a further significant[229] source, namely from the fundamental rights laid down in 'international treaties for the protection of human rights on which the Member States have collaborated or of which they are signatories',[230] in particular the European Convention for the Protection of Human Rights and Fundamental Freedoms (ECHR),[231] which has been ratified by all the Member States of the Community.[232] It is not possible here to consider the vexed question as to whether the Community, without having formally acceded to the ECHR, is now directly bound by the substantive provisions of the Convention.[233] In any event, the Court of Justice appears to consider that the Community is not directly bound by the

---

221 See Zuleeg, *Rechtsprechung*, p. 239, who considers that the wording could be taken to indicate that the Court reaches its decisions on the basis of the lowest common denominator; Bahlmann, p. 10, takes the view that the theory of a 'maximum standard' is not borne out of the (previous) case-law of the Court; see also the distinction drawn in the interpretation of Pescatore, *Schutz der Grundrechte*, pp. 130 et seq. (discussion).

222 As to the objections to the idea of a 'maximum standard', see Sasse, p. 58.

223 See, to this effect, Dauses, *JöR 1982*, p. 12.

224 See the leading judgment of 15 July 1964 in Case 6/64 *Costa* v. *ENEL* [1964] ECR 585 (at p. 594).

225 Schwarze, *Abstraktion*, p. 235; Weber, p. 969.

226 See, however, the criticism expressed by Ress & Ukrow, p. 502, in which it is contended that the Court of Justice, in its judgment of 21 September 1989 in Joined Cases 46/87 and 227/88 *Hoechst* v. *Commission* [1989] ECR 2859, reduced the protection of fundamental rights by the Community to the lowest common denominator or even, in the absence of such a denominator, refused the protection of fundamental rights.

227 See Beutler, *Grundrechtsschutz*, p. 1475; Weber, p. 969; for a critical view of this approach, see Sasse, p. 62.

228 Kutscher, *Schutz von Grundrechten*, p. 46.

229 Occasionally, acts of the Community institutions, such as the Joint Declaration by the European Parliament, the Council and the Commission on fundamental rights of 5 April 1977 (OJ 1977 C 103, p. 1) are stated to constitute a source of the protection of fundamental rights by the Community; see Mestmäcker et al., p. 75; Schermers, pp. 252 et seq.; Schwarze, *EuGRZ 1986*, p. 294.

230 Case 44/79 *Hauer* [1979] ECR 3727 (at p. 3745).

231 BGBl. 1952 II 686; see, for example, the judgments of 10 July 1984 in Case 63/83 *Regina* v. *Kirk* [1984] ECR 2689 (at p. 2718) and of 26 June 1980 in Case 136/79 *National Panasonic* v. Commission [1980] ECR 2033 (at p. 2057).

232 See BGBl. 1990 II, Fundstellennachweis B, p. 243.

233 Those authors who contend that the Community is bound include Schermers, p. 251; Tomuschat, *EuR 1990*, p. 357; Bleckmann, *Bindung*, pp. 79 et seq.; Pescatore, *Schutz der Grundrechte*, pp. 70 et seq.; the undecided include Schwarze, *EuGRZ 1986*, p. 297; those against the contention include Feger, *DÖV 1987*, pp. 329 et seq.; Klein, *Bedeutung*, p. 137; Beutler, *Grundrechtsschutz*, pp. 1485 et seq.

ECHR, just as it regards the common constitutional traditions of the Member States as merely a starting-point for the 'discovery' of fundamental rights under Community law.[234]

As to the relationship between 'common constitutional traditions' and 'international treaties' as sources of law, it has recently been stated that the Court of Justice, in its judgment of 21 September 1989 in Joined Cases 46/87 and 227/88 *Hoechst* v. *Commission*,[235] has now made it clear that both sources rank *equally*.[236] The Court is said to have held that the general principles of Community law were to be safeguarded in accordance both with the common constitutional traditions of the Member States *and* with international treaties for the protection of human rights. Formerly, in contrast, it is said to have placed greater weight on the common constitutional traditions of the Member States, and merely to have 'had regard to' international treaties.[237]

It is not possible to subscribe to that view. For one thing, the finding that the two sources of law rank equally presupposes that they can be divorced from one another; but this is not the case. The common constitutional traditions find *likewise* expression in the ECHR. Furthermore, the wording used by the Court of Justice in the judgment in Joined Cases 46/87 and 227/88 *Hoechst* is to be found also in an earlier case,[238] yet was not repeated in the interim period.[239]

The development by the Court of Justice of the protection of fundamental rights under Community law on a case-by-case basis has been accompanied by the evolution of the case-law of the German Federal Constitutional Court, which initially rejected the standard of fundamental rights adopted at Community level,[240] subsequently adopted a wait-and-see attitude,[241] and finally took a positive view of it;[242] that standard ultimately enabled it in principle to decline to review secondary Community law against the criterion of the fundamental rights laid down in the Basic Law. In the field of Community law,[243] therefore, direct

---

234 See the typical wording used in the Court's judgment of 13 July 1989 in Case 5/88 *Wachauf* [1989] ECR 2609 (at p. 2639): 'In safeguarding those rights, the Court *has to look to* the constitutional traditions common to the Member States ... . International treaties concerning the protection of human rights on which the Member States have collaborated or to which they have acceded *can also supply guidelines* to which regard should be had in the context of Community law' (emphasis added).

235 [1989] ECR 2859.

236 Ress & Ukrow, p. 501.

237 *ibid.*

238 See the judgment of 26 June 1980 in Case 136/79 *National Panasonic* v. *Commission* [1980] ECR 2033 (at p. 2057).

239 See n. 234, above.

240 See BVerfGE 37, p. 271 (headnote).

241 BVerfGE 52, p. 187 (at p. 203).

242 BVerfGE 73, p. 339 (at p. 340) (headnote).

243 In areas falling outside the ambit of Community law, the Member States are not bound by the fundamental rights contained in Community law; see the judgments of the Court of Justice of 11 July 1985 in Joined Cases 60 and 61/84 *Cinéthèque* [1985] ECR 2605 (at p. 2627) and 30 September 1987 in Case 12/86 *Demirel* [1987] ECR 3719 (at p. 3754), and the Opinion of Advocate-General Mancini in Case 352/85 *Bond van Adverteerders* [1988] ECR 2085 (at p. 2122); as to the necessary demarcation between the Community field and that of the Member States, see Weiler, *FS Pierre Pescatore*, pp. 821 *et seq.*; Weiler, *Methods of Protection*, pp. 595–617; Schwartz, *Liberté d'expression*, pp. 177 *et seq.*; Everling, *Beitrag*, pp. 172 *et seq.*; see also the Commission's

claims may be brought against the EC with regard to the guaranteeing of fundamental rights.[244]

(ii) Restrictions on fundamental rights

The fundamental rights guaranteed by Community law are subject, as is familiar in German law,[245] to certain restrictions. Specific limitations, grafted onto the individual fundamental right in question, have been formulated, as in the case of the fundamental right itself, by means of assessments carried out on the basis of constitutional comparisons, and having regard to the ECHR.[246] In general terms, the Court has held that the fundamental rights recognized by it are not absolute but must be considered in relation to their social function.[247]

The susceptibility to limitation of fundamental rights under Community law is itself subject to certain restrictions. As long ago as 17 December 1970 in the judgment in Case 25/70 Köster[248] the Court examined whether a restriction of a fundamental right which was permissible in principle imposed an excessively onerous burden on the person concerned and thus ultimately violated the right in question.[249] In examining that question, the Court was concerned with the principle of necessity, which represents an element of the Community law principle of proportionality.[250] The prohibition of excessive restrictions on fundamental rights has been reiterated by the Court of Justice in subsequent decisions, in which it has at the same time held such restrictions to be contrary to the prohibition against interference with the essential substance ('Wesensgehalt') of fundamental rights,[251] but without thereby deciding sufficiently clearly in favour of the theory of the 'relative substance' ('Theorie vom relativen

---

(cont.)

answer to Written Question No. 2898/90 (OJ 1991 C 85, p. 44) on the position of conscientious objectors to military service in Greece and on the complaint raised in that connection concerning an infringement by Greece of Art. 9 of the ECHR: the matter was stated to lie outside the jurisdiction of the Commission.

244 In Grundrechte, p. 48, Feger uses the term 'Anspruchsgegner' (adversary against whom a claim may be made).

245 See Maunz & Zippelius, pp. 156 et seq.

246 See primarily in that regard the Court's judgments of 13 December 1979 in Case 44/79 Hauer [1979] ECR 3727 (at pp. 3745 et seq.) and 14 May 1974 in Case 4/73 Nold v. Commission [1974] ECR 491 (at pp. 507 et seq.).

247 See the judgments of 13 July 1989 in Case 5/88 Wachauf [1989] ECR 2609 (at p. 2639) and 11 July 1989 in Case 265/87 Schräder [1989] ECR 2237 (at p. 2268).

248 [1970] ECR 1161.

249 ibid., at pp. 1177 et seq.

250 For a definition of the principle of proportionality, see the judgment of 11 July 1989 in Case 265/87 Schräder [1989] ECR 2237 (at pp. 2269).

251 Judgments of 13 July 1989 in Case 5/88 Wachauf [1989] ECR 2609 (at p. 2639), of 11 July 1989 in Case 265/87 Schräder [1989] ECR 2237 (at p. 2268) and of 13 December 1979 in Case 44/79 Hauer [1979] ECR 3727 (at p. 3747); as to the question of the restriction of limitations on fundamental rights under Community law, see also Dauses, JöR 1982, p. 5; Thiel, p. 280; Kutscher, Grundsatz, p. 94; Schwarze, Europäisches Verwaltungsrecht II, p. 705; Ress, Grundsatz, pp. 39 et seq.; Pollak, p. 45.

Wesensgehalt') of fundamental rights.[252] The Court has further described as a limitation on the restriction of fundamental rights under Community law the requirement that restrictions on fundamental rights must 'in fact correspond to objectives of general interest pursued by the Community'.[253]

(iii) Interpretation consistent with fundamental rights

The fundamental rights guaranteed by Community law may make their effects felt not only by the Court's possibly declaring legislative acts of the Community institutions unlawful. They may also contribute towards avoiding the taint of illegality, in so far as where more than one interpretation of a Community legislative act of the Community is possible, preference is given to the one which does not violate the fundamental rights guaranteed by Community law. The Court of Justice has emphasized with particular clarity the need for an interpretation which is consistent with fundamental rights in its judgment of 21 September 1989 in Joined Cases 46/87 and 227/88 Hoechst,[254] where it held that Article 14 of Regulation No. 17 'cannot be interpreted in such a way as to give rise to results which are incompatible with the general principles of Community law and in particular with fundamental rights'.[255] The Court had previously held, on 18 May 1989 in Case 249/86 Commission v. Germany,[256] that Regulation No. 1612/68 was to be interpreted in the light of the right to respect for family life enshrined in Article 8 of the ECHR, which forms part of the fundamental rights guaranteed by Community law.[257] Lastly, in the judgment of 13 July 1989 in Case 5/88 Wachauf, the Court imposed upon the national authorities the obligation, when applying Community rules, to exercise the discretionary powers retained by them 'in a manner consistent with the requirements of the protection of fundamental rights'.[258]

Express recognition of the need for Community law to be interpreted and applied in conformity with fundamental rights is, indeed, a new phenomenon.[259] However, the Court of Justice did in fact use this method before. An example of this is to be found in the judgment of 27 October 1976 in Case 130/75 Prais v. Council,[260] in which it construed Article 27 of the Staff Regulations of Officials consistently with the fundamental right to freedom of religion.[261] Thus,

---

252 That evidently appears, however, to be the interpretation applied by Pernice in: Grabitz, Kommentar zum EWGV, Art. 164, n. 73, to the case-law of the Court of Justice; as to the theories advanced in German law regarding the absolute and relative substance of fundamental rights, see Hendrichs in: von Münch, Grundgesetz-Kommentar, Art. 19, n.25.

253 Judgment of 13 December 1979 in Case 44/79 Hauer [1979] ECR 3727 (at p. 3747); see also the judgments referred to in n. 251, above.

254 [1989] ECR 2859.

255 ibid., at p. 2923.

256 [1989] ECR 1263.

257 ibid., at p. 1290.

258 [1989] ECR 2609 (at p. 2640).

259 This is correctly stated by Everling, EuR 1990, p. 208.

260 [1976] ECR 1589.

261 Pernice, JZ 1977, p. 780, rightly describes the judgment as an example of interpretation in conformity with fundamental rights; for a further example, see the judgment of 12 November 1969 in Case 29/69 Stauder [1969] ECR 419 (at p. 425).

interpretation in conformity with fundamental rights must be regarded as a basic canon of construction of Community law.

(c) Implications for the cultural field

The aforementioned purpose of the protection of fundamental rights under Community law, namely the legitimation of the sovereign authority of the Community institutions,[262] means that that protection of fundamental rights must extend as far as the exercise of Community powers requires.[263] The consequence of this for the cultural field is that any extension of the exercise of Community powers in that field must be accompanied by a corresponding extension of the protection of fundamental rights. The authority of the Community and the protection of fundamental rights must at all times be co-extensive. The idea that the protection afforded by the Community to funda-mental rights should be restricted merely to fundamental rights with an economic connotation[264] must be rejected for the same reasons as the idea that the cultural field is excluded from the scope of Community competence.[265] The approach of the Court of Justice likewise assumes the comprehensive validity of fundamental rights at Community level.[266]

Admittedly, commentators have stated from time to time that certain spheres of fundamental rights are 'impervious to any possible encroachment by the exercise of Community powers',[267] that interference with, for example, religious and ideological freedom are 'scarcely conceivable',[268] that the emergence in Community law of classic fundamental rights issues is 'fairly unlikely'[269] and that certain classic fundamental rights are incapable of being violated by the Community, owing to its restricted powers.[270] What all those statements have in common, however, is that they merely describe the probability of violations of fundamental rights by the Community institutions,[271] without seeking to restrict the compass of fundamental rights under Community law. Such discussions are of limited value, however, since they relate to the state of

---

262 See 'The development of fundamental rights', pp 212 et seq., above.

263 What is involved here is the protection of fundamental rights in relation solely to the exercise of competence by the Community institutions in a manner which is in principle permissible. The fact that the fundamental rights of individuals may also (indeed, precisely) be violated where the Community acts *ultra vires* is pointed out by Klein, *Bedeutung*, p. 145.

264 e.g. see the Italian Government's contention in Case 118/75 *Watson and Belmann* [1976] ECR 1185 (at p. 1192) that there exists no specific relationship between Art. 8 of the ECHR and the sphere of economic activity governed by the Treaty.

265 For a more detailed analysis, see 'Conclusions in relation to the cultural field', pp. 193 et seq., above.

266 See, to take but one example, the judgment of 18 May 1989 in Case 249/86 *Commission v. Germany* [1989] ECR 1263 (at p. 1290), in which the Court referred to the passage in the preamble to the Single European Act relating to fundamental rights.

267 Ipsen, *Europäisches Gemeinschaftsrecht*, p. 721.

268 Kropholler, p. 129.

269 Pescatore, *Schutz der Grundrechte*, p. 67.

270 Kutscher, *Schutz von Grundrechten*, p. 45.

271 It is only from this standpoint that it is possible to speak of the 'Community relevance' of fundamental rights; for a concurring view, see Pernice, *Grundrechtsgehalte*, p. 52.

development of Community law at a given time and are, moreover, subject to the limitations of the observer's imagination.

So, it must be assumed that the Community institutions are capable of violating *any* fundamental right[272] and, consequently, that *all* fundamental rights, whether enshrined in the common constitutional traditions of the Member States or in international treaties for the protection of human rights, apply in Community law, albeit in a form which is geared to the needs of the Community and to be developed by the Court of Justice.

Hitherto, it has been very rare for the violations of fundamental cultural rights to form the subject-matter of proceedings before the Court of Justice.[273] However, the quota rules contained in the 'television directive' of 3 October 1989[274] show – even though they were unlawful in any event for want of an appropriate legal basis[275] – that a violation by the Community institutions of, for example, the fundamental right to broadcasting freedom is possible.[276] Thus, the relative silence of the EEC Treaty on the subject of fundamental rights[277] has turned out in the result to be a benefit: had it laid down a list of fundamental rights, that list would in all probability have been restricted to fundamental rights with some economic connotation,[278] and this would at the very least have made it more difficult for other fundamental rights in the cultural field not been expressly guaranteed to have been recognized, if not precluded such recognition altogether.

3. THE SPHERE OF COMPETENCE OF THE MEMBER STATES

(a) Introduction

Even in the federal State of the Federal Republic of Germany, where the allocation of powers between the Federation and the *Länder* depends in principle on the subject-matter concerned,[279] it is impossible to draw a fine dividing line between areas of competence,[280] and so it cannot be ruled out that the Federation may, 'in

---

272 See also, to this effect, Klein, *Bedeutung*, p. 145; EP-Doc. A2-3/89/Part B, p. 33.

273 See, however, the judgment of 27 October 1976 in Case 130/75 *Prais* v. *Council* [1976] ECR 1589, concerning the fundamental right to religious freedom.

274 OJ 1989 L 298, p. 23.

275 See in this regard 'The binding force and legality of the quota rules', pp. 163 *et seq.*, above.

276 See Magiera, *Ansätze*, p. 23, who subscribes to the view that this constitutes a breach of fundamental rights; see also Engel, pp. 243 *et seq.*, who maintains that this would constitute a violation of Art. 10 of the ECHR.

277 The 'classic' fundamental rights dealt with here do not include the fundamental freedoms provided for by the Treaty (for a concurring view, see Streinz, *Grundrechtsprobleme*, pp. 122 *et seq.*), despite the fact that they may exhibit many similarities (see in that regard Bleckmann, *GS Christoph Sasse*, pp. 665 *et seq.*).

278 Since the potential relevance of Community law *per se* to fundamental rights has clearly exceeded what the draftsmen of the EEC Treaty could imagine (see Bahlmann, p. 3; Pescatore, *Schutz der Grundrechte*, p. 64; Dauses, *JöR 1982*, p. 2), it cannot be taken that any list of fundamental rights would have contained rights other than fundamental economic rights.

279 See Bleckmann, *DÖV 1986*, p. 126; Memminger, p. 849.

280 See Stern, p. 676; Bothe in: AK-GG, Art. 70, nn. 21 *et seq.*; also, as a prime example, the criticism by the Bundesrat (Federal Council) of a claim to competence in relation to the promotion of sport asserted by the Federation, BR-Drs. 221/91 (Beschluß).

legislating, encroach upon another field'.[281] In the relationship between the Community and the Member States, which is characterized primarily by the objectives and tasks which have been assigned to the Community, without any link to any specific subject-matter, 'encroachment' upon the spheres of competence reserved to the Member States represents quite simply the typical manifestation of the exercise of Community competence.[282] Accordingly, the question which arises here (even more than in German law) is whether, in the exercise of Community powers, the 'encroachment' upon alien[283] spheres of competence should take place with moderation, and with the least possible interference with those spheres of competence.[284]

A great deal of support for this proposition is to be found in the literature. It is argued, for example, that, in exercising their powers, the Community institutions may 'not unnecessarily encroach upon national legal systems',[285] that they must consider the effects which their acts may have on the legislative powers remaining to the Member States,[286] and that, in the context of the approximation of legislation, the restriction of national powers must not be disproportionate to the benefit to be gained in terms of Community policy, but rather that, the greater the emphasis of a subject on matters falling outside the ambit of economic activity, the more restrained should be the use by the Community of its powers.[287] An argument on the same lines is that the Community should naturally be required to show restraint when exercising its powers in fields involving 'competence which is only partially related to economic matters'.[288]

(b) The issue as regards Germany

In the Federal Republic of Germany, non-intervention in spheres of national competence must arguably benefit not only the Federation but also the *Länder*. There is nothing very special in this, given that, in other Member States, regional authorities are similarly entrusted with the performance of internal tasks.[289] However, the Federal Republic of Germany is the only Member State of the

---

281 BVerfGE 61, p. 149 (at p. 205).

282 See in that regard 'Conclusions in relation to the cultural field', pp. 193 *et seq.*, above.

283 National legal systems are 'alien' to the Community inasmuch as they do not 'belong' to the Community legal order; it should be borne in mind, however, that the Community legal order is to a considerable extent defined by the fact that it 'acts upon' the national legal systems (see 'Conclusions in relation to the cultural field', pp. 193 *et seq.*, above). It is misleading, therefore, to suggest in this context that the Community is 'basically' or 'in principle' lacking in competence, though that is the view expressed by Klein & Beckmann, p. 186.

284 See, to that effect, the Federal Constitutional Court, BVerfGE 61, p. 149 (at p. 205).

285 Wohlfahrt, *Rechtsordnung*, p. 175.

286 See Ossenbühl, p. 46; also, to the same effect, Fiedler, pp. 165 *et seq.*, and Hilf, ZaöRV 1975, p. 58.

287 See Jarass, p. 93.

288 See Schröder, p. 50.

289 e.g. see Art. 117 of the Italian Constitution; Art. 148 of the Spanish Constitution; Art. 3 *ter* of the Belgian Constitution; for a basic appraisal, see Blanke, *Föderalismus und Integrationsgewalt.*

European Community which is organized on a federal basis. The status of the *Länder* as States[290] distinguishes the Federal Republic of Germany from all other Member States.[291] According to the case-law of the Federal Constitutional Court, that status presupposes that the *Länder* 'retain, as part of their intrinsic patrimony, an inalienable nucleus of tasks of their own'.[292] Now, in view of the numerous transfers of competence from the *Länder* to the Federation and the EC which have occurred,[293] that nucleus appears to be secured only by powers in the cultural field, by the so-called 'cultural sovereignty'[294] of the *Länder*.[295]

It is feared by some that any further restriction of 'cultural sovereignty' could jeopardize the status of the *Länder* as States, i.e. the status of the Federal Republic of Germany as a federation.[296] The question thus arises whether Community law imposes on the exercise of powers by the Community institutions any special limitations, aimed at ensuring the status as a federation of the Federal Republic of Germany. The safeguarding of that status would seem in any case to impose only very slight restrictions on the exercise by the Community institutions of their powers, since it could only qualify for protection if there were an immediate threat to Germany's federal status, and could not be safeguarded against individual legal acts falling short of such a threat.

It is necessary to consider whether there is any direct or indirect obligation on the part of the Community institutions to observe the federative principle ('Bundesstaatsprinzip') governing the status of the Federal Republic of Germany as a federal State. The idea that the Community is directly bound by national constitutional principles – no matter what its theoretical basis – is now generally rejected,[297] and could, moreover, not be squared with the case-law of the Court of

---

290 The Federal Constitutional Court has recognized the status of the *Länder* as States; see, for example, BVerfGE 34, p. 9 (at p. 19); for a critical view of the nature of the *Länder* as States, see Hesse, p. 85, n. 1.

291 See, to take just two examples, Blanke, *Bundesländer*, pp. 53 et seq.; Siedentopf, *Europa 1992*, p. 241.

292 BVerfGE 34, p. 9 (at p. 20).

293 Nass, pp. 287 et seq., considers that it is not the EC but the Federation and the *Länder* themselves which have most contributed to the latters' loss of powers.

294 As to this term, see BVerfGE 37, p. 314 (at p. 322); BVerfGE 6, p. 309 (at p. 354).

295 That is the view advanced by numerous academic legal authors; e.g. see Hufen, p. 1, who regards culture as the pillar and central point of the existence of the Federal State; Bethge, p. 26, to whom cultural sovereignty lies 'at the heart' of the federal system; Eiselstein, *NVwZ 1989*, p. 330, who considers that the status of the *Länder* as States in their own right continues in essence to be safeguarded only by culture; Dörr, *NWVBl. 1988*, p. 293, who argues that, outside the ambit of their cultural sovereignty, the *Länder* possess hardly any other significant legislative powers.

296 See, to that effect, Dörr, op. cit., p. 293; Ipsen, *GS Wilhelm Karl Geck*, p. 352; Vitzthum, p. 289.

297 See Vitzthum, p. 287; Blanke, *Bundesländer*, p. 61; Ress, *EuGRZ 1986*, p. 550; Henrichs, p. 423; Schwan, p. 49; Rengeling, *ZHR 1988*, p. 462; Bleckmann, *Europarecht*, p. 180, appears to take a different view, contending that the Community institutions must have regard to whatever powers are open to the States under their constitutions; see also Zuleeg, *JöR 1971*, pp. 31-35, who infers from the first paragraph of Art. 247 of the EEC Treaty a restriction of Community law's claim to validity in terms of fundamental constitutional principles.

Justice. The Court has been at pains to emphasize, from an early stage, the independence[298] of the Community legal order,[299] and it has subsequently expressly declared that the validity of a Community measure cannot be challenged on the ground that it runs counter to the principles of a national constitutional structure.[300]

Whilst it cannot be said, therefore, that the Community is directly bound by the federative principle, the question remains whether any such binding force may be indirectly inferred from any general principle of federalism inherent in Community law and arising from the common constitutional traditions of the Member States. This is necessarily conditional on at least a predominant number of Member States being organized in a manner comparable to the federal structure of the Federal Republic of Germany. However, as has already been said, this is not the case. Consequently, it is not possible to discern in Community law any general principle of federalism such as to guarantee to the German *Länder* a 'patrimony' of powers inherent to them.[301]

No specific direct or indirect restrictions on the exercise by the Community institutions of their powers can therefore be inferred from the federal status of the Federal Republic of Germany. However, the powers of the German *Länder*, and thus the federal status of the Federal Republic of Germany, may benefit indirectly from a general duty on the part of the Community to have regard to the spheres of competence of the Member States.[302] The possible theoretical basis for such a duty is discussed below.

(c) Basis under Community law for a duty to have regard to national spheres of competence

(i) The principle of proportionality

The existence of the principle of proportionality in Community law is beyond

---

298 Not only the independence of Community law but also the need for it to be applied uniformly throughout the entire territory of the Community is advanced as an argument against its being bound by individual national constitutional principles; see R. Geiger, *Stellung der Bundesländer*, p. 62; a different view is clearly taken by Hailbronner, *JZ 1990*, pp. 152 *et seq.*, who contends that the exercise of their powers by the Community institutions must generally take account of the basic structures of the federal system of the Federal Republic of Germany.

299 See the judgment of 15 July 1964 in Case 6/64 *Costa* v. *ENEL* [1964] ECR 585 (at pp. 593 *et seq.*).

300 Judgment of 17 December 1970 in Case 11/70 *Internationale Handelsgesellschaft* [1970] ECR 1125 (at p. 1134); recently confirmed in the judgment of 17 October 1989 in Joined Cases 97-99/87 *Dow Chemical Ibérica and Others* v. *Commission* [1989] ECR 3165 (at p. 3191).

301 See also, to the same effect, Ress, *EuGRZ 1986*, p. 551; Blanke, *Bundesländer*, p. 61; R. Geiger, *Stellung der Bundesländer*, p. 62; Rengeling, *ZHR 1988*, p. 462; Siedentopf, *DÖV 1988*, p. 983; for a different view, see Hailbronner, *JZ 1990*, p. 152.

302 The *Länder* cannot assert their own rights against the EC, since the Community and its institutions are – as Ipsen puts it in *FS Walter Hallstein*, p. 256 – afflicted with 'State blindness'; see also, to the same effect, as regards the principle of subsidiarity, Ress, *EuGRZ 1987*, p. 362; Badura, p. 126.

dispute.[303] It derives its particular significance from the fact that its effect is similar to that of a fundamental right.[304] Schwarze goes so far as to contend that the 'aim of the principle of proportionality [is] ... to protect the freedom of the individual against the restrictions of the State'.[305] The principle of proportionality in Community law is comparable in substance with that employed in the German legal system.[306] This came to the fore particularly clearly in the judgment of 11 July 1989 in Case 265/87 Schräder. In that case, the Court of Justice summarized the principle of proportionality with regard to certain financial charges imposed on economic operators by stating that such charges are only lawful if they are appropriate and necessary for meeting the objectives legitimately pursued by the legislation in question. It held that, where there is a choice between several appropriate measures, the least onerous measure must be used, and, in addition, that the charges imposed must not be disproportionate to the aims pursued.[307] The Court of Justice manifestly took over the three elements of appropriateness, necessity and adequacy from the German legal system.[308]

The relevance, emphasized above, of the principle of proportionality to fundamental rights is shown by the way in which it protects the *individual* against measures adopted by the Community institutions imposing a burden of some kind. It is now proposed to discuss whether the principle of proportionality is also capable of operating so as to protect the *Member States* against legislative measures enacted by the Community institutions within the national sphere of competence. Hitherto, no such function appears to have been ascribed to the principle of proportionality in the case-law of the Court of Justice.[309] However, academics have from time to time advanced the view that the principle of proportionality must be regarded as restricting the exercise of Community competence where this conflicts with the competence of the Member States.[310] According to Bleckmann, the importance of the principle of proportionality even extends to the comprehensive setting of the principles of the rule of law which the

303 e.g. see the judgments of the Court of Justice of 19 June 1980 in Joined Cases 41, 121 and 796/79 *Testa* [1980] ECR 1979 (at p. 1997) and of 11 July 1989 in Case 265/87 *Schräder* [1989] ECR 2237 (at p. 2269), in which it held that the principle of proportionality is one of the general principles of Community law; for a detailed analysis of the principle of proportionality in Community law, see Schwarze, *Europäisches Verwaltungsrecht*, vol. II, pp. 690–842.

304 Pernice in: Grabitz, *Kommentar zum EWGV*, Art. 164, n.101, describes the principle of proportionality as 'the key to the protection of fundamental rights in Community law'; a similar view is expressed by Schwarze, op. cit., p. 841, who contends that the significance of the principle of proportionality in Community law is comparable to that of fundamental rights in German law.

305 Schwarze, op. cit., p. 838.

306 See also, to the same effect, Schiller, p. 929; Ress, *Grundsatz*, p. 38; Schwarze, op. cit., p. 832.

307 [1989] ECR 2237 (at p. 2269).

308 See Zuleeg, *Rechtsprechung*, p. 238, who was the Judge-Rapporteur in Case 265/87 *Schräder*; Schmidt, p. 4.

309 For a concurring view, see Schröder, p. 51.

310 e.g. see Ossenbühl, pp. 47 *et seq.*; Delbrück, *Rundfunkhoheit*, pp. 57 *et seq.*; Hailbronner, *JZ* 1990, p. 152; Steindorff, *Grenzen*, p. 32; Everling, *EuR* 1990, pp. 216 *et seq.*; Ipsen, *GS Wilhelm Karl Geck*, p. 353; Langeheine in: Grabitz, *Kommentar zum EWGV*, Art. 100, n.12 (concerning the form and extent of the approximation of laws); Schröder, p. 51, expresses doubts on the point; Schwarze, in *Europäisches Verwaltungsrecht*, vol. II, p. 841, is equivocal, stating that the significance of the principle of proportionality is also evident in cases of interference with the actual interests of the Member States.

Community is required to observe not only in relation to individuals but also, in his view, in its dealings with Member States.[311]

As against the view that the principle of proportionality is applicable in the context of the division of powers between the Community and the Member States, it may be objected, first, that the EEC Treaty constitutes a definitive, self-contained set of rules, leaving no room for the principle of proportionality. That view is supported by the fact that the EEC Treaty has expressly adopted elements of the principle of proportionality in the constituent elements of various individual provisions, for example Article 8a(1) ('*erforderliche* Maßnahmen' ('necessary measures') in the German text), Article 67(1) ('*necessary* to ensure the proper functioning of the common market') and Article 235 ('if action by the Community should prove *necessary*'/'take the *appropriate* measures').

That view could be accepted without hesitation if it were possible to state that the EEC Treaty lays down relatively precise rules regarding the content and scope of Community legislation. However, that is not the case. The EEC Treaty merely affords the Community institutions a more or less specific framework for action[312] in bringing about the 'genuinely political unification process'.[313] Basically, the Community legislature enjoys – obviously within the framework of the powers conferred by the Treaty and interpreted in each case in accordance with the Treaty objectives[314] – a discretion which has been recognized by the Court of Justice,[315] and within the scope of which it might be possible to take into account, on the basis of the principle of proportionality, the sphere of competence retained by the Member States.[316] This is not at odds with the case-law of the Court of Justice. Whilst the Court has stated that the principle of proportionality constitutes one of the *general* principles of Community law,[317] this does not in principle prevent it from possessing a comprehensive significance going beyond the protection of the individual.

If, therefore, the Court of Justice were to hold that the principle of proportionality is applicable to the protection of the national sphere of competence, the Community legislature would be obliged to choose, from amongst a series of measures each of which is equally appropriate for the attainment of the objective pursued in a given case, the one which least restricts the sphere of competence of the Member States. Furthermore, such a measure

---

311 Bleckmann, *Europarecht*, pp. 178 *et seq.*

312 For a more detailed analysis of the indeterminate nature of the rules contained in the EEC Treaty, see Clever, pp. 144 *et seq.*; as to the characterization of the EEC Treaty as a framework treaty, 'The results of the EEC Treaty', pp. 200 *et seq.*, above.

313 See Magiera, *GS Wilhelm Karl Geck*, p. 511.

314 This is pointed out by Everling, *FS Karl Doehring*, p. 195.

315 See the judgments of 30 May 1989 in Case 20/88 *Roquette Frères* v. *Commission* [1989] ECR 1553 (at p. 1588), of 17 May 1988 in Case 84/87 *Erpelding* [1988] ECR 2647 (at p. 2673), of 9 July 1985 in Case 179/84 *Bozzetti* [1985] ECR 2301 (at p. 2322), of 22 May 1985 in Case 13/83 *European Parliament* v. *Council ('Common transport policy')* [1985] ECR 1513 (at p. 1596) and of 29 February 1984 in Case 37/83 *Rewe-Zentral* [1984] ECR 1229 (at p. 1249).

316 It is generally true to say that, the greater the discretion enjoyed by the institution in question, the greater the significance of the principle of proportionality, and conversely, that the greater the precision with which the provisions of a legislative act are laid down, the more limited the significance of the principle; see Jakobs, p. 138.

317 See n. 303, above.

could not unreasonably encroach on the competence of the Member States; in the scarcely imaginable 'extreme case' of its so doing, it would have to remain unimplemented.[318]

It would be necessary in such circumstances, however, to pay particular regard to the fact that the determination, expressed in the Treaty itself, that active steps be taken by the Community institutions, and thus the basic permissibility of 'encroachment' onto national legal systems, remains unchallenged. It would not be permissible, for example, to claim that the rules on the free movement of goods, or the competition rules, are inapplicable in specific fields solely on the ground that those fields have a particular cultural significance which affects the sphere of competence of the Member States.[319] It is moreover doubtful whether the Court of Justice, with a view to leaving national spheres of competence untouched, would regard compliance with the principle of proportionality as justiciable. In its judgment of 11 July 1989 in Case 265/87 *Schräder*, it held that, by virtue of the wide discretionary powers conferred on the Community legislature in matters concerning the Common Agricultural Policy, the legality of a measure adopted in that sphere can be affected only if the measure is 'manifestly inappropriate' having regard to the objective pursued.[320] Thus the discretion of the Community legislature relates in this connection not only to the choice to be made from amongst a number of proportionate measures but also to the conditions governing proportionality.

It is questionable, however, whether the Court of Justice would concur with such an application of the principle of proportionality. The derivation from German law of the Community law principle of proportionality suggests that the principle should be accorded the same significance in the relationship between the EC and the Member States as it has in that between the Federal German State and the *Länder*. With regard to that latter relationship, the Federal Constitutional Court held on 22 May 1990 that the 'restrictions (deriving from the principle of the rule of law) on interference by the State in the legal sphere of the individual ... (were) not applicable to the relationship in respect of competence between the Federal State and the *Länder*'.[321] It observed that this was particularly the case as regards the principle of proportionality.[322] The Court stated that considerations concerning the concepts of freedom and restriction could not be applied to the division of powers between the Federal State and the *Länder*.[323] The situation in this regard is not the same, therefore, as in the case of the guarantee of local government, the structure of which is 'comparable to that of fundamental rights'[324] and which is protected, according to the case-law of the Federal Constitutional Court, against disproportionate encroachment on the part of the Federal State or the *Länder*.[325]

---

318 See Schröder, p. 51.
319 However, this is apparently the view taken by Ipsen, *GS Wilhelm Karl Geck*, p. 354.
320 [1989] ECR 2237 (at p. 2270).
321 BVerfGE 81, p. 310; fifth headnote.
322 *ibid.*
323 *ibid.*, p. 338; for a different view, see Stettner, pp. 397 *et seq.*
324 Blümel, p. 268.
325 See the decision of 7 October 1980, BVerfGE 56, p. 298 (at pp. 313 *et seq.*); Knemeyer, *Kommunalrecht*, p. 36.

Support for the appraisal undertaken here of the prospective position of the Court of Justice regarding the application of the principle of proportionality to the relationship between the EC and the Member States is to be found in a comment on the principle of proportionality made by Judge Kapteyn of the European Court of Justice: 'Moreover, the principle of proportionality is applicable to the relationship between the Community and its citizens. We are not speaking of a principle aimed at limiting the powers of the Community *vis-à-vis* the Member States'.[326]

(ii) The principle of Community loyalty

In addition to the principle of proportionality, the principle of Community loyalty ('Gemeinschaftstreue') may be regarded as a further starting point for the establishment of a duty on the part of the Community institutions to have regard to the competence of the Member States. That principle is not contained in any written Community law, having instead been conceptualized by academics;[327] it has been recognized in the case-law of the Court of Justice, although the term 'Community loyalty' has not been used in any of the Court's decisions. The Court has referred to the 'principle'[328] or 'general rule'[329] 'imposing on Member States and the Community institutions mutual duties of genuine cooperation and assistance'.[330] In the view of the Court, that principle finds expression in Article 5 of the EEC Treaty.[331] In addition, reference has at times been made in the literature to Article 6(2) of the EEC Treaty as evidencing the existence of a general duty requiring the Community institutions to act in good faith *vis-à-vis* the aims of the Community.[332]

Whilst, therefore, it appears undeniable that the Community owes a duty to act in good faith *vis-à-vis* the Member States,[333] the question arises whether that duty encompasses an obligation to have regard to the spheres of competence of the Member States and to encroach as little as possible upon them. No direct indication to that effect is to be found in the relevant case-law of the Court of Justice.[334] However, a number of commentators infer from the principle of Community loyalty such a duty to have regard to the competence of the Member States.[335]

---

326 Kapteyn, p. 39.
327 See Grabitz in: *idem, Kommentar zum EWGV*, Art. 5, n.15.
328 Judgments of 2 February 1989 in Case 94/87 *Commission* v. *Germany* [1989] ECR 175 (at p. 192), 15 January 1986 in Case 52/84 *Commission* v. *Belgium* [1986] ECR 89 (at p. 105) and 10 February 1983 in Case 230/81 *Luxembourg* v. *Parliament* [1983] ECR 255 (at p. 287).
329 Judgment of 15 January 1986 in Case 44/84 *Hurd* [1986] ECR 29 (at p. 81).
330 See the judgments cited in nn. 328 and 329, above.
331 *ibid.*
332 See Zuleeg in: GBTE, *Kommentar zum EWGV*, Art. 6, n.7; Ossenbühl, p. 41.
333 For a concurring view, see also Jarass, pp. 93 *et seq.*; Ossenbühl, p. 45.
334 See nn. 328 and 329, above.
335 e.g. see Ipsen, *GS Wilhelm Karl Geck*, pp. 352 *et seq.*; Ossenbühl, p. 46; Jarass, p. 94; and also, arguably, Hilf, *ZaöRV 1975*, p. 58, according to whom it is incumbent on all of the parties involved at all times to bear in mind the possible effects which the rules they propose may have on areas falling outside their own legal order. Everling, in *FS Karl Doehring*, p. 195, regards the principle of Community loyalty as merely an 'extreme' limit of the division of powers.

This appears, in principle, to be the correct view. An encroachment which is *mala fide* or unfair on the competence of the Member States must necessarily be impermissible. Since it is expressed in such general terms, the principle of Community loyalty does not constitute a manageable yardstick. It is essential, therefore, to determine the criteria according to which the exercise by the Community institutions of their powers in a given case may be judged unfair or in bad faith. The principle of proportionality is once again involved here, since it appears inconceivable that a measure which is proportionate in relation to the competence of the Member States could be regarded as *mala fide*, just as, conversely, it appears inconceivable that a disproportionate measure encroaching on the sphere of competence of the Member States could be held to be in conformity with the principle of Community loyalty.

Thus the substance of the principle of proportionality and the principle of Community loyalty coincide, at least as regards the point at issue here, i.e. non-interference in areas of national competence.[336] To that extent, the principle of *bona fide* Community cooperation possesses no independent significance going beyond that of the principle of proportionality.[337] However, it follows from this that the reservations expressed about the applicability of the principle of proportionality[338] must also apply to the principle of Community loyalty.

(iii) The principle of subsidiarity

The principle of subsidiarity should also be discussed as the last basis for a possible obligation on the part of the Community institutions to have regard to the sphere of competence of the Member States. The principle of subsidiarity is now once again 'on everybody's lips',[339] having previously been described as a manifestation of a 'fashion of which people are beginning to tire'.[340] However, the present debate about the principle of subsidiarity is no longer concerned with German constitutional law – as were the statements quoted in the preceding sentence – but with European Community law. The principle of subsidiarity is developing, as a result, into the 'key concept underlying discussion of European policy'.[341] In the context of the impending revision of the Community Treaties, efforts are being made to provide for the express incorporation of the principle of subsidiarity in Community law.[342] Under the law as it already stands, however, calls are being

---

336 See also, to the same effect, Delbrück, *Rundfunkhoheit*, p. 58; Ossenbühl, p. 48; Hailbronner, *JZ 1990*, p. 152; Bleckmann, *Europarecht*, p. 178.

337 For a different view, see Schröder, p. 50, who argues that, from a systematic point of view, the determination of proportionality in relation to individual cases may most readily be based on the principle of Community loyalty enshrined in Art. 5 of the EEC Treaty.

338 See 'The principle of proportionality', immediately above.

339 This expression was already being used as long ago as 1963, by Herzog in *Der Staat 1963*, p. 399.

340 See Isensee, p. 9.

341 As Heintzen, p. 317, has aptly described it; see also, to the same effect, Wilke & Wallace, p. 1.

342 See the conclusions of the Foreign Ministers of the Member States, Europe Documents No. 1666, 6 December 1990; Commission Opinion of 21 October 1990 on the proposal for amendment of the Treaty establishing the European Economic Community with a view to political union, COM(90) 600, p. 13; resolutions of the European Parliament on the principle of

made – particularly by the *Länder* of the Federal Republic of Germany – for the principle of subsidiarity to be put into effect.[343] Such calls are being encouraged by the Community institutions themselves, which have declared themselves in favour of the observance of the principle of subsidiarity.[344]

However, the consensus to which all this testifies is merely verbal.[345] The understanding of the principle which prevails in the German *Länder* diverges considerably from that of the Commission. Whilst the *Länder* expect the principle of subsidiarity predominantly to mean the exercise of restraint by the Community institutions and non-interference with their powers,[346] the principle of subsidiarity is understood within the Commission as constituting a rational principle

---

(cont.)

subsidiarity dated 12 July 1990, OJ 1990 C 231, p. 163, and 21 November 1990, OJ 1990 C 324, p. 167; concluding statement of 30 November 1990 made at the conference in Rome of the parliaments of the European Community, EA 1991, D 21 *et seq.*, Nos 23-25; resolution of the Bundesrat (German Federal Council) on the establishment of Europe as a federal entity within the framework of political union, BR-Drs. 780/90 (Beschluß); see, now, Art. 3b of the EC Treaty as recast by the Treaty on European Union, signed on 7 February 1992, OJ 1992 C 191, p. 1.

343 See Schelter, pp. 217 *et seq.*; Stoiber, *EA 1987*, p. 551; the Munich declaration of the Conference of Minister-Presidents of 21-23 October 1987 on 'Federalism in the European Community – General Principles', para. I.2 (roneo copy); see also, as a prime example, the resolution of the Bundesrat on the communication from the Commission of the European Communities concerning Community action to promote rural tourism, BR-Drs. 223/91, in which the Bundesrat stated that the Commission was laying claim to powers which it did not possess or which did not take adequate account of the principle of subsidiarity; see also Hailbronner, *JZ 1990*, p. 153.

344 e.g. see the working programme of the Commission for 1991, *EC Bulletin* Supplement 1/91, p. 16, para. 3; the declaration by the President of the Commission, Jacques Delors, made at a meeting in Bonn with the Minister-Presidents of the German *Länder* on 19 May 1988, EA 1988, D 340 *et seq.*; in particular, the communication from the Commission concerning its action programme relating to the implementation of the Community charter of basic social rights for workers, COM(89) 568, p. 4, which states: 'In accordance with the principle of subsidiarity whereby the Community acts when the set objectives can be reached more effectively at its level than at that of the Member States ...'; Wägenbaur, *Rechtsprechung*, p. 172, who states that the Commission is increasingly recognizing the importance of the principle of subsidiarity for relations between the Community and the Member States; see also the Council resolution of 28 January 1991 on the Green Paper on the urban environment, OJ 1991 C 33, p. 4, para. 3; conclusions of the Council and the Ministers for Education meeting within the Council of 6 October 1989 on cooperation and Community policy in the field of education in the run-up to 1993, OJ 1989 C 277, p. 5, para. 2; Council decision of 21 December 1990 concerning the Media programme, OJ 1990 L 380, p. 37, twenty-second recital in the preamble.

345 For the substantive variants, see Heintzen, p. 318.

346 Schrenk, p. 392, takes the same view; e.g. see the Munich declaration of the Conference of Minister-Presidents (see n. 343, above), in which it was stated that the assumption of new tasks by the EC must be 'imperatively necessary in the interests of citizens'; see also the declaration of the Conference of Minister-Presidents, held in Munich on 20-21 December 1990, on 'Strengthening Federalism in Germany and Europe', para. III.1, according to which the EC can only be competent if a given task exceeds the powers existing at the lower level; see also, on the other hand, the submission by the Land of Baden-Württemberg concerning a resolution on the protection of the environment in the internal market, BR-Drs. 327/90, para. II.2, which contended that the principle of subsidiarity involves 'an appropriate division of tasks between the different levels of the Community'.

governing the allocation of tasks.[347] That difference has been cautiously expressed in the statement by Jacques Delors that he too supports the principle of subsidiarity, 'perhaps not in the exact sense applied to that term in German constitutional law, yet nevertheless in the sense that matters should only be regulated at European level if they can be better and more appropriately regulated at that level'.[348] In view of the lack of conceptual clarity, it is worth briefly examining the way in which the principle of subsidiarity has developed.

According to the generally accepted view, the principle of subsidiarity as we now know it originates from Catholic social doctrine;[349] its 'classic' formulation[350] appeared in Pope Pius XI's 1931 encyclical *Quadragesimo Anno*.[351] According to that formulation, it offends in particular against the concept of equity 'for a larger and higher organization to arrogate to itself functions which can be performed efficiently by smaller and lower bodies'. It is further stated that 'the true aim of all social activity should be to help individual members of the social body, but never to destroy or absorb them'.[352] It follows from this that the higher level should not appropriate a task unless and until it has first attempted, without success, to support the lower level in its own attempts to fulfil that task, that is to say, it has tried to place that lower level in a position of being able to act.[353]

That interpretation supports the view of the German *Länder* that the application of the principle of subsidiarity must be reflected generally in restraint on the part of the Community institutions when exercising their powers.[354] That view appears especially cogent with regard to Community activities in the cultural field, which – as has been demonstrated[355] – are characterized by the particular relevance of fundamental rights.[356] Häberle calls in straightforward terms for the recognition of a 'principle of subsidiarity in the cultural field',[357] whilst Rovan regards culture as a field which is, without any doubt, 'particularly

---

347 e.g. see Schmidhuber & Hitzler, p. 276, who contend that, under the principle of subsidiarity, the level at which action should in each case be taken is that at which it is possible 'to produce the best result at the least expense'; see also the quotation from the Commission communication on the Community charter of basic social rights (see n. 344, above); EC Commission, 'Communication on the Framework for Community Action in the 1990s in the Fields of Research and Development', SEC(89) 675 (reproduced as BR-Drs. 364/89), p. 7, according to which the Community should act if the relevant objectives can be more effectively achieved at Community level.

348 EA 1988, D 341.

349 See, to cite but a few examples, Millgramm, p. 744; Zuck, pp. 3 *et seq.*; Stadler, p. 12; Isensee, pp. 18 *et seq.*

350 According to Isensee, p. 18.

351 Published in English translation by the Catholic Truth Society (London, 1931).

352 *ibid.*, at p. 37.

353 For a concurring view, see V. Constantinesco, *Integration 1990*, p. 168.

354 In a similar vein, Kapteyn, p. 42, contends that the autonomy of the individual and social levels must be protected against unnecessary intervention by the State; Blanke, *ZG 1991*, p. 135, argues in favour of a system of protection for the Member States and the regions; Pechstein, *DÖV 1991*, p. 536, submits that the lower levels should enjoy maximum protection.

355 See 'The significance of fundamental rights in relation to the cultural field', pp. 211 *et seq.*, above.

356 As to the connection between fundamental rights and the principle of subsidiarity, see Merten, in: Benda et al., p. 780; Isensee, p. 313; Stadler, p. 81.

357 Häberle, *Europa in kulturverfassungsrechtlicher Perspektive*, p. 66.

ill-suited to centralistic rules imposed from above',[358] and as an area in which it is especially necessary to have regard to the principle of subsidiarity.[359]

It should be borne in mind, however, that the subsidiarity principle is of general application,[360] and that it constitutes, moreover, a principle of social philosophy founded on 'arguments based on the general rationality of mankind'.[361] Independent proof is therefore needed that it applies as a *legal* principle binding the Community institutions.

Since no express mention of the principle of subsidiarity is to be found in Community law, its general validity must be ascertained from indirect references. The first of these is contained in Article 130r(4) of the EEC Treaty, which requires the Community to 'take action relating to the environment to the extent to which the objectives referred to in paragraph 1 can be attained better at Community level than at the level of the individual Member States'. That wording has in fact been interpreted by numerous[362] commentators as an expression of the principle of subsidiarity.[363] This is surprising, in view of the meaning of the principle of subsidiarity mentioned above, because Article 130r(4) of the EEC Treaty cannot be interpreted as conferring priority on lower levels, since the wording of the provision is geared solely to the better fulfilment of tasks. It is the quality of the performance of the task which constitutes the object of protection and the criterion governing its allocation; there is nothing whatever to suggest any possible intention to protect lower levels, for example in the form of an additional restrictive proviso stating that the Community may *only* take action if it is better able to attain an objective than the Member States. This is all the more significant in that the absence of such a proviso affects the 'feel' of the language used, and can thus hardly be based on an unintended omission.[364] Some academics either overlook this[365] or underestimate its significance.[366]

Consequently, it comes as no surprise to find other commentators who conversely avoid linking the concept of the principle of subsidiarity to Article 130r(4) of the EEC Treaty and refer instead to the 'principle of the appropriate level for taking action'[367] or the 'principle of the optimum level of operation'[368] or describe the article in question simply as the 'better' clause.[369] Although it is necessary to conclude, therefore, that the principle of subsidiarity is not expressed by Article 130r(4) of the EEC Treaty, the use of the expression 'principle of subsidiarity' is – as Krämer rightly states – 'in no way objectionable, as long as no

---

358 Rovan, p. 104.
359 *ibid.*
360 See V. Constantinesco, *Integration* 1990, p. 168; Süsterhenn, p. 149.
361 See Süsterhenn, p. 142.
362 Schrenk, p. 392, goes too far in suggesting that this is virtually the universally held view.
363 e.g. see Wilke & Wallace, p. 3; Tomuschat, *F.I.D.E. Reports*, p. 40; Mischo, p. 685; Dauses, *BayVBl. 1989*, p. 615; Glaesner, *Umwelt*, p. 8; Merten, p. 34; V. Constantinesco, *Integration 1990*, p. 170; Knemeyer, *DVBl. 1990*, p. 450; Oschatz, p. 69.
364 The French and German versions of the Treaty likewise contain no such proviso.
365 e.g. Nicolaysen, *Europarecht I*, p. 128, who simply adds the word 'only'.
366 e.g. Klein, *VVDStRL 50 (1991)*, p. 73, who adds the word 'only' in parentheses.
367 See Grabitz & Zacker, pp. 299 and 302; Vitzthum, p. 287.
368 See Pernice, *DV 1989*, p. 35.
369 See Scheuing, *EuR 1989*, p. 164.

inferences are drawn from the concept of subsidiarity'.[370] It appears doubtful, however, whether this can be resisted. Lerche, for example, warns against the widespread 'tendency to decant global formulae into a positive constitution, in order thereafter to precipitate specific products'.[371]

Expressions of the principle of subsidiarity have been discerned not only in Article 130r(4) of the EEC Treaty but also in various other provisions of the Treaty. Articles 6 and 67,[372] 100,[373] 118a,[374] 128,[375] 130g,[376] 130t,[377] 189,[378] and 235[379] have been mentioned in this connection. Whilst it is questionable whether those provisions really bear the 'imprint' of the principle of subsidiarity, rather than merely according – more or less by chance – with the principle of subsidiarity, evidence would still be needed that the articles in question constitute the expression of a principle which underlies the Treaty *generally* and which the Community institutions are required to observe as a restriction on their competence. If general conclusions are to be drawn from individual rules, then both the analogy and the converse conclusion present themselves as logically equivalent.[380]

Any decision in favour of one solution rather than the other needs, therefore, to be justified with particular cogency. The principles governing the division of powers under the Treaty are particularly relevant in this regard. As has already been pointed out, Community law is geared towards dynamic development and expansion.[381] This would involve conflict with the recognition of a principle of subsidiarity necessitating the specific determination of the appropriate level in each individual case, since the dynamic of integration would be impeded.[382] The principle of subsidiarity, as a restriction on the exercise of competence, does not 'fit in' with the present system of European Community competence.[383] The appropriate level for taking action is determined in principle by Community law itself.[384]

This accords with the 'Community Charter of Basic Social Rights for Workers'[385] adopted by the Heads of State or Government of 11 Member States, the sixteenth recital in the preamble to which provides that, pursuant to the

---

370 Krämer, p. 142.

371 Lerche, p. 76. In a different connection, Herzog, *JuS 1967*, p. 194, likewise describes as extraordinary the process of inferring legal consequences from a device which was originally intended to serve an explanatory purpose only.

372 See Glaesner, *Umwelt*, p. 8.

373 See R. Geiger, *Stellung der Bundesländer*, p. 63; V. Constantinesco, *Integration 1990*, p. 168.

374 See Dauses, *BayVBl. 1989*, p. 615; Wilke & Wallace, p. 27.

375 See Dauses, op. cit.

376 See Giscard d'Estaing, p. 64.

377 See Dauses, op. cit.; Wilke & Wallace, p. 27.

378 See, in relation to directives, R. Geiger, *Stellung der Bundesländer*, p. 63; Jacqué & Weiler, p. 203; Kapteyn, p. 38.

379 See Dauses, op. cit.; R. Geiger, *Stellung der Bundesländer*, p. 63; Glaesner, *Umwelt*, p. 8.

380 See also Herzog, *Der Staat 1963*, p. 412; Zuck, p. 56.

381 See 'The dynamic of Community law', pp. 200 *et seq.*, above,

382 See also, in the same vein, Blanke, *ZG 1991*, p. 141.

383 See also Heintzen, p. 319; for a similar view, see Blanke, op. cit., p. 143.

384 See also Pernice, *DV 1989*, p. 34.

385 See the document bearing the same title (Office for Official Publications of the EC, Luxembourg, 1990).

principle of subsidiarity, the Member States and their regional authorities, and, within the framework of its powers, the European Community, are to be competent to achieve the realization of the social rights described in the Charter. That wording reflects the fact that, whilst the principle of subsidiarity may possibly have 'been a factor in the division of tasks and powers when the Community was established',[386] and the allocation of competence by the Treaty may itself be regarded as an expression of the principle of subsidiarity,[387] it cannot be recognized as a principle of law binding on the Community institutions which they are obliged to observe when exercising their powers.[388]

4. Restrictions Imposed by Public International Law

(a) Introduction

Restrictions on the exercise of Community competence in the cultural field arise not only from Community law itself but also from the rules of public international law, to which the Community is undeniably subject in its relations with third countries and international organizations.[389] In addition to its general obligations under international law, the Community is under a duty to respect its commitments under international agreements.[390] The following concise statements are restricted to a complex of problems which, in the context of Community practice, has become important in the cultural field, namely the question whether, and to what extent, the Community is bound by a principle of free trade under international law.

It is feared in some quarters that completion of the internal market will lead to free trade on the part of third countries being generally impaired by the Community: a situation encapsulated by the expression 'Fortress Europe'.[391] Specifically, the Community has been accused of infringing the principle of free trade by adopting the quota rules contained in the television directive.[392] That complaint is voiced principally by persons in the United States, who fear a deterioration in the export prospects of their domestic film industry.[393] The course adopted by the Community in this connection has been described as blatantly protectionist, unjustified and discriminatory towards the US and non-EC film industry.[394] The quota rules have also been criticized by European commentators, especially in Germany. According to Bullinger, for instance, the

---

386 Everling, *FS Karl Doehring*, p. 193.
387 See Pechstein, *DÖV 1991*, p. 539.
388 See also Bleckmann, *ZRP 1990*, p. 268; Eiselstein, *ZRP 1991*, p. 22.
389 See Simma & Vedda in: Grabitz *Kommentar zum EWGV*, Art. 210, n.17; also Everling, *Wirtschaftsbeziehungen*, p. 177, who describes this conclusion as 'banal, but not superfluous, since it frequently happens that insufficient regard is paid to it.
390 See, in relation to Community law relating to external economic matters, Everling, *ibid.*, p. 187.
391 See in that regard Müller-Huschke, p. 17.
392 For further details in that regard, see 'The binding force and legality of the quota rules', pp. 163 *et seq.*, above.
393 e.g. see Kleinsteuber, p. 550.
394 According to the United States trade delegate Carla Hills, NZZ, 13 October 1989.

quota rules are 'redolent of the spirit of French cultural *dirigisme*',[395] whilst Everling describes them as 'objectionable on the grounds of their culturally protectionist tendency'.[396]

At Community level, fears about a 'Fortress Europe' have been noted and attempts have been made to allay them. Thus the Presidency of the European Council held in Rhodes on 2–3 December 1988 stated that the internal market would not close itself off from the world outside, and that the Europe of 1992 would be a partner, not a 'Fortress Europe'.[397] The Commission has also confirmed the Community's interest in open and free world trade,[398] which is accounted for by the Community's heavy dependence on exports[399] and touched upon in the EEC Treaty itself (e.g. in the sixth recital in the preamble and in Article 110).

In discussing the protectionist conduct of the Community – especially as regards the quota rules – it is necessary to distinguish political arguments from legal ones. Where, for example, German commentators describe protectionism generally as 'economically inefficient'[400] or express the view that the quota rules are not a sensible measure of industrial policy, preferring instead active financial stimulation,[401] they are engaging in the political argument. The comments set forth below are concerned, however, solely with the legal aspects of the debate.

(b) The principle of free trade

(i) General public international law

The question arises, first of all, whether there exists any general rule of public international law requiring the Community to open its market to third countries. No such rule can be discerned. Instead, the position is governed by considerations of State sovereignty, the effect of which is in principle that, under international law, 'each State (may) freely stipulate the "conditions of entry" '.[402] This legal conclusion is bolstered by the practice of States whereby they resort to uniformly interventionist means in order to protect their domestic markets.[403] This can be seen particularly clearly in the field of agriculture, in which protectionism represents an almost 'universal principle'.[404]

It follows that the extent to which third countries may invoke freedom of trade under international law in their dealings with the Community depends on the existence and specific formulation of bilateral and multilateral rules set out in international agreements. This point is analyzed below by reference to the General

---

395 Bullinger, *Werbung und Quotenregelung*, p. 97.
396 Everling, *EuR 1990*, p. 217.
397 *EC Bulletin* 12/1988, para. 1.1.10.
398 *EC Bulletin* 10/1988, para. 1.2.3.
399 *ibid.*; see also Vedder in: Grabitz, *Kommentar zum EWGV*, introductory comments on Arts 110 *et seq.*, n.5; Hilf, *Europa '92*, p. 15.
400 See Oppermann & Beise, p. 451.
401 See Frohne, p. 396.
402 Meessen, p. 88.
403 See in that regard Adamantopoulos, p. 12.
404 See Rhein, p. 72.

Agreement on Tariffs and Trade (GATT),[405] the 'most important international instrument regulating world trade'.[406]

(ii) The General Agreement on Tariffs and Trade

As regards GATT – by contrast with the ECHR, for example[407] – it is undisputed that the Community is directly bound by its substantive provisions.[408] Generally, the Community is described as a *de facto* party' to it;[409] in a few rare cases, consideration has even been given to the idea of the Community having *de jure* membership of GATT.[410] That raises the question whether GATT may be said to contain a principle of free trade which might prevent, in principle, the adoption by the Community of measures in the cultural field which have protectionist objectives and affect international trade in goods.[411]

Put in those general terms, the question may be answered unhesitatingly in the affirmative: according to its preamble, the fundamental aim of GATT is to work towards 'reciprocal and mutually advantageous arrangements directed to the substantial reduction of tariffs and other barriers to trade and to the elimination of discriminatory treatment in international commerce'. The liberalization of international trade thus described is aimed at the attainment of various more remote goals which are also specified in the preamble, including the raising of living standards, the achievement of full employment and the expansion of the production and exchange of goods. All in all, therefore, it seems appropriate to describe the progressive liberalization of international trade as the 'basic idea'[412] or 'fundamental consensus'[413] underlying GATT.

It does not follow from this, however, that GATT has imposed on the contracting parties any direct obligation to liberalize trade or even to adopt '*laissez-faire*' liberalism.[414] Instead, GATT restricts itself merely to certain measures, such as the obligation under Article I to afford most-favoured-nation treatment, which are designed ultimately to *bring about* free trade.[415] In addition, GATT does in fact contain numerous exemptions and protective provisions[416] considered necessary 'in a world made up of relatively disparate trading partners'.[417]

---

405 Reproduced in 55–61 UNTS; Cmd. 7258.
406 See Vedder in: Grabitz, *Kommentar zum EWGV*, Art. 113, n. 192.
407 See, in that regard, 'The development of fundamental rights', pp. 212 *et seq.*, above.
408 See von Bogdandy, p. 15.
409 e.g. see Vedder in: Grabitz, *Kommentar zum EWGV*, Art. 113, n. 195; Benedek, p. 191.
410 See Bourgeois in: GTE, *Kommentar zum EWGV*, Art. 110, n. 3.
411 As it presently stands, GATT is concerned only with the movement of goods; see Bourgeois in: GTE, *Kommentar zum EWGV*, Art. 113, n. 173; Benedek, p. 37; for a critical view, see von Bogdandy, p. 15. Negotiations regarding the provision of services are being conducted in the context of the Uruguay Round; see Benedek, p. 38.
412 See Senti, p. 257.
413 See Benedek, p. 47.
414 See Petersmann, *EWG als GATT-Mitglied*, p. 132.
415 See Smeets, p. 196.
416 For further details, see Petersmann, op. cit., p. 132.
417 See Rhein, p. 78, who uses this as an argument against 'complete free trade'.

It is consequently impossible to draw any specific conclusions from the 'basic idea' of GATT with regard to the compatibility with GATT of individual measures adopted by the Community institutions. Instead, it is necessary in each case to undertake a precise analysis in the light of the individual Treaty provisions.

As regards the cultural field, it should be stated, first, that the cultural policy aims of a given measure do not fall to be considered in the context of that analysis. This is apparent, first, from Article IV of GATT, which expressly makes special provision for cinematographic films, doubtless because, as Jackson has stated, that product 'was more related to domestic cultural policies than to economics and trade',[418] and also from Article XX of GATT, paragraph (f) of which allows the imposition by the contracting parties of measures for the protection of national treasures of artistic, historic or archaeological value, subject however to the requirement that they are not applied in a manner which would constitute arbitrary or unjustifiable discrimination or a disguised restriction on international trade.

As regards, in particular, the television directive, von Bogdandy has shown that in the final analysis it infringes Article IV(b) of GATT, since it differentiates between supplying countries by favouring specific States which are not members of the Community[419] and consequently breaches the principle of most-favoured nation treatment.[420] Even if the quota rules were to be regarded as conforming with GATT, however, they could nevertheless serve as an example illustrating the general danger of the infringement of GATT provisions by Community measures in the cultural field.

In order to avoid that danger, the Community institutions must restrict themselves to measures for the promotion, in financial terms or otherwise, of areas of cultural trade selected *ad hoc*[421] or systematically defined, in a way which is permissible under Community law and unobjectionable in principle from the standpoint of GATT. Individual examples of *ad hoc* promotion have already been described at greater length above;[422] an instance of a systematic approach taking the form of a measure to promote Community industrial policy is to be found in the MEDIA programme of 21 December 1990,[423] which is expressly designed to foster the development of the European audio-visual industry, and which is aimed, according to Article 2, *inter alia* at increasing 'European production and distribution companies' share of world markets'.

---

418 Jackson, p. 293.

419 See Art. 6(1)(b) and (c) of the television directive (OJ 1989 L 298, p. 23).

420 von Bogdandy, p. 16; this is also, evidently, the view of Petersmann, *Uruguay Round*, p. 205, who refers, in connection with the television directive, to 'discriminatory market-sharing arrangements'. Doubts regarding its compatibility with GATT are also expressed by M. Seidel, *Europäische Rundfunkzone*, p. 145, and Everling, *EuR 1990*, pp. 217 *et seq.*

421 Oppermann, *Länderkulturhoheit*, p. 81, regards such acts as ultimately permissible under Community law, since he contends that culture constitutes the 'fundamental reason for European integration'.

422 See 'Individual measures', pp. 74 *et seq.*, above.

423 OJ 1990 L 380, p. 37.

Chapter 2

THE
COMMUNITY LAW
FRAMEWORK
FOR NATIONAL CULTURAL POLICY

I. THE BASIC PRINCIPLE

Part 3 of this work describes, in the light of the case-law of the Court of Justice, individual problems arising as a result of the application of Community law in the cultural field. It has emerged that measures regarded by the Member States as falling within their national cultural policy have to be assessed against the provisions of Community law, and must either be adapted or dispensed with, as the case may be. However, that does not alter the fact that competence for the formulation of national cultural policy, particularly in the narrower cultural field, lies in principle with the Member States.[1] The Court of Justice has defined the influence of Community law on the spheres of policy retained by the Member States by stating that the exercise of powers transferred to the Community is not limited by the fact that it may affect matters which do not *as such* fall within the competence of the Community institutions.[2]

The following section seeks, by means of individual conclusions drawn in Part 3 of this work in relation to the narrower cultural field, to define the framework of Community law which national cultural policy is required to respect.

---

1   See, to cite but one example, Everling, *Instrumente*, p. 23.

2   See the leading judgment of 3 July 1974 in Case 9/74 *Casagrande* [1974] ECR 773 (at p. 779); for a more detailed analysis of the division of powers, see 'Division of powers in the cultural field between the Community and the Member States', pp. 187 *et seq.*, above.

II. RESTRICTIONS IMPOSED BY COMMUNITY LAW

1. INTRODUCTION

Community law, which takes precedence over national law,[3] restricts the Member States' room for manoeuvre, primarily through those provisions of the Treaty which are directly applicable to the Member States and which require them to act, or to refrain from acting, in a particular manner. Such provisions include, first and foremost, the general prohibition of discrimination on grounds of nationality laid down in the first paragraph of Article 7 of the EEC Treaty,[4] as well as the fundamental freedoms enshrined in the Treaty and the rules on State aid. Member States may in addition find themselves restricted by provisions which are not addressed to them but to individuals. That possibility was indicated by the Court of Justice in its judgment of 10 January 1985 in Case 229/83 *Leclerc*,[5] in which it held that it was only the absence of a Community competition policy in the book sector which prevented it from inferring from Article 85 of the EEC Treaty, in conjunction with Article 5, the existence of a rule prohibiting the enactment of legislation on the fixing of book prices.[6] The following analysis is restricted, however, to an examination of the rules of Community law addressed to the Member States concerning the general prohibition of discrimination and the fundamental freedoms enshrined in the Treaty.

2. THE GENERAL PROHIBITION OF DISCRIMINATION

(a) Basics

The most significant restriction applied by Community law to national cultural policy may be said to reside in the general prohibition laid down in the first paragraph of Article 7 of the EEC Treaty, which has been described, by reason of its fundamental importance, as 'a *leitmotiv* of the entire Treaty'[7] and precludes, within the scope of application of the Treaty, all discrimination on grounds of nationality. This is because of the particular temptation, in fostering and promoting national culture, to apply nationality as a distinguishing criterion. However, the prohibition of discrimination laid down by the first paragraph of Article 7 of the EEC Treaty covers not only overt discrimination but also all forms of covert discrimination which, although based on criteria which appear to be neutral,[8] in

---

3   Judgment of the Court of Justice of 15 July 1964 in Case 6/64 *Costa* v. *ENEL* [1964] ECR 585 (at p. 594).

4   That prohibition applies both to the Community and to the Member States; see Zuleeg in: GTE, *Kommentar zum EWGV*, Art. 7, n. 18.

5   [1985] ECR 1.

6   *ibid.*, at p. 33; for a more detailed analysis, see 'The permissibility of price maintenance by order of the State', pp. 177 *et seq.*, above.

7   Wohlfahrt in: WEGS, *Die EWG*, Art. 7, n. 1.

8   See the judgment of the Court of Justice of 3 February 1982 in Joined Cases 62 and 63/81 *Seco* v. *Evi* [1982] ECR 223 (at p. 235).

fact achieve the same result.[9] The question whether there exists any *intention* to circumvent the prohibition of discrimination by applying apparently neutral criteria is irrelevant; the prohibition is sufficiently contravened if the application of such criteria leads 'in fact to the same result'[10] as overt discrimination on grounds of nationality.[11]

Discrimination prohibited by the first paragraph of Article 7 of the EEC Treaty may take the form not only of the different treatment of comparable situations but also of the treatment in the same way of situations which are not comparable.[12] The latter case involves at the same time covert discrimination.[13] Furthermore, discrimination on grounds of nationality, as prohibited under the Treaty, may be said to exist only where unequal treatment, based on nationality, of comparable situations, or equal treatment of dissimilar situations, is not objectively justified.[14]

(b) Influence on the Member States' room for manoeuvre in the field of cultural policy

The extent to which that general prohibition of discrimination may restrict the Member States' room for manoeuvre in the field of cultural policy is examined in greater detail below. This analysis deals first with measures which are overtly based on nationality, and thereafter with covert forms of discrimination.

(i) Overt discrimination

One example of measures overtly based on nationality in the field of cultural policy is to be found in the composition of national sports teams.[15] Another

---

9   Judgments of the Court of Justice of 30 May 1989 in Case 33/88 *Allué and Coonan* [1989] ECR 1591 (at p. 1610) and of 12 February 1974 in Case 152/73 *Sotgiu* [1974] ECR 153 (at p. 164).

10   *ibid.*

11   See also Zuleeg in: GTE, *Kommentar zum EWGV*, Art. 7, n. 5; a different view is expressed in Grabitz in: *idem*, *Kommentar zum EWGV*, Art. 7, n. 15.

12   Zuleeg in: GTE, *Kommentar zum EWGV*, Art. 7, n. 1.

13   See the judgment of the Court of Justice of 3 February 1982 in Joined Cases 62 and 63/81 *Seco* v. *Evi* [1982] ECR 223 (at p. 235), in which the extension by a Member State of a financial charge imposed on persons established in that State to persons established in another Member State who provided services in the first State was described as covert discrimination, since they were already liable to a comparable charge in their own State and thus ultimately had to bear a heavier burden than those established in the first State; in other words, similar treatment was being applied to dissimilar circumstances.

14   As the Court stated in its judgment of 12 February 1974 in Case 152/73 *Sotgiu* [1974] ECR 153 (at p. 164), in which it held that there was no covert discrimination on grounds of nationality where the unequal treatment in question could be justified by objective differences; see also the judgment of 16 October 1980 in Case 147/79 *Hochstrass* v. *Court of Justice* [1980] ECR 3005 (at p. 3019); Zuleeg in: GTE, *Kommentar zum EWGV*, Art. 7, n. 2; for a different view, see Grabitz in: *idem*, *Kommentar zum EWGV*, Art. 7, n. 11, and Marticke, p. 60, with whom it is only possible to concur in so far as it is more difficult to discern objective grounds for overt differentiation on grounds of nationality than for covert discrimination.

15   For a more detailed analysis, see 'Freedom of movement for professional sportspersons', pp. 168 *et seq.*, above.

example is national laws to promote the domestic film industry, which require or have in the past required, in certain fields, nationals of the country in question to be involved in the production of the films promoted.[16]

Both these examples have manifested themselves at Community level. As regards the composition of national teams, mention should be made of the judgments of the Court of Justice of 12 December 1974 in Case 36/74 *Walrave and Koch*[17] and of 14 July 1976 in Case 13/76 *Donà* v. *Mantero*;[18] as for the promotion of national film industries, reference is made to the Commission Decision of 21 December 1988 on aid granted by the Greek Government to the film industry for the production of Greek films.[19] In addition, the Commission has initiated State aid proceedings under Article 93(2) of the EEC Treaty in relation to the draft law presented by the German Government extending and amending the Film Promotion Law.[20]

Both cases are characterized by the fact that the complete exclusion, or at least the exclusion from certain major fields, of nationals of other Member States appears at first sight to be justified. However, it is also a feature common to both cases that they do not fall outside the scope of Community law by reason, for example, of the absence of any economic nexus. Such a nexus is clearly visible in the case of measures to promote film production which are expressly designed, as in German law, to further the economic, and not the cultural, aspects of film-making.[21] An economic dimension is also unmistakeably present, however, in the composition of national teams.[22]

Nevertheless, the Court of Justice has sought, where the composition of national teams is concerned, to apply a 'restriction on the scope of the provisions' of Community law.[23] That wording has been rightly interpreted as indicating that the Court of Justice was not seeking to apply any ground of justification *within* the scope of Community law, but rather that it removed the national provisions in question entirely from the scope of application of Community law.[24] The reason for this is that there was no possibility of justifying the provisions at issue within the scope of application of Community law.

This is clear if the matter is considered in the light of the basic principles of the general prohibition of discrimination, according to which, in the case of the composition of national teams, the overt criterion that they be made up of

---

16 Evidently, the only such requirements which still continue to exist at the present time are those laid down by the German Law on measures to promote German films (the Film Promotion Law) of 18 November 1986 (BGBl. I 2047), especially in Art. 15(2)(4); see Europe-Agence Internationale No. 5658 of 31 January 1992, p. 12.

17 [1974] ECR 1405.

18 [1976] ECR 1333.

19 OJ 1989 L 208, p. 38.

20 BT-Drs. 12/2021 of 30 January 1992; for further details, see Friccius, pp. 806 *et seq.* See also Europe-Agence Internationale No. 5658 of 31 December 1992, p. 12.

21 See the statement of reasons of the German Government in relation to the Draft Second Law amending the Film Promotion Law, BT-Drs. 12/2021 of 30 January 1992, p. 14.

22 For a more detailed analysis, see 'Freedom of movement for professional sportspersons', pp. 168 *et seq.*, above.

23 Judgment of 12 December 1974 in Case 36/74 *Walrave and Koch* [1974] ECR 1405 (at p. 1419).

24 See, to that effect, Marticke, p. 60.

nationals of the country concerned could be justified only on an objective ground. It goes without saying that that objective ground is not that a national team should consist only of nationals of the country concerned. That would be a circular argument.[25] The ground justifying unequal treatment must exist independently of the mere intention to discriminate.

In actual fact, however, the only reason for restricting membership of a national team to nationals of the country concerned is to be found in the very fact of possession of that nationality, which enables a nation to identify with the team in question in victory and in defeat and thereby to develop or assert its national identity.[26] If, therefore, the composition of national teams for sports purposes involves the nurturing of national identity, then the point of contact with the restriction of the scope of Community law applied by the Court of Justice must in the final analysis be the existence of the Member States and their national identity as such, as recognized by Community law.[27] So long as the Community is made up of States, it will continue to be necessary, on the basis of the case-law of the Court of Justice, and despite the reservations expressed at greater length above,[28] to accept the feelings engendered by membership of a nation and by official national consciousness, even where participation in the relevant events has some economic significance. Care should nonetheless be taken in that regard to ensure that the restriction of the scope of application of Community law is consonant with the principle of proportionality.

The above remarks cannot apply, however, to the field of film promotion, since that sphere does not involve – as in the case of national teams – merely the national consciousness of the collaboration of nationals of the country concerned. Instead, the promotion of a national film industry is primarily concerned – as the German Government has stated – with 'the way in which we put across to ourselves our society, our identity, our ideas',[29] i.e. the portrayal of the national cultural area.[30] However, it is not necessary for those purposes to lay down the criterion of possession of the nationality of the country concerned, which is a *legal* status and amounts at best to a rebuttable presumption of the fitness of the person possessing it to represent the national cultural area. Accordingly, insistence on possession of the nationality of the country concerned cannot be justified in the case of national rules designed to promote the portrayal of the national cultural area, since nationality is not an appropriate means of attaining the goal pursued.

---

25 For a more detailed analysis in this regard, see 'Freedom of movement for professional sportspersons', pp. 168 *et seq.*, above.

26 See, to this effect, Klose, p. 159.

27 See, to cite but one example, the first sentence of Art. 36 of the EEC Treaty, which refers to the protection of *national* treasures possessing artistic, historic or archaeological value.

28 See the final paras of 'Freedom of movement for professional sportspersons', pp. 168 *et seq.*, above.

29 See the statement of reasons submitted in relation to the Draft Second Law amending the Film Promotion Law, BT-Drs. 12/2021 of 30 January 1992, p. 14.

30 See Art. 15(2)(4) of the Film Promotion Law, according to which German films may be directed not only by those possessing German nationality but also by members of the German cultural area.

(ii) Covert discrimination

Whilst we have hitherto been concerned with national measures relating to cultural policy which are overtly linked to possession of the nationality of the Member State concerned, it is now proposed to examine the permissibility under Community law of rules which are linked to criteria other than nationality and, although ostensibly affording equal treatment to nationals of the Member State concerned and nationals of other Member States affected by the criterion in question, actually amount to covert discrimination on grounds of nationality.

An instance of this is once again to be found in measures for the promotion of national films. Only very rarely do they overtly impose the criterion of possession of the nationality of the country concerned, but they may require, for example, that the producer be resident in that country, that the film be shot in studios situated in that country, or that it be produced in the national language.[31] Such requirements will be contrary to the prohibition of discrimination on grounds of nationality if they in fact lead to the same result as rules based overtly on nationality and cannot be justified on objective grounds.

Of the three requirements referred to immediately above, the first two can be distinguished as acceptable from the standpoint of Community law, provided that the Commission declares, pursuant to Article 92(3)(c) of the EEC Treaty, that the film promotion measure in question is compatible in principle with the Common Market.[32] This is because the criteria that the producer must be resident in the country concerned and that the film must be shot in studios situated in that country are linked to the existence of State aid, which is indeed concerned with State measures to promote the *domestic* economy.[33]

On the other hand, the third requirement, namely that a film be produced in the national language, gives rise to problems. That condition is in principle liable to result in covert discrimination on grounds of nationality, since nationals of the State concerned are as a general rule more likely to be able to satisfy the language requirement than foreigners.[34] The question therefore arises whether that condition attaching to the promotion of a film can be justified on any objective ground.

The representation of the national cultural area, referred to above, falls to be considered as one such objective ground. This is because Community law does not in principle preclude the Member States from preserving their national culture. This was stated by the Court of Justice in its judgment of 28 November 1989 in Case 379/87 *Groener*[35] in relation to a national policy for the promotion of the national and first official language in the public education system,[36] and even the

---

31 e.g. see Art. 15 of the Film Promotion Law.

32 That possibility is referred to by the Commission in its decision of 21 December 1988 on aid granted by the Greek Government to the film industry for the production of Greek films; see OJ 1989 L 208, p. 40.

33 In practice, even the Commission is prepared to assume that it is compatible with Community law to make the grant of aid subject to the condition that the film which is being promoted is shot and made in studios situated in the State granting the aid; see *ibid.*

34 For a concurring view, see Sparr, p. 35.

35 [1989] ECR 3967.

36 *ibid.*, at p. 3993.

Commission regards the promotion of the national language as a legitimate interest of the Member States.[37]

However, the Member States are required in that regard to confine themselves to measures which are proportionate in relation to the implementation of the policy pursued.[38] This was denied by the Commission in its above-mentioned decision regarding the requirement that the original version of a film should be produced in Greek: it stated that it should be made possible, notably by dubbing techniques, for persons without a command of Greek to take part in the making of a Greek film.[39] The question whether 'the link between language and acting and between language and actors (is) of essential significance for the production of a specific Greek film'[40] ultimately depends on the quality of the dubbing.

In sum, it may therefore be stated that measures adopted by the Member States which in practice treat their own nationals more favourably than other EC nationals do not contravene the prohibition of discrimination, provided that they are designed to safeguard national culture and are proportionate.[41]

3. THE FUNDAMENTAL FREEDOMS

(a) The prohibition of discrimination and the exceptions thereto

(i) General considerations

According to the wording of the general prohibition of discrimination laid down by the first paragraph of Article 7 of the EEC Treaty, it is applicable 'without prejudice to any special provisions contained [in the Treaty]'. Specific forms of the general prohibition of discrimination are to be found within the EEC Treaty in the provisions on freedom of movement for workers and freedom to provide services[42] and also in those on freedom of establishment.[43] In contrast, the free movement of goods, in particular the prohibition of quantitative restrictions on imports and measures having equivalent effect set out in Article 30 of the EEC Treaty, does not constitute an embodiment of the general prohibition of discrimination, since the prohibition is linked not to the nationality of the producer or trader but to the origin of the goods.[44] Consequently, where reference is made hereafter simply to the prohibition of discrimination, that distinction must be borne in mind.

The prohibition of discrimination embodied in all fundamental freedoms is

---

37   See the Commission decision, op cit., n. 32.

38   Judgment of the Court of Justice of 28 November 1989 in Case 379/87 *Groener* [1989] ECR 3967 (at pp. 3993 *et seq.*).

39   See n. 32, above.

40   Sparr, p. 35, answers this in the affirmative – unlike the Commission.

41   This is also, in the final analysis, the conclusion reached by Sparr, p. 35; however, he is obliged to resort to extralegal arguments in order to justify that conclusion, since he does not regard it as possible to justify on objective grounds overt or covert discrimination based on nationality (p. 26).

42   As the Court of Justice held in its judgment of 12 December 1974 in Case 36/74 *Walrave and Koch* [1974] ECR 1405 (at p. 1418).

43   Zuleeg in: GTE, *Kommentar zum EWGV*, Art. 7, n. 20.

44   For a concurring view, see Bleckmann, *Europarecht*, p. 504.

subject, as a result of express provisions of the Treaty, to certain exceptions, which may also be of significance in relation to cultural policy measures adopted by the Member States. These include Articles 36, 48(3) and (4), 55 and 56 (in conjunction with Article 66). A common feature of all the derogations in the Treaty from the prohibition of discrimination is that they must be construed strictly and cannot be relied on for economic purposes.[45]

(ii) The permissibility of the protection of national treasures

The first sentence of Article 36 of the EEC Treaty is the only provision of Community law which expressly takes account of the cultural concerns of the Member States; it therefore merits a brief examination. That provision allows the Member States to apply prohibitions or restrictions on imports, exports or goods in transit justified on grounds of the protection of national treasures of artistic, historic or archaeological value. The Court of Justice has rejected a broad interpretation of the protection of national treasures permitted by that provision. For example, it does not cover the protection of creativity and cultural diversity in the national field of book publishing.[46]

Competence to define what constitutes a national treasure of artistic, historic or archaeological value lies in principle with the individual Member States, since the safeguarding of 'their' cultural heritage is involved.[47] This does not, however, prevent national decisions from being reviewed in the light of Community law,[48] as is clear from the prohibition of arbitrary discrimination and disguised restrictions on trade expressly laid down in the second sentence of Article 36 of the EEC Treaty.

Within the limits traced by the Court of Justice, the Member States still have leeway in future to impose restrictions on the free movement of goods pursuant to the first sentence of Article 36 of the EEC Treaty. Admittedly, the Commission has submitted proposals for two legal acts relating to the export of national cultural goods out of the Community and the return of cultural objects unlawfully removed from the territory of a Member State,[49] which are designed to take account of the removal of internal border controls with effect from 1 January 1993. However, those acts will not remove the Member States' power in future to pray in aid that they are acting to protect national treasures referred to in the first sentence of Article 36 of the EEC Treaty.[50]

The rules proposed by the Commission are intended merely to supplement Member States' provisions relating to the protection of the national cultural heritage.[51] Moreover, unlike in the case of other protected national objects, the

---

45   e.g. see, as regards Art. 36 of the EEC Treaty, 'Principles', pp. 144 et seq., above, and, as regards Art. 56, 'Permissible restrictions on the free movement of television broadcasts', pp. 157 et seq., above.
46   See 'Principles', pp. 144 et seq., above.
47   As the Commission rightly stated in its Communication on 'The Protection of National Treasures Possessing Artistic, Historic or Archaeological Value: Needs Arising from the Abolition of Frontiers in 1992', COM(89) 594, p. 4.
48   For a concurring view, see Pescatore, RDTE 1985, p. 457.
49   OJ 1992 C 53, pp. 8 and 11 respectively; COM(91) 447.
50   COM(91) 447, p. 2.
51   ibid., p. 5.

harmonization throughout the Community of the corresponding national rules would not eliminate recourse to the possibility, afforded by the first sentence of Article 36 of the EEC Treaty, of restricting the free movement of goods on grounds of the protection of national treasures, since a Community-wide standard of protection does not mean that there is such a thing as Community treasures. Not until the existence of Community treasures is recognized, replacing the individual national treasures, will recourse to the first sentence of Article 36 of the EEC Treaty be rendered superfluous.[52]

(b) The prohibition of restrictions and the exceptions thereto

(i) General considerations

It has become recognized in the meantime that there is inherent, at least within the ambit of the free movement of goods and freedom to provide services, a general prohibition of restrictions which goes beyond the prohibition of discrimination. As a result of the recognition by Community law of such a widely construed sphere of freedom, it has become necessary to allow the Member States, within specific limits, to invoke public interests in order to justify the application, without distinction, of rules which, whilst non-discriminatory, nevertheless restrict intra-Community trade.[53] However, in so far as such rules affect domestic and imported products, or, as the case may be, nationals and non-nationals in completely the same way – i.e. to the extent to which they do not impose on foreign trade more onerous changes or rearrangements – the Court of Justice does not reason on the basis of whether the rules in question are justified by the public interest, but instead applies a less stringent test, namely, whether such rules are 'consistent with the objectives of public interest pursued by the Treaty'.[54]

The demarcation between non-discriminatory and covertly discriminatory rules gives rise to difficulties, since, formally, both types of rules are applicable without distinction.[55] One test for non-discriminatory rules is to be found in the judgment of the Court of Justice of 20 February 1979 in Case 120/78 ('Cassis de Dijon'), in which it held that it was necessary to accept certain obstacles to trade within the Community 'resulting from disparities between the national laws relating to the marketing of the products in question'.[56] In the final analysis, this addresses the fact that the application of national rules stops at the frontier, and

---

52 As the Commission has rightly pointed out (see n. 47, above).

53 See 'Principles', pp. 139 et seq., above, and 'Permissible restrictions on the free movement of television broadcasts', pp. 157 et seq., above.

54 See the judgment of 23 November 1989 in Case C-145/88 *Torfaen Borough Council* [1989] ECR 3851 (at p. 3889); see also 'Influence on Member States' decisions regarding cultural policy', pp. 142 et seq., above.

55 This is rightly pointed out by Sparr, p. 44; however, the distinction drawn by him between cases in which the exercise of basic freedoms is prevented (covert discrimination) and those in which it is merely rendered more difficult (no discrimination) is not convincing; for an example of the existence of covert discrimination despite equality of treatment, see the judgment of the Court of Justice of 6 November 1984 in Case 177/83 *Kohl* [1984] ECR 3651 (at p. 3663).

56 [1979] ECR 649 (at p. 662).

thus the fact that the Community still consists of different States possessing legal systems whose effectiveness is limited to their territory.

Consequently, a non-discriminatory rule, applicable without distinction, may in principle be said to exist where it applies in fact, and not merely formally, to nationals or domestic products. However, the application of such a rule may give rise to covert discrimination if the public interest concerned has already been taken into account in similar rules adopted by the other Member State.[57]

As we have already observed with regard to the restrictions entailed by the prohibitions of discrimination attaching to the fundamental freedoms enshrined in the Treaty, the public interest justification may not be invoked for economic purposes.[58]

(ii) Asserting the cultural interests of the Member States

This raises the question of the extent to which it is open to the Member States to rely on grounds of cultural policy in order to justify non-discriminatory rules, applying without distinction, which impede intra-Community trade. Here again, it is necessary to distinguish between cases in which an obstacle affects domestic and foreign trade factors alike and those in which certain more onerous burdens are imposed on the latter.

The first group of cases formed the subject-matter of the judgments of the Court of Justice of 11 July 1985 in Joined Cases 60 and 61/84 *Cinéthèque*[59] and of 23 November 1989 in Case C-145/88 *Torfaen Borough Council*.[60] In the first of those judgments, the Court classified the priority afforded to the exploitation of films in cinemas as unobjectionable under Community law, without giving any further reasons for its view.[61] It made a similar finding in the second judgment, concerning a ban on Sunday trading. Accordingly, it may be stated that measures adopted by the Member States on grounds of cultural policy which fall within the ambit of the cases dealt with here will be compatible with Community law if they are proportionate and do not run counter to the general objectives of the Treaty.

On the other hand, national rules which impose a more onerous burden on foreign traders than on domestic traders can be justified only on the ground of a public interest recognized by the Court of Justice. The Court has expressly stated on a number of occasions in recent times that even obstacles to the fundamental freedoms which are motivated by considerations of cultural policy may be valid under Community law. In its judgment of 26 February 1991 in Case C-154/89 *Commission* v. *France*,[62] it held that the appreciation of places and things of historical interest and the widest possible dissemination of knowledge of the artistic and cultural heritage of a Member State are capable of justifying a

---

57 See, in relation to freedom to provide services, 'Permissible restrictions on the free movement of television broadcasts', pp. 157 *et seq.*, above.

58 For a concurring view, see Currall, p. 173.

59 [1985] ECR 2605.

60 [1989] ECR 3851.

61 [1985] ECR 2605 (at p. 2626).

62 [1991] ECR I-659.

restriction on freedom to provide services.[63] In the judgment of 25 July 1991 in Case C-288/89 *Collectieve Antennevoorziening Gouda* ('*Mediawet*'),[64] it expressed with even greater clarity the view that a national cultural policy may constitute a mandatory requirement relating to the general interest.[65]

The fact that in those cases cultural policy requirements were recognized as possibly being mandatory requirements relating to the general interest cannot, however, be interpreted as meaning that the Member States are henceforth at liberty to invoke generally the cultural policy objectives of national rules in order to neutralize, under Community law, their restrictive effect on the fundamental freedoms. Whilst the determination of the objectives of national cultural policy is a matter for the Member States,[66] that does not mean that rules described by the Member States as relating to cultural policy are exempt from scrutiny under Community law.

Such scrutiny involves, first of all, the determination of the real aim lying behind the general cultural policy motive. As has already been stated, that aim may on no account be economic in nature. If a non-economic objective is involved, however, the proportionality of the relevant rules must be comprehensively examined. The fact that the aim is being pursued in the context of a national cultural policy is in any event irrelevant for the purposes of the assessment of the real aim from the standpoint of Community law. This was made clear by the Court of Justice in the judgment in Case C-288/89 ('*Mediawet*'),[67] in which it held that a cultural policy *understood in that sense* may constitute a mandatory requirement relating to the general interest.[68] In so stating, the Court was referring to the submissions of the Netherlands Government, in which it had specified the substance of the cultural policy pursued by it in the media sector.[69]

To sum up, it may be stated, therefore, that the Member States are not in principle precluded from restricting the exercise of basic freedoms in order to protect their cultural interests, provided that domestic and external trade are treated in the same way, the objective pursued is of a non-economic nature and the measures adopted do not go beyond what is necessary in order to achieve that objective.

---

63   [1991] ECR I-659, para. 17.
64   [1991] ECR I-4007.
65   *ibid.*, para. 23.
66   See 'The basic principle', pp. 237 *et seq.*, above.
67   [1991] ECR I-4007.
68   *ibid.*, para. 23.
69   *ibid.*, para. 22.

Chapter 3

THE LEGAL SIGNIFICANCE
OF INDIVIDUAL FORMS OF ACTION
IN THE CULTURAL FIELD

I. INTRODUCTION

It is apparent from the survey of Community activity in the cultural field contained in Part 2 of this work that in the three spheres of education and training, science, and culture in the narrower sense, considerable use is made, to a greater or lesser extent, of forms of action for which no express provision is made in the EEC Treaty. Indeed, as regards the Council and the Commission, it may be stated that binding legal acts of the kind referred to in Article 189 of the EEC Treaty, or proposals submitted by the Commission in relation to them, form, at least in the fields of education and training and of culture in the narrower sense, the exception rather than the rule. At Council level, regarded as the level combining acts of the Council in its capacity as an institution and joint action by the Member States which relates in terms of its form or substance to the Community, it is resolutions which predominate.[1] The Commission frequently addresses communications to the other Community institutions, whilst the European Parliament likewise acts by means of resolutions.

This finding raises the question of the legal significance of the forms of action referred to. The subject is generally shrouded in considerable uncertainty, reflected, in particular, by the fact that the forms of action in question are

---

[1] Mention should be made here of a further form of action at Council level, namely 'conclusions', which features to an appreciable extent; however, they appear to differ from resolutions only inasmuch as they are even less subject to formal requirements; see also Craeyenest, p. 128, who considers that conclusions are analogous to resolutions; also Everling, *GS Léontin-Jean Constantinesco*, p. 138, who, having mentioned conclusions in n. 29, goes on to refer to them simply as resolutions.

described as 'soft law'[2] – a term which is not a legal concept but a notion possessing 'the diffuse and deliberately provocative nature of a catchphrase',[3] and on which there exists considerable differences of opinion.[4] Consequently, certain academics rightly advise against the use of the term.[5]

The legal substance of the forms of action in question is examined in greater detail below. The first part of the analysis discusses general principles applying only to acts of the Community institutions. It is followed by a more specific examination of the individual forms of action in respect of each institution, in the course of which consideration is also given to joint action by the Member States.

II. GENERAL OBSERVATIONS ON THE ACTS OF THE COMMUNITY INSTITUTIONS

1. The Binding Force of the Act in Question

The concept of an 'act' in the widest sense of the term covers all activities of the Community institutions, whether or not they are binding and whether or not they are of a legal nature. Before any differentiation is made between legal and non-legal acts, it is necessary to distinguish between acts which are binding and those which are not. This is because any statement concerning the binding force of an act must apply equally to legal and non-legal acts: on the one hand, a non-binding act is non-binding in every respect, i.e. from both a legal and a non-legal standpoint; on the other hand, an act which has binding force may be binding both from a legal and a non-legal point of view. A finding that an act has binding force should not in any circumstances be taken to mean that it is necessarily binding *in law*,[6] since not only binding legal obligations are conceivable but also non-legal obligations – social, moral, religious or political obligations, for example.[7]

As regards the criteria for determining whether an act is binding, the decisive factor is the intention, if any, on the part of the author of the act to give it binding

---

2   e.g. see Lenz, *Zuständigkeiten und Initiativen*, pp. 186 *et seq.*; Wägenbaur, *EuR 1990*, p. 140; Oppermann, *Europäisches Gemeinschaftrecht und Deutsche Bildungsordnung*, p. 21.

3   Thürer, p. 433.

4   See, on the one hand, Thürer, p. 434, who considers that it includes norms 'which, whilst not binding in law, nevertheless have certain legal effects or come close to being law'; Ehricke, p. 1907, who describes 'soft law' as being 'the commitment – similar to a legal commitment – embodied by a norm jointly created or supported by a subject of international law which in fact, however, is not binding in law'; a contrary view is taken by Heusel, p. 317, who contends that the phrase 'soft law' should be used only for obligations which are worded in especially soft terms but which nonetheless constitute legal obligations.

5   See Schröder, p. 41; also, from the specific standpoint of Community law, Everling, *GS Léontin-Jean Constantinesco*, p. 150.

6   See primarily in that regard Bothe, *NYIL 1980*, pp. 67 *et seq.*; *idem, FS Hans-Jürgen Schlochauer*, pp. 768 *et seq.*

7   See Bothe, *NYIL 1980*, pp. 65 *et seq.*

force.[8] The question whether there exists an intention to give an act binding force needs to be determined in each individual case by interpretation. One significant indication of an intention to give an act binding force is the degree of precision and particularity of the formulation of the act in question. An act which lacks precision in the way in which it is formulated will not only not be binding in law but will have no binding force whatever,[9] whilst even a non-legal act may contain provisions which are precise and specific and capable of having binding force.[10] It is therefore obvious that for an act to have binding legal force it must exhibit the same precision in its formulation.[11]

A finding that an act is binding in some way or other is not in itself enough to characterize that act; it merely represents a notional intermediate step and cannot really be separated in practice from the question of the legal or non-legal nature of the binding force of the act, which is considered below.

2. The Legal Nature of an Act

(a) The need to distinguish between legal and non-legal acts

The question has been raised in relation to public international law whether it may not be futile to seek to differentiate between norms of a legal nature and those of a non-legal nature.[12] That question arises because of the special nature of international law: subjects of international law cannot in principle be compelled to comply with it, whether international law is complied with depends on the will of its subjects to observe it,[13] and there is no obligatory authority dealing with the interpretation of international law.[14] The position is different, however, at least in the latter respect, in the field of European Community law. According to Article 164 of the EEC Treaty, the Court of Justice of the European Communities is to ensure that 'in the interpretation and application of this Treaty the law is observed'.

Thus the function entrusted to the Court is solely to ensure observance of the law, and not compliance with non-legal norms. For that reason alone, the opening question in this section must be answered in the negative: as far as the field of

---

8   See also Everling, *Probleme*, p. 422; *idem, GS Léontin-Jean Constantinesco*, p. 155; Morand, p. 627, who states: 'Il faut examiner si l'organe communautaire a manifesté d'une façon ou d'autre son intention de se lier lui-même ou de lier les destinataires de l'acte' (It is necessary to examine whether the Community institution has indicated in any way its intention to bind itself or to bind the addressees of the act).

9   As is rightly pointed out by Heusel, p. 237.

10   *ibid.*, p. 159.

11   See the judgment of the Court of Justice of 10 April 1984 in Case 108/83 *Luxembourg* v. *European Parliament* [1984] ECR 1945, in which the Court held that a resolution of the European Parliament was effective in law on the ground of its 'specific and precise decision-making character' (at p. 1958); see also Glaesner, *Einführung*, p. 49, who states that, in order to have legal effects, a decision must be sufficiently precise in terms of its substance and particularity.

12   See Thürer, p. 440.

13   *ibid.*

14   See Hailbronner, *Entwicklungstendenzen*, p. 23.

Community law is concerned, the question whether a norm is or is not of a legal nature cannot be left open. There are no blurred transitions between law and non-law. The binding force of an act must be either legal or non-legal.[15] It is not legitimate, by reason of practical difficulties in determining the nature of a binding act, to refer to a 'twilight zone' between law and non-law.[16]

(b) Criteria for distinguishing between legal and non-legal acts

In view of the foregoing statement that, in order for an act to have binding force, it is essential that it should have been intended to have such force, it follows that the nature of its binding effects is also dictated by the intention of the institution which adopts the act.[17] The position is the same where the question is not specifically whether an act is to have legally binding force but the general one of whether it is actually intended to have any legal effect. That view accords with the case-law of the Court of Justice, which has held that legal protection must be available under Article 173 of the EEC Treaty 'in the case of all measures adopted by the institutions, whatever their nature or form, which are intended to have legal effects'.[18]

However, it is only possible to have regard to the intention of the institution which adopts the act if that intention is apparent from the act under consideration. The decisive factor in that regard is the way in which the addressee of the act may reasonably be expected to understand it.[19] A claim made *ex post* that the act in question merely involved 'declarations of intent having political rather than legal significance'[20] is irrelevant.[21] Where an act does not contain a clear statement by the institution adopting it as to the nature of the effect which it is designed to have, that effect is to be determined by means of interpretation.[22] In that regard, the form of an act may at best serve as an indication.[23] Primarily, however, it is necessary to look at its 'meaning, subject-matter and content'[24] – in other words, to

---

15   As is correctly stated by Thürer, p. 441; Bothe, *NYIL 1980*, p. 94; Heusel, p. 287.

16   Although that is the line taken by Tomuschat, *ZaöRV 1976*, p. 484.

17   See also Bothe, *NYIL 1980*, pp. 67 and 94; Heusel, p. 291; Wellens & Borchardt, p. 296; Morand, p. 627.

18   Judgment of 31 March 1971 in Case 22/70 *Commission* v. *Council* ('AETR') [1971] ECR 263 (at p. 277); with particular regard to acts of the European Parliament, see the judgment of 23 April 1986 in Case 294/83 *Les Verts* v. *European Parliament* [1986] ECR 1339 (at p. 1366); Opinion of Advocate-General Lenz of 25 April 1991 in Joined Cases C-213/88 and C-39/89 *Luxembourg* v. *European Parliament* [1991] ECR I-5643.

19   See Daig in: GBTE, *Kommentar zum EWGV*, Art. 189, n. 83.

20   As the Council argued in Case 22/70 *Commission* v. *Council* [1971] ECR 263 (at p. 267).

21   In its judgment of 31 March 1971 in Case 22/70 *Commission* v. *Council* ('AETR') [1971] ECR 263 (at p. 278), the Court consequently held that the proceedings of the Council could not have been simply the expression or the recognition of voluntary coordination, but were designed to lay down a course of action binding on both the institutions and the Member States, and thus produced specific legal effects.

22   See also Heusel, p. 291.

23   e.g. see Daig in: GBTE, *Kommentar zum EWGV*, Art. 189, nn. 54 and 83 (*in fine*); Wellens & Borchardt, p. 301.

24   L.-J. Constantinesco, p. 588, in relation to the demarcation of legal acts *inter se*. This does not prevent the same criteria from being used to differentiate between legal and non-legal acts.

focus on the 'content of a decision according to its substance and specific terms'.[25]

The Court of Justice likewise assesses the legal effects of an act primarily in the light of its content. Thus it held in its judgment of 14 December 1962 in Joined Cases 16/62 and 17/62 *Confédération Nationale des Producteurs de Fruits* v. *Council*[26] that it could not restrict itself to considering the official title of a measure, but must first take into account its object and content.[27] In its judgment of 24 October 1973 in Case 9/73 *Schlüter*,[28] it found, in relation to a resolution adopted by the Council, that that resolution could not '*by reason of its content*, create legal consequences'.[29] In its judgment of 10 April 1984 in Case 108/83 *Luxembourg* v. *Parliament*,[30] the Court stated in relation to a resolution of the European Parliament that '*consideration of the content* of the resolution' revealed that it produced legal effects.[31] Finally, in its judgment of 13 December 1989 in Case C-322/88 *Grimaldi*,[32] it held that the choice of form cannot alter the nature of a measure, but that it is necessary to ascertain whether the content of a measure is in fact consistent with the form attributed to it.[33]

The decisive nature of the content of an act, but not of its form or designation, is confirmed by the second paragraph of Article 173 of the EEC Treaty, which provides for the possibility that a 'decision' within the meaning of the fourth paragraph of Article 189 of the Treaty may be adopted 'in the form of a regulation'. In addition to the possibility that the act as a whole may be wrongly described, it is conceivable that an act which in principle is correctly designated may contain elements the legal nature of which proves to be different from that suggested by its description.[34] By the same token, it is conceivable that a legal act may contain provisions of a non-legal nature.

Consequently, whether an act is legal or non-legal will depend on the specific interpretation of the measure in question; it is not possible, in principle, to lay down any rules of general application. In particular, there can be no presumption, *in cases of doubt*, that the Community institutions intended to adopt a *legal* act. Admittedly, the entire EEC Treaty is intended to bring about integration through law.[35] It is not possible, however, to state with any certainty whether, in an individual case, a Community institution intended to make use of powers to adopt

---

25 Glaesner, *Einführung*, p. 49. A different view is expressed by Zuleeg, *JöR 1971*, p. 14, who argues that, if it appears from its designation that a decision is intended not to have binding force, then for reasons of legal clarity no greater weight should be attached to the wording of its contents.

26 [1962] ECR 471.

27 *ibid.*, at p. 478.

28 [1973] ECR 1135.

29 *ibid.*, at p. 1161; emphasis added.

30 [1984] ECR 1945.

31 *ibid.*, at p. 1958; emphasis added.

32 [1989] ECR 4407.

33 *ibid.*, at p. 4420.

34 See the judgment of 14 December 1962 in Joined Cases 16 and 17/62 *Confédération Nationale* [1962] ECR 471 (at p. 479); Grabitz, *Quellen des Gemeinschaftsrechts*, p. 96.

35 Bleckmann, *RIW 1991*, p. 219; see also, to the same effect, Zuleeg, *NVwZ 1987*, p. 281, who contends that the EC is a legal community, and that the political will which finds expression at supranational level must therefore assert itself in the Member States principally through the vehicle of law; also Karl, p. 598, who argues in favour of the primacy of the principle that relations within the Community are shaped on the basis of binding legal rules.

legal acts which are provided for in the Treaty or conferred by it. Exceptionally, however, the legal nature of an act must be inferred where it is intended to introduce some change in the *legal* sphere.[36]

(c) Determination of the ability of an act to have legal effects

The Court of Justice assesses whether an act of a Community institution may have legal effects when considering the admissibility of an application for its annulment. That the act is capable of having such effects is therefore necessary in order for the application to be admissible.[37] That does not preclude the possibility that, in the specific circumstances of a given case, whether an act is capable of having legal effects, and thus whether an action for its annulment is admissible, may depend on whether the action is well-founded.[38] However, when the action fails on the merits, the Court of Justice will dismiss it not on the ground that it is inadmissible but on the general ground that it is unfounded.[39]

In principle, therefore, the question whether an act is capable of having legal effects falls to be distinguished from questions of substantive law, particularly those relating to competence. As a general rule, the fact that an act is unlawful affects not its ability to have legal effects but merely whether it may be declared void.[40]

---

36   Heusel, p. 291.

37   e.g. see the judgment of 17 December 1984 in Case 135/84 *F.B.* v. *Commission* [1984] ECR 3577 (at p. 3579), in which it was held that an action for the annulment of a letter from the Director-General of the Commission's Legal Service was inadmissible; the judgment of 10 April 1984 in Case 108/83 *Luxembourg* v. *European Parliament* [1984] ECR 1945 (at p. 1958), in which the Court ruled that an application for the annulment of a resolution of the European Parliament was admissible; and the judgment of 31 March 1971 in Case 22/70 *Commission* v. *Council* ('*AETR*') [1971] ECR 263 (at p. 278), in which an action against a proceeding of the Council was held to be admissible.

38   e.g. see the judgment of 22 September 1988 in Joined Cases 358/85 and 51/86 *France* v. *European Parliament* [1988] ECR 4821 (at p. 4851); also the judgment of 10 February 1983 in Case 230/81 *Luxembourg* v. *European Parliament* [1983] ECR 255 (at p. 285). Both cases concerned the distinction to be drawn between the internal organizational powers of the European Parliament and legal acts adopted by it having external effect.

39   That, in any event, was the conclusion reached in the judgment of 22 September 1988 in Case 358/85 *France* v. *European Parliament* [1988] ECR 4821 (at p. 4858).

40   Zuleeg, *JöR 1971*, p. 14, appears to take a different view. He states, in relation to the power to adopt non-binding acts, that an unlawful act which might otherwise be thought, on the basis of its contents, to be binding has, in any event, no legal basis and cannot be binding on the Member States. Whilst it is not possible generally to subscribe to this view, it does not exclude the possibility that acts at Community level may be not only capable of annulment but void *ab initio*; for a more detailed analysis, see Daig in: GBTE, *Kommentar zum EWGV*, Art. 173, n. 11; judgment of the Court of Justice of 10 September 1957 in Joined Cases 1 and 14/57 *Usines à Tubes de la Sarre* v. *High Authority* [1957] ECR 105 (at p. 113), in which the Court described an 'opinion' delivered by the High Authority pursuant to para. 4 of Art. 54 of the ECSC Treaty as lacking any existence, by reason of the absence of a statement of reasons, and as non-existent in law.

3. The Permissibility of an Act

The comprehensive definition of what is meant by the term 'act',[41] and the ability of the Community institutions *in practice* to avail themselves of their various powers of action,[42] raise the question of the extent to which such an act is in fact permitted by the EEC Treaty. Two possibilities must be examined in this regard: it may be thought, on the one hand, that the EEC Treaty makes exclusive provision for every act adopted by the Community institutions, and thus, in the final analysis, all powers conferred on the Community institutions, and, on the other hand, that it merely governs those powers to act which are expressly specified and otherwise allows the Community institutions complete latitude. The first of those alternatives would result in the illegality of many of the acts which arise in practice in the Community and which are of importance for the purpose of its functioning.[43]

Irrespective of the logical objections to such an argument, that ground alone justifies the view that the EEC Treaty *cannot* be based on the first model described above. This view is supported by the literature, according to which the conferment by the Treaty of powers on the Community institutions[44] restricts the activities of the institutions only in relation to sovereign acts intended to be binding on the Member States or individuals.[45] As is demonstrated below, it is not possible to infer from the Treaty any more extensive restriction on acts of the institutions undertaken pursuant to the powers conferred on them.

The starting-point for this line of argument is to be found in the second indent of Article 155 of the EEC Treaty, which gives the Commission the task of '[formulating] recommendations or [delivering] opinions on matters dealt with in this Treaty, if it expressly so provides or if the Commission considers it necessary'. According to the fifth paragraph of Article 189 of the Treaty, recommendations and opinions 'have no binding force', which should be read as 'no binding force *in law*', since there is nothing to indicate that the EEC Treaty is also intended to cover obligations of a non-legal nature. The power of the Commission to adopt such 'non-binding' acts is thus restricted – given the reference to the 'matters dealt with in this Treaty' – solely by the collective competence of the Community.

However, conclusions regarding a *general* power on the part of the Community institutions to undertake non-binding acts may be drawn from the second indent of Article 155 of the EEC Treaty only if that provision in itself constitutes not a

---

41 See 'The binding force of the Act in question', pp. 250 *et seq.*, above.

42 See 'Determination of the ability of an act to have legal effects', immediately above, in which it is stated that the permissibility, i.e. the legality, of an act is in principle to be distinguished from its ability to have effects.

43 Magiera, *Jura 1989*, p. 598, refers by way of example to fiscal acts, informal acts, practical acts, legal acts of an organizational nature and internal administrative acts.

44 As to the so-called 'principle of limited individual powers', see the more detailed analysis contained in 'Nature and scope of institutional competence', pp. 196 *et seq.*, above.

45 See Bleckmann, *Europarecht*, p. 70; *idem, DÖV 1977*, p. 616; to the same effect, Klein & Bleckmann, p. 188, n. 84; also Oppermann, *Europarecht*, p. 169; Grabitz in: *idem, Kommentar zum EWGV*, Art. 189, n. 75.

'conferred power'[46] but, on the contrary, a confirmation by the Treaty that the conferment of such a power is not in fact required in the case of recommendations and opinions. If it were a 'conferred power', then (for example) the Council, on whom no general power to formulate recommendations and deliver opinions is expressly conferred, would be empowered only to make recommendations pursuant to the third subparagraph of Article 43(2) and Article 206b of the Treaty, and to deliver opinions pursuant to Article 236.

That extraordinary consequence, which contradicts the importance of the Council in the system established by the Treaty and cannot be reconciled with its general power to adopt legally binding acts,[47] can be avoided if the second indent of Article 155 of the EEC Treaty is interpreted as constituting not a *limit* on the powers of the Commission but rather, as the wording of the article itself suggests, as conferring on the Commission the obligatory *task* of 'activating integration by means of recommendations or opinions',[48] which is supplementary to its monopoly power to initiate measures.[49] No such obligation is imposed on the Council. However, this does not prevent it from formulating recommendations or delivering opinions in the context of the collective competence of the Community.[50]

Whilst, as is contended here, recommendations and opinions fall within an area of Community competence for which no specific attribution of powers is needed, that does not preclude the allocation to that area not only of recommendations and opinions of the Commission and the Council but also of all other acts of the Community institutions which are not binding on Member States or individuals.

It follows, therefore, that only sovereign acts of the Community institutions which are binding on Member States and individuals need to be specifically authorized under the Treaty. On the other hand, there is no need for the conferment by the Treaty of a power to adopt acts which are not legally binding, i.e. a power to lay down non-legal obligations and to adopt acts which are not binding in any way.

Lastly, it is necessary to examine whether the Community institutions are completely unfettered in the field just described, or whether they are obliged, even there, to observe certain limits. First, the statement by Morand that the Community institutions enjoy 'pouvoirs presque illimités' (almost unlimited powers) in that regard[51] does not take matters any further. Bleckmann advances the view that, even if no individual conferment of powers is needed under the

---

46   This is clearly the view taken by Hummer in: Grabitz, *Kommentar zum EWGV*, Art. 155, n. 30, according to whom the provision contained in the second indent of Art. 155 of the Treaty is *constitutive* in conferring the power to formulate recommendations and to deliver opinions; see also Oppermann, *Europarecht*, p. 183, who refers to 'the conferment of the power to formulate recommendations'.

47   See also to this effect Zuleeg, *JöR 1971*, p. 17, n. 91, who considers that the general power vested in the Commission to formulate recommendations and deliver opinions 'should apply *a fortiori* to the Council'.

48   See Hummer in: Grabitz, *Kommentar zum EWGV*, Art. 155, n. 28.

49   *ibid.*, n. 40.

50   Oppermann, *Europarecht*, p. 183, is thus incorrect in stating that the competence of the Council does not include a broad power to make recommendations comparable with that conferred on the Commission.

51   Morand, p. 623.

Treaty, all measures adopted by the Community institutions which are not binding on the Member States or individuals must nevertheless have some basis in the Treaty.[52] He perceives that basis as consisting of all the objectives of the EEC Treaty, including its preamble, to which he refers as 'tasks' and reformulates as specific powers of action under the doctrine of 'implied powers'.

The question whether such efforts on the theoretical level are necessary does not require an answer here. Suffice it to say that it is possible to concur with Bleckmann's contention that the collective competence of the Community represents the limit within which all acts of the Community institutions – including those without any binding force – are to be undertaken.[53] This is borne out by the second indent of Article 155 of the EEC Treaty, by which the Commission's power to formulate non-binding recommendations or deliver opinions is expressly restricted to the 'matters dealt with in this Treaty'.

III. RESOLUTIONS AT COUNCIL LEVEL

1. THE LEGAL SIGNIFICANCE OF RESOLUTIONS AND THE DETERMINATION OF THE IDENTITY OF THE AUTHOR

(a) The legal significance of a resolution as a form of action

If it were found necessarily to be the case that the very designation of an act as a 'resolution' meant that it was incapable of possessing any legal significance, then there would be no point in undertaking any more detailed examination of the legal significance of resolutions at Council level.[54] Even in the light of the remarks made above concerning the criteria for distinguishing between legal and non-legal acts,[55] this possibility cannot be dismissed *ab initio*, since the designation of an act does constitute an indication of whether it is intended to be binding. It is important to stress, however, that its designation is only *one* indication. Consequently, it is impossible to accept in its entirety Everling's statement that the designation of an act at Council level as a 'resolution' must frequently be taken to mean that it cannot have been intended to be binding.[56] That view amounts to a presumption against any intention to create binding legal effects, and cannot therefore be reconciled with the case-law of the Court of Justice, according to which no decisive significance can be attached to such a designation.[57] In addition to taking account of the designation of a given act, it will be necessary in each individual case, therefore, to evaluate and construe the act in its entirety.

---

52 Bleckmann, *DÖV 1977*, p. 616; a similar view is expressed by him in *Europarecht*, p. 70; however, he takes a different line on the power of the European Parliament to adopt resolutions of a political nature (*ibid.*, at p. 59), stating that the Parliament may adopt such resolutions even on issues lying completely outside the sphere of competence of the EC.

53 For a concurring view, see Hiermaier, p. 91; Kaiser, *EuR 1980*, p. 112.

54 Morand, p. 625, describes this as the traditional view.

55 See 'Criteria for distinguishing between legal and non-legal acts', pp. 252 *et seq.*, above.

56 Everling, *GS Léontin-Jean Constantinesco*, p. 155.

57 See 'Criteria for distinguishing between legal and non-legal acts', pp. 252 *et seq.*, above.

That is not to say, of course, that the designation of an act as a 'resolution' cannot in an individual case become the deciding factor, as may well have been the case with the judgment of 13 November 1964 in Joined Cases 90 and 91/63 *Commission* v. *Luxembourg and Belgium.*[58] In that judgment, the Court held that the time-limits laid down in a Council resolution for the adoption of certain legal acts did not have the same effect as the time-limits provided for in the Treaty. It stated that that intention on the part of the authors of the resolution was clear 'from the fact that they adopted it under a style and form which are not those of the binding measures of the Council within the meaning of Article 189 of the Treaty'.[59] Since the text of the resolution in question[60] was in practice concerned exclusively with the fixing of the time-limits referred to, and did not contain in addition any provision whatever indicating whether it was intended to be legally or non-legally binding, or indeed to have any binding force at all, the issue fell to be determined in the light of its designation.[61]

The legal significance of resolutions adopted at Council level has not been affected by Article 3(3) of the Acts concerning the conditions of accession of new Member States,[62] even though they confirm the general permissibility of such measures under primary Community law.[63] Article 3(3) provides that the new Member States 'are in the same situation as the present Member States in respect of declarations or resolutions of, or other positions taken up by, the Council and in respect of those concerning the European Communities adopted by common agreement of the Member States'. Accordingly, the new Member States undertake to 'observe the principles and guidelines deriving from those declarations, resolutions or other positions' and to 'take such measures as may be necessary to ensure their implementation'.

The view rightly taken by commentators – and confirmed by the Court of Justice in the judgment of 15 January 1986 in Case 44/84 *Hurd*[64] – is that Article 3(3) of the Acts of Accession has not altered the view to be taken of the acts to which it refers, and in particular that it does not attach to them any additional legal effectiveness over and above that which they originally possessed.[65] Consequently, there are objections to the contention that the provisions of Article 3(3) of the Acts of Accession have 'created expectations of a lesser and lower standard of conduct'[66]

---

58 [1964] ECR 625.

59 *ibid.*, at p. 631.

60 ABl. EG Nr. 30/1006 (1962); the text does not appear to have been translated into English.

61 Consequently, Bothe, in *FS Hans-Jürgen Schlochauer*, p. 765, goes too far in citing that decision as support for the argument that the choice of designation *necessarily* indicates a desire to avoid the attribution of binding legal force, whilst nevertheless conceding that an act bearing – for instance – the designation 'programme' may constitute, 'depending on the nature of the matter, a regulation, directive or decision'.

62 e.g. see the Act concerning the conditions of accession of the Kingdom of Spain and the Portuguese Republic and the adjustments to the Treaties, OJ 1985 L 302, p. 23.

63 For a more detailed analysis, see Wenig in: Grabitz, *Kommentar zum EWGV*, Art. 173, n. 50.

64 [1986] ECR 29 (at p. 79).

65 e.g. see Everling, *GS Léontin-Jean Constantinesco*, p. 148; Heusel, p. 163; Wuermeling, p. 202; for a different view, see Bothe, *FS Hans-Jürgen Schlochauer*, p. 772.

66 See Bothe, *ibid.*

or even resulted in the 'establishment, by a manner akin to a general clause, of a minimum standard of consequential obligations'.[67] If the function of Article 3(3) is to make it impossible 'for a new Member State to rely on the fact that it was not present when such legal acts were adopted',[68] and that provision therefore places new Member States in every respect under the obligations imposed on the original Member States, as is evidenced by its very wording, there can be no basis for making abstract assumptions about the binding nature of the acts concerned. It is only by examining each individual act that enlightenment may be gleaned about the imposition of any obligations on the original Member States and hence on the new Member States as well.

Lastly, the attempt which has been made to take account of Article 3(3) of the Acts of Accession as an expression of the subjective motivation of the Member States when determining whether they intended to create binding obligations must likewise be rejected.[69] Since Article 3(3) relates only to previously adopted resolutions, it may at most provide an indication of the view as to the binding nature of the resolutions in question which was held by the original Member States *at the time of the accession* of the new Member States. However, whether that view is the right one falls to be determined in the light of each individual resolution.

(b) The determination of the identity of the author of a resolution

Resolutions at Council level may be adopted at the instigation of any of three different authors: by the Council alone, by the representatives of the Governments of the Member States (meeting within the Council) alone, or by both jointly.[70] Since resolutions at Council level invariably attribute, in their title, responsibility for the act in question to one of the three authors referred to, no problem appears to arise in that regard: the body described in the title of a resolution as its author must be regarded as its originator.[71] The position might conceivably be different in the case of an inadvertent false designation.

However, this unequivocal finding has not always been accepted. In particular, Italy has sought to characterize acts of the Council – the cases involved an acceleration decision[72] and a directive[73] – as international agreements. The Council itself advanced the view in Case 22/70 ('AETR')[74] that the underlying proceedings of the Council were nothing more than a coordination of policies amongst Member States within the framework of the Council.[75] In the first two

---

67 See Millarg, p. 182.
68 Judgment of the Court of Justice in Case 44/84 *Hurd* [1986] ECR 29 (at p. 79).
69 That, however, is the position adopted by Wuermeling, p. 203.
70 Bothe wrongly suggests, in *FS Hans-Jürgen Schlochauer*, p. 770, that in this case the question of the identity of the author is left open.
71 See also, to the same effect, Zuleeg, *Das Recht der EGen*, p. 27.
72 Judgment of the Court of Justice of 18 February 1970 in Case 38/69 *Commission* v. *Italy* [1970] ECR 47.
73 Judgment of the Court of Justice of 18 March 1980 in Case 91/79 *Commission* v. *Italy* (the 'detergents' case) [1980] ECR 1099.
74 [1971] ECR 263.
75 *ibid.*, at p. 276.

cases, the Court of Justice countered that argument correctly (although its reasoning was not altogether convincing) by stating that a measure which is in the nature of a Community decision on the basis of its objective and of the institutional framework within which it has been drawn up cannot be described as an 'international agreement'.[76]

Whilst the reference to the *institutional framework* within which the measure is drawn up must be regarded as a material factor, the reference to the *objective* of the measure, which is supplemented by statements regarding the powers of the Community institutions in the sector concerned, seems to point in the wrong direction.[77] The reason for this is that questions of competence may possibly affect the legality of an act – even, in certain circumstances, its existence – but cannot answer the question as to the identity of its author unless no author is named in the act. The determination of the identity of the author of a given act is therefore not open to interpretation to the same extent as (in accordance with what has been submitted above) the nature of the act in question. It must be granted, however, that the Court of Justice clearly took into account the above-mentioned considerations regarding the substantive content of the acts at issue only in order to lend support to a solution which was already apparent from the designation of the authors of those acts in the acts themselves.

If, therefore, the mere fact that the author is named in the act in question is decisive, it cannot properly be stated, for example, that the 'Council' has adopted 'decisions of the representatives of the Member States meeting within the Council'.[78] As will be shown below, a precise designation of the author is essential for the purposes of the legal assessment of an act adopted at Council level.

2. RESOLUTIONS OF THE COUNCIL

(a) Sphere of competence

As has been indicated in general terms above,[79] the Council's power to adopt resolutions is limited, regardless of the nature and degree of the binding force which they are intended to have, by the collective competence of the Community. Where, in adopting a resolution, the representatives of the Governments of the Member States do so by invoking their joint capacity as the Community institution known as 'the Council', it may be assumed that they are attributing the subject-matter dealt with in the resolution to the sphere of collective Community competence.[80] It is not possible, however, to draw any more far-reaching conclusions. In particular, the designation of the Council as the author of

---

76 [1970] ECR 47 (at p. 56).

77 See also the judgment of 31 March 1971 in Case 22/70 *Commission* v. *Council* ('*AETR*') [1971] ECR 263 (at p. 278), in which it was held that the Council's proceedings dealt with a matter falling within the power of the Community, and that the Member States *could not* therefore act outside the framework of the Community institutions.

78 That, however, is what is stated by Wagner, pp. 228 and 307.

79 See 'The permissibility of an act', pp. 255 *et seq.*, above.

80 See also, to the same effect, Wellens & Borchardt, p. 299.

an act cannot in any way be taken to indicate whether, and to what extent, the resolution in fact falls within the sphere of Community competence.[81]

(b) Characteristics of the resolutions in question

In order to be able to assess the legal significance of Council resolutions, it is necessary in principle to interpret each individual resolution.[82] This does not, however, make it impossible to seek out and identify characteristics common to all or some of the resolutions which are indicative of their legal significance. This analysis will be confined to resolutions relating to the cultural field, as representative of resolutions in general.

First, nearly all Council resolutions are published under the heading '(Information), Council' in the C series of the *Official Journal of the European Communities*, which contains 'Information and Notices', but not, it would appear, in the L series, which contains 'Legislation'. No more significance can be inferred from this with regard to the legal significance of resolutions than from the designation 'resolution' itself, since the way in which an act is published is patently due to the fact that it is entitled 'resolution', and, moreover, the Treaty itself does not lay down any rules on the distinction between the L series and the C series of the *Official Journal*.

Greater significance may be attached, with regard to the existence of intent to give an act binding legal force, to the fact that the procedural rules laid down in the Treaty have been complied with and the extent to which this has been done. It is possible in that regard to class resolutions in three categories: the first category covers resolutions which are solely based in general terms on the Treaties or the EEC Treaty and which in other respects scarcely fulfil any other formal requirements.[83] The second category contrasts with the first by reason of the fact that the European Parliament[84] and also, occasionally, the Economic and Social Committee[85] were consulted before the resolution was adopted. The third category covers resolutions which, as regards their form, can hardly be distinguished from binding legal acts of the type referred to in Article 189 of the EEC Treaty, except by the fact that they bear the designation 'resolution' and are published in the C series (rather than the L series) of the *Official Journal*. In

---

81   Dewost goes too far, therefore, in stating (p. 328) that 'Si *l'auteur* de la résolution est *le Conseil* le contenu de cette décision politique relève du domaine communautaire ...' (If the *author* of the resolution is *the Council*, the content of that policy decision falls within the Community sphere).

82   See 'The legal significance of a "resolution" as a form of action', pp. 259 *et seq.*, above.

83   e.g. see the Resolution of 18 December 1979 on linked work and training for young persons (OJ 1980 C 1, p. 1), the Resolution of 5 June 1989 on continuing vocational training (OJ 1989 C 148, p. 1) and the Resolution of 18 December 1990 on the comparability of vocational training qualifications (OJ 1991 C 109, p. 1).

84   e.g. see the Resolution of 14 January 1974 on an initial outline programme of the European Communities in the field of science and technology (JO 1974 C 7, p. 6).

85   e.g. see the Resolution of 6 June 1974 on the mutual recognition of diplomas, certificates and other evidence of formal qualifications (OJ 1974 C 98, p. 1) and the Resolution of 11 July 1983 concerning vocational training policies in the European Communities in the 1980s (OJ 1983 C 193, p. 2).

particular, such resolutions are based not solely in general terms on the EEC Treaty but on specific Treaty provisions.

A conspicuous – indeed, it would appear, to date the only[86] – example of this category is the Resolution of 25 July 1983 on framework programmes for Community research, development and demonstration activities and a first framework programme 1984-1987,[87] which was based on Article 235 of the EEC Treaty. The recitals in its preamble expressly state – as is customary in the case of measures based on Article 235 – that 'the Treaty ... does not provide the specific powers of action required for the adoption of this resolution'. This manner of proceeding, whilst unusual, is permissible: resolutions constitute 'appropriate measures' within the meaning of Article 235 of the EEC Treaty.[88]

Even in the case of such a formalized resolution, approximating on the face of it to a binding legal act, further arguments are needed in order to establish the existence of binding legal force. Glaesner considers, on the basis of an analysis of its contents, that Articles 1 to 3 of the resolution in question may have legal effects, since they lay down, 'in a substantiated form, the procedures and general criteria applying to future framework programmes'.[89] On the other hand, he does not regard the framework programme adopted in conjunction with the resolution as having been adequately substantiated.[90]

To sum up, it may thus be stated that the degree of precision with which a resolution is formulated, and the extent to which it is given concrete or substantive form, will provide guidance as to the existence and extent to which it is *binding*, whilst the extent to which procedural requirements have been complied with may be taken as an indication of the desire of its author to give it binding force *in law*.

(c) The case-law of the Court of Justice

There exists no self-contained body of case-law of the Court of Justice concerning the legal significance of Council resolutions; nor is this to be expected in the future, since, as has already been repeatedly emphasized, it is scarcely possible to draw any conclusions which hold good in general for all resolutions. Instead, each individual resolution must be considered on its own merits. However, it is possible to discern certain judgments of the Court which provide indications as to the legal significance of individual Council resolutions. An impression of the varying legal significance of Council resolutions may be gleaned from a survey of those judgments.

The starting-point is to be found in a resolution adopted by the Council at The Hague on 3 November 1976, the object of which was the extension of the Member States' fishing zones to 200 miles.[91] Annex VI to that resolution, which

---

86 According to a search carried out in the EC's CELEX data bank.
87 OJ 1983 C 208, p. 1.
88 See Grabitz in: *idem, Kommentar zum EWGV*, Art. 235, n. 83; Schwartz in: GBTE, *Kommentar zum EWGV*, Art. 235, n. 296, tends to reject this view.
89 Glaesner, *Einführung*, p. 51.
90 *ibid.*
91 OJ 1981 C 105, p. 1.

was not published in the *Official Journal*,[92] provided that the Member States were not in principle to take any unilateral measures to protect their fisheries resources and that, in the event of such measures nevertheless becoming necessary, the Member States were, before adopting them, to seek the approval of the Commission, which was to be consulted at every stage. Annex VI to the so-called Hague Resolution, referred to henceforth simply as 'the Resolution', has been before the Court of Justice on several occasions. In all of its decisions, the Court assumed that the Resolution had binding legal effects on the Member States. The Court held that it was not contested that the Resolution was binding on the Member States[93] and that the Member States must comply with the procedural and substantive conditions laid down by the Resolution.[94] The Court consistently described the Resolution as a 'legal act',[95] and regarded the provisions of the Resolution as forming part of 'the substantive and procedural rules of Community law'.[96]

However, it is impossible to discern with complete clarity the grounds on which the Resolution was held to be binding.[97] Admittedly, the Court expressly concurred with the Commission's view that the Resolution made 'specific the duties of co-operation which the Member States assumed under Article 5 of the EEC Treaty when they acceded to the Community'.[98] However, it remains an open question whether the binding nature of the Resolution consequently derives from Article 5 of the EEC Treaty or from the Resolution itself. In the final analysis, it may be said that Council resolutions which appear to render specific the duty of cooperation laid down in Article 5 of the EEC Treaty may at least give rise, via Article 5, to legal effects which are binding on the Member States.[99]

A different kind of legal significance was attributed by the Court to a Council resolution in its judgment of 4 February 1975 in Case 169/73 *Compagnie Continentale* v. *Council*.[100] In that case, the Council had informed commercial operators in a resolution of the contents of a regulation which it was planning to adopt, in order to enable them to prepare for and adapt to the new provisions at the earliest opportunity. In so doing, however, it failed to draw attention to a provision of Community law which was capable of affecting the rules set out in the draft regulation to the detriment of the commercial operators concerned, and which

---

92   e.g. it is set out in the judgment of 16 February 1978 in Case 61/77 *Commission* v. *Ireland* [1978] ECR 417 (at pp. 444–445).

93   Judgment of 10 July 1980 in Case 32/79 *Commission* v. *United Kingdom* [1980] ECR 2403 (at p. 2432).

94   Judgment of 14 February 1984 in Case 24/83 *Gewiese and Mehlich* [1984] ECR 817 (at p. 832).

95   [1980] ECR 2403 (at p. 2437).

96   Judgment of 30 November 1982 in Case 287/81 *Noble Kerr* [1982] ECR 4053 (at p. 4073).

97   As Glaesner aptly points out in *Einführung*, p. 50.

98   Judgment of 4 October 1979 in Case 141/78 *France* v. *United Kingdom* [1979] ECR 2923 (at p. 2942); see also – albeit not with the same clarity – the judgment of 16 February 1978 in Case 61/77 *Commission* v. *Ireland* [1978] ECR 417 (at pp. 449 *et seq.*).

99   It should be noted, however, that resolutions which do not have any binding legal force are not as a general rule accorded, via Art. 5 of the EEC Treaty, 'legal effect through the back door, so to speak' (Bothe, *FS Hans-Jürgen Schlochauer*, p. 772).

100 [1975] ECR 117.

subsequently did have just such an adverse effect. In the action for damages subsequently brought by one of the undertakings concerned, the Court of Justice criticized the Council on the ground that 'it ought to have issued a reminder as to the provision in question and expressed reservations as to its possible application'.[101] Although the Court ultimately held that the action was unsuccessful, by reason of the absence of a causal link between the failure of the Council to fulfil its obligations and the damage which had occurred, it is apparent that even where resolutions do not have any binding legal force, they may have legal effects in so far as they fall to be regarded as constituting conduct on the part of the Council giving rise to liability.

Other decisions of the Court of Justice place more stress on the significance of individual resolutions from the point of view of policy considerations. In its judgment of 15 June 1978 in Case 149/77 *Defrenne*,[102] it described the Council Resolution of 21 January 1974 concerning a social action programme[103] as a specific instance of the legislative programme for social policy contained in Articles 117 and 118 of the EEC Treaty.[104] In the judgment of 13 December 1979 in Case 44/79 *Hauer*,[105] it described the Council Resolution of 21 April 1975 concerning new guidelines designed to balance the market in table wines[106] as a 'factor [in German, 'Rechtsakt'] which makes it possible to perceive the Community policy pursued in that field'.[107] In its judgment of 3 February 1976 in Case 59/75 *Manghera*,[108] the Court likewise attributed primarily policy significance to a Council resolution. It held, with regard to a time-limit specified in the resolution for the elimination of certain State monopoly rights, that such a time-scale could not prevail over that contained in the Treaty.[109]

It may thus be concluded from that case-law, first, that Council resolutions for the planning of Community policy may be of (policy) significance and, secondly, that provisions of the EEC Treaty cannot be rendered ineffective by the adoption of a mere resolution.

(d) The legal significance of the resolutions in question

Whilst Council resolutions cannot generally produce *primary* effects – as in the rare case of the 'Hague Resolution', to which reference is made above – rendering them tantamount to legal acts of the kind described in Article 189 of the EEC Treaty, but have instead chiefly significance in the sphere of policy, nevertheless, the possibility of their having *secondary* legal effects cannot be ruled out. As has been already shown by reference to the case-law of the Court of Justice, Council resolutions may possess significance in relation to Articles 5 and 215 of the EEC Treaty. Apart from their significance in the context of the duty of Community

---

101 [1975] ECR 117 (at p. 134).
102 [1978] ECR 1365.
103 OJ 1974 C 13, p. 1.
104 [1978] ECR 1365 (at p. 1376).
105 [1979] ECR 3727.
106 OJ 1975 C 90, p. 1.
107 [1979] ECR 3727 (at p. 3748).
108 [1976] ECR 91.
109 *ibid.*, at p. 102.

loyalty between Member States and the possibility that they may found liability on the part of the Community, Council resolutions may have other secondary legal effects. Such legal effects may be subsumed under the term 'Tatbestandswirkung', borrowed from German general administrative law,[110] which describes the effects of resolutions by virtue of their being not legal norms or legal acts but legally relevant facts.

However, it is possible here to discuss only some of the legal evidence of such effects. In particular, it is not proposed to analyze the possible significance of Council resolutions in relation to discretionary decisions of the Council[111] and the interpretation of secondary Community law by the Court of Justice.[112] Instead, first, a closer look will be taken at the role played by Council resolutions in the Community legislative process, before examining, by reference to the first paragraph of Article 7 in conjunction with Article 128 of the EEC Treaty, the extent to which the Court of Justice takes Council resolutions into account as legally relevant facts.

(i) The role played by Council resolutions in the Community legislative process

The Community legislative process does not begin with the submission of formal proposals by the Commission. On the contrary, a Commission proposal is itself the result of a policy selection process which is influenced from many sides.[113] Practical experience shows that the Commission's 'monopoly power to initiate measures'[114] is a monopoly only from a formal standpoint. From a substantive point of view, it is primarily the Council which influences, by means of resolutions, the future shape of Community policy.[115] By virtue of their nature, the significance of Council resolutions of this kind is exerted primarily in policy fields which have not hitherto been much developed by Community law. On the other hand, Council resolutions are tied to the collective competence of the Community. It is for that reason that Council resolutions in the field of education and training are primarily concerned with vocational training, whereas resolutions relating to general educational matters are generally adopted jointly by the Council and the representatives of the Governments meeting within the Council.[116]

---

110 Jabloner & Okresek, p. 221, transpose this term into the field of international law, in order to describe the secondary effects of measures of so-called 'soft law'; for a more detailed analysis of the term, see Erichsen in: Erichsen & Martens, p. 220; Koja, p. 533.

111 See in that regard the Opinion of Advocate-General Lenz in Case 68/86 *United Kingdom* v. *Council* [1988] ECR 855 (at p. 887, section 59).

112 See the judgment of 24 October 1973 in Case 43/72 *Merkur* [1973] ECR 1055 (at p. 1072). Everling advances the view, in *Probleme*, p. 425, that resolutions may be taken into consideration in order to interpret legal acts adopted pursuant to them, provided that it is clear that the Council was in fact guided by them.

113 For a more detailed analysis in that regard, see Glaesner, *Einführung*, pp. 38 *et seq.*

114 Hummer in: Grabitz, *Kommentar zum EWGV*, Art. 155, n. 40.

115 See, to the same effect, Dewost, p. 328; also, in general terms, Wellens & Borchardt, pp. 302 *et seq.*; Glaesner, *Einführung*, p. 39.

116 See 'The Council', pp. 40 *et seq.*, above.

The Council's power to initiate policy measures is not only a practical phenomenon but finds expression in the EEC Treaty.[117] According to Article 152 of the Treaty, the Council 'may request the Commission to undertake any studies the Council considers desirable for the attainment of the common objectives, and to submit to it any appropriate proposals'. The Council has, moreover, occasionally made use in resolutions of its power to request the Commission to submit proposals.[118] By means of the adoption of resolutions, therefore, the Council fulfils its task of 'giving concrete form to the undefined objectives of the Treaty'.[119]

(ii) Effects of Council resolutions by virtue of their being legally relevant facts in connection with the first paragraph of Article 7 of the EEC Treaty

Council resolutions have 'Tatbestandswirkung' by commanding attention, as 'legally relevant facts',[120] in connection with provisions of Community law. A significant example of the effect of resolutions as surrounding facts was provided by the Court of Justice in its judgment of 13 February 1985 in Case 293/83 *Gravier*.[121] In order to substantiate its view that access to vocational training fell within the scope of the EEC Treaty and was thus subject to the prohibition of discrimination set out in the first paragraph of Article 7, the Court took account of the stage reached in the progressive development of the common vocational training policy provided for in Article 128 of the Treaty. In turn, the Court determined the stage reached in the development of the common vocational training policy by reference to various Community texts, including the Resolution of the Council of 11 July 1983 on vocational training policies in the European Community in the 1980s.[122]

That resolution serves, therefore, in conjunction with the other acts taken into account by the Court of Justice, to provide information about the stage reached in the development of the common vocational training policy. The legal effects which it has are not direct, but are merely created indirectly by the fact that it contributes to the process of giving concrete form to the scope of application of the EEC Treaty.[123] It is only the first paragraph of Article 7 of the EEC Treaty which itself has legal effects, by prohibiting, within the scope of application of the Treaty, any discrimination on grounds of nationality.

---

117 See Beutler et al., *3rd ed.*, p. 120, according to whom Art. 152 of the EEC Treaty has, with the adoption of Council resolutions, acquired particular significance as a means of bringing influence to bear upon the Commission in accordance with the Treaty.

118 e.g. see the Resolution of 18 December 1990 on the comparability of vocational training qualifications (OJ 1991 C 109, p. 1), in which the Council invites the Commission 'to submit proposals taking account of this Resolution ...' (point 5(b)).

119 Bleckmann, *FS Hans Kutscher*, p. 28.

120 Jabloner & Okresek, p. 221.

121 [1985] ECR 593.

122 OJ 1983 C 193, p. 2.

123 See also, in that regard, the final paras of 'The scope of the EEC Treaty', pp. 115 *et seq.*, above.

3. Resolutions Adopted by the Representatives of the Governments of the Member States

(a) Sphere of competence

In accordance with the above finding that, in the exercise of its power to adopt resolutions, the Council is confined within the bounds of collective Community competence, the Member States are in principle subject to a complementary restriction requiring them to stay within the area of competence remaining to them – but with two qualifications. First, Community law itself contains various provisions which require joint action by the Governments of the Member States,[124] and thus relate not to the status of the Member States under the statutory-law components of the Treaty but to their capacity as parties to a treaty concluded under international law.[125] Secondly, there is the vexed question whether it is open to the Member States to act by way of a bilateral international agreement where the action to be taken could also be based on Article 235 of the EEC Treaty.[126] It is not proposed to deal here with those two qualifications – as to the first, because the basis for joint action by the Member States lies in the Treaties themselves and therefore problems are hardly likely to arise, and as to the second, because it appears to be a hypothetical rather than an actual restriction.

(b) Characteristics of the resolutions in question

Resolutions adopted by the representatives of the Governments of the Member States – here, too, it is proposed to consider only those relating to the cultural sphere – do not differ from Council resolutions in point of the manner of their publication: they are published in the C series of the *Official Journal of the European Communities* under the heading '(Information), Council'. However, that is the only thing which they have in common with Council resolutions. As far as can be seen, none of the resolutions of the Governments of the Member States contains any reference to the EEC Treaty or any of the other treaties. At most, they occasionally refer to documents of the European Council.[127] For the rest, also, it is practically impossible to discern any common characteristics as to their form. One striking point, however, is that a certain – albeit small – proportion of the resolutions indicate that they were adopted by the 'representatives of the Governments of the Member States',[128] whilst the overwhelming majority of them state that they were adopted by the 'Ministers *meeting within the Council*'. It may well be true that those

---

124 e.g. Arts 167, 168a and 216 of the EEC Treaty, Art. 11 of the Merger Treaty, and the second para. of Art. 1 of the Statute of the EIB.

125 See, with regard to the distinction between the contractual and statutory components of treaties establishing international organizations, Mosler, p. 5.

126 Schwartz in: GBTE, *Kommentar zum EWGV*, Art. 235, nn. 181 *et seq.*, maintains that they are not so entitled to act; Hilf, *Maßnahmen*, p. 252, and Gulmann, pp. 244 *et seq.*, take the view that they may in principle.

127 e.g. see the Resolution of 17 February 1986 on the establishment of transnational cultural itineraries (OJ 1986 C 44, p. 2) and the Resolution of 6 June 1974 on cooperation in the field of education (OJ 1974 C 98, p.2).

128 See 'The representatives of the Governments of the Member States', pp. 67 *et seq.*, above.

formulations reflect the ministerial view of the respective closeness of the various resolutions to Community law.[129] However, such differences can be no more than marginal – after all, even in the first case, the government representatives purport to act in their common capacity as representatives of the Member States of the EC. What is primarily involved, therefore, is a difference in terminology.[130]

(c) The case-law of the Court of Justice

The case-law of the Court of Justice includes principally two noteworthy decisions concerning resolutions of the representatives of the Governments of the Member States: the judgment of 8 April 1976 in Case 43/75 *Defrenne*[131] and the judgment of 15 January 1986 in Case 44/84 *Hurd*.[132] In *Defrenne*, the Court confirmed the view which it had already taken with regard to resolutions of the Council,[133] namely that a resolution cannot extend a time-limit laid down by the EEC Treaty. The procedure for amending the Treaty would have to be followed in order to extend such a time-limit.[134] In the Court's view, however, the position may in certain circumstances be different where it is sought, by means of a resolution of the Member States, to bring forward a time-limit laid down in the Treaty.[135]

Whilst the second decision was not specifically concerned with an act of the government representatives described as a 'resolution', it is nonetheless of significance in this context. The Court was requested in that decision to rule pursuant to Article 177 of the EEC Treaty on whether the agreements concluded between the Member States on the setting-up of the European Schools fell to be regarded as acts of the Community institutions, and thus as falling within its interpretational jurisdiction. The Court held in that regard that the European Schools were set up, not on the basis of the Community Treaties or on the basis of measures adopted by the Community institutions, but on the basis of international agreements concluded by the Member States. It held that the mere fact that those agreements were linked to the Community and to the functioning of its institutions did not mean that they had to be regarded as an integral part of Community law, the uniform interpretation of which throughout the Community falls within the jurisdiction of the Court.[136]

The fact that the agreements in issue did not fall within any field of 'Community law', however defined – the term 'Community law' is not in fact used in the EEC Treaty – cannot be regarded as having led the Court to reach the conclusions it did; what must instead be regarded as the decisive factor was that the Court saw no way in which the agreements could possibly be described as 'measures adopted by the Community institutions' within the meaning of Article 177 of the Treaty. It follows that, for the purposes of any legal classification of

---

129 See, to that effect, Wellens & Borchardt, p. 299.
130 That view appears to be shared by Kaiser, *FS Carl Friedrich Ophüls*, p. 115.
131 [1976] ECR 455.
132 [1986] ECR 29.
133 See the final paragraphs of 'The case-law of the Courts of Justice', pp 262 *et seq.*, above.
134 [1976] ECR 455 (at p. 478).
135 *ibid.*: 'without prejudice to its possible effects as regards encouraging and accelerating the full implementation of Art. 119'.
136 [1986] ECR 29 (at pp. 76 *et seq.*).

resolutions of the representatives of the Governments of the Member States, there is nothing to be gained, save, at most, from a descriptive standpoint, from general discussion of whether resolutions adopted by the representatives of the Governments must be ascribed to the sphere of 'Community law'.[137] The only significant factor is the question as to which field of application is opened up by the individual provisions of the Treaty.[138]

Against this background, the characterization of joint acts of the government representatives as 'decisions of the Council, albeit not in the strict sense'('uneigentliche Ratsbeschlüsse')[139] or as 'decisions of the institutions, albeit not in the strict sense' ('uneigentliche Organbeschlüsse')[140] is misleading, since, conceptually, it assumes such acts form part of Community law and that cannot be proved. This is also true of the contention that the joint acts of the government representatives have an 'aura' of EC law and must be regarded as forming part of the 'Community patrimony'.[141]

(d) The legal significance of the resolutions in question

Since resolutions adopted by the representatives of the Governments of the Member States cannot be ascribed to the Community institutions, they can have direct legal effects only in the intergovernmental sphere. That must be the position if they are to be regarded as international agreements. If so, they are subject to the rules of municipal law relating to the conclusion of such treaties.[142] Two distinct rules are contained in that regard in Article 59(2) of the German Basic Law. Treaties which regulate the political relations of the Federal Republic of Germany or relate to matters covered by, or requiring acts of, federal legislation have to receive assent in the form of a federal law; as regards administrative agreements, however, reference is made merely to the provisions concerning the federal administration. It should be noted that non-compliance with the mandatory constitutional procedure does not in principle affect the validity of

---

137 However, that is the view taken by Millarg, p. 181, who has coined the term 'tertiary Community law'; his approach is supported by Hiermaier, p. 100; Bothe, *FS Hans-Jürgen Schlochauer*, p. 762; Zuleeg, *JöR 1971*, p. 21; Kaiser, *FS Carl Friedrich Ophüls*, p. 124, who states somewhat obscurely that decisions adopted by the government representatives meeting within the Council constitute, in the broader sense, 'decisions of the Communities' and 'one of the sources of the law of the European Communities'; and Bebr, p. 534. The contrary view is expressed by Bülow, p. 32; Wuermeling, pp. 80 *et seq.*; and Magiera, *Jura 1989*, p. 596, who describes the resolutions in question as acts which merely *relate to Community law* and distinguishes between them and legal acts undertaken jointly by the Member States for which express provision is made in the Treaty, which he describes as falling within *Community law in the broader sense*.

138 e.g. see Art. 155 of the EEC Treaty, dealing with 'the measures taken by the institutions pursuant (to this Treaty)'; the first para. of Art. 169, relating to the failure of a Member State 'to fulfil an obligation under this Treaty'; the first para. of Art. 175, which is concerned with cases of failure to act 'in infringement of this Treaty'; and subpara. (a) of the first para. of Art. 177, which deals with 'the interpretation of this Treaty'.

139 e.g. see Wagner, p. 229; Nicolaysen, *Europarecht I*, p. 130.

140 e.g. see Zuleeg, *Das Recht der Europäischen Gemeinschaften*, p. 28.

141 See Oppermann, *Europarecht*, p. 186.

142 L.-J. Constantinesco, p. 546.

an agreement under international law by virtue of Article 27 of the Vienna Convention on the Law of Treaties. In so far as a resolution adopted by the government representatives is intended merely to be non-legally binding, Article 59(2) of the Basic Law does not apply: that provision is solely concerned with the establishment, alteration or suspension of *legal* relations.[143]

Whilst it is true that resolutions of the government representatives may have direct legal effects only as between States, such acts are not protected against repercussions from Community law. In its judgment of 15 January 1986 in Case 44/84 *Hurd*,[144] the Court of Justice held that Article 5 of the EEC Treaty might be applicable where a measure taken to implement an agreement concluded between the Member States outside the scope of the Treaties were to impede 'the implementation of a provision of the Treaties or of secondary Community law or the functioning of the Community institutions'.[145]

4. RESOLUTIONS ADOPTED JOINTLY BY THE COUNCIL AND BY THE GOVERNMENT REPRESENTATIVES MEETING WITHIN THE COUNCIL

(a) Sphere of competence

Where the government representatives act within the Council '*uno actu*'[146] both as the Council, in its capacity as a Community institution, and as the representatives of the Governments of the Member States meeting within the Council, it is open to them to exhaust both the competence conferred on them by the Community and the competence which they enjoy as Member States. There are two possible reasons for such 'hybrid' decision-making: first, the government representatives, or perhaps merely some of them,[147] may have taken the view that the content of a resolution *actually* had a bearing on both the Community and the Member States' spheres of competence.[148] Secondly, *doubts* as to the correct form of collective competence – whether in relation to the resolution as a whole or to individual parts of it – may determine the choice of the 'hybrid' form in which the resolution is adopted.[149] Although this will not necessarily preclude its annulment on the ground of lack of powers under the second sentence of the first paragraph of Article 173 of the EEC Treaty,[150] it will prevent it from being a complete nullity, that is to say, under both Community law and international law.

In so far as it can be clearly inferred from the resolution that particular parts of it can be ascribed to particular functions of the government representatives, it is possible, for the purposes of legal assessment, notionally to split the resolution

---

143 Maunz in: MDHS, *Kommentar zum GG*, Art. 59, n. 11.

144 [1986] ECR 29.

145 *ibid.*, at p. 81.

146 This expression is to be found in Mosler, p. 7.

147 Everling, in *Probleme*, p. 418, contends that the 'hybrid' form of adopting decisions is used where there is no unanimity between the government representatives regarding their collective competence; examples of this are given by Bothe in *FS Hans-Jürgen Schlochauer*, p. 762.

148 e.g. see Wellens & Borchardt, p. 299.

149 e.g. see Magiera, *Jura 1989*, p. 596.

150 That, however, is the view taken in Schweitzer in: Grabitz, *Kommentar zum EWGV*, Art. 146, n. 18.

into two acts undertaken by two different authors.[151] Where a resolution cannot be severed in that way, however, the only feasible alternative will be to ascribe the entire text of the resolution both to the Council and to the government representatives. That appears also to be the view taken by the Court of Justice, which, in its judgment of 24 October 1973 in Case 9/73 *Schlüter*,[152] described the Resolution of the Council and of the Representatives of the Governments of the Member States of 22 March 1971 on the attainment by stages of economic and monetary union within the Community[153] as a 'Council resolution' and examined its contents with a view to ascertaining the existence of legal effects which might be relied on by Community nationals before the national courts.[154]

(b) Characteristics of the resolutions in question

The resolutions adopted in the cultural field by the Council and the representatives of the Governments of the Member States meeting within the Council are of a relatively informal nature; in particular, their legal basis is at most stated to be 'the Treaties establishing the European Communities'[155] and scarcely ever the EEC Treaty.[156] A special feature of the resolutions adopted in the field of education and training is that a great many of them draw an express distinction between measures to be implemented at Community level and those to be implemented by the individual Member States, and provide that the implementation of such measures by the Member States is to be subject in part to 'the limits of their own specific educational policies and structures'[157] or, in addition, to 'the constitutional and financial limits' to which the Member States are subject.[158] Such reservations not only reflect the view of the government representatives that the sphere of competence of the Member States is affected; they also indicate the absence of any intention, either between the Member States or at Community level, to impose binding legal obligations.

(c) The case-law of the Court of Justice

As far as can be seen, there are no decisions of the Court relating specifically to the legal nature of resolutions of the Council and of the representatives of the Governments meeting within the Council. As has already been observed, the Court appears to ignore, when carrying out judicial review, the fact that the

---

151 This also appears to be the view taken by Wuermeling, pp. 243 *et seq.*
152 [1973] ECR 1135.
153 OJ, English Special Edition, Second Series IX, p. 40.
154 [1973] ECR 1135 (at p. 1161).
155 e.g. see the Resolution of 3 June 1985 containing an action programme on equal opportunities for girls and boys in education (OJ 1985 C 166, p. 1).
156 See, however, the Resolution of 9 June 1986 on consumer education in primary and secondary schools (OJ 1986 C 184, p. 21).
157 e.g. see the Resolution of 24 May 1988 on the European dimension in education (OJ 1988 C 177, p. 5).
158 e.g. see the Resolution of 22 May 1989 on school provision for children of occupational travellers (OJ 1989 C 153, p. 1).

resolution in question was adopted by recourse to the 'hybrid' form of decision-making and to treat the resolution as having been adopted by the Council alone.[159] That manner of proceeding arises because of the split between collective Community and Member State competence and the resulting restriction of the jurisdiction of the Court.

(d) The legal significance of the resolutions in question

Legal significance may attach to resolutions of the Council and of the representatives of the Governments meeting within the Council, either for the reasons stated for Council resolutions[160] or for those given for resolutions adopted by the government representatives.[161] Where a resolution contains parts which are capable of being severed and attributed to the Council and the government representatives, legal effects may be inferred from both sets of reasons at the same time. It does not appear permissible to consider that the 'hybrid' form of decision-making cannot give rise to legal effects simply because 'measures which are material under Community law ... [can] only be taken by the Community institutions'.[162] According to what is stated above,[163] the special characteristic of the 'hybrid' form of decision-making is *not* that the representatives of the Governments of the Member States are seeking to take action within the sphere of competence of the Community but instead that they are intending, where the position with regard to competence is unclear, to adopt a further decision circumspectly and *uno actu* by means of the adoption of a corresponding Council resolution. In so doing, they are consciously accepting that one or other of the two acts combined in the resolution might be unlawful or even non-existent.

IV. COMMISSION COMMUNICATIONS

1. Introduction

The Commission calls a great many of its acts 'communications'; they are so multifarious that it must be doubted from the outset whether it is possible to speak of them as a *single* form of act at all. There are, for example, communications which are necessary for the purposes of applying provisions of Community law and report on the occurrence of specific events.[164] Other communications give notice

---

159 See the concluding paragraphs of 'Sphere of competence', pp. 270 *et seq.*, above.
160 See 'The legal significance of the resolutions in question', pp. 264 *et seq.*, above.
161 See 'The legal significance of the resolutions in question', pp. 269 *et seq.*, above.
162 See Glaesner, *Umwelt*, p. 4.
163 See 'Sphere of competence', pp. 270 *et seq.*, above.
164 e.g. see the Communication pursuant to Council Regulation (EEC) No. 3832/90 of 20 December 1990, applying tariff preferences for 1991 in respect of textile products originating in developing countries (OJ 1991 C 116, p. 2), which gives notice of the exhaustion of certain quotas.

of decisions reached by the Commission.[165] Yet further communications are published in the course of the preparation of decisions, for example in competition[166] and State aid[167] cases. Such communications have to do with the administrative activities of the Commission in the narrower sense of the term, and may be described as 'information communications'.[168] There is a further group, consisting of communications (which could be termed 'guideline communications'[169]) which set forth, from the Commission's point of view, the case-law of the Court of Justice in specific fields and the approach which it is proposing to adopt in the future, particularly in dealing with Treaty infringements by the Member States.[170]

Neither of the groups of communications referred to above appear to play any role in the cultural field. In that sphere, it is 'programme communications' which predominate.[171] These include communications in which plans – of a more or less concrete nature – for future action by the Commission in a specific field are elaborated and submitted to the other Community institutions, and also, in some cases, to 'interested parties',[172] for discussion.[173] It is self-evident that those communications also contain the Commission's views on matters of Community law, and thus to some extent resemble guidance communications; programme communications, however, are designed to serve a different purpose and are clearly distinguishable from guideline communications. The question whether, and to what extent, legal significance attaches to such programme communications is considered in the next section.

---

165 e.g. see the Communication pursuant to Art. 115 of the EEC Treaty (OJ 1990 C 161, p. 6), containing notice by the Commission of authorization granted by it to Italy to exempt certain goods in free circulation from Community treatment, and the Communication concerning State aid (OJ 1990 C 159, p. 13), containing notice by the Commission of the closure of a procedure against Spain under Art. 93(2) of the Treaty.

166 e.g. see the Communication pursuant to Art. 19(3) of Regulation No. 17 of the Council (OJ 1991 C 116, p. 6), in which the Commission invites all interested third parties to submit their comments on the proposed grant of an exemption.

167 e.g. see the Communication regarding a tariff structure for natural gas prices in the Netherlands (OJ 1983 C 327, p. 3), inviting all parties concerned to submit their comments within a specified period prior to the opening of a procedure under Art. 93(2) of the EEC Treaty; see in that regard the judgment of the Court of Justice in Case 169/84 *Cofaz* [1986] ECR 391 (at p. 410).

168 This term is to be found in Meier, p. 1306.

169 *ibid.*; as to this form of communication, see also Schmitt von Sydow, pp. 667 *et seq.*; Ayral, pp. 677 *et seq.*

170 e.g. see the Communication concerning the consequences of the judgment given by the Court of Justice on 20 February 1979 in Case 120/78 ('*Cassis de Dijon*') (OJ 1980 C 256, p. 2); see also the general reference by the Commission in the White Paper entitled 'Completing the Internal Market', COM(85) 310, section 155, to the need for more systematic action to eliminate unjustified trade barriers and to the proposed publication, to that end, of communications 'setting out the legal situation'.

171 As to that term, see Meier, p. 1305, n. 22.

172 See the Communication from the Commission, 'Green Paper on Copyright and the Challenge of Technology', COM(88) 172, p. 16.

173 For detailed information regarding communications in the cultural field, see the sections on the activities of the Commission contained in Part 2, above.

2. THE LEGAL SIGNIFICANCE OF COMMUNICATIONS

(a) The significance of communications in the legislative process

In its communication of 14 October 1981 entitled 'The Institutional Structure of the Community',[174] the Commission stated, with regard to its practice of submitting programme communications, that it normally submitted to the European Parliament and to the Council 'communications setting out the most serious problems in the field under consideration'.[175] It intended to intensify that practice, in order to formulate its proposals in the light of the policy discussions thus initiated.[176] It is clear from this that – as has been stated above concerning the role played by Council resolutions in the Community's legislative process[177] – a formal Commission proposal constitutes not the starting-point of a Commission initiative but its culmination. Communications are an instrument by which the Commission fulfils its task, laid down in general terms in the third indent of Article 155 of the EEC Treaty, of participating 'in the shaping of measures taken by the Council and by the European Parliament'.[178] Even the communications themselves, however, do not represent the commencement of a Commission initiative; they conclude the preparatory work done by the services of the Commission.[179]

To sum up, it will be seen, therefore, that programme communications constitute a means available to the Commission of safeguarding its power of initiation which, whilst not expressly provided for in the Treaty, appears nevertheless to be taken for granted and is in any event permissible. Such communications, like other pronouncements made in the course of the process for the formulation of intended measures, are as a rule neither designed to have nor capable of having direct legal effects.[180] However, this does not mean that they are prevented from doing so by the fact that they are entitled 'communications':[181] here too, it is not the title of a measure which determines whether it has legal effects.[182]

(b) Further evidence of the possible legal significance of communications

Whilst there can be no question of programme communications having direct legal effects, they may nonetheless have certain indirect legal effects ('Tatbestandswirkungen').[183] The functional connection between communications and

---

174 *EC Bulletin* Supplement 3/82.

175 *ibid.*, at p. 10.

176 *ibid.*

177 See 'The role played by Council resolutions in the Community legislative process', pp. 265 *et seq.*, above.

178 For a more detailed analysis, see Schweitzer in: Grabitz, *Kommentar zum EWGV*, Art. 155, n. 40.

179 For further details, see Ipsen, *Europäisches Gemeinschaftsrecht*, pp. 488 *et seq.*

180 See also, to the same effect, L.-J. Constantinesco, p. 579.

181 For a concurring view, see Oppermann, *Europarecht*, p. 187.

182 See in that regard 'Criteria for distinguishing between legal and non-legal acts', pp. 252 *et seq.*, above.

183 As to this term, see 'The legal significance of the resolutions in question', pp. 264 *et seq.*, above.

subsequent proposals of the Commission as described above may justify the attribution of possible indirect legal effects, inherent in the Commission's *proposals*, to the *communications* as well. Two possible cases in which Commission proposals may have indirect legal effect are worth discussing.

In its judgment of 30 September 1982 in Case 108/81 *Amylum* v. *Council*,[184] the Court of Justice took into account, *inter alia*, a Commission proposal in holding that a commercial undertaking could not rely, for the purposes of contesting the retroactive effect of a provision of Community law, on the principle of the *protection of legitimate expectations*. It held that, prior to the adoption of the contested measure, the applicant had become aware, from the publication of the Commission's proposal in the *Official Journal*, that it was to have retroactive effect.[185] Here, the Court followed the Opinion of Advocate-General Reischl, in which he had concluded that the Commission's proposal could 'certainly be regarded as a factor relevant to the question of the protection of legitimate expectations'.[186]

Whilst in that case the principle of the protection of legitimate expectations was held not to apply in the light of a Commission proposal, the Court's judgment of 12 July 1989 in Case 161/88 *Binder*[187] concerned the converse question whether any legitimate expectations could be founded on a Commission proposal which was ultimately not adopted by the Council. In that case, the Court answered that question in the negative on the ground that the plaintiff in the proceedings before the national court, as a commercial trader engaged essentially in import-export operations, could reasonably be expected 'to ascertain, by reading the relevant *Official Journals*, the Community duty applicable to the operations which he carries out'.[188] Furthermore, according to the case-law of the Court, legitimate expectations may not be placed on acts of the Community institutions where those acts are capable of being altered by the institutions in the exercise of their discretion.[189] In the case of Commission proposals, however, such alteration may occur at any time prior to the adoption of such proposals by the Council, under Article 149(3) of the EEC Treaty.

Yet even if significance were to be attached to a Commission proposal for the purposes of establishing the existence of legitimate expectations, it would be doubtful whether such effects could simply be transposed to Commission communications. There are principally two reasons why this should not be possible. First, communications are significantly more remote from the legal measures subsequently to be adopted, and are, for that reason alone, hardly likely to destroy or found any legitimate expectations as to particular conduct on the part of the Community institutions. The decisive point appears, however, to be the fact that frequently the Commission's programme communications are not published

---

184 [1982] ECR 3107.
185 *ibid.*, at p. 3133.
186 *ibid.*, at p. 3149.
187 [1989] ECR 2415.
188 *ibid.*, at p. 2439.
189 Judgment of 14 February 1990 in Case C-350/88 *Delacre and Others* v. *Commission* [1990] ECR I-395 (at p. 426).

in the *Official Journal*[190] and, since accordingly they are not addressed to the world at large, cannot be regarded as the basis for legitimate expectations on the part of third parties. In this regard, however, as is invariably the case, matters will ultimately turn on all the circumstances of each individual case.

A further instance in which Commission proposals may possibly have indirect legal effects arises out of the basic structure of the division of powers between the Community and the Member States. The legislative procedure followed by the Community in the sphere of concurrent powers has been cited above as an example of the inherent dynamic of Community law, and it has been shown that a concurrent Community power is transformed into exclusive competence when it is *exercised*.[191]

The question arises, therefore, whether the transmission to the Council of a Commission proposal in a specific field can in itself be regarded as constituting the *exercise* of concurrent Community competence. Support for that proposition may possibly be found in the judgment of the Court of Justice of 5 May 1981 in Case 804/79 *Commission* v. *United Kingdom*,[192] in which the Court described certain Commission proposals as representing 'the point of departure for concerted Community action'.[193] Whilst the Court's decision concerned the exclusive competence of the Community,[194] that does not prevent the finding in question from also being applied in the field of concurrent competence. However, the submission of a Commission proposal will not generally be regarded as sufficient to transform a concurrent power into an exclusive power of the Community, since it is possible that the proposal will either not be accepted at all or will be adopted only after a lengthy period has elapsed or in a totally changed form. Nevertheless, it would seem that the possibility of such an interpretation being applied in an individual case cannot be wholly excluded.

This raises the further question whether similar effects can be attributed to Commission communications themselves. Basically, the objection to that proposition is that communications are generally only preparatory in nature. Communications not only set forth the Commission's legislative programmes but also frequently deal with whether Community rules should be adopted at all. In the latter case, at least, there can be no question of any exercise of concurrent Community competence. The position may be different in individual cases involving relatively specific legislative programmes.

---

190 See, by way of exception, the Communication on the development of European standardization, 'Action for Faster Technological Integration in Europe' (OJ 1991 C 20).

191 See 'The results of the EEC Treaty', pp. 200 *et seq.*, above, *in fine*.

192 [1981] ECR 1045.

193 *ibid.*, at p. 1075.

194 *ibid.*, at pp. 1075 *et seq.*: 'As this is a field reserved to the powers of the Community, within which Member States may henceforth act only as trustees of the common interest ...'.

V. RESOLUTIONS OF THE EUROPEAN PARLIAMENT

1. Outward Form and Scope of Application

Resolutions constitute the typical form in which acts are adopted by the European Parliament, not only in the cultural field but generally. It is basically possible to distinguish two groups of resolutions. The first consists of resolutions which become necessary in the context of the Community legislative process, whether by reason of the mandatory or optional consultation of the European Parliament or in the context of the cooperation procedure provided for by Article 149(2) of the EEC Treaty; such resolutions are consequently referred to as 'legislative resolutions'.[195] The second group comprises resolutions adopted by the Parliament on its own initiative, which may appropriately be referred to as 'initiative resolutions'. They are conditional either on the tabling of a motion for a resolution by members of the Parliament[196] or on the submission of an own-initiative report by a Parliamentary committee.[197]

Whilst the scope of the first group of resolutions is laid down by the EEC Treaty, the second group is not referred to in any of the Treaties. However, the Parliament makes extensive use of its ability to adopt initiative resolutions, not least in the cultural field.[198] In so doing, the Parliament occasionally exceeds – sometimes manifestly, sometimes less obviously – the bounds of collective Community competence; however, a detailed examination of that phenomenon falls outside the scope of this work. As is stated above in relation to the permissibility of acts of the Community institutions,[199] the Parliament, in so doing, strays outside the limits of its powers. It is not possible to concur with Klein's contention that 'recourse by the European Parliament to powers for the purposes of dealing with political events throughout the world'[200] can be justified by an 'interpretation agreement concluded by the Member States',[201] since the Member States are obliged to observe the Community legal order even where they work together in concert; any changes which they may wish to make to Community law are subject to the procedure for amending the Treaty which is laid down in Article 236 of the EEC Treaty.[202]

It is likewise necessary to reject Bleckmann's approach of inferring from the democratic principle enshrined in Community law that the Parliament's political mandate authorizes it to adopt resolutions on subjects lying wholly outside the sphere of competence of the EC,[203] since it is impossible to prove that the democratic principle required the collective competence of the Community to be exceeded. To argue that there is nothing in the Treaty limiting the matters which may be debated and made the subject of resolutions adopted at Parliamentary

---

195 See the Rules of Procedure of the European Parliament (OJ 1995 L 293), Rule 58(2).
196 *ibid.*, Rule 45.
197 *ibid.*, Rule 148.
198 See, in each case, the sections relating to the European Parliament in Part 2 of this work.
199 See 'The permissibility of an act', pp. 255 *et seq.*, above.
200 Klein, *Vertragsauslegung*, p. 105.
201 *ibid.*, at p. 104.
202 See also, to the same effect, Steinberger, p. 18.
203 Bleckmann, *Europarecht*, p. 59.

sessions[204] is to misunderstand the division of powers between the Community and the Member States. That such *ultra vires* acts are not justiciable by reason of their lack of legal significance does not alter the fact that they are unlawful.

However, the Parliament's obligation to respect the collective competence of the Community has been loosened to a certain extent by the Single European Act. The first sentence of Article 30(4) of the Single European Act provides for the European Parliament to be closely involved in European Political Cooperation. According to the second sentence of Article 30(4) of the Act, the Presidency of European Political Cooperation is to ensure 'that the views of the European Parliament are duly taken into consideration'. Consequently, it will frequently be possible to justify acts which exceed the collective competence of the Community by reference to the mandatory involvement of the Parliament in European Political Cooperation. In addition, the Parliament will have to be allowed the right to express its views on matters which should in its opinion be included within the sphere of Community competence, by means of the amendment of the Treaty, even though the Parliament's right to be consulted, in the context of the procedure for amending the Treaty, pursuant to the second paragraph of Article 236 of the Treaty extends, according to the wording of that provision, only to draft amendments already submitted by the Commission or the Member States.

To sum up, it may therefore be concluded that the European Parliament is empowered to adopt 'simple parliamentary decisions'[205] in the form of resolutions, but that, in so doing, it is bound in principle (i.e. subject to the considerations described above) by the collective competence of the Community, and, as Magiera has established in relation to German constitutional law,[206] may not exercise that power in a manner which detracts from the autonomous powers of the other institutions.

2. THE ROLE OF THE RESOLUTIONS IN QUESTION IN THE COMMUNITY LEGISLATIVE PROCESS

In common with resolutions adopted at Council level and Commission communications, own-initiative resolutions of the European Parliament play a role in the Community legislative process. Frequently it would appear that acts of the Community can be traced back to a resolution of the Parliament, as, for example, in the case of Community activity in the narrower cultural field.[207] Generally, however, it will be difficult to demonstrate a clear causal link.[208]

In this respect, too, it is apparent that the Commission's 'monopoly power to initiate measures' is limited to the submission of formal proposals for the

---

204 As is contended by Elles, p. 413.

205 As to the meaning of this term, see Steinberger, p. 33; as regards German constitutional law, see Magiera, *Parlament und Staatsleitung*, pp. 210 *et seq.*

206 Magiera, op. cit., p. 217.

207 See 'The European Parliament', pp. 66 *et seq.*, above; see also, in general terms, Glaesner, *Einführung*, p. 40.

208 See also, to the same effect, Jacobs & Corbett, p. 181.

initiation of the legislative process. In advance of such proposals, the European Parliament can bring its ideas to bear, since the Commission does not have a 'monopoly in ideas'.[209]

---

209 See Jacobs & Corbett, p. 180.

Chapter 4

POSSIBLE DEVELOPMENTS
IN COMMUNITY LAW
IN THE CULTURAL FIELD

I. INTRODUCTION

Possible developments in Community law in the cultural field can be discussed
not only on the basis of the law currently in force but also with regard to the
forthcoming amendments to the Treaty. Whilst Treaty amendments providing for
Community competence in the cultural field, particularly in the sphere of culture
in the narrower sense of the term, appear likely,[1] the specific form of the alterations
to be made and the date of their entry into force remain uncertain. Furthermore, a
discussion of the desirability of cultural competence at Community level lies
outside the scope of the present work. It is necessary, therefore, to deal with the
question of possible developments in Community law in the cultural field solely
on the basis of the law currently in force.

   That question is not of equal interest with regard to each of the three sectors of
the cultural field, namely education and training, science, and culture in the
narrower sense of the term. Whilst the fields of education and training and science
have a more-or-less assured basis in the Treaties, the field of culture in the narrower
sense is scarcely mentioned in them at all.[2] Consequently, the question arises in
relation to that field in particular as to what room is afforded by Community law
for any further development. It is clear from the way in which Community law has
developed to date that the absence of any mention of a matter in the Treaty has not

---

1   See Title XV ('Tourism') and Title XIX ('Culture') of the provisions concerning the EEC
Treaty which are contained in the 'Draft Treaty on Union' produced by the Luxembourg
Presidency, the English language version of which is published in Europe-Agence Internationale,
Documents Nos 1722 and 1723 of 5 July 1991; see also, since then, Title IX ('Culture') of Part 3
of the EC Treaty in the version contained in the Treaty on European Union signed on 7 February
1992 (OJ 1992 C 191, p. 1, at p. 24).
2   See above, under 'Introduction' at pp. 31 *et seq.*, 49 *et seq.*, and 63 *et seq.*

prevented the Community institutions from opening up new areas for Community policy.

There follows below, therefore, a discussion of whether, and to what extent, the narrower cultural field falls to be considered for an independent Community policy, taking the form of something more than a mere 'side-effect',[3] as it were, of the exercise of powers under the Treaty,[4] and going beyond *ad hoc* financial assistance measures on the part of the Commission[5] which lack any legal basis and possibly do not even require one.[6] The first part of the discussion seeks to demonstrate, by way of example, how the development of new fields of policy takes place in practice in the Community. There then follows a discussion from a legal standpoint of the possibility of developing a 'flanking policy' in the narrower cultural field.

II. THE DEVELOPMENT OF 'FLANKING POLICIES' IN THE COMMUNITY

The term 'flanking policies' has come into use to signify autonomous policy areas which, whilst not expressly referred to in the Treaties establishing the Communities, are nonetheless laid claim to by the Community institutions as areas within their competence.[7] The characteristic of 'flanking', i.e. the element of the policies in question providing protection and lateral cover,[8] indicates that the autonomy of those policy areas is not so extensive that they have no bearing on the integration of the Member States of the Community. On the contrary, the function of such policies clearly lies in the very fact that they are intended to secure and underpin the integration process. There follows below a more detailed analysis of the development of a 'flanking policy' with reference to the field of environmental protection, since that field provides a particularly good illustration of such development, in the light not only of the legislation adopted by the Community institutions but also of the case-law of the Court of Justice.

---

3   That is the term used by Grabitz & Sasse, p. 97, in relation to the possibility, prior to the Single European Act, of taking environmental problems into consideration in the exercise of Community competence.

4   For a more detailed analysis, see 'The modalities of the exercise of Community competence in the cultural field', pp. 205 *et seq.*, above.

5   For a more detailed discussion of these activities, see the concluding passages of 'Individual Measures', pp. 74 *et seq.*, above; Flesch, *EG -Informationen 5/1991*, p. 3.

6   Fiedler, pp. 172 *et seq.*, adopts a critical approach to the question whether such financial activities on the part of the Commission continue to fall below the threshold of 'significant new Community action', within the meaning of Point IV.3(c) of the Joint Declaration by the European Parliament, the Council and the Commission on various measures to improve the budgetary procedure (OJ 1982 C 194, p. 1), which require the adoption of a basic regulation providing for the use of the means laid down in the budget; see also Glaesner, *Einführung*, p. 40, who refers to a declaration in the minutes relating to that provision stating that 'significant new Community action' was not to include pilot action on the part of the Commission.

7   e.g. see L.-J. Constantinesco, pp. 256 *et seq.*; Lauwaars, p. 100; Beutler et al., *3rd ed.*, pp. 77 *et seq.*; R. Böhm, p. 328.

8   See *Webster's Third New International Dictionary* (1981 edition) under 'flank': 'to shelter or protect a side of', 'to stand or be situated at the side of'.

The political impetus for the development of an environmental policy at Community level was provided by the Paris Summit Conference of 19–21 October 1972. In the final declaration the Heads of State or Government emphasized 'the importance of a Community environmental policy' and invited the Community institutions 'to establish before 31 July 1973 a programme of action accompanied by a precise timetable'.[9] That passage from the final declaration must be regarded as giving concrete form to the introductory observations, which expressed the need to avoid seeing economic expansion as an end in itself and stated that such expansion must result in an improvement in the quality of life as well as in standards of living.[10] The Heads of State or Government regarded it as appropriate, for the purposes of putting the action programme into effect, to 'utilize to the maximum all of the provisions of the Treaties, including Article 235 of the EEC Treaty'.[11]

The above outline illustrates the procedure followed at Community level: the starting-point for Community activity is not the question as to what possibilities for action are afforded by the EEC Treaty; instead, the starting-point is the recognition of a substantive problem needing, by reason of its Community-wide dimension or its significance for the integration process, to be dealt with at Community level. Because of the potential for cross-border environmental pollution,[12] the field of environmental protection represents a particularly illuminating example.[13] Only at a subsequent stage is an examination undertaken of the question as to which forms of possible action are available under Community law for the Community-wide resolution of the problem in question. The rules of Community law are thus brought in to serve policy objectives; the possibilities for action by the Community institutions within the framework of the policy objectives in question are limited by the conditions laid down in the individual enabling provisions of the Treaty.

In the environmental field, it has been primarily Articles 100 and 235 of the EEC Treaty which have been used as a legal basis, sometimes individually[14] and sometimes jointly.[15] It is scarcely possible to conceive of any legal objections to the application of Article 100 of the Treaty.[16] The Court of Justice has held that it

---

9   *EC General Report* 6/1972, p. 14.

10   *ibid.*, at p. 8.

11   *ibid.*, at p. 18.

12   See in that regard Scheuing, *EuR 1989*, p. 153; Behrens, p. 22.

13   e.g. see Haneklaus, p. 1136, who states that, faced with pressing environmental problems, the Community decided to develop a Community environmental policy. Scheuing writes in *EuR 1989*, p. 153, that the Heads of State or Government were unable to escape the realization that Community solutions were needed, and according to Grabitz & Zacker, p. 297, the environmental problems had been recognized early on at European level.

14   e.g. see the Council Directive of 20 March 1970 on the approximation of the laws of the Member States relating to measures to be taken against air pollution by gases from positive-ignition engines of motor vehicles (OJ, English Special Edition 1970 (I), p. 171) (Art. 100) and the Council Directive of 2 April 1979 on the conservation of wild birds (OJ 1979 L 103, p. 1) (Art. 235).

15   e.g. see the Council Directive of 4 May 1976 on pollution caused by certain dangerous substances discharged into the aquatic environment of the Community (OJ 1976 L 129, p. 23).

16   For a concurring view, see Nicolaysen, *Environmental policy*, p. 112.

is 'by no means ruled out that provisions on the environment may be based on Article 100 of the Treaty',[17] since, in the absence of harmonization of national legislative provisions relating to environmental protection, competition could appreciably be distorted.[18] Whilst the application of Article 100 of the EEC Treaty in the field of environmental protection was conditional on the requirement that the provisions laid down in individual Member States must directly affect the Common Market, Article 235 of the Treaty conferred on the Community institutions the power to act in cases in which the 'direct effect on the common market ... (was) scarcely discernible'[19] and which were therefore concerned for their own sake with the protection of the environment.[20] The legislative zenith in that regard was reached with the Council Directive of 2 April 1979 on the conservation of wild birds.[21] Having regard to the Community objective laid down by Article 235 of the EEC Treaty, the preamble to the directive recited, without stating any further grounds, that the conservation of wild birds naturally occurring in the European territory of the Member States was 'necessary to attain, within the operation of the common market, the Community's objectives regarding the improvement of living conditions, a harmonious development of economic activities throughout the Community and a continuous and balanced expansion'.[22]

By contrast, the reasons given for using Article 235 of the Treaty as well as Article 100 in the Council Directive of 17 December 1979 on the protection of groundwater against pollution caused by certain dangerous substances[23] are more informative. The preamble states that it is necessary 'for this approximation of laws to be accompanied by Community action in the sphere of environmental protection and improvement of the quality of life'.[24] That wording refers to the European Communities' first Programme of Action on Environmental Protection of 22 November 1973,[25] the preamble to which states that the EEC's task, laid down in Article 2 of the EEC Treaty, of promoting throughout the Community a harmonious development of economic activities and a continuous and balanced expansion 'cannot now be imagined in the absence of an effective campaign to combat pollution and nuisances or of an improvement in the quality of life and the protection of the environment'.[26] It goes on to state that improvement in the quality of life and the protection of the natural environment are among the fundamental tasks of the Community.[27]

---

17   Judgment of 18 March 1980 in Case 91/79 *Commission* v. *Italy* [1980] ECR 1099 (at p. 1106).

18   *ibid.*

19   See Zuleeg, *ZfW 1975*, p. 136.

20   See Usher, p. 5.

21   OJ 1979 L 103, p. 1.

22   *ibid.*, sixth recital in the preamble.

23   OJ 1980 L 20, p. 43.

24   *ibid.*, fifth recital in the preamble.

25   OJ 1973 C 112, p. 1, adopted as a 'Declaration of the Council of the European Communities and of the Representatives of the Governments of the Member States meeting in the Council'.

26   *ibid.*, fourth recital in the preamble.

27   *ibid.*, fifth recital in the preamble.

Whilst that wording created a further link between the economic development and expansion referred to in Article 2 of the Treaty and Community environmental protection, express reference was made a little later on in the action programme to the improvement of the living and working conditions referred to in the preamble to the EEC Treaty.[28] That paved the way for an independent Community environmental policy, whose sole connection with the economic dimension of the Community apparently lay in the fact that the achievement of that economic dimension *cannot ... be imagined* in the absence of ... an improvement in the quality of life and the protection of the environment'.[29]

The permissibility of the development of a 'flanking policy' in the environmental field was confirmed by the Court of Justice in its judgment of 7 February 1985 in Case 240/83 *ADBHU*,[30] in which it held that the Council directive at issue in that case fell within the scope of environmental protection, 'which is one of the Community's essential objectives'.[31] That wording appears to refer to the third recital in the preamble to the EEC Treaty, in which the constant improvement of living and working conditions is likewise described as an 'essential objective'. It followed that environmental protection constituted not merely an aspect to be borne in mind in the context, and within the limits, of the other provisions of the Treaty but an 'objective of general interest' capable of placing limits on the fundamental freedoms enshrined in the Treaty.[32] Accordingly, it was logical to recognize the protection of the environment as a 'mandatory requirement' which may limit the application of Article 30 of the Treaty and thus restrict the free movement of goods.[33] The 'crowning achievement' of the Community's 'flanking environmental policy' was its express incorporation in the EEC Treaty as a result of the Single European Act.[34]

On looking back to the starting-point of the development described above, namely the 1972 Paris Summit Conference, it appears that the political will to pursue an autonomous Community policy in the environmental field, as manifested at that conference, was realized with the aid of Community law and with the approval of the Court of Justice. Seen in general terms, the practical consequence of that finding is that the development of 'flanking policies' of the Community ultimately depends on the Member States' having the common political will to implement a given policy. In this connection, Article 235 of the EEC Treaty has the function of serving as the legal basis for action which goes beyond the confines of the other provisions of the Treaty and hence characterizes the 'flanking policies'. It is apparent from the appreciable increase in the use made of Article 235 of the Treaty in the Community legislation adopted prior to the entry into force of the Single European Act[35] that the Community was addressing

---

28 OJ 1973 C 112, p. 1, introduction to Part I of the Annex.
29 op. cit., n. 26; emphasis added.
30 [1985] ECR 531.
31 *ibid.*, at p. 549.
32 *ibid.*, with reference to the 'principle of free trade'.
33 Judgment of the Court of Justice of 20 September 1988 in Case 302/86 *Commission* v. *Denmark* [1988] ECR 4607 (at p. 4630).
34 See Art. 25 of the Single European Act (OJ 1987 L 169, p. 11).
35 See Grabitz in: *idem, Kommentar zum EWGV*, Art. 235, n. 9; as to developments prior to 1 September 1975, see Everling, *EuR 1976, Sonderheft*, pp. 6 *et seq.*

itself increasingly to areas of responsibility which did not appear to warrant comprehensive treatment at Community level under the other provisions of the Treaty. Subject to any amendment of the Treaties,[36] it is anticipated that that trend will be given fresh impetus in the course of the completion of the internal market.

This empirical finding may reduce the significance of any *legal* discussion of the possibility of developing a 'flanking policy' in the narrower cultural field. However, it does not remove the need for such a discussion, since the law operates as the means of realizing policy ideas at Community level.

III. THE POSSIBILITY OF DEVELOPING A COMMUNITY 'FLANKING POLICY' IN THE CULTURAL FIELD

1. The Conditions for the Application of Article 235 of the EEC Treaty

In order to consider the possibility of developing a 'flanking policy' in the cultural field, it is necessary to examine the conditions laid down for the application of Article 235 of the EEC Treaty, constituting as it does the decisive provision governing the opening up of new policy fields. Article 235 provides that the Council, acting unanimously on a proposal from the Commission and after consulting the European Parliament, is to take the appropriate measures if 'action by the Community should prove necessary to attain, in the course of the operation of the common market, one of the objectives of the Community and this Treaty has not provided the necessary powers'.

All the conditions for the application of Article 235 of the Treaty give rise to problems to a certain extent, and are capable of having a bearing on whether it is possible to develop a 'flanking policy' in the narrower cultural field. However, 'the key problem of interpretation' is what is meant by 'the objectives of the Community',[37] which Article 235 is to help to attain. The fact that its conditions of application look towards the objectives of the Community makes Article 235 fundamentally different from all of the other enabling provisions of the Treaty. Consequently, the analysis undertaken below focuses on the aspect of 'the objectives of the Community'. Following that analysis, it is proposed briefly to discuss what significance is to be attached to the necessary link, expressed in

---

36 According to the 'Draft Treaty on Union' published by Europe-Agence Internationale, Documents Nos 1722 and 1723 of 5 July 1991, Art. 235 of the EEC Treaty was expected to take the following form: '(1) Should it prove that attainment of one of the objectives of the Community calls for action by the Community in one of the fields covered by Articles 3 [and 3a] and this Treaty has not provided the necessary powers, the Council shall, acting unanimously on a proposal from the Commission and after receiving the assent of the European Parliament, adopt the appropriate measures while taking into account the principle of subsidiarity as defined in Article 3b. (2) The Council shall determine, under the conditions laid down in paragraph 1, what shall be covered by decisions to be taken by qualified majority.' In the text as finally signed on 7 February 1992, Art. 235 was left unamended; see the Treaty on European Union, OJ 1992 C 191, p. 1.

37 According to Everling, *EuR 1976, Sonderheft*, p. 9; he refers, however, not to the objectives 'of the Community' (which is the wording used in Art. 235) but to objectives 'of the Treaty'.

Article 235, between Community measures and 'the course of the operation of the common market'.

2. THE REQUIREMENT OF A COMMUNITY OBJECTIVE IN THE CULTURAL FIELD

(a) The objectives of the Community

The question of the objectives of the Community within the meaning of Article 235 of the EEC Treaty will be investigated in two stages. The first stage will involve an examination of what objectives the Community has in fact been set; in the second stage, an analysis will be undertaken of whether the concept of an objective, as the term is used in Article 235 of the Treaty, contains any element which diverges from the compass of the Community objectives as established in the first stage, in particular, whether it has a restricted content.

(i) The objectives of the Community in general

The EEC Treaty lays down objectives to be achieved by the Community, and imposes on it tasks[38] of varying degrees of abstraction,[39] drawing no apparent distinction between the objectives 'of the Community' and the objectives 'of the Treaty'.[40] Parts 2-4 of the Treaty lay down objectives for the Community which may be described as specific[41] or sectoral[42] objectives. According to the classification undertaken by Magiera, objectives of a general nature are contained in the preamble to the EEC Treaty and in the principles set out in Part 1 of the Treaty.[43] Whilst no further problems appear to arise in relation to the category of specific Treaty objectives, nor as regards Article 3 of the Treaty,[44] Article 2 and the preamble to the Treaty need to be considered more closely.

It is not disputed that Article 2 of the Treaty lays down objectives of the Community. This has been acknowledged by the Court of Justice, which referred,

---

38   It does not appear possible to draw any distinction between the objectives and the tasks of the Community; see Magiera, *GS Wilhelm Karl Geck*, p. 514; Zuleeg in: GTE, *Kommentar zum EWGV*, Art. 2, n. 1, where reference is made to the judgment of the Court of Justice of 29 September 1987 in Case 126/86 *Zaera* [1987] ECR 3697 (at p. 3715), in which the Court refers, in connection with Art. 2 of the Treaty, which describes the *task* of the Community, to the *aims* laid down in that provision. From a theoretical standpoint, however, it must be conceded that the purpose of a task is invariably the achievement of an objective; see Köck, *FS Ingaz Seidl-Hohenveldern*, p. 280.

39   See in that regard Magiera, op cit., p. 514.

40   Henckel von Donnersmarck, p. 51, n. 44, considers that it is possible to draw conclusions in relation to Art. 235 from the varying terminology used in the EEC Treaty; that approach is rightly criticized by Behrens, p. 270; the correct view is consequently that expressed by Everling, op. cit., n. 37.

41   See Magiera, op. cit., n. 38, p. 514.

42   See L.-J. Constantinesco, p. 274.

43   See Magiera, op. cit., n. 38, p. 514.

44   In its judgment of 12 July 1973 in Case 8/73 *Massey-Ferguson* [1973] ECR 897 (at p. 907), the Court of Justice held that Art. 3 of the EEC Treaty sets out objectives of the Community; a similar *dictum* is to be found in the earlier judgment of 21 February 1973 in Case 6/72 *Continental Can* [1973] ECR 215 (at p. 244).

in its judgment of 29 September 1987 in Case 126/86 *Zaera*,[45] to 'the aims laid down' in Article 2.[46]

However, there are problems inherent in the question whether the five general objectives of the Community set out in Article 2, which are to be achieved 'by establishing a common market and progressively approximating the economic policies of Member States', are solely economic in nature. The significance of that question attaches primarily to the last of the general objectives laid down in Article 2, namely the promotion of 'closer relations between the States' – an aim which may also contain a cultural element.

Steindorff, for example, argues that, according to Article 2 of the EEC Treaty, 'Community competence [is] restricted to the economic field'.[47] In so stating, he relies *inter alia* on the judgment of the Court of Justice of 12 December 1974 in Case 36/74 *Walrave and Koch*,[48] in which it held that, having regard to the objectives of the Community, the practice of sport was subject to Community law only in so far as it constituted an economic activity within the meaning of Article 2 of the Treaty.[49] That finding was repeated almost verbatim by the Court in its judgment of 5 October 1988 in Case 196/87 *Steymann*.[50]

It would be going too far, however, to infer from this that the Community pursues only economic objectives, since it must be borne in mind that the decisions in question were solely concerned with the legal classification of the conduct of private persons and the applicability of individual provisions of the Treaty. The economic objectives of Article 2 of the Treaty are clearly not such as to necessitate the inclusion within the scope of Community law of the non-economic activities of private individuals. It is only in that sense that the *dicta* of the Court fall to be understood. The facts of the cases in question were not such as to indicate any more far-reaching, fundamental comment on the scope of Article 2 of the EEC Treaty.

It must be concluded, therefore, that Article 2 of the Treaty contains no indication to the effect that the five general objectives set out in it are restricted to economic matters. In particular, the objective of the promotion of closer relations between the Member States of the Community is not limited to the promotion of economic relations.[51]

There is scant room for any doubt that the preamble to the EEC Treaty contains objectives; indeed, the preamble plainly sets out what have been termed 'ultimate objectives'[52] or 'long-term aims'.[53] However, the contention that those objectives constitute objectives of the Community has from time to time been challenged. The first commentator to question it was clearly Gericke, who advanced the view that the objectives contained in the preamble could be attributed only to the

---

45 [1987] ECR 3697.
46 *ibid.*, at p. 3715.
47 Steindorff, *Grenzen*, p. 37; see also, to the same effect, R. Böhm, p. 107.
48 [1974] ECR 1405.
49 *ibid.*, at p. 1417.
50 [1988] ECR 6159 (at p. 6172).
51 See also, to the same effect, Zuleeg in: GTE, *Kommentar zum EWGV*, Art. 2, n. 16; Grabitz in: *idem*, *Kommentar zum EWGV*, Art. 2, n. 8.
52 L.-J. Constantinesco, p. 274.
53 Langeheine, p. 231.

parties to the EEC Treaty, and not to the Community established by it. According to Gericke, the preamble prepares the way, conceptually, for the establishment of the EEC, and ranges over what may be termed a pre-Community sphere. In his view, the formulation of Community objectives commences with Article 1 of the Treaty.[54] That view has had,[55] and continues to have, its adherents.[56]

However, the very wording used by Gericke betrays his doubts about his theory: in so far as 'the parties to the Treaty (manifested) the will, the resolve ... the intention to achieve certain objectives, these (remained) *initially* their own national objectives – *common* objectives, it is true, since otherwise the conclusion of the Treaty could not have come about, but nevertheless *not yet immediate* objectives of the *Community* as a supranational institution'.[57] Even Gericke seems to have felt that the common objectives of the Member States were also objectives of the Community, even if they were not initially so, i.e. probably before the Treaty was concluded, possibly not yet immediately. It has been objected to Gericke's view that in most cases the objectives of the Member States and of the Community are identical.[58]

That objection does not go far enough, however. As far as the objectives formulated in the preamble are concerned, it is not merely in most cases, but in all cases, that the objectives of the Member States and those of the Community are identical. The objectives of all the Member States laid down in the preamble *are* the objectives of the Community – they embody the 'fundamental will of the Community'.[59] In this context, what has been said about the distinction drawn by some commentators between a 'Community policy' and a 'common policy'[60] applies *mutatis mutandis*. The preamble constitutes not merely a document to be ascribed to the groundwork leading up to the EEC Treaty, laying down common objectives of the Member States by way of motives and expectations,[61] but an integral part of the Treaty which, whilst couched in abstract terms, is nevertheless legally binding.[62]

The Court of Justice has affirmed that view[63] by using the preamble as a means of interpretation and also by expressly inferring from it tasks, that is to say objectives, of the Community the achievement of which is incumbent on the Community institutions.[64] That interpretation is also indirectly confirmed by the

---

54 Gericke, pp. 32 *et seq.*
55 Schumacher, p. 542; Tomuschat, *EuR 1976, Sonderheft*, p. 61, n. 65, regarded Gericke's view as 'not hitherto rebutted'. He has since argued that the preamble unquestionably forms part of the objectives of the Community; see *idem, F.I.D.E. Reports*, p. 30.
56 e.g. see Dorn, p. 114.
57 Gericke, p. 33; emphasis added.
58 See Behrens, p. 268.
59 See Matthias, p. 21.
60 See 'Principles underlying the powers of action of the Community institutions', pp. 128 *et seq.*, above.
61 As to these concepts, see, for example, Schumacher, p. 542.
62 Magiera, *GS Wilhelm Karl Geck*, p. 515; Zuleeg in: GTE, *Kommentar zum EWGV*, Preamble, n. 1; Schepers, pp. 356 *et seq.*
63 e.g. see the judgment of 13 July 1966 in Case 32/65 *Italy* v. *Commission* [1966] ECR 389 (at p. 405): 'Article 85 as a whole should be read in the context of the provisions of the preamble to the Treaty which clarify it'.
64 Opinion 1/76 of 26 April 1977 [1977] ECR 741 (at p. 758).

third paragraph of Article 131 of the EEC Treaty,[65] which refers to 'the principles set out in the preamble to this Treaty'. According to the case-law of the Court of Justice, the word 'principle' is used, in the language of the Treaty, 'in order to indicate the fundamental nature of certain provisions'.[66] The Court has held that it is not permissible to reduce that concept to the rank of a vague declaration.[67]

To sum up, therefore, both Article 2 of the EEC Treaty and the preamble to the Treaty are to be taken into account for the purposes of ascertaining the objectives of the Community. Those objectives are subject to the same dynamic as that inherent in Community law as a whole,[68] i.e. their significance may change[69] and they may now permit or require measures which in former times could not yet have been taken into consideration.

(ii) The objectives of the Community within the meaning of Article 235 of the EEC Treaty

In the light of the foregoing discussion of the objectives of the Community, it is necessary to justify separate treatment of the question of the objectives of the Community *within the meaning of Article 235 of the EEC Treaty*, since the wording of Article 235 provides no evidence to suggest that the objectives of the Community, as referred to in that article, could have any other meaning than that indicated above. Article 235 does not refer to 'indirect' or 'direct' objectives, to 'general' or 'specific' objectives, or to 'abstract' or 'concrete' objectives, but merely to 'objectives'. In so far as the question raised nevertheless requires discussion, the reason is to be found in the numerous attempts made in the literature to limit the scope of Article 235 by means of a narrow construction of the term 'objective'. Recourse to the preamble in order to determine Community objectives within the meaning of Article 235 of the Treaty is perceived as a threat potentially resulting in 'all of the special confines of competence' being 'washed away'[70] or in a 'disregard of the predetermined structures'.[71]

It is necessary to examine, as the first argument in favour of restricting the concept of 'objectives' contained in Article 235, the contention that the objectives set out in Article 2 of the Treaty and in its preamble are too general.[72] As has already been established above, however, Article 235 makes no distinction between general and specific objectives. This means that the general nature of the objectives is not an appropriate criterion for narrowing the scope of Article 235, in the absence of any explanation as to the extent to which the very generality of an objective prevents it from falling within the framework of Article 235. It is moreover doubtful whether the individual objectives set out in the preamble and in Article 2 of the EEC Treaty are really as general as has been alleged. Schwartz has

---

65 For a concurring view, see also Magiera, op. cit., n. 62, p. 515.
66 Judgment of 8 April 1976 in Case 43/75 *Defrenne* [1976] ECR 455 (at p. 474).
67 *ibid.*
68 See in that regard 'The dynamic of Community law', pp. 200 *et seq.*, above.
69 e.g. see Behrens, p. 269; Henckel von Donnersmarck, pp. 50 *et seq.*
70 Zuleeg, *Der Staat 1978*, p. 43.
71 Henckel von Donnersmarck, p. 50.
72 See, with regard to Art. 2 of the EEC Treaty, Everling, *EuR 1976, Sonderheft*, p. 9; as regards the preamble, see, for example, Gericke, p. 32.

shown that this is not the case as regards the great majority of the objectives mentioned in the preamble.[73] However, even the objective of laying 'the foundations of an ever closer union among the peoples of Europe' contained in the preamble, which Schwartz regards as insufficiently precise, must be accepted as constituting an objective within the meaning of Article 235, since both that objective and the other objectives laid down in the preamble self-evidently need, to a greater or lesser extent, to be given some concrete form. That concrete form is provided *by* the relevant legal instrument adopted on the basis of Article 235 of the Treaty by the Council, which thus has the task of giving them substance.

A further argument for restricting the concept of objectives within the meaning of Article 235 of the Treaty is derived from Article 2. That article provides two means of achieving the five general objectives which it lays down: the establishment of a common market and the approximation of the economic policies of the Member States. It has been inferred from this that the objectives set out in Article 2 may be achieved *only* by those two means,[74] and that the concept of objectives embodies, to a certain extent, an inherent limitation restricting the vehicle by which they are to be achieved to the means expressly referred to.[75] One judgment of the Court of Justice appears, at first sight, to support that view.[76] In its judgment of 29 September 1987 in Case 126/86 *Zaera*,[77] it held that the objectives laid down in Article 2 of the Treaty were concerned with the existence and functioning of the Community, and that they were to be achieved 'through the establishment of the common market and the progressive approximation of the economic policies of Member States'.[78]

As against this, it may be objected, however, that the object of the Court's decision was not the extent of Community competence but the different question as to whether the general objectives laid down in Article 2 of the Treaty impose specific legal obligations on the Member States and/or confer rights on which individuals may rely. The Court rejected that objection on the grounds quoted above. In the final analysis, it emphasized only the special nature of provisions laying down objectives as descriptions of states of affairs aspired to in the future, which still have to be achieved and hence cannot be regarded as a basis for present rights and obligations. It is not possible to draw from the judgment in *Zaera* any more extensive inferences, particularly as regards the means available to the Community for achieving the objectives of the Treaty.

In support of his view that the objectives referred to in Article 235 of the Treaty must be interpreted restrictively in the light of the two vehicles mentioned in Article 2, Everling puts forward an argument based on comparative linguistics. He concludes from the French text of the Treaty, which renders the German word

---

73 Schwartz in: GBTE, *Kommentar zum EWGV*, Art. 235, n. 119.

74 e.g. see Steindorff, *Grenzen*, p. 47; Schwartz in: GBTE, *Kommentar zum EWGV*, Art. 235, n. 81; Everling, *EuR 1976, Sonderheft*, p. 11; Gericke, p. 24; Grabitz in: *idem, Kommentar zum EWGV*, Art. 235, n. 23.

75 This view is apparently shared by Fiedler, p. 168: whilst acknowledging that the objectives laid down in Art. 2 of the EEC Treaty are very widely framed, he argues that Art. 235 is intended to cover only activities 'which have at least indirect effects on the economy'.

76 Steindorff, *Grenzen*, pp. 46 *et seq.*, relies on that decision.

77 [1987] ECR 3697.

78 *ibid.*, at pp. 3715 *et seq.*

'Ziele' as 'objets', not as 'objectives', that Article 235 is intended to refer to 'objectives in the form given to the term by the *subject-matters* of the Treaty'.[79] However, this linguistic comparison is clearly being used not as the basis for his view but in order to shore up a preconceived opinion. If this were not the case, Everling would have had to take into account the other language versions of the Treaty, and would have found, for example, that the English version refers to 'objectives', despite the fact that, in English, the word 'objects' is capable of having the same connotation as the French 'objets', that the Italian text of the Treaty refers to 'scopi', a term which can be translated as 'objectives' or 'purposes' but not as 'subject-matter', and that the Dutch term 'doelstellingen' is likewise to be translated as 'objectives'. Accordingly, a comparison of the texts of the Treaty, all of which are equally binding,[80] does not produce any clear result.

Grabitz considers, however, that Everling's interpretation is borne out by the scheme of the Treaty.[81] He contends that Article 235 constitutes a competence-conferring provision, and that, as such, it has the function of promoting the fulfilment of the tasks of the Community, defined in the most general terms in Article 2 as 'establishing a common market' and 'approximating the economic policies of Member States' and more specifically in the fields of activity set out in Article 3 and in other individual provisions of the Treaty. The wording of Article 235 likewise indicates, he argues, that the attainment of the objectives must be necessary 'in the course of the operation of the common market'. This means, in his view, that the objectives must in any event have some bearing on the tasks described in general terms in Article 2 of the Treaty.[82]

The following objections may be raised in opposition to that view. In describing the function of Article 235 of the Treaty as a competence-conferring provision, Grabitz assumes that the term 'tasks' is a restricted one, which is precisely what he is seeking to establish. Moreover, he takes as evidence in support of his interpretation another element of Article 235, namely the attainment of objectives 'in the course of the operation of the common market'.[83] This shows that the notion of a Community objective, viewed in isolation, clearly cannot support the restrictive interpretation thus advocated. If, however, the 'objectives of the Community' constitute an independent element of Article 235, then those objectives must also be ascertained independently, that is to say, without recourse to other elements of Article 235.

Consequently, it must be assumed that the term 'objectives of the Community' in Article 235 of the Treaty means all the objectives of the Community, as described above. It is precisely because it relates to the objectives of the Community that – as has already been stated – Article 235 stands out from the

---

79 Everling, *EuR 1976, Sonderheft*, p. 10 (emphasis added); for a concurring view, see Grabitz in: *idem, Kommentar zum EWGV*, Art. 235, n. 22.

80 Schweitzer in: Grabitz, *Kommentar zum EWGV*, Art. 248, n. 5.

81 Grabitz in: *idem, Kommentar zum EWGV*, Art. 235, n. 23.

82 *ibid.*; see also, to the same effect, Schwartz in: GBTE, *Kommentar zum EWGV*, Art. 235, n. 81, in which it is contended that the five main objectives laid down in Art. 2 of the Treaty may not be promoted with the aid of Art. 235 by measures which cannot be attributed to one of those two means, and that the machinery of Art. 2 may not be circumvented.

83 Bleckmann, *Europarecht*, p. 207, likewise takes this element into account in order more precisely to define the objectives of the Community.

other provisions of the Treaty, and to that extent represents in some degree – in addition to 'establishing a common market' and 'approximating the economic policies of Member States' – a further means of attaining the objectives of the Community. The position occupied by Article 235 within the scheme of the Treaty lends support to this view: as a 'general' provision,[84] to use a mathematical metaphor, it is a factor placed before the brackets.

Therefore, the notion of a Community objective as it appears in Article 235 of the EEC Treaty cannot be restricted to the means of attainment provided for in Article 2. Thus it is not possible to limit the scope of Article 235 by reference to the notion of an objective. At best, the fact that Article 235 links Community measures to 'the course of the operation of the common market' could lend support to a possible restriction of its scope of application.[85]

(b) The objectives of the Community in the cultural field

Now that it has been established that the objectives of the Community are to be found not only in the specific provisions of the Treaty but also in the preamble and in Article 2, and that those objectives are not subject to any inherent restrictions imposed by Article 2, the question remains as to which of the objectives laid down by the Treaty could be used to implement a 'flanking policy' of the Community in the cultural field. The view has on occasion been advanced in the literature that in order for culture to come under the Community umbrella there would need to be a new objective, which is not contained in Community law as it stands at present. It is contended in this connection that Article 235 of the EEC Treaty does not permit the formulation of new objectives.[86] Other authors infer from the reality of Community law the more pragmatic conclusion that, if it has proved possible to bring environmental protection under the Community umbrella, then it is only logical to hold that this would also be possible for culture.[87] There is a minority of writers who tend more positively to support the application of Article 235 of the Treaty to cultural matters.[88]

As far as the possibility of setting cultural objectives is concerned, it is necessary to look more closely at the preamble and Article 2 of the EEC Treaty. The objectives in the preamble which primarily fall to be considered are those concerning the laying of foundations of an ever closer union among the peoples of Europe and the constant improvement of living conditions, the wide formulation of which is such that neither excludes the cultural dimension.[89] In Article 2, it is above all the objective of promoting closer relations between the Member States which goes beyond the economic field and offers scope for a cultural dimension.

---

84   Art. 235 appears in Part Six of the Treaty, entitled 'General and final provisions', and is not a final provision.

85   See in this regard 'The attainment of objectives "in the course of the operation of the common market" ', pp. 295 *et seq.*, below.

86   e.g. see L.-J. Constantinesco, p. 260; in the result, this is also the view taken by Bleckmann, *Europarecht*, p. 207.

87   See Tomuschat, *F.I.D.E. Reports*, p. 30; Fiedler, p. 169; de Witte, *Cultural policy*, p. 204.

88   e.g. see Schröder, p. 55.

89   For a concurring view, see Magiera, *Emergence*, p. 16.

Whilst the objective of the improvement of living conditions sheds no light on the form which a cultural objective is to take – although the concept of living conditions unquestionably has a cultural dimension – it is possible to identify a cultural objective with sufficient precision in the objective of closer relations between the peoples or Member States of the Community. According to that objective, the task, and thus the aim, of the Community must be regarded as the promotion of mutual knowledge of the various cultures, e.g. by means of exchange programmes, the furtherance of knowledge of foreign languages or the promotion of tourism. The scope of that objective does not extend to levelling out the differences between cultures, since the existence of different cultural areas at present and in the future is implicit, just as the existence of different European peoples and of different States is implicit in the preamble and in Article 2 of the EEC Treaty respectively.

The cultural objective of the Community has been secured by the adoption of the Single European Act. In the preamble to the Act, the Contracting Parties express their will 'to transform relations as a whole among their States into a European Union, in accordance with the Solemn Declaration of Stuttgart of 19 June 1983'. Article 1 of the Act expressly imposes on the Community the objective of contributing, together with European Political Cooperation, 'to making concrete progress towards European unity'. The objective of achieving the union of the peoples of Europe has thus been given concrete shape in a legally binding way.[90] The Solemn Declaration of Stuttgart,[91] referred to in the preamble, contains a section on cultural cooperation which, like the Declaration as a whole, has, since the adoption of the Single European Act, constitued a binding objective of the Community.[92]

Hitherto, it is only seldom that legal acts in the narrower cultural field have been adopted on the basis of Article 235 of the EEC Treaty. However, the few acts which it is possible to mention in that regard indicate that the Community institutions and also – via the Council – the Member States have ideas consistent with the cultural aim of the Community discussed above. Thus the Council Decision of 16 June 1988 adopting the first phase of the 'Youth for Europe' action programme for the promotion of youth exchanges in the Community[93] states that youth exchanges are an appropriate method of teaching young people more about the European Community and its Member States.[94] However, as if that statement were too bold in its scope, a further clause adds that youth exchanges 'thus contribute to the training and preparation of young people for adult and working life'. Clearer language is used in the Council Decision of 28 July 1989 establishing an action programme to promote foreign language competence in the European Community (LINGUA).[95] In that decision, the advantage of greater

---

90 See also Grabitz in: *idem, Kommentar zum EWGV*, SEA, n. 12; *idem, Integration* 1986, p. 97.
91 *EC Bulletin* 6/1983, pp. 26 *et seq.*
92 This is probably also the view taken by Grabitz in: *idem, Kommentar zum EWGV*, SEA, n. 12, who states that the Declaration has been raised to the rank of a binding statement of the objective 'of European unification'.
93 OJ 1988 L 158, p. 42.
94 *ibid.*, ninth recital in the preamble.
95 OJ 1989 L 239, p. 24.

competence in foreign languages is described as including the enhancement of understanding and solidarity between the peoples which go to make up the Community, whilst preserving the linguistic diversity and cultural wealth of Europe.[96]

Consequently, the development of a 'flanking policy' of the Community in the cultural field may be considered, subject to an examination of the other constituent elements of Article 235 of the EEC Treaty, to fall within the framework of the cultural objective of the Community described above. This is evident, since the interpenetration of European cultures appears particularly suited to a 'flanking' of the integration process. The Member States have apparently recognized the need for the integration process to be flanked in some way by Community measures in the cultural field, and have begun – albeit still hesitantly – to adopt the corresponding acts based on Article 235 of the Treaty.

Finally, if one returns to the parallel drawn with the development of the environmental policy of the Community, the cultural policy of the Community cannot be said to be still in its initial stage. The Court of Justice has recently acknowledged the right of Member States to impose limits on the fundamental freedoms, subject to certain conditions, with a view to protecting specific cultural interests,[97] just as it has recognized that environmental protection represents a 'mandatory requirement'.[98] In addition, it held in its judgment of 30 May 1989 in Case 242/87 *Commission* v. *Council* ('*Erasmus*')[99] that the general objectives of the Community included the achievement of a people's Europe,[100] thereby confirming in a general way the cultural objective of the Community as described above, just as it has described environmental protection as an (essential) objective of the Community.[101] If, as may be anticipated, an express cultural policy is inserted into the EEC Treaty by way of amendment thereto, that would complete the parallel with the field of environmental protection.

3. The Attainment of Objectives 'In the Course of the Operation of the Common Market'

It is necessary, lastly, to examine whether the development of a flanking policy in the narrower cultural field may find itself confronted with obstacles resulting from the link which measures based on Article 235 of the EEC Treaty must have with the 'course of the operation of the common market'. That condition in Article 235 remains the subject of debate;[102] but the exchange of arguments has now

---

96 OJ 1989 L 239, p. 24, eighth recital in the preamble.

97 See 'Freedom of movement of tourist guides', pp. 147 *et seq.*, above, and 'Permissible restrictions on the free movement of television broadcasts', pp. 157 *et seq.*, above.

98 For a more detailed analysis, see 'The development of "flanking policies" in the Community', pp. 282 *et seq.*, above.

99 [1989] ECR 1425.

100 *ibid.*, at p. 1456; as to the concept of a 'people's Europe', see Niedobitek, pp. 2–7.

101 For a more detailed analysis, see 'The development of "flanking policies" in the Community', pp. 282 *et seq.*, above.

102 Grabitz in: *idem, Kommentar zum EWGV*, Art. 235, n. 54.

essentially taken place,[103] and it is not anticipated that any new arguments will be advanced in support of any one view or another. Furthermore, what is involved here appears primarily to be an academic controversy without any practical relevance. Nevertheless, there follows an attempt to express a brief view on this point, based on the assumption that the words 'in the course of the operation of the common market' possess independent significance.[104] In so far as Everling regarded those words as dispensable,[105] this was only because he had already interpreted the phrase 'objectives of the Community' in Article 235 of the Treaty in a restrictive manner which might, if at all, have been brought about by the phrase 'in the course of the operation of the common market'.

The comprehensive link between Article 235 of the Treaty and the attainment of objectives, as described above, would be significantly impaired if the Community institutions were restricted by Article 235 to measures which have as their subject-matter the establishment of the Common Market within the meaning of Article 2 of the Treaty – particularly if the second of the two instruments referred to in that article, namely the approximation of the economic policies of Member States, were dispensed with – or to measures which affect the functioning of the Common Market, and then only directly.[106] Certain academics suggest, therefore, that the concept of the Common Market used in Article 2 of the EEC Treaty should not be used in Article 235 of the Treaty, and that it should instead be based on a wider notion,[107] embracing in particular the approximation of economic policies, which 'cannot be excluded when Article 235 of the EEC Treaty is applied'.[108]

However, the development in Article 235 of a notion of the Common Market which diverges from that found in Article 2 is justified only if it would appear impossible otherwise to apply any meaningful interpretation to the phrase in question. Yet that is not the case.

This is because the need to establish an extended notion of the Common Market arises only if the link between Community measures and the 'operation of the common market' is conceived as a material limitation of the scope of Article 235 of the Treaty.[109] If that were so, a narrow construction of the concept of the 'Common Market' would lead to the result that the measures taken to coordinate the economic policies of the Member States, for example, were impermissible on the basis of Article 235 of the EEC Treaty. However, as against this view, the reference in Article 235 to the objectives of the Community would in those circumstances have been superfluous, in the same way that Article 100 of the Treaty contains no reference to the objectives of the Community. Since, however, Article 235

---

103 See the survey of the different schools of thought in Schwartz in: GBTE, *Kommentar zum EWGV*, Art. 235, nn. 141 *et seq.*

104 For a concurring view, see Eiden, p. 110.

105 Everling, *EuR 1976, Sonderheft*, p. 11.

106 See Tomuschat, *EuR 1976, Sonderheft*, p. 65.

107 e.g. see M. Seidel, *DVBl. 1989*, p. 445, who submits that Art. 235 covers the whole of the Community's tasks, in particular the coordination of economic, social and societal policies, together, above all, with activities which must necessarily be undertaken by the Community for reasons connected with the flanking of the integration process.

108 Nicolaysen, *Europarecht* I, p. 134.

109 For a concurring view, see Grabitz in: *idem, Kommentar zum EWGV*, Art. 235, n. 57.

expressly mentions the objectives of the Community, it must be assumed that it is the attainment of objectives, not the safeguarding of the operation of the Common Market, which is central to that article,[110] and consequently that the aim of Article 235 is clearly different from that pursued by Article 100. As Schwartz has rightly stated, Article 235 may well help the Common Market to operate, but that is not the aim of that provision.[111] It cannot be accepted, therefore, that Article 235 of the Treaty is restricted, as regards its subject-matter, to measures directly or indirectly concerned with the establishment or operation of the Common Market. There is no need for the concept of the Common Market in Article 235 to be interpreted more broadly than the same concept when it is contained in Article 2.

If, however, the concept of the Common Market in Article 235 of the Treaty is to be equated with the same concept as that appearing in Article 2,[112] the question arises as to the meaning which should be attached to the phrase 'in the course of the operation' of the Common Market. Since we have ruled out the possibility that the subject-matter of Article 235 is restricted to the direct or indirect functioning of the Common Market, it can only be assumed that the function of that phrase is to preclude measures which interfere with the basic structures and functioning of the Common Market.[113] That function is expressed more clearly in the other language versions of the Treaty than by the German version, which reads 'im Rahmen des Gemeinsamen Marktes' (within the framework of the Common Market). Thus, in terms similar to the English text, the French text reads 'dans le fonctionnement du marché commun' and the Italian 'nel funzionamento del mercato commune'. Consequently, measures based on Article 235 of the Treaty must fit harmoniously into the framework of the Common Market predetermined by the Treaty.[114] Thus the objective of the establishment and sound operation of the Common Market takes precedence over the other objectives of the Community. In the final analysis, therefore, the sole function of the words 'in the course of the operation of the common market' is to lay down a ranking order for Community objectives for the purposes of the scope of application of Article 235 and to entrust to the Community institutions the task of giving priority to and taking due care of the functioning of the Common Market, which ultimately turns out to be a transverse task to be borne in mind in the pursuit of objectives.

All in all, it is impossible to infer from the link between the attainment of objectives and the 'course of the operation of the common market' any significant obstacles to the realization of a flanking policy in the narrower cultural field. The only measures which are prohibited are those which would result in a regression of the Common Market.[115]

---

110 See also, to the same effect, R. Böhm, p. 111; a different view is taken by Henckel von Donnersmarck, p. 43, who argues that the words 'in the course of the operation of the common market' form the cornerstone of Art. 235 of the Treaty.

111 Schwartz in: GBTE, *Kommentar zum EWGV*, Art. 235, n. 156.

112 See also *ibid.*, n. 149.

113 See also the concurring view expressed by Magiera, *GS Wilhelm Karl Geck*, p. 519; Schwartz in: GBTE, *Kommentar zum EWGV*, Art. 235, n. 161; Grabitz in: *idem, Kommentar zum EWGV*, Art. 235, n. 62; Gericke, p. 43.

114 See also Schwartz in: GBTE, *Kommentar zum EWGV*, Art. 235, n. 158.

115 See Magiera, op. cit., n. 113, p. 519.

BIBLIOGRAPHY

Italicised material in book or journal titles indicate the shortened form by which entries are referred to in the text.

Adamantopoulos, Konstantinos
  Das Subventionsrecht des GATT in der EWG, Cologne (*inter alia*) 1988.
AK-GG
  See Reihe Alternativkommentare.
Arnull, Anthony
  What Shall We Do on Sunday?, ELR 1991, 112-124.
Avenarius, Hermann
  Zugangsrechte von EG-Ausländern im Bildungswesen der Bundesrepublik
    Deutschland, NVwZ 1988, 385-393.
Ayral, Michel
  Quelques observations concernant l'impact des communications de la
    Commission, in: Schwarze, J. et al. (eds), The 1992 Challenge at National
    Level, Baden-Baden 1990, 677-678.
Badura, Peter
  Bewahrung und Veränderung demokratischer und föderativer
    Verfassungsprinzipien der in Europa verbundenen Staaten, ZSR 1990, half-
    vol.1, 115-134.
Bahlmann, Kai
  Der Grundrechtsschutz in der Europäischen Gemeinschaft, EuR 1982, 1-20.
Bärmann, Johannes
  Die Europäischen Gemeinschaften und die Rechtsangleichung, JZ 1959,
    553-560.
Battis, Ulrich
  Freizügigkeit und Beschäftigung in der öffentlichen Verwaltung, in: Magiera,
    S. (ed.), Das Europa der Bürger in einer Gemeinschaft ohne Binnengrenzen,
    Baden-Baden 1990, 47-59.
Bebr, Gerhard
  Acts of Representatives of the Governments of the Member States, SEW 1966,
    529-545.
Beckedorf, Ingo, & Henze, Thomas
  Neuere Entwicklungen in der Bildungspolitik der Europäischen
    Gemeinschaft, NVwZ 1993, 125-130.

Becker, Jürgen
  Der Buchhandel im europäischen Binnenmarkt, EG-Magazin 10/1989, 20–23.
Becker, Ulrich
  Der Gestaltungsspielraum der EG-Mitgliedstaaten im Spannungsfeld zwischen
  Umweltschutz und freiem Warenverkehr, Baden-Baden 1991.
Behrens, Fritz
  Rechtsgrundlagen der Umweltpolitik der Europäischen Gemeinschaften,
  Berlin 1976.
Bekemans, Léonce, & Balodimos, Athanassios
  Le traité de Maastricht et l'éducation, la formation professionnelle et la culture,
  RMUE 2/1993, 99–142.
Benda, Ernst et al. (eds)
  Handbuch des Verfassungsrechts der Bundesrepublik Deutschland, Berlin &
  New York 1983.
Benedek, Wolfgang
  Die Rechtsordnung des GATT aus völkerrechtlicher Sicht, Berlin (*inter alia*)
  1990.
Berggreen, Ingeborg
  Diskussionsbeitrag, in: Battis, U. (ed.), Europäischer Binnenmarkt und
  nationaler öffentlicher Dienst, Regensburg 1989, 81.
  Das Bildungswesen in Europa nach Maastricht, *RdJB 1992*, 436–450.
Berggreen, Ingeborg, & Hochbaum, Ingo
  Bildung, Ausbildung und Kultur, in: Borkenhagen, Franz H.U. et al. (eds), Die
  deutschen Länder in Europa, Baden-Baden 1992, 47–60.
Bernhardt, Rudolf
  Zur Auslegung des europäischen Gemeinschaftsrechts, in: Grewe, W. G. et al.
  (eds), Europäische Gerichtsbarkeit und nationale
  Verfassungsgerichtsbarkeit, FS Hans Kutscher, Baden-Baden 1981, 17–24.
Bethge, Herbert
  Die Rolle der Länder im deutschen Bundesstaat und ihre rechtlichen
  Einflußmöglichkeiten auf die nationale Gemeinschaftspolitik, in: Kremer,
  H. A. (ed.), Die Bundesrepublik Deutschland und das Königreich Spanien
  1992 – Die Rolle der Länder und der Comunidades Autónomas im
  Europäischen Integrationsprozeß, Munich 1989, 22–50.
Betz, Jürgen
  Die EG-Fernsehrichtlinie – Ein Schritt zum europäischen Fernsehen?, Media
  Perspektiven 1989, 677–688.
Beutler, Bengt
  Grundrechtsschutz, in: von der Groeben, H. et al. (eds), Kommentar zum EWG-
  Vertrag, 3rd ed., Baden-Baden 1983, 1461–1499.
  Aufenthaltsrechtliche Stellung von Ausländern im Rahmen der
  Bildungsmigration, *RdJB 1989*, 150–156.
Beutler, Bengt et al.
  Die Europäische Gemeinschaft – Rechtsordnung und Politik, *3rd ed.*, Baden-
  Baden 1987.
  Die Europäische Union – Rechtsordnung und Politik, *4th ed.*, Baden-Baden
  1993.

Bieber, Roland
Die Ausgaben der Europäischen Gemeinschaften, *EuR 1982*, 115-132.
Zur *Rolle der Mitgliedstaaten* bei der Ausfüllung von Lücken im EG-Recht, in:
Bieber, R., & Ress, G. (eds), Die Dynamik des Europäischen
Gemeinschaftsrechts, Baden-Baden 1987, 283-310.
On the Mutual Completion of Overlapping Legal Systems: The Case of the
European Communities and the National Legal Orders, *ELR 1988*,
147-158.
Educational aspects of research and technology policies, in: de Witte, B. (ed.),
European Community Law of Education, Baden-Baden 1989, 83-93.

Bindschedler, Rudolf L.
Rechtsfragen der europäischen Einigung, Basel 1954.

BK
See Kommentar zum Bonner Grundgesetz (Bonner Kommentar)

Blanke, Hermann-Josef
Die *Bundesländer* im Spannungsverhältnis zwischen Eigenstaatlichkeit und
Europäischer Integration, in: Heckmann, D., & Meßerschmidt, K. (eds),
Gegenwartsfragen des Öffentlichen Rechts, Berlin 1988, 53-81.
Föderalismus und Integrationsgewalt, Berlin 1991.
Das Subsidiaritätsprinzip als Schranke des Europäischen
Gemeinschaftsrechts?, *ZG 1991*, 133-148.
Der Unionsvertrag von Maastricht – Ein Schritt auf dem Weg zu einem
europäischen Bundesstaat?, *DÖV 1993*, 412-423.
Europa auf dem Weg zu einer *Bildungs- und Kulturgemeinschaft*, Cologne (*inter
alia*) 1994.

Blaukopf, Kurt
Musik in der Mediamorphose – Plädoyer für eine kulturelle Marktwirtschaft,
Media Perspektiven 1989, 552-558.

Bleckmann, Albert
Die Beihilfenkompetenz der Europäischen Gemeinschaften, *DÖV 1977*,
615-619.
Teleologie und dynamische Auslegung des Europäischen Gemeinschaftsrechts,
EuR 1979, 239-260.
Zum Ermessensmißbrauch im europäischen Gemeinschaftsrecht, in: Grewe,
W. G. et al. (eds), Europäische Gerichtsbarkeit und nationale
Verfassungsgerichtsbarkeit, *FS Hans Kutscher*, Baden-Baden 1981, 25-41.
Die Freiheiten des Gemeinsamen Marktes als Grundrechte, in: Bieber, R. et al.,
(eds), Das Europa der zweiten Generation, *GS Christoph Sasse*, vol. I, Baden-
Baden 1981, 665-684.
Die *Bindung* der Europäischen Gemeinschaft an die Europäische
Menschenrechtskonvention, Cologne 1986.
Zur Bindung der Länder an die Ziele der Bundespolitik, *DÖV 1986*, 125-132.
Die Ausnahmen der Dienstleistungsfreiheit nach dem EWG-Vertrag, *EuR
1987*, 28-50.

Die *Bindungswirkung* der Praxis der Organe und der Mitgliedstaaten der EG bei
der Auslegung und Lückenfüllung des Europäischen Gemeinschaftsrechts:
Die Rolle des Art. 5 EWG-Vertrag, in: Bieber, R., & Ress, G. (eds), Die
Dynamik des Europäischen Gemeinschaftsrechts, Baden-Baden 1987,
161-227.
Europarecht, 5th ed., Cologne (*inter alia*) 1990.
Politische Aspekte der europäischen Integration unter dem Vorzeichen des
Binnenmarktes 1992, *ZRP 1990*, 265-268.
Das Verhältnis des Gerichtshofs zur Kommission der Europäischen
Gemeinschaften, *RIW 1991*, 218-224.

Blümel, Willi
Wesensgehalt und Schranken des kommunalen Selbstverwaltungsrechts, in:
von Mutius, A. (ed.), Selbstverwaltung im Staat der Industriegesellschaft,
FG Georg Christoph von Unruh, Heidelberg 1983, 265-303.

Böhm, Johann
Die Europäische Union - Gefahr oder Chance für den Föderalismus in
Deutschland?, BayVBl. 1993, 545-551.

Böhm, Reinhard
Kompetenzauslegung und Kompetenzlücken im Gemeinschaftsrecht,
Frankfurt am Main 1985.

Börner, Bodo
Kompetenz der EG zur Regelung einer Rundfunkordnung, ZUM 1985,
577-587.

Börsenverein des deutschen Buchhandels (ed.), Buch und Buchhandel in Zahlen,
Ausgabe 1989/1990, Frankfurt am Main 1990.

Bogdan, Michael
Free Movement of Tourists within the EEC?, J.W.T.L. 1977, 468-475.

Borchmann, Michael
Der Artikel 235: Generalklausel für EG-Kompetenzen, in: Borkenhagen, Franz
H. U. et al. (eds), Die deutschen Länder in Europa, Baden-Baden 1992,
100-105.

Bothe, Michael
Legal and Non-Legal Norms - A Meaningful Distinction in International
Relations?, *NYIL 1980*, 65-95.
'Soft Law' in den Europäischen Gemeinschaften?, in: von Münch, I. (ed.),
Staatsrecht - Völkerrecht - Europarecht: *FS Hans-Jürgen Schlochauer*, Berlin &
New York 1981, 761-775.

Boulouis, Jean
Sur la notion de politique commune et ses implications juridiques, in:
Schwarze, J., & Schermers, H. G. (eds), Structure and Dimensions of
European Community Policy, Baden-Baden 1988, 55-59.

Bueckling, Adrian
Nationale Abwehrfront gegen Weiterverbreitung ausländischer TV-
Programme stürzt in Raten, ZUM 1988, 288-290.

Bullinger, Martin
Rundfunkordnung im Bundesstaat und in der Europäischen Gemeinschaft,
AfP 1985, 257-265.

Werbung und Quotenregelung zwischen nationalem und europäischem Rundfunkrecht, in: Stern, K. et al., Eine Rundfunkordnung für Europa – Chancen und Risiken, Munich 1990, 85-100.

Bülow, Erich
Das Verhältnis des Rechts der europäischen Gemeinschaften zum nationalen Recht, in: Aktuelle Fragen des europäischen Gemeinschaftsrechts, Europarechtliches Kolloquium 1964, Stuttgart 1965, 28-59.

Buss, Wolfgang
7 Jahre bildungspolitische Zusammenarbeit in der Europäischen Gemeinschaft: Erfolge und Mißerfolge, in: Schmitz-Wenzel, H. (ed.), Bildungspolitik in der Europäischen Gemeinschaft, Baden-Baden 1980, 17-24.

Classen, Claus Dieter
Bildungspolitische Förderprogramme der EG – Eine kritische Untersuchung der vertragsrechtlichen Grundlagen, *EuR 1990*, 10-19.
Diskussionsbeitrag, in: Magiera, S. (ed.), Das Europa der Bürger in einer Gemeinschaft ohne Binnengrenzen, Baden-Baden 1990, 180.
Maastricht und die Verfassung: kritische Bemerkungen zum neuen 'Europa-Artikel' 23 GG, *ZRP 1993*, 57-61.

Clever, Friedrich
Ermessensmißbrauch und détournement de pouvoir nach dem Recht der Europäischen Gemeinschaften, Berlin 1967.

Cloos, Jim et al.
Le Traité de Maastricht – Genèse, Analyse, Commentaires, Brussels 1993.

Cludius, Stefan
Die Kompetenzen der Europäischen Gemeinschaft für den Bereich der Bildungspolitik, Frankfurt am Main 1995.

Constantinesco, Léontin-Jean
Das Recht der Europäischen Gemeinschaften, vol. I: Das institutionelle Recht, Baden-Baden 1977.

Constantinesco, Vlad
Compétences et Pouvoirs dans les Communautés Européennes, Paris 1974.
Subsidiarität: Zentrales Verfassungsprinzip für die Politische Union, *Integration 1990*, 165-178.
La structure du Traité instituant l'Union européenne, *CDE 1993*, 251-284.

Constantinesco, Vlad et al. (eds)
Traité sur l'Union européenne, Paris 1995.

Corbett, Richard
The Treaty of Maastricht, Harlow 1993.

Cornu, Marie
Compétences culturelles en Europe et principe de subsidiarité, Brussels 1993.

Currall, Julian
Some Aspects of the Relation between Articles 30-36 and Article 100 of the EEC Treaty, with a Closer Look at Optional Harmonisation, YEL 1984, 169-205.

da Cruz Vilaça, José Luis, & Piçarra, Nuno
Are There Material Limits to the Revision of the Treaties on the European
Union?, Bonn 1994.

Damiani, Alessandro
Tendances de la recherche en Europe: Le programme - cadre est adopté, RMC
1987, 369–377.

Damm, Renate
Rechtsprobleme des grenzüberschreitenden Fernsehens, in: Schwarze, J. (ed.),
Fernsehen ohne Grenzen, Baden-Baden 1985, 175–187.

Dauses, Manfred A.
Der Schutz der Grundrechte in der Europäischen Gemeinschaft, JöR 1982,
1–22.
Grundlagen der Rechtsprechung des Gerichtshofes - Auswirkungen auf Bund
und Länder, BayVBl. 1989, 609–617.
(ed.), Handbuch des EG-Wirtschaftsrechts, Loseblatt, Munich 1994.

de Crayencour, J.-P.
Die Europäische Gemeinschaft und die Freizügigkeit der freien Berufe,
Brussels 1983.

Dehousse, Renaud
Community Competences: Are there Limits to Growth?, in: idem (ed.), Europe
After Maastricht - An Ever Closer Union?, Munich 1994, 103–125.
From Community to Union, in: idem (ed.), Europe After Maastricht - An Ever
Closer Union?, Munich 1994, 5–15.

Delannay, Philippe
Anmerkungen zu dem Urteil des Gerichtshofs vom 12. Dezember 1974, Rs.
36/74 (Walrave & Koch), CDE 1976, 209–226.

Delbrück, Jost
Die Rundfunkhoheit der deutschen Bundesländer im Spannungsfeld zwischen
Regelungsanspruch der Europäischen Gemeinschaft und nationalen
Verfassungsrecht, Frankfurt am Main 1986.
Rundfunkrecht und Wettbewerbsrecht vor dem Forum des europäischen
Gemeinschaftsrechts, in: Hoffmann-Riem, W. (ed.), Rundfunk im
Wettbewerbsrecht, Baden-Baden 1988, 244–251.

Demaret, Paul
The Treaty Framework, in: O'Keeffe, David & Twomey, Patrick M., (eds), Legal
Issues of the Maastricht Treaty, London (inter alia) 1994, 3–11.

Demaret, Paul, & Ernst de la Graete, Brigitte
Mesures nationales d'ordre public et circulation des personnes entre Etats
membres, CDE 1983, 261–303.

de Moor, Anne
Article 7 of the Treaty of Rome Bites, The Modern Law Review 1985, 452–459.

de Nanclares, José Martín-Pérez
Die EG-Fernsehrichtlinie, Frankfurt am Main (inter alia) 1995.

Deringer, Arved
Europäisches Gemeinschaftsrecht und nationale Rundfunkordnung, ZUM
1986, 627–638.

de Witte, Bruno
The *Scope of Community Powers* in Education and Culture in the Light of
Subsequent Practice, in: Bieber, R., & Ress, G. (eds), Die Dynamik des
Europäischen Gemeinschaftsrechts, Baden-Baden 1987, 261-281.
Cultural policy: The complementary of negative and positive integration, in:
Schwarze, J. (ed.), Structure and Dimensions of European Community
Policy, Baden-Baden 1988, 195-204.
Cultural Policy Limits to Fundamental Rights, in: Kaufmann, A. et al.,
Rechtsstaat und Menschenwürde, *FS Werner Maihofer*, Frankfurt am Main
1988, 651-667.
Educational Equality for Community Workers and their Families, in: de Witte,
B. (ed.), European Community Law of Education, Baden-Baden 1989,
71-79.
Cultural linkages, in: Wallace, W. (ed.), The Dynamics of European Integration,
London & New York 1990, 192-210.

de Witte, Bruno, & Post, Harry
Educational and Cultural Rights, in: Cassese, A. et al. (eds), Human Rights and
the European Community: The Substantive Law, Baden-Baden 1991,
123-176.

Dewost, Jean-Louis
Décisions des Institutions en vue du développement des Compétences et des
Instruments juridiques, in: Bieber, R., & Ress, G. (eds), Die Dynamik des
Europäischen Gemeinschaftsrechts, Baden-Baden 1987, 321-342.

de Zwaan, J. W.
The Single European Act: Conclusion of a Unique Document, CML Rev. 1986,
747-765.

Dicke, Klaus
Eine europäische Rundfunkordnung für welches Europa?, Media Perspektiven
1989, 193-199.

Dietz, Adolf
Das *Urheberrecht* in der Europäischen Gemeinschaft, Baden-Baden 1978.
Harmonisierung des europäischen Urheberrechts, in: Ress, G. (ed.),
Entwicklung des Europäischen Urheberrechts, Baden-Baden 1989, 57-67.

Dittmann, Armin, & Fehrenbacher, Claus
Die bildungsrechtlichen Harmonisierungsverbote (Art. 126 Abs. 4, 127 Abs. 4
EGV) und ihre Bedeutung für die nationale 'Bildungshoheit', RdJB 1992,
478-493.

Dohms, Rüdiger
Die Kompetenz der EG im Bereich der allgemeinen Bildung nach Art. 126
EGV, RdJB 1992, 451-468.

Dörr, Dieter
Die Europäischen Gemeinschaften und die Deutschen Bundesländer, *NWVBl.
1988*, 289-294.
Das Deutsche Beamtenrecht und das Europäische Gemeinschaftsrecht, *EuZW
1990*, 565-571.
Aussprache, *VVDStRL 1994*, 125.

Dorn, Dietrich-W.
Art. 235 EWGV – Prinzipien der Auslegung, Kehl 1986.

Durand, Claire-Françoise
Le Traité sur l'Union européenne (Maastricht, 7 février 1992) – Quelques
réflexions, in: Commentaire Megret, Le droit de la CEE, 2nd ed., vol. 1,
Brussels 1992, 357–445.

Eberle, Carl-Eugen
Das europäische Recht und die Medien am Beispiel des Reundfunkrechts, AfP
1993, 422–429.

Ehlers, Dirk
Die Einwirkungen des Rechts der Europäischen Gemeinschaften auf das
Verwaltungsrecht, DVBl. 1991, 605–613.

Ehmke, Horst
Wirtschaft und Verfassung, Karlsruhe 1961.
Prinzipien der Verfassungsinterpretation, VVDStRL 20 (1963), 53–102.

Ehricke, Ulrich
'Soft law' – Aspekte einer neuen Rechtsquelle, NJW 1989, 1906–1908.

Eiden, Christoph
Die Rechtsangleichung gemäß Art. 100 des EWG-Vertrages, Berlin 1984.

Eiselstein, Claus
Verlust der Bundesstaatlichkeit?, NVwZ 1989, 323–330.
Europäische Verfassungsgebung, ZRP 1991, 18–24.

Elles, Lady Diana
Auslegung der Verträge unter dem Einfluß der Praxis in den EG-Organen, in:
Bieber, R., & Ress, G. (eds), Die Dynamik des Europäischen
Gemeinschaftsrechts, Baden-Baden 1987, 410–414.

Emiliou, Nicholas
Subsidiarity: An Effective Barrier Against 'the Enterprise of Ambition'?, ELR
1992, 383–407.

Engel, Christoph
Europäische Konvention über grenzüberschreitendes Fernsehen, ZRP 1988,
240–247.

Erichsen, Hans-Uwe, & Martens, Wolfgang (eds)
Allgemeines Verwaltungsrecht, 8th ed., Berlin & New York 1988.

Everling, Ulrich
Das *Niederlassungsrecht* im Gemeinsamen Markt, Berlin & Frankfurt am Main
1963.
Die allgemeine Ermächtigung der Europäischen Gemeinschaft zur
Zielverwirklichung nach Art. 235 EWG-Vertrag, *EuR 1976, Sonderheft*,
2–26.
Das europäische Gemeinschaftsrecht im Spannungsfeld von Politik und
Wirtschaft, in: Grewe, W. G. et al. (eds), Europäische Gerichtsbarkeit und
nationale Verfassungsgerichtsbarkeit, *FS Hans Kutscher*, Baden-Baden 1981.

Zur rechtlichen Wirkung von Beschlüssen, Entschließungen, Erklärungen und Vereinbarungen des Rates oder der Mitgliedstaaten der Europäischen Gemeinschaft, in: Lüke, G. (ed.), Rechtsvergleichung, Europarecht und Staatenintegration: *GS Léontin-Jean Constantinesco*, Cologne (*inter alia*) 1983, 133-156.

Das Recht in den internationalen *Wirtschaftsbeziehungen* der EG, in: Hilf, M., & Petersmann, E.-U. (eds), GATT und Europäische Gemeinschaft, Baden-Baden 1986, 175-202.

Rechtsvereinheitlichung durch Richterrecht in der Europäischen Gemeinschaft, *RabelsZ 50 (1986)*, 193-232.

Gestaltungsbedarf des Europäischen Rechts, *EuR 1987*, 214-235.

Probleme atypischer Rechts- und Handlungsformen bei der Auslegung des europäischen Gemeinschaftsrechts, in: Bieber, R., & Ress, G. (eds), Die Dynamik des Europäischen Gemeinschaftsrechts, Baden-Baden 1987, 417-429.

Die rechtlichen *Instrumente* zur Verwirklichung des europäischen Binnenmarkts im Bereich des Buchhandels, in: Becker, J. (ed.), Der Buchhandel im Europäischen Binnenmarkt, Frankfurt am Main 1989, 13-28.

Die *Rechtsprechung* des Europäischen Gerichtshofes zur Freizügigkeit im öffentlichen Dienst, in: Battis, U. (ed.), Europäischer Binnenmarkt und nationaler öffentlicher Dienst, Regensburg 1989, 23-44.

Zur föderalen Struktur der Europäischen Gemeinschaft, in: Hailbronner, K. et al. (eds), Staat und Völkerrechtsordnung, *FS Karl Doehring*, Berlin (*inter alia*) 1989, 179-198.

Brauchen wir 'Solange III'?, *EuR 1990*, 195-227.

Von der Freizügigkeit der Arbeitnehmer zum Europäischen Bürgerrecht?, *EuR 1990, Beiheft 1*, 81-103.

Der *Beitrag* des Europäischen Gerichtshofs zur europäischen Grundrechtsgemeinschaft, in: Stern, K. (ed.), 40 Jahre Grundgesetz, Munich 1990, 167-180.

Zur Rechtsprechung des Europäischen Gerichtshofs über die Beschäftigung von EG-Ausländern in der öffentlichen Verwaltung, *DVBl. 1990*, 225-231.

Reflections on the Structure of the European Union, *CML Rev. 1992*, 1053-1077.

Kompetenzordnung und Subsidiarität, in: Werner Weidenfeld (ed.), Reform der Europäischen Union, Gütersloh 1995, 166-176.

Fastenrath, Ulrich
Regelungskompetenzen der EG-Mitgliedstaaten im Bereich gemeinsamer Politiken, NJW 1983, 494-495.

Feger, Dieter
Die *Grundrechte* im Recht der Europäischen Gemeinschaften - Bestand und Entwicklung -, Frankfurt am Main 1984.

Die Normsetzung auf dem Gebiet der Grundrechte in den Europäischen Gemeinschaften - Der Europäische Gerichtshof (EuGH) als Rechtsetzungsorgan, *DÖV 1987*, 322-334.

Feuchthofen, Jörg E., & Brackmann, Hans-Jürgen
  Berufliche Bildung im Maastrichter Unionsvertrag, RdJB 1992, 468-477.
Fezer, Karl-Heinz, & Grosshardt, Holger R.
  Die Buchpreisbindung im Europäischen Binnenmarkt, RIW 1991, 141-150.
Fiedler, Wilfried
  Impulse der Europäischen Gemeinschaft im kulturellen Bereich - Rechtliche
    Grundlagen und politische Fortentwicklung, in: Magiera, S. (ed.), Das
    Europa der Bürger in einer Gemeinschaft ohne Binnengrenzen, Baden-
    Baden 1990, 147-177.
Fischer-Dieskau, Christian
  Ziele und Methoden europäischer Forschungspolitik, in: Meessen, K. M. (ed.),
    Öffentliche Aufträge und Forschungspolitik, Baden-Baden 1979, 35-41.
Flesch, Colette
  Braucht Europa eine eigene Kulturpolitik?, EG-Informationen 5/1991, 3-4.
  Was kann Kultur für Europa leisten?, EG Informationen 10/1992, 1-2.
Flynn, James
  Vocational Training in Community Law and Practice, YEL 1988, 59-85.
  Gravier: Suite du Feuilleton, in: de Witte, B. (ed.), European Community Law of
    Education, Baden-Baden 1989, 95-112.
Forch, Stefan
  Freizügigkeit für Studienreferendare, NVwZ 1987, 27-31.
Franzone, Daniel
  L'économie et la culture dans l'approche communautaire de la radiodiffusion,
    RMC 1988, 274-278.
Frey, Bruno S., & Serna, Angel
  Der Preis der Kunst, in: Michel, K. M., & Spengler, T. (eds), Kursbuch, March
    1990, 105-113.
Friccius, Enno
  Zur Novellierung des Filmförderungsgesetzes, Media Perspektiven 1991,
    806-809.
Friden, Georges
  Recent Developments in EEC Intellectual Property Law: The Distinction
    between Existence and Exercise Revisited, CML Rev. 1989, 193-217.
Frohne, Ronald
  Die Quotenregelungen im nationalen und im europäischen Recht, ZUM 1989,
    390-396.
Frowein, Jochen Abr.
  Die Herausbildung europäischer Verfassungsprinzipien, in: Kaufmann, A.
    (ed.), Rechtsstaat und Menschenwürde, FS Werner Maihofer, Frankfurt am
    Main 1988, 149-158.
  Bundesrat, Länder und europäische Einigung, in: Bundesrat (ed.), Vierzig Jahre
    Bundesrat, Baden-Baden 1989, 285-302.
Gallwas, Hans-Ullrich
  Bildungsförderalismus in der Europäischen Gemeinschaft unter rechtlichen
    Aspekten, Verantwortung und Leistung, Heft 21, May 1990.
Gau, Doris
  Kultur als Politik, Munich 1990.

GBTE
See von der Groeben, Hans, von Boeckh, Hans, Thiesing, Jochen, &
Ehlermann, Claus-Dieter (eds).

Geiger, Rudolf
Die *Stellung der Bundesländer* im Europäischen Gemeinschaftsrecht und ihre
Rechtsschutzmöglichkeiten gegen Rechtsakte der Gemeinschaft, in:
Kremer, H. A. (ed.), Die Landesparlamente im Spannungsfeld zwischen
europäischer Integration und europäischem Regionalismus, Munich 1988,
51-71.
EG-Vertrag - Kommentar zum Vertrag zur Gründung der Europäischen
Gemeinschaft, 2nd ed., Munich 1995.

Geiger, Willi
Zur europäischen Geschichte der Grundrechte, in: Fürst, W. et al. (eds),
Festschrift für Wolfgang Zeidler, vol. 2, Berlin & New York 1987,
1401-1414.

Geißler, Birgit
Staatliche Kunstförderung nach Grundgesetz und Recht der EG, Berlin 1995.

Gericke, Hans-Peter
Allgemeine Rechtsetzungsbefugnisse nach Artikel 235 EWG-Vertrag,
Hamburg 1970.

Gerold, Rainer
Die Zusammenarbeit in Forschung und Technologie im Rahmen der
Europäischen Gemeinschaft, WissR 1987, 64-71.

Gesser, Ulrich
Änderungen im Freizügigkeitsrecht der EG-Arbeitnehmer und ihrer
Familienangehörigen, EuZW 1991, 435-438.

Giscard d'Estaing, Valéry
La règle d'or du fédéralisme européen, R.A.E. 1/1991, 63-66.

Glaesner, Hans-Joachim
Die *Einführung* und Entwicklung neuer Politiken in der Europäischen
Gemeinschaft, in: Schwarze, J. (ed.), Gesetzgebung in der Europäischen
Gemeinschaft, Baden-Baden 1985, 31-53.
Gemeinschaftspolitik im Bereich von Wissenschaft und Technologie, in:
Schwarze, J., & Bieber, R. (eds), Das europäische Wirtschaftsrecht vor den
Herausforderungen der Zukunft, Baden-Baden 1985, 55-83.
Les objectifs de la Communauté économique européenne - origine et
développements, in: Schwarze, J., & Schermers, H. G. (eds), Structure and
Dimensions of European Community Policy, Baden-Baden 1988, 13-23.
Umwelt als Gegenstand einer Gemeinschaftspolitik, in: Rengeling, H.-W.
(ed.), Europäisches Umweltrecht und europäische Umweltpolitik, Cologne
(*inter alia*) 1988, 1-11.

Goerlich, Helmut
'Formenmißbrauch' und Kompetenzverständnis, Tübingen 1987.

Goerlich, Helmut, & Bräth, Peter
Europäische Freizügigkeit und nationaler Ämterzugang, *DÖV 1987*,
1038-1049.
Zur europäischen Freizügigkeit im öffentlichen Sektor, *NVwZ 1989*, 330-332.

Gölter, Georg
  Kein kulturelles Einheitseuropa, MittHV 1989, 133-137.
Gormley, Laurence
  The Rule of Reason and Culture, *ELR 1985*, 440-445.
  Anmerkungen zum Urteil des Gerichtshofs vom 23. November 1989, Rs. 145/
    88, *CML Rev. 1990*, 141-150.
Grabitz, Eberhard
  Gemeinschaftsrecht bricht nationales Recht, Hamburg 1966.
  Methoden der Verfassungspolitik in der Gemeinschaft, in: Bieber, R. et al.
    (eds), Das Europa der zweiten Generation, *GS Christoph Sasse*, vol. I, Baden-
    Baden 1981, 105-114.
  Quellen des Gemeinschaftsrechts: Rechtshandlungen der Gemeinschaftsorgane, in:
    Kommission der EG (ed.), Dreißig Jahre Gemeinschaftsrecht, Luxembourg
    1983, 91-117.
  Das politische Ermessen des Rates - Zum Urteil des Gerichtshofs in Sachen
    Verkehrspolitik -, *Integration 1985*, 103-107.
  Die Einheitliche Europäische Akte: Rechtliche Bewertung, *Integration 1986*,
    95-100.
  Europäisches Verwaltungsrecht - Gemeinschaftsrechtliche Grundsätze des
    Verwaltungsverfahrens, *NJW 1989*, 1776-1783.
  (ed.): *Kommentar zum EWG-Vertrag*, Munich (4. Ergänzungslieferung Juni
    1990).
Grabitz, Eberhard, & Hilf, Meinhard (eds)
  Kommentar zur Europäischen Union, Loseblatt, Munich.
Grabitz, Eberhard, & Sasse, Christoph
  Umweltkompetenz der Europäischen Gemeinschaften, Berlin 1977.
Grabitz, Eberhard, & Zacker, Christian
  Die neuen Umweltkompetenzen der EWG, NVwZ 1989, 297-303.
GTE
  See von der Groeben, Hans, Thiesing, Jochen, & Ehlermann, Claus-Dieter
    (eds)., *Kommentar zum EWG-Vertrag*
Gulich, Joachim
  Rechtsfragen grenzüberschreitender Rundfunksendungen, Baden-Baden 1990.
  Reichweite und *Grenzen* der Dienstleistungsfreiheit für Rundfunkveranstalter
    in der Europäischen Gemeinschaft, in: Hopt, K. J. (ed.), Europäische
    Integration als Herausforderung des Rechts, Essen 1991, 297-302.
Gulmann, Claus
  Member State measures for enlarging the scope of the treaties, in: Bieber, R., &
    Ress, G. (eds), Die Dynamik des Europäischen Gemeinschaftsrechts, Baden-
    Baden 1987, 241-249.
Häberle, Peter
  Verfassungslehre als Kulturwissenschaft, Berlin 1982.
  Vom *Kulturstaat* zum Kulturverfassungsrecht, in: *idem* (ed.),
    Kulturstaatlichkeit und Kulturverfassungsrecht, Darmstadt 1982, 1-59.
  Europa in kulturverfassungsrechtlicher Perspektive, in: Graf Vitzthum, W. (ed.),
    Grundrechtsschutz im nationalen und internationalen Recht, Werner von
    Simson zum 75. Geburtstag, Baden-Baden 1983, 41-67.

Sonn- und Feiertagsrecht im Verfassungsstaat, in: Wilke, J. (ed.), Mehr als ein Weekend?, Paderborn (*inter alia*) 1989, 27–74.
Buchbesprechung: Hermann-Josef Blanke, Europa auf dem Weg zu einer Bildungs- und Kulturgemeinschaft, *DVBl.* 1995, 761–762.

Hablitzel, Hans
Subsidiaritätsprinzip und Bildungskompetenzen im Vertrag über die Europäische Union, Regensburg 1994.

Hackspiel, Sabine
Opferentschädigung und Europäisches Gemeinschaftsrecht, NJW 1989, 2166–2171.

Hailbronner, Kay
Entwicklungstendenzen des Wirtschaftsvölkerrechts, Konstanz 1983.
Die deutschen Bundesländer in der EG, *JZ 1990*, 149–158.
Zur Entwicklung der Freizügigkeit in der Europäischen Gemeinschaft – Rechtsprechung und Rechtspolitik, *ZAR 1990*, 107–114.
Die soziale Dimension der EG-Freizügigkeit – Gleichbehandlung und Territoralitätsprinzip, *EuZW 1991*, 171–180.
Europa 1992 – Freizügigkeit für Studenten und Auszubildende in der Europäischen Gemeinschaft, *JuS 1991*, 9–18.

Hailbronner, Kay et al.
Handkommentar zum EU-Vertrag, Loseblatt, Cologne (*inter alia*) ('HandKommEUV').

Hallstein, Walter
Die echten *Probleme* der europäischen Integration, Kiel 1965.
Die EWG – Eine *Rechtsgemeinschaft*, in: Oppermann, T. (ed.), Walter Hallstein – Europäische Reden, Stuttgart 1979, 341–348.

Handoll, John
Article 48 (4) EEC and Non-National Access to Public Employment, *ELR 1988*, 223–241.
Foreign Teachers and Public Education, in: de Witte, B. (ed.), European Community Law of Education, Baden-Baden 1989, 31–50.

Haneklaus, Winfried
Zur Verankerung umweltpolitischer Ziele im EWG-Vertrag, DVBl. 1990, 1135–1141.

Hartley, Trevor C.
La libre circulation des etudiants en droit communautaire, CDE 1989, 325–344.

Heintzen, Markus
Subsidiaritätsprinzip und Europäische Gemeinschaft, JZ 1991, 317–323.

Henckel von Donnersmarck, Guidotto Graf
Planimmanente Krisensteuerung in der Europäischen Wirtschaftsgemeinschaft, Frankfurt am Main & Berlin 1971.

Henrichs, Helmut
Gemeinschaftsrecht und nationale Verfassungen – Organisations- und verfahrensrechtliche Aspekte einer Konfliktlage, EuGRZ 1990, 413–423.

HER
See von der Groeben, Thiesing & Ehlermann, *Handbuch des Europäischen Rechts.*

Herzog, Roman
Subsidiaritätsprinzip und Staatsverfassung, *Der Staat 1963*, 399–423.
Zwischenbilanz im Streit um die bundesstaatliche Ordnung, *JuS 1967*, 193–200.

Hesse, Konrad
Grundzüge des Verfassungsrechts der Bundesrepublik Deutschland, 17th ed., Heidelberg 1990.

Heusel, Wolfgang
'Weiches' Völkerrecht, Baden-Baden 1991.

Hiermaier, Werner
Der Einfluß der Europäischen Gemeinschaft auf das Deutsche Bildungswesen, in: Birk, H.-J. et al. (eds), Kulturverwaltungsrecht im Wandel, Stuttgart, Munich & Hannover 1981, 81–110.

Hilf, Meinhard
Auswirkungen auf die Gemeinschaftsrechtsordnung – Stellungnahme zum Beschluß des Bundesverfassungsgerichts vom 29. Mai 1974, *ZaöRV 1975*, 51–66.
Die Freizügigkeit des Berufsfußballspielers innerhalb der Europäischen Gemeinschaft, *NJW 1984*, 517–523.
Maßnahmen zur Erweiterung des Wirkungsbereichs der Verträge, in: Bieber, R., & Ress, G. (eds), Die Dynamik des Europäischen Gemeinschaftsrechts, Baden-Baden 1987, 251–260.
Europa '92 – Festung oder Partner?, in: *idem* (ed.), EG und Drittstaatsbeziehungen nach 1992, Baden-Baden 1991, 9–15.
Europäische Union: Gefahr oder Chance für den Föderalismus in Deutschland, Österreich und der Schweiz?, *VVDStRL 1994*, 7–25.

Hochbaum, Ingo
Die Hochschulpolitik der Europäischen Gemeinschaften, *WissR 1986*, 206–219.
Enteignung der Bundesländer?, *DUZ 20/1987*, 20–21.
Politik und Kompetenzen der Europäischen Gemeinschaften im Bildungswesen, *BayVBl. 1987*, 481–490.
Die Aktion der EG-Kommission zur Liberalisierung des öffentlichen Dienstes, *ZBR 1989*, 33–40.
The *Federal Structure* of Member States as a Limit to Common Educational Policy: The Case of Germany, in: de Witte, B. (ed.), European Community Law of Education, Baden-Baden 1989, 145–158.
Zum Mitmachen verpflichtet?, *DUZ 8/1989*, 11–12.
Die Liberalisierung des öffentlichen Dienstes im Binnenmarkt, *Der Staat 1990*, 577–598.

Hochbaum, Ingo, & Eiselstein, Claus
Die Freizügigkeitsrechte des Art. 48 EWG-Vertrag und der öffentliche Dienst, Verantwortung und Leistung, Heft 17, May 1988.

Hoffmann-Riem, Wolfgang
Europäisierung des Rundfunks – aber ohne Kommunikationsverfassung?, in: *idem* (ed.), Rundfunk im Wettbewerbsrecht, Baden-Baden 1988, 201–223.

Rundfunk in Europa zwischen Wirtschafts- und Kulturfreiheit, in: Nicolaysen, G., & Quaritsch, H. (eds), Symposion für Hans Peter Ipsen zur Feier des 80. Geburtstages, Baden-Baden 1988, 75-83.

Rundfunkrecht neben Wettbewerbsrecht, Baden-Baden 1991.

Huber, Bertold

Die Entwicklung des Ausländer-, Asyl- und Arbeitserlaubnisrechts in den Jahren 1987/88, NJW 1988, 3059-3069.

Huber, Ernst Rudolf

Wirtschaftsverwaltungsrecht, 2nd ed., vol. 2, Tübingen 1954.

Zur Problematik des Kulturstaats, Tübingen 1958.

Hufen, Friedhelm

Gegenwartsfragen des Kulturföderalismus, BayVBl. 1985, 1-7 and 37-43.

Ipsen, Hans Peter

Als Bundesstaat in der Gemeinschaft, in: von Caemmerer, E. et al. (eds), Probleme des Europäischen Rechts, FS *Walter Hallstein*, Frankfurt 1966, 248-265.

Europäisches Gemeinschaftsrecht, Tübingen 1972.

Die Rolle des Prozeßrichters in der Vorrang-Frage – Zur Bedeutung des II. Simmenthal-Urteils (Rs. 106/77) des Europäischen Gerichtshofs, *EuR 1979*, 223-238.

Rundfunk im Europäischen Gemeinschaftsrecht, Frankfurt am Main & Berlin 1983.

Europäische Verfassung – Nationale Verfassung, *EuR 1987*, 195-213.

Der 'Kulturbereich' im Zugriff der Europäischen Gemeinschaft, in: Fiedler, W., & Ress, G. (eds), Verfassungsrecht und Völkerrecht: *GS Wilhelm Karl Geck*, Cologne (*inter alia*) 1989, 339-354.

Ischreyt, Heinz

Deutsche Kulturpolitik, Bremen 1964.

Isensee, Josef

Subsidiaritätsprinzip und Verfassungsrecht, Berlin 1968.

Jabloner, Clemens, & Okresek, Wolf

Theoretische und praktische Anmerkungen zu Phänomenen des 'soft law', Österr. Zeitschrift für öffentliches Recht und Völkerrecht 1983, 217-241.

Jackson, John H.

World Trade and the Law of GATT, Indianapolis (*inter alia*) 1969.

Jacobs, Francis, & Corbett, Richard

The European Parliament, Harlow 1990.

Jacqué, Jean-Paul

Liberté d'information, in: Cassese, A. et al. (eds), Human Rights and the European Community: The Substantive Law, Baden-Baden 1991, 309-363.

Jacqué, Jean-Paul, & Weiler, Joseph H. H.

On the Road to European Union – A New Judicial Architecture: An Agenda for the Intergovermental Conference, CML Rev. 1990, 185-207.

Jakobs, Michael Ch.

Der Grundsatz der Verhältnismäßigkeit, Cologne (*inter alia*) 1985.

Jarass, Hans D.

EG-Recht und nationales Rundfunkrecht – Zugleich ein Beitrag zur Reichweite der Dienstleistungsfreiheit, EuR 1986, 75-94.

Kaiser, Joseph H.
Die im Rat vereinigten Vertreter der Regierungen der Mitgliedstaaten, in:
    Hallstein, W., & Schlochauer, H.-J. (eds), Zur Integration Europas, *FS Carl
    Friedrich Ophüls*, Karlsruhe 1965, 107–124.
Modi der Integration – Ökonomische Elemente und juristische Relevanz, in:
    von Caemmerer, E. et al. (eds), Probleme des Europäischen Rechts, *FS Walter
    Hallstein*, Frankfurt am Main 1966, 266–274.
Grenzen der EG-Zuständigkeit, *EuR 1980*, 97–118.

Kampf, Roger
Die 'richtige' Rechtsgrundlage der Richtlinie über das Aufenthaltsrecht der
    Studenten, EuR 1990, 393–404.

Kapteyn, P. J. C.
Community Law and the Principle of Subsidiarity, R.A.E. 2/1991, 35–43.

Karl, Joachim
Zur Rechtswirkung von Protokollerklärungen in der Europäischen
    Gemeinschaft, JZ 1991, 593–599.

Keßler, Werner K.
Die Filmwirtschaft im Gemeinsamen Markt, Berlin 1976.

Klein, Eckart
Die materielle *Bedeutung* der Europäischen Menschenrechtskonvention für das
    Europäische Gemeinschaftsrecht, in: Mosler, H. et al. (eds),
    Grundrechtsschutz in Europa, Berlin & Heidelberg 1977, 133–145.
Vertragsauslegung und 'spätere Praxis' Internationaler Organisationen, in:
    Bieber, R., & Ress, G. (eds), Die Dynamik des Europäischen
    Gemeinschaftsrechts, Baden-Baden 1987, 101–112.
Der Verfassungsstaat als Glied einer europäischen Gemeinschaft, *VVDStRL 50
    (1991)*, 56–96.
Hochschulpolitik nach Maastricht, *MittHV 1992*, 262–264.

Klein, Eckart, & Beckmann, Martina
Neuere Entwicklungen des Rechts der Europäischen Gemeinschaften, DÖV
    1990, 179–189.

Klein, Eckart, & Haratsch, Andreas
Neuere Entwicklungen des Rechts der Europäischen Gemeinschaften – 1. Teil–,
    DÖV 1993, 785–798.

Kleinsteuber, Hans J.
Unfaire Handelspraktiken oder Kulturpolitik?, Media Perspektiven 1990,
    549–557.

Klose, Martin
Die Rolle des Sports bei der Europäischen Einigung, Berlin 1989.

Knecht, Wolfdietrich
Das EWG-Kartellrecht in der Praxis, Wien 1988.

Knemeyer, Franz-Ludwig
Subsidiarität – Föderalismus, Dezentralisation, *DVBl. 1990*, 449–454.
Bayerisches *Kommunalrecht*, 7th ed., Stuttgart (*inter alia*) 1991.

Knolle, H.
Die gemeinsame Politik der Berufsausbildung in der Europäischen
    Wirtschaftsgemeinschaft, BArbBl. 1963, 379–382.

Köck, Heribert Franz
Vertragsinterpretation und Vertragsrechtskonvention, Berlin 1976.
Die 'implied powers' der Europäischen Gemeinschaften als Anwendungsfall
der 'implied powers' internationaler Organisationen überhaupt, in:
Böckstiegel, K.-H. et al. (eds), Völkerrecht – Recht der Internationalen
Organisationen – Weltwirtschaftsrecht, *FS Ignaz Seidl-Hohenveldern*,
Cologne (*inter alia*) 1988, 279–299.

Koja, Friedrich
Allgemeines Verwaltungsrecht, 2nd ed., Wien 1986.

Kommentar zum Bonner Grundgesetz (Bonner Kommentar), Heidelberg, Stand
61. Lieferung (October/November 1990).

Kommission der Europäischen Gemeinschaften (ed.)
The *Conditions of Service of Teachers* in the European Community, Luxembourg
1988.
Europa im Wandel: Die kulturelle Herausforderung, Brussels & Luxembourg
1988.

Konow, Gerhard
Bildungs- und Kulturpolitik in der Europäischen Gemeinschaft, *RdJB 1989*,
118–129.
Bildungspolitik nach 'Maastricht', *RdJB 1992*, 428–435.
Zur Europäischen Forschungspolitik nach Maastricht, *WissR 1993, Beiheft 11*,
40–61.

Köstlin, Thomas
Die Kulturhoheit des Bundes, Berlin 1989.

Koszuszeck, Helmut
Freier Dienstleistungsverkehr und nationales Rundfunkrecht, ZUM 1989,
541–547.

Krämer, Ludwig
Einheitliche Europäische Akte und Umweltschutz: Überlegungen zu einigen
neuen Bestimmungen im Gemeinschaftsrecht, in: Rengeling, H.-W. (ed.),
Europäisches Umweltrecht und europäische Umweltpolitik, Cologne (*inter
alia*) 1988, 137–162.

Kraushaar, Reinhold
Zur Kompetenz der Kommissionen der Europäischen Gemeinschaften zum
Erlaß von Verordnungen, DÖV 1959, 726–731.

Kraußer, Hans-Peter
Das Prinzip begrenzter Ermächtigung im Gemeinschaftsrecht als
Strukturprinzip des EWG-Vertrages, Berlin 1991.

Kreile, Johannes
Die Anforderungen an den Jugendschutz im grenzüberschreitenden
Rundfunk, ZUM 1989, 407–413.

Kropholler, Jan
Die Europäischen Gemeinschaften und der Grundrechtsschutz, EuR 1969,
128–146.

Kuch, Hansjörg
Das Ringen um eine europäische Medienordnung. Ein Beitrag aus der Sicht der Länder, in: Scholl-Latour, P. (ed.), On-Line '89, Kongreß II: Kabel- und Satellitenkommunikation in Europa, Velbert 1989, Abschnitt II - 21, 1-14.

Kunig, Philip
Der Schutz des Sonntags im verfassungsrechtlichen Wandel, Berlin & New York 1989.

Kutscher, Hans
Thesen zu den Methoden der Auslegung des Gemeinschaftsrechts, aus der Sicht eines Richters, in: Gerichtshof der Europäischen Gemeinschaften (ed.), Begegnung von Justiz und Hochschule am 27 und 28 September 1976, Luxembourg 1976, I-1-I-56.
Der *Schutz von Grundrechten* im Recht der Europäischen Gemeinschaften, in: *idem* et al., Der Grundrechtsschutz im Europäischen Gemeinschaftsrecht, Heidelberg 1982, 35-50.
Zum *Grundsatz* der Verhältnismäßigkeit im Recht der Europäischen Gemeinschaften, in: Kutscher, H. et al., Der Grundsatz der Verhältnismäßigkeit in europäischen Rechtsordnungen, Heidelberg 1985, 89-97.

Kuyper, Pieter Jan
Anmerkungen zu dem Urteil des Gerichtshofs vom 10 Januar 1985 (Leclerc), Rs. 229/83, CML Rev. 1985, 787-811.

Lagrange, Maurice
Les pouvoirs de la Haute Autorité et l'application dù Traité de Paris, RDP 77 (1961), 40-58.

Lambers, Hans-Jürgen
Subsidiarität in Europa - Allheilmittel oder juristische Leerformel?, EuR 1993, 229-242.

Lane, Robert
New Community Competences under the Maastricht Treaty, CML Rev. 1993, 939-979.

Langbein, Heike Birgit
Die Buchpreisbindung in der EWG, Frankfurt am Main 1989.

Langeheine, Bernd
Abgestufte Integration, EuR 1983, 227-260.

Larenz, Karl
Methodenlehre der Rechtswissenschaft, 6th ed., Berlin (*inter alia*) 1991.

Läufer, Thomas
Die Organe der EG - Rechtsetzung und Haushaltsverfahren zwischen Kooperation und Konflikt, Bonn 1990.

Laursen, Finn, & Vanhoonacker, Sophie (eds)
The Intergovernmental Conference on Political Union, Dordrecht 1992.

Lauwaars, R. H.
Art. 235 als Grundlage für die flankierenden Politiken im Rahmen der Wirtschafts- und Währungsunion, EuR 1976, 100-129.

Lecheler, Helmut
Nationaler öffentlicher Dienst und europäisches Freizügigkeitsrecht, in: Battis,
  U. (ed.), Europäischer Binnenmarkt und nationaler öffentlicher Dienst,
  Regensburg 1989, 127-141.
Öffentliche Verwaltung in den Mitgliedstaaten nach Maßgabe der 'Dynamik
  der Europäischen Integration', DV 1989, 137-149.
Die *Interpretation* des Art. 48 Abs. 4 EWGV und ihre Konsequenzen für die
  Beschäftigung im (nationalen) öffentlichen Dienst, Berlin 1990.
Die Konsequenzen des Art. 48 Abs. 4 EWGV für den nationalen öffentlichen
  Dienst, ZBR 1991, 97-102.

Lenaerts, Koen
ERASMUS: Legal Basis and Implementation, in: de Witte, B. (ed.), European
  Community Law of Education, Baden-Baden 1989, 113-125.
Education in European Community Law after 'Maastricht', CML Rev. 1994,
  7-41.
Subsidiarity and Community Competences in the Field of Education, CJEL
  1994/95, 1-28.

Lenz, Brigitte
The Public Service in Article 48 (4) EEC with Special Reference to the Law in
  England and in the Federal Republic of Germany, LIEI 1989/2, 75-122.

Lenz, Carl Otto
Entwicklung und unmittelbare Geltung des Gemeinschaftsrecht, *DVBl. 1990*,
  903-910.
Zuständigkeiten und Initiativen der Europäischen Gemeinschaft im Bereich des
  Bildungswesens im Lichte der Rechtsprechung des Gerichtshofs (EuGH),
  in: Magiera, S. (ed.), Das Europa der Bürger in einer Gemeinschaft ohne
  Binnengrenzen, Baden-Baden 1990, 183-208.
Die *Rechtsordnung der Europäischen Gemeinschaft*, in: Die Soziale Ordnung des
  Europäischen Binnenmarktes - Einheit oder Vielfalt?, Veröffentlichungen
  der Walter-Raymond-Stiftung, vol. 30, Cologne 1991, 67-93.
(ed.): *EG-Vertrag*, Wien 1994.

Lerche, Peter
Föderalismus als nationales Ordnungsprinzip, VVDStRL 21 (1964), 66-104.

Levi Sandri, Lionello
Europäische Arbeitsmarktpolitik unter Berücksichtigung der Aufgaben der
  Berufsausbildung, in: Deutscher Industrie- und Handelstag (ed.),
  Berufsausbildung im Europäischen Raum, Bonn 1964, 22-33.

Lichtenberg, Hagen
Freizügigkeit und Bildungswesen in der Europäischen Gemeinschaft an der
  Schwelle zum gemeinsamen Binnenmarkt, in: Baur, J. F. et al. (eds),
  Festschrift für Ernst Steindorff, Berlin & New York 1990, 1269-1286.

Lochner, Norbert
Was bedeuten die Begriffe Harmonisierung, Koordinierung und Gemeinsame
  Politik in den Europäischen Verträgen?, ZStW 1962, 35-61.

Loman, J. M. E. et al.
Culture and Community Law - Before and after Maastricht, Deventer & Boston
  1992.

Lonbay, Julian
Education and Law: The Community Context, ELR 1989, 363-387.

Louis, Jean-Victor
Free Movement of Tourists and Freedom of Payments in the Community: The
Luisi-Carbone Judgment, *CML Rev. 1984*, 625-637.
Die *Rechtsordnung* der Europäischen Gemeinschaften, 2nd ed., Brussels 1990.

Maaß, Kurt-Jürgen
Die Bildungspolitik der Europäischen Gemeinschaft, Bonn 1978.

Maggiore, Matteo
Herstellung und Verbreitung audiovisueller Informationen im Gemeinsamen
Markt, Luxembourg 1990.

Magiera, Siegfried
Parlament und Staatsleitung in der Verfassungsordnung des Grundgesetzes,
Berlin 1979.
Die Haushaltsbefugnisse des Europäischen Parlaments – Ansatz zur
parlamentarischen Mitregierung auf Gemeinschaftsebene?, in: von Münch,
I. (ed.), Staatsrecht – Völkerrecht – Europarecht, *FS Hans-Jürgen Schlochauer*,
Berlin & New York 1981, 829-853.
Die Europäische Gemeinschaft auf dem Wege zu einem Europa der Bürger,
DÖV 1987, 221-231.
Als *Bundesstaat* in der Europäischen Gemeinschaft, in: *idem* & Merten, D. (eds),
Bundesländer und Europäische Gemeinschaft, Berlin 1988, 11-19.
Die Einheitliche Europäische Akte und die Fortentwicklung der Europäischen
Gemeinschaft zur Europäischen Union, in: Fiedler, W., & Ress, G. (eds),
Verfassungsrecht und Völkerrecht, *GS Wilhelm Karl Geck*, Cologne (*inter
alia*) 1989, 507-530.
Die Rechtsakte der EG-Organe, *Jura 1989*, 595-606.
The *Emergence* of a 'Europe of Citizens' in a Community without Frontiers,
Speyer 1989.
Rechtliche Grundfragen einer werdenden europäischen Rundfunkordnung, in:
Stern, K. et al., Eine Rundfunkordnung für Europa – Chancen und Risiken,
Munich 1990, 51-74.
Ansätze für ein Europa der Bürger in der Rechtsordnung der Europäischen
Gemeinschaft, in: *idem* (ed.), Das Europa der Bürger in einer Gemeinschaft
ohne Binnengrenzen, Baden-Baden 1990, 13-25.
Kompetenzgrenzen und Strukturprinzipien der Europäischen Gemeinschaft,
in: Bracher, K. D. et al. (eds), Staat und Parteien – *FS Rudolf Morsey*, Berlin
1992, 211-236.

Maihofer, Werner
Zur Notwendigkeit einer europäischen Kulturföderation, in: Weidenfeld, W.
et al.: Europäische Kultur: das Zukunftsgut des Kontinents, Gütersloh
1990, 59-96.

Marticke, Hans-Ulrich
Ausländerklauseln und Spielertransfer aus europarechtlicher Sicht, in: Will, M.
R. (ed.), Sport und Recht in Europa, Saarbrücken 1988, 53-79.

Matthias, Annette
Integrationsrechtliche Probleme im Recht der Europäischen Gemeinschaften,
Berlin 1979.

Matthies, Heinrich
Die Verfassung des Gemeinsamen Marktes, in: Bieber, R. et al. (eds), Das
Europa der zweiten Generation, GS Christoph Sasse, vol. I, Baden-Baden
1981, 115-130.

Maunz, Theodor, Dürig, Günter, Herzog, Roman, & Scholz, Rupert (*inter alia*)
Grundgesetz, Kommentar, vol. III, 28. Ergänzungslieferung, Munich 1990.

Maunz, Theodor, & Zippelius, Reinhold
Deutsches Staatsrecht, 28th ed., Munich 1991.

McMahon, Bryan M.E.
Case 379/87 (Groener), CML Rev. 1990, 129-139.

MDHS
See Maunz, Theodor, Dürig, Günter, Herzog, Roman, & Scholz, Rupert (*inter
alia*).

Meessen, Karl Matthias
Vom Anti-Protektionismus zur Fortentwicklung der internationalen
Wirtschaftsordnung, in: Vorstand des Arbeitskreises Europäische
Integration (ed.), Neuer Protektionismus in der Weltwirtschaft und EG-
Handelspolitik, Baden-Baden 1985, 81-97.

Meier, Gert
Die 'Mitteilung' er Kommission: Ein Instrument der Normensetzung der
Gemeinschaft?, in: Baur, J. F. et al. (eds), Festschrift für Ernst Steindorff,
Berlin & New York 1990, 1303-1312.

Memminger, Gerhard
Bedeutung des Verfassungsrechtsstreits zur EG-Rundfunkrichtlinie, DÖV
1989, 846-850.

Merten, Detlef
Die Beteiligung der Bundesländer an der Setzung europäischen
Gemeinschaftsrechts, in: Kloepfer, M. et al., Die Bedeutung der
Europäischen Gemeinschaften für das deutsche Recht und die deutsche
Gerichtsbarkeit, Berlin 1989, 31-49.

Mestmäcker, Ernst-Joachim
Wege zur Rundfunkfreiheit in Europa, in: *idem* (ed.), Offene Rundfunkordnung,
Gütersloh 1988, 9-43.
Zur Anwendung von Kartellaufsicht und Fachaufsicht auf urheberrechtliche
Verwertungsgesellschaften und ihre Mitglieder, in: Leßmann, H. et al. (eds),
Festschrift für Rudolf Lukes, Cologne (*inter alia*) 1989, 445-460.
Zur Rechtsstellung urheberrechtlicher Verwertungsgesellschaften im
europäischen Wettbewerbsrecht, in: Löwisch, M. et al. (eds), Beiträge zum
Handels- und Wirtschaftsrecht, *FS Fritz Rittner*, Munich 1991, 391-404.

Mestmäcker, Ernst-Joachim et al.
Der Einfluß des europäischen Gemeinschaftsrechts auf die deutsche
Rundfunkordnung, Baden-Baden 1990.

Meyer, Albert
  Die europäische Integration und das deutsche Beamtenrecht, BayVBl. 1990,
    97–100.
Meyer-Cording, Ulrich
  Die europäische Integration als geistiger Entwicklungsprozeß, in: Greiß, F., &
    Meyer, F. W., Wirtschaft, Gesellschaft und Kultur, FG Alfred Müller-
    Armack, Berlin 1961, 291–319.
Millarg, Eberhard
  Die Anwendung des Rechts der Europäischen Gemeinschaften in Dänemark,
    Großbritannien, Irland und Norwegen, EuR 1972, 179–187.
Millgramm, Karl-Heinz
  Föderalismus und Individuum, DVBl. 1990, 740–748.
Mischo, Jean
  Un rôle nouveau pour la Cour de Justice?, RMC 1990, 681–686.
Morand, Charles-Albert
  Les recommendations, les resolutions et les avis du droit communautaire, CDE
    1970, 623–644.
Mortelmans, Kamiel
  Article 30 of the EEC Treaty and Legislation Relating to Market
    Circumstances: Time to Consider a New Definition?, CML Rev. 1991,
    115–136.
Mosler, Hermann
  National- und Gemeinschaftsinteressen im Verfahren des EWG-Ministerrats,
    ZaöRV 1966, 1–32.
Möwes, Bernd, & Schmitt-Vockenhausen, Monika
  Europäische Medienordnung im Lichte des Fernsehübereinkommens des
    Europarats und der EG-Fernsehrichtlinie 1989, EuGRZ 1990, 121–129.
Müller, Joachim A.
  Dienstleistungsmonopole im System des EWGV, Baden-Baden 1988.
Müller-Graff, Peter-Christian
  Wettbewerbsbeschränkungen durch Gesetz: Preisbindungspflicht bei
    Büchern, *EuR 1985*, 293–308.
  Dienstleistungsfreiheit und Erbringungsformen grenzüberschreitender
    Dienstleistungen, in: Leßmann, H., & Großfeld, B., & Vollmer, L. (eds),
    Festschrift für Rudolf Lukes, Cologne (*inter alia*) 1989, 471–493.
Müller-Huschke, Wolfgang
  Eine 'Festung Europa'?, Baden-Baden 1991.
Nass, Klaus Otto
  Staaten oder Regionen? Die Bundesländer in der Europäischen Gemeinschaft,
    in: Mestmäcker, E.-J. et al. (eds), Eine Ordnungspolitik für Europa, FS Hans
    von der Groeben, Baden-Baden 1987, 285–302.
Nicolaysen, Gert
  Environmental policy before the Single European Act, in: Schwarze, J., &
    Schermers, H. G. (eds), Structure and Dimensions of European Community
    Policy, Baden-Baden 1988, 111–115.
  Europarecht I, Baden-Baden 1991.

Niedobitek, Matthias
Pläne und Entwicklung eines Europas der Bürger, Speyer 1989.

O'Keeffe, David
Equal Rights for Migrants: The Concept of Social Advantages in Article 7 (2), Regulation 1612/68, YEL 1985, 93-123.

Oldekop, Dieter
Die Richtlinien der EWG, Göttingen 1968.

Oliver, Peter
Non-Community Nationals and the Treaty of Rome, *YEL 1985*, 57-92.
A Review of the Case Law of the Court of Justice on Articles 30 to 36 EEC in 1985, *CML Rev. 1986*, 325-357.
Free Movement of Goods in the EEC, 2nd ed., London 1988.

Ophüls, Carl Friedrich
Über die Auslegung der Europäischen Gemeinschaftsverträge, in: Greiß, F., & Meyer, F. W. (eds), Wirtschaft, Gesellschaft und Kultur, *FG Alfred Müller-Armack*, Berlin 1961, 279-290.
Die Europäischen Gemeinschaftsverträge als *Planverfassungen*, in: Kaiser, J. H. (ed.), Planung I, Baden-Baden 1965, 229-245.
Staatshoheit und Gemeinschaftshoheit – Wandlungen des Souveränitätsbegriffs, in: Recht im Wandel, *FS Carl Heymanns Verlag*, Cologne (*inter alia*) 1965, 519-590.

Oppermann, Thomas
Kulturverwaltungsrecht, Tübingen 1969.
Die Europäische Gemeinschaft als parastaatliche Superstruktur, in: Stödter, R., & Thieme, W. (eds), Hamburg – Deutschland – Europa, FS Hans Peter Ipsen zum siebzigsten Geburtstag, Tübingen 1977, 685-699.
Europäische Integration und das deutsche Grundgesetz, in: Berberich, Th. et al. (eds), Neue Entwicklungen im öffentlichen Recht, Stuttgart (*inter alia*) 1979, 85-101.
Europäisches Gemeinschaftsrecht und Deutsche Bildungsordnung, Bonn 1987.
Von der *EG-Freizügigkeit* zur gemeinsamen europäischen Ausbildungspolitik? Die 'Gravier'-Doktrin des Gerichtshofes der Europäischen Gemeinschaften, Berlin & New York 1988.
Europarecht, Munich 1991.
Die deutsche *Länderkulturhoheit* und EG-Aktivitäten in Bildung, Forschung und technologischer Entwicklung, in: Vogel, B. (ed.), Föderalismus in der Bewährung, Cologne 1992, 73-84.

Oppermann, Thomas, & Beise, Marc
Chancen für eine neue Welthandelsordnung?, EA 1991, 449-460.

Oschatz, Georg-Berndt
EG-Rechtsetzung und deutscher Föderalismus, in: Merten, D. (ed.), Föderalismus und Europäische Gemeinschaften, Berlin 1990, 63-80.

Ossenbühl, Fritz
Rundfunk zwischen nationalem Verfassungsrecht und europäischem Gemeinschaftsrecht, Frankfurt am Main 1986.

Pechstein, Matthias
Die Mitgliedstaaten der EG als 'Sachwalter des gemeinsamen Interesses',
Baden-Baden 1987.
Die Bedeutung von Protokollerklärungen zu Rechtsakten der EG, EuR 1990,
249-268.
Diskussionsbeitrag, in: Hopt, K. J. (ed.), Europäische Integration als
Herausforderung des Rechts, Essen 1991, 303.
Subsidiarität der EG-Medienpolitik?, DÖV 1991, 535-542.
Pernice, Ingolf
Religionsrechtliche Aspekte im Europäischen Gemeinschaftsrecht, JZ 1977,
777-781.
Grundrechtsgehalte im Europäischen Gemeinschaftsrecht, Baden-Baden 1979.
Kompetenzordnung und Handlungsbefugnisse der Europäischen
Gemeinschaft auf dem Gebiet des Umwelt- und Technikrechts, DV 1989,
1-54.
Europäische Union: Gefahr oder Chance für den Föderalismus in Deutschland,
Österreich und der Schweiz?, DVBl. 1993, 909-924.
Maastricht, Staat und Demokratie, DV 1993, 449-488.
Pertek, Jacques
Un arret d'une grande importance sur des questions de principe, Anmerkungen
zum Urteil des Gerichtshofs vom 30. Mai 1989 in der Rs. 242/87
(ERASMUS), RTDE 1991, 132-137.
Pescatore, Pierre
Der Schutz der Grundrechte in den Europäischen Gemeinschaften und seine
Lücken, in: Mosler, H. et al. (eds), Grundrechtsschutz in Europa, Berlin,
Heidelberg & New York 1977, 64-75.
Aspects judiciaires de l'"acquis communautaire', RTDE 1981, 617-651.
Le commerce de l'art et le Marché commun, RTDE 1985, 451-462.
Petersmann, Ernst-Ulrich
Die EWG als GATT-Mitglied - Rechtskonflikte zwischen GATT-Recht und
Europäischem Gemeinschaftsrecht, in: Hilf, M. & idem (eds), GATT und
Europäische Gemeinschaft, Baden-Baden 1986, 119-174.
The Uruguay Round of Multilateral Trade Negotiations and the Single European
Market 1992, in: Hilf, M. (ed.), EG und Drittstaatsbeziehungen nach 1992,
Baden-Baden 1991, 195-212.
Pieroth, Bodo, & Kampmann, Bernd
Außenhandelsbeschränkungen für Kunstgegenstände, NJW 1990,
1385-1390.
Pollak, Christiana
Verhältnismäßigkeitsprinzip und Grundrechtsschutz in der Judikatur des
Europäischen Gerichtshofs und des Österreichischen
Verfassungsgerichtshofs, Baden-Baden 1991.
Pracht, Daniel
Die grenzüberschreitende Informations- und Rundfunkfreiheit nach
allgemeinem Völkerrecht, dem Recht der Europäischen Gemeinschaften
und dem Grundgesetz der Bundesrepublik Deutschland, Dissertation,
Osnabrück 1989.

Rabe, Hans-Jürgen
Das Verordnungsrecht der Europäischen Wirtschaftsgemeinschaft, Hamburg 1963.

Rambow, Gerhard
Möglichkeiten und Grenzen der Verbraucherpolitik im Gemeinsamen Markt, EuR 1981, 240–252.

Reich, Norbert
Die *Rundfunkhoheit* der Bundesländer im Spannungsfeld zwischen Regulierungsanspruch der EG und deutschem Verfassungsrecht, in: Joerges, Ch., & Sieveking, K. (eds), Europäische Integration, Nationalstaat und regionale Politikkompetenzen, ZERP – DP 2/1987, Bremen 1987, 65–73.
Förderung und Schutz diffuser Interessen durch die Europäischen Gemeinschaften, Baden-Baden 1987.
Rundfunkrecht und Wettbewerbsrecht vor dem Forum des europäischen Gemeinschaftsrechts, in: Hoffmann-Riem, W. (ed.), Rundfunk im Wettbewerbsrecht, Baden-Baden 1988, 224–243.
Die Bedeutung der Binnenmarktkonzeption für die Anwendung der EWG-Wettbewerbsregeln, in: Baur, J. F. et al. (eds), *Festschrift für Ernst Steindorff*, Berlin & New York 1990, 1065–1084.

Reihe Alternativkommentare
Kommentar zum Grundgesetz für die Bundesrepublik Deutschland, 2nd ed., vol. 2, Neuwied 1989.

Reinert, Patrick
Grenzüberschreitender Rundfunk im Spannungsfeld von staatlicher Souveränität und transnationaler Rundfunkfreiheit, Frankfurt am Main 1990.

Reischl, Gerhard
Die *Rechtsprechung des Gerichtshofs* der Europäischen Gemeinschaften zum Urheberrecht im Gemeinsamen Markt, in: Ress, G. (ed.), Entwicklung des Europäischen Urheberrechts, Baden-Baden 1989, 45–55.
Europäisches Urheberrecht und gewerblicher Rechtsschutz im Lichte der Rechtsprechung des EuGH, Saarbrücken 1990.

Rengeling, Hans-Werner
Der Grundrechtsschutz in der Europäischen Gemeinschaft und die Überprüfung der Gesetzgebung, *DVBl. 1982*, 140–144.
Grundlagen des Subventionsrechts und Kompetenzen aus der Sicht von Bund und Ländern, *ZHR 1988*, 455–571.

Renzsch, Wolfgang
Deutsche Länder und europäische Integration, Aus Politik und Zeitgeschichte B 28/90, 28–39.

Ress, Georg
Der *Grundsatz* der Verhältnismäßigkeit im deutschen Recht, in: Kutscher, H. et al., Der Grundsatz der Verhältnismäßigkeit in europäischen Rechtsordnungen, Heidelberg 1985, 5–51.
Die Europäischen Gemeinschaften und der deutsche Föderalismus, *EuGRZ 1986*, 549–558.

Das deutsche Zustimmungsgesetz zur Einheitlichen Europäischen Akte – Ein
Schritt zur 'Föderalisierung' der Europapolitik, *EuGRZ 1987*, 361-367.
Kultur und Europäischer Binnenmarkt, Stuttgart (*inter alia*) 1991.
Die neue Kulturkompetenz der EG, *DÖV 1992*, 944-955.
Die Zulässigkeit von *Kulturbeihilfen* in der Europäischen Union, in:
Randelzhofer, A. et al. (eds), Gedächtnisschrift für Eberhard Grabitz,
Munich 1995, 595-629.

Ress, Georg, & Bieber, Roland
Die Dynamik des EG-Rechts als Rechtsproblem, in: Bieber, R., & Ress, G.
(eds), Die Dynamik des Europäischen Gemeinschaftsrechts, Baden-Baden
1987, 13-29.

Ress, Georg, & Ukrow, Jörg
Neue Aspekte des Grundrechtsschutzes in der Europäischen Gemeinschaft,
EuZW 1990, 499-505.

Rhein, Eberhard
Wie protektionistisch ist die EG?, in: Vorstand des Arbeitskreises Europäische
Integration (ed.), Neuer Protektionismus in der Weltwirtschaft und EG-
Handelspolitik, Baden-Baden 1985, 69-80.

Riegel, Reinhard
Zum Anwendungsbereich der Art. 48 ff. EWGV, *NJW 1978*, 468-470.
Die Einwirkung des europäischen Gemeinschaftsrechts auf die
Eigentumsordnung der Mitgliedstaaten, *RIW 1979*, 744-749.

Roth, Wulf-Henning
Grenzüberschreitender Rundfunk und Dienstleistungsfreiheit, *ZHR 1985*,
679-692.
Die Harmonisierung des Dienstleistungsrechts in der EWG, *EuR 1986*,
340-369.
Grundfreiheiten des Gemeinsamen Marktes für kulturschaffende Tätigkeiten
und kulturelle Leistungsträger, *ZUM 1989*, 101-110.
Niederlassungs- und Dienstleistungsfreiheit für Autoren, Verlage und Buchhändler
im EG-Binnenmarkt, in: Becker, J. (ed.), Der Buchhandel im Europäischen
Binnenmarkt, Frankfurt am Main 1989, 39-57.
Die Entwicklung der deutschen Fernsehwerbemärkte: EG-Fernsehrichtlinie
und deutsches Kartellrecht, *AfP 1991*, 504-510.

Rovan, Joseph
Überlegungen und Vorschläge zur europäischen Kulturpolitik, in:
Weidenfeld, W. et al., Europäische Kultur: das Zukunftsgut des Kontinents,
Gütersloh 1990, 97-116.

Rupp, Hans Heinrich
Verfassungsprobleme auf dem Weg zur Europäischen Union, ZRP 1990, 1-4.

Sasse, Christoph
Der Schutz der Grundrechte in den Europäischen Gemeinschaften und seine
Lücken, in: Mosler, H. et al. (eds), Grundrechtsschutz in Europa, Berlin (*inter
alia*) 1977, 51-63.

Sattler, Andreas
Das Prinzip der 'funktionellen Integration' und die Einigung Europas,
Göttingen 1967.

Scharf, Albert
Fernsehen ohne Grenzen – Die Errichtung des Gemeinsamen Marktes für den Rundfunk, in: Magiera, S. (ed.), Entwicklungsperspektiven der Europäischen Gemeinschaft, Berlin 1985, 147-163.

Schelter, Kurt
Subsidiarität – Handlungsprinzip für das Europa der Zukunft, EuZW 1990, 217-219.

Schepers, Stefan
The Legal Force of the Preamble to the EEC Treaty, ELR 1981, 356-361.

Scherer, Joachim
Europäisches Niederlassungsrecht für Freiberufler, WiVerw 1987, 159-178.

Schermers, Henry G.
The European Communities Bound by Fundamental Human Rights, CML Rev. 1990, 249-258.

Schermers, Henry G., & Waelbroeck, Denis
Judicial Protection in the European Communities, 4th ed., Deventer (inter alia) 1987.

Scheuing, Dieter H.
Das Niederlassungsrecht im Prozeß der Integration, JZ 1975, 151-159.
Umweltschutz auf der Grundlage der Einheitlichen Europäischen Akte, EuR 1989, 152-192.

Scheuner, Ulrich
Staatszielbestimmungen, in: Schnur, R. (ed.), Festschrift für Ernst Forsthoff, 2nd ed., Munich 1974, 325-346.

Schiller, Klaus-Volker
Der Verhältnismäßigkeitsgrundsatz im Europäischen Gemeinschaftsrecht nach der Rechtsprechung des EuGH, RIW 1983, 928-930.

Schima, Bernhard
Das Subsidiaritätsprinzip im Europäischen Gemeinschaftsrecht, Wien 1994.

Schlochauer, Hans-Jürgen
Der Gerichtshof der Europäischen Gemeinschaften als Integrationsfaktor, in: von Caemmerer, E. et al. (eds), Probleme des Europäischen Rechts, FS Walter Hallstein, Frankfurt am Main 1966, 431-452.

Schlotfeld, Walter
Die Rechtsnatur der 'Allgemeinen Grundsätze zur Berufsausbildung' der EWG, in: Deutscher Industrie- und Handelstag (ed.), Berufsausbildung im Europäischen Raum, Bonn 1964, 54-64.

Schmidhuber, Peter M.
Die Politik der EG-Kommission zur Freizügigkeit der Arbeitnehmer und zum Beschäftigungszugang in der öffentlichen Verwaltung der Mitgliedstaaten, in: Battis, U. (ed.), Europäischer Binnenmarkt und nationaler öffentlicher Dienst, Regensburg 1989, 109-121.

Schmidhuber, Peter M., & Hitzler, Gerhard
Die Planungskompetenz der Europäischen Gemeinschaft beim Ausbau der europäischen Infrastrukturen, DÖV 1991, 271-278.

Schmidt, Reiner
Wirtschaftsstandort Bundesrepublik aus verfassungs- bzw.
verwaltungsrechtlicher Sicht, WUR 1990, 1–6.

Schmidt-Räntsch, Jürgen
Erlaß von Förderprogrammen durch den Rat der EG aufgrund Art. 128
EWGV, NJW 1989, 3071–3072.

Schmitt von Sydow, Helmut
La place des communications dans la politique de la Commission: les objectifs
poursuivis, in: Schwarze, J. et al. (eds), The 1992 Challenge at National
Level, Baden-Baden 1990, 667–676.

Schneider, Hans
Autonome Satzung und Rechtsverordnung, in: Hefermehl, W., & Nipperdey,
H. C. (eds), Festschrift für Philipp Möhring, Munich & Berlin 1965,
521–541.

Schrenk, Gundolf
Mitgliedstaatliche und gemeinschaftliche Handlungsebene in der
europäischen Umweltpolitik, NuR 1990, 391–395.

Schröder, Meinhard
Europäische Bildungspolitik und bundesstaatliche Ordnung, Baden-Baden
1990.

Schroeder, Werner
Sport und Europäische Integration, Munich 1989.

Schulz, Axel
Die Teilhabe von Ausländern an der Hochschulausbildung, ZAR 1987, 72–77.

Schumacher, Detlef
Die Ausfüllung von Kompetenzlücken ein Verfassungsrecht der Europäischen
Gemeinschaften, AWD 1970, 539–545.

Schuster, Günter
Gemeinsame Politik im Bereich von Wissenschaft und Technologie, in: von der
Groeben, H. et al., Kommentar zum EWG-Vertrag, 3rd ed., Baden-Baden
1983, 1527–1537.

Schwan, Hartmut Heinrich
Die deutschen Bundesländer im Entscheidungssystem der Europäischen
Gemeinschaften, Berlin 1982.

Schwartz, Ivo E.
EG-Rechtsetzungsbefugnisse, insbesondere nach Artikel 235 – ausschließlich
oder konkurrierend?, *EuR 1976, Sonderheft*, 27–44.
Die *Liberalisierung* der nationalen Hörfunk- und Fernsehsysteme aufgrund der
Regeln des Gemeinschaftsrechts, in: Seidel, M. (ed.), Hörfunk und
Fernsehen im gemeinsamen Markt, Baden-Baden 1983, 147–164.
Fernsehen ohne Grenzen – Die Errichtung des Gemeinsamen Marktes für den
Rundfunk, in: Magiera, S. (ed.), Entwicklungsperspektiven der
Europäischen Gemeinschaft, Berlin 1985, 121–145.
Zur *Debatte* über das EG-Grünbuch: Weitere Aktionen der Kommission, in:
Schwarze, J. (ed.), Rundfunk und Fernsehen im Lichte der Entwicklung des
nationalen und internationalen Rechts, Baden-Baden 1986, 99–118.

Zur Zuständigkeit der Europäischen Gemeinschaft im Bereich des Rundfunks, in: Arbeitskreis Werbefernsehen der Deutschen Wirtschaft (ed.), Europafernsehen und Werbung, Baden-Baden 1987, 79–90.

EG-Rechtsetzungsbefugnis für das Fernsehen, *ZUM 1989*, 381–389.

La *liberté d'expression* (Art. 10 CEDH) et la libre prestation des services (Art. 59 Traité CEE) dans le domaine de la radiodiffusion télévisuelle, in: Cassese, A., & Clapham, A. (eds), Transfrontier Television in Europe: The Human Rights Dimension, Baden-Baden 1990, 165–188.

Rundfunk, EG-Kompetenzen und ihre Ausübung, *ZUM 1991*, 155–167.

Subsidiarität und EG-Kompetenzen – Der neue Titel 'Kultur' – Medienvielfalt und Binnenmarkt, *AfP 1993*, 409–421.

Schwarze, Jürgen
Die Befugnis zur *Abstraktion* im europäischen Gemeinschaftsrecht, Baden-Baden 1976.

Funktionen des Rechts in der Europäischen Gemeinschaft, in: *idem* (ed.), Gesetzgebung in der Europäischen Gemeinschaft, Baden-Baden 1985, 9–30.

Rundfunk und Fernsehen in der Europäischen Gemeinschaft, in: *idem* (ed.), Fernsehen ohne Grenzen, Baden-Baden 1985, 11–44.

Schutz der Grundrechte in der Europäischen Gemeinschaft, *EuGRZ 1986*, 293–299.

Europäisches Verwaltungsrecht, vol. II, Baden-Baden 1988.

Rechtsstaatlichkeit und Grundrechtsschutz als Ordnungspostulate der Europäischen Gemeinschaft, in: Kaufmann, A. et al. (eds), Rechtsstaat und Menschenwürde, *FS Werner Maihofer*, Frankfurt am Main 1988, 529–548.

Schweitzer, Michael
Rechtsetzung durch die Europäischen Gemeinschaften und Kompetenzverlust in den Mitgliedstaaten, in: Kremer, H. A. (ed.), Die Landesparlamente im Spannungsfeld zwischen europäischer Integration und europäischem Regionalismus, Munich 1988, 20–40.

EG-Kompetenzen im Bereich von Kultur und Bildung, in: Merten, D. (ed.), Föderalismus und Europäische Gemeinschaften, Berlin 1990, 147–159.

Schweitzer, Michael, & Hummer, Waldemar
Europarecht, 3rd ed., Neuwied & Frankfurt 1990.

Séché, Jean-Claude
Libre prestation des services et allocations de devises aux touristes, CDE 1984, 706–713.

Sedemund, Jochim, & Montag, Frank
Europäisches Gemeinschaftsrecht, NJW 1988, 601–609.

Seidel, Lore
'Fernsehen ohne Grenzen', NVwZ 1991, 120–125.

Seidel, Martin
Die *Dienstleistungsfreiheit* in der neuesten Rechtsentwicklung, in: Schwarze, J. (ed.), Der Gemeinsame Markt, Bestand und Zukunft in wirtschaftsrechtlicher Perspektive, Baden-Baden 1987, 113–136.

Europäische Rundfunkzone für die nationalen Hörfunk- und Fernsehsysteme oder gemeinschaftseinheitliches Rundfunksystem? Zu neueren Entwicklungen der europäischen Rundfunkpolitik, in: Scherer, J. (ed.), Nationale und europäische Perspektiven der Telekommunikation, Baden-Baden 1987, 133–148.

Umweltrecht der Europäischen Gemeinschaft – Träger oder Hemmnis des Fortschritts?, *DVBl 1989*, 441–448.

Senti, Richard

GATT als System der Welthandelsordnung, Zürich 1986.

Siedentopf, Heinrich

Europäische Gemeinschaft und kommunale Beteiligung, *DÖV 1988*, 981–988.

Die europäische Integration: Bestand und Perspektiven, *VOP 1991*, 12–13.

Europa 1992 – Traum oder Trauma für die kommunale Selbstverwaltung?, in: *idem* (ed.), Verwaltungsgerichtsbarkeit – Umweltschutz – Kommunale Selbstverwaltung, Speyer 1991, 227–248.

Siedentopf, Heinrich, & Huber, Norbert

Präambeln, Vorsprüche und Zweckbestimmungen in den Rechtsordnungen der westlichen Welt, in: Hill, H. (ed.), Gesetzesvorspruch, Heidelberg 1988, 37–76.

Sieveking, Klaus

Die sozialrechtliche Stellung der EG-Ausländer, in: Zuleeg, M. (ed.), Ausländerrecht und Ausländerpolitik in Europa, Baden-Baden 1987, 101–122.

Skouris, Wassilios

La Liberté d'établissement et de prestation de services en matière d'enseignement, in: de Witte, B. (ed.), European Community Law of Education, Baden-Baden 1989, 21–29.

Slot, Piet Jan

State Aids in the Cultural Sector, Bonn 1994.

Smeets, Heinz-Dieter

Importschutz und GATT, Bern & Stuttgart 1987.

Sommermann, Karl-Peter

Staatsziel 'Umweltschutz' mit Gesetzesvorbehalt?, DVBl. 1991, 34–36.

Sørensen, Max

Berührungspunkte zwischen der Europäischen Menschenrechtskonvention und dem Recht der Europäischen Gemeinschaften, EuGRZ 1978, 33–36.

Sparr, Jürgen

Kulturhoheit und EWG-Vertrag, Baden-Baden 1991.

Späth, Lothar

1992: Der Traum von Europa, Stuttgart 1989.

Speyer, Stefan

Anwendung der Cassis-de-Dijon-Doktrin und Spaltbarkeit reglementierter Tätigkeiten als neue Etappen der Dienstleistungsfreiheit, EuZW 1991, 588–590.

Stadler, Hans

Subsidiaritätsprinzip und Föderalismus, Freiburg in der Schweiz 1951.

Starkle, G.
Extension du principe de non-discrimination en droit communautaire au ressortissant d'un Etat membre licitement installé dans un autre Etat membre, CDE 1984, 672-695.

Staudenmayer, Dirk
Mittelbare Auswirkungen des Gemeinschaftsrechts auf das Bildungswesen, *WissR 1994*, 249-281.
Europäische Bildungspolitik - vor und nach Maastricht -, *BayVBl. 1995*, 321-330.

Stauffenberg, Franz Ludwig Graf, & Langenfeld, Christine
Maastricht - ein Fortschritt für Europa?, ZRP 1992, 252-259.

Stein, Torsten
Die *Autorität* des Europäischen Gemeinschaftsrechts, in: *idem* (ed.), Die Autorität des Rechts, Heidelberg 1985, 53-76.
Die *Querschnittsklausel* zwischen Maastricht und Karlsruhe, in: Ole Due et al. (eds), Festschrift für Ulrich Everling, vol. II, Baden-Baden 1995, 1439-1453.

Steinberger, Helmut
Der Verfassungsstaat als Glied einer europäischen Gemeinschaft, VVDStRL 50 (1991), 9-55.

Steindorff, Ernst
Berufssport im Gemeinsamen Markt, *RIW 1975*, 253-255.
Berufsfreiheit für nicht-wirtschaftliche Zwecke im EG-Recht, *NJW 1982*, 1902-1905.
Ausbildungsrechte im EG-Recht, *NJW 1983*, 1231-1233.
Dienstleistungsfreiheit im EG-Recht, *RIW 1983*, 831-839.
Reichweite der Niederlassungsfreiheit, *EuR 1988*, 19-32.
Grenzen der EG-Kompetenzen, Heidelberg 1990.

Steiner, Josephine
Recipients of Services - Some More Equal Than Others, ELR 1985, 348-352.

Stern, Klaus
Das Staatsrecht der Bundesrepublik Deutschland, 2nd ed., vol. I, Munich 1984.

Stettner, Rupert
Grundfragen einer Kompetenzlehre, Berlin 1983.

Stock, Martin
Europäisches Medienrecht im Werden - Probleme und Chancen, RuF 1989, 180-202.

Stoiber, Edmund
Stellungnahme zum Beitrag von Prof. A. Deringer, *ZUM 1986*, 672-673.
Auswirkungen der Entwicklung Europas zur Rechtsgemeinschaft auf die Länder der Bundesrepublik Deutschland, *EA 1987*, 543-552.

Streil, Jochen
Der Beitrag des Gerichtshofs der Europäischen Gemeinschaften zur Entwicklung des Sozialrechts in der Gemeinschaft, in: Lichtenberg, H. (ed.), Sozialpolitik in der EG, Baden-Baden 1986, 95-116.

Streinz, Rudolf
Die *Auswirkungen des Europäischen Gemeinschaftsrechts* auf die Kompetenzen der deutschen Bundesländer, in: Heckmann, D., & Meßerschmidt, K. (eds), Gegenwartsfragen des Öffentlichen Rechts, Berlin 1988, 15-51.
Grundrechtsprobleme im Gemeinschaftsrecht, in: Kremer, H. A. (ed.), Die Landesparlamente im Spannungsfeld zwischen europäischer Integration und europäischem Regionalismus, Munich 1988, 120-154.
Europarecht, 2nd ed., Heidelberg 1995.

Stremmel, Jörg
Die Forschungs- und Technologiepolitik der Europäischen Gemeinschaft, Aachen 1988.

Strohmeier, Rudolf W.
Grundzüge der europäischen Bildungspolitik, GdWZ 1992, 69-72.

Sturm, Fritz
Belgisches Kabelfernsehen vor dem Forum des Europäischen Gerichtshofs, AfP 1980, 190-194.

Süsterhenn, Adolf
Das Subsidiaritätsprinzip als Grundlage der vertikalen Gewaltenteilung, in: Maunz, T. (ed.), Vom Bonner Grundgesetz zur gesamtdeutschen Verfassung, FS Hans Nawiasky, Munich 1956, 141-155.

Taschner, Hans Claudius
Rechtsangleichung in der Bewährung?, in: Lüke, G., et al. (eds), Rechtsvergleichung, Europarecht und Staatenintegration, GS Léontin-Jean Constantinesco, Cologne (*inter alia*) 1983, 765-780.

Teske, Wolfgang
BAföG und EG-Recht, EuZW 1991, 54-55.

Thiel, Jürgen Michael
Europa 1992: Grundrechtlicher Eigentumsschutz im EG-Recht, JuS 1991, 274-281.

Thieme, Werner
Die *Kulturordnung* im Grundgesetz als föderalistisches Problem, in: Annales Universitatis Saraviensis, Rechts- und Wirtschaftswissenschaften, VIII 1960, Saarbrücken 1961, 59-74.
Der Student als sozialrechtliches Problem, in: Fiedler, W., & Ress, G. (eds), Verfassungsrecht und Völkerrecht, *GS Wilhelm Karl Geck*, Cologne (*inter alia*) 1989, 897-914.

Thürer, Daniel
'Soft Law' - eine neue Form von Völkerrecht?, ZSR 1985, half-vol. 1, 429-453.

Tomuschat, Christian
Der Vorbehalt der Ausübung öffentlicher Gewalt in den Berufsfreiheitsregelungen des EWG-Vertrages und die freie Advokatur im Gemeinsamen Markt, *ZaöRV 1967*, 53-93.
Die Charta der wirtschaftlichen Rechte und Pflichten der Staaten, *ZaöRV 1976*, 444-491.
Die Rechtsetzungsbefugnisse der EWG in Generalermächtigungen, insbesondere in Art. 235 EWGV, *EuR 1976, Sonderheft*, 45-73.

Le principe de proportionnalité: Quis iudicabit? - L'affaire Watson, *CDE 1977*, 97-102.

Rechtliche Aspekte des Gemeinschaftshandelns im Bereich der Kultur, in: *F.I.D.E. Reports* of the 13th Congress, Vol. 1, Athens 1988, 17-64.

Aller guten Dinge sind III?, *EuR 1990*, 340-361.

Traversa, Enrico
L'interdiction de discrimination en raison de la nationalité en matière d'accès à l'enseignement, RTDE 1989, 45-69.

Trute, Hans-Heinrich, & Groß, Thomas
Rechtsvergleichende Grundlagen der europäischen Forschungspolitik, WissR 1994, 203-248.

Usher, John
The Development of Community Powers after the Single European Act, in: White, R., & Smythe, B. (eds), Current Issues in European and International Law, London 1990, 3-18.

van Craeyenest, Felix
La nature juridique des résolutions sur la coopération en matière d'éducation, in: de Witte, B. (ed.), European Community Law of Education, Baden-Baden 1989, 127-133.

van der Woude, Marc, & Mead, Philip
Free Movement of the Tourist in Community Law, CML Rev. 1988, 117-140.

Verstrynge, Jean-Fraçois
Un espace européen de la créativité, R.A.E. 3/1991, 66-72.

Vitzthum, Wolfgang Graf
Der Föderalismus in der europäischen und internationalen Einbindung der Staaten, AöR 1990, 281-304.

Völker, Stefan
Passive Dienstleistungsfreiheit im Europäischen Gemeinschaftsrecht, Berlin 1990.

von Bogdandy, Armin
Europäischer Protektionismus im Medienbereich, EuZW 1992, 9-17.

von Borries, Reimer
Gedanken zur Tragweite des Subsidiaritätsprinzips im Europäischen Gemeinschaftsrecht, in: Everling,Ulrich et al. (eds), Europarecht, Kartellrecht, Wirtschaftsrecht - FS Arved Deringer, Baden-Baden 1993, 22-39.

von der Groeben, Hans, von Boeckh, Hans, Thiesing, Jochen, & Ehlermann, Claus-Dieter (eds)
Kommentar zum EWG-Vertrag, 3rd ed., vols. 1 & 2, Baden-Baden 1983.

von der Groeben, Hans, Thiesing, Jochen, & Ehlermann, Claus-Dieter (eds)
Kommentar zum EWG-Vertrag, 4th ed., vols. 1, 3 & 4, Baden-Baden 1991.
Handbuch des Europäischen Rechts, Baden-Baden (as at November 1986).

von Meibom, Hanspeter
Lückenfüllung bei den Europäischen Gemeinschaftsverträgen, NJW 1968, 2165-2170.

von Münch, Ingo (ed.)
  Grundgesetz-Kommentar, vol. 1 (Präambel bis Art. 20), 3rd ed., Munich
    1985.
von Simson, Werner
  Rechtsetzungsaufträge in der Europäischen Gemeinschaft, in: Schwarze, J.
    (ed.), Gesetzgebung in der Europäischen Gemeinschaft, Baden-Baden 1985,
    55-72.
von Wilmowsky, Peter
  Zugang zu öffentlichen Leistungen anderer Mitgliedstaaten, ZaöRV 1990,
    231-281.
Waelbroeck, D.
  Application des règles de concurrence du Traité de Rome à l'autorité publique,
    RMC 1987, 25-34.
Wägenbaur, Rolf
  L'Europe des citoyens – Quelques considérations sur un sujet d'actualité, in:
    'Haristirion' – Mélanges en l'honneur du Professeur Georges M. Papahadzis,
    Athens & Komotini 1989, 469-485.
  Die deutsche Universität und die Europäische Gemeinschaft, MittHV 1989,
    138-145.
  Die Einbeziehung der Hochschulen in den europäischen Integrationsprozeß,
    EuR 1990, 135-142.
  Die Rechtsprechung des Europäischen Gerichtshofs auf den Gebieten Umwelt
    und Gesundheit, Kultur und Bildung, in: Merten, D. (ed.), Föderalismus
    und Europäische Gemeinschaften, Berlin 1990, 161-173.
  Auf dem Wege zur Bildungs- und Kulturgemeinschaft, in: Randelzhofer, A. et al.
    (eds), Gedächtnisschrift für Eberhard Grabitz, Munich 1995, 851-865.
Wagner, Heinz
  Grundbegriffe des Beschlußrechts der Europäischen Gemeinschaften, Cologne
    (inter alia) 1965.
Wallace, Rebecca, & Goldberg, David
  The EEC Directive on Television Broadcasting, YEL 1989, 175-196.
Wallenfels, Dieter
  Das System der Preisbindung für Verlagserzeugnisse im EG-Binnenmarkt, in:
    Becker, J. (ed.), Der Buchhandel im Europäischen Binnenmarkt, Frankfurt
    am Main 1989, 71-83.
Weatherill, Stephen
  Discrimination on Grounds of Nationality in Sport, YEL 1989, 55-92.
Weber, Albrecht
  Die Grundrechte im Integrationsprozeß der Gemeinschaft in vergleichender
    Perspektive, JZ 1989, 965-973.
Weberling, Johannes
  Die Rechtsprechung der Europäischen Gerichtshöfe zum Wissenschaftsrecht
    in den Jahren 1989 und 1990, WissR 1991, 123-139.
WEGS
  See Wohlfahrt, Ernst, Everling, Ulrich, Glaesner, Hans Joachim, & Sprung,
    Rudolf.

Weiler, Joseph H. H.
The European Court at a Crossroads: Community Human Rights and Member State Action, in: Capotorti, F. et al. (eds), Du droit international au droit de l'integration, *FS Pierre Pescatore*, Baden-Baden 1987, 821-842.
Methods of Protection: Towards a Second and Third Generation of Protection, in: Cassese, A. et al. (eds), Human Rights and the European Community: Methods of Protection, Baden-Baden 1991, 555-642.

Wellens, K. C., & Borchardt, G. M.
Soft Law in European Community Law, ELR 1989, 267-321.

Wemmer, Benedikt
Die neuen Kulturklauseln des EG-Vertrages, Frankfurt am Main 1996.

Wenger, Klaus
Euro-Fernsehen oder Euro-Flimmern?, EA 1989, 545-552.

Wiesand, Andreas Johannes
Kunst ohne Grenzen?, Cologne 1987.

Wilke, Marc, & Wallace, Helen
Subsidiarity: Approaches to Power-Sharing in the European Community, RIIA Discussion Paper No. 27, London 1990.

Wittkowski, Bernd
Bildungsrechtliche Folgen des Maastricht-Vertrages aus deutscher Sicht, RdJB 1994, 317-325.

Wittweiler, Bernhard
Europäischer Binnenmarkt 1992 und Sinfonieorchester, ZUM 1990, 557-562.

Wohlfahrt, Ernst
Von der Befugnis der Organe der Europäischen Wirtschaftsgemeinschaft zur Rechtsetzung, *JIR 1961*, 12-32.
Europäische und deutsche *Rechtsordnung*, Göttingen 1965.

Wohlfahrt, Ernst, Everling, Ulrich, Glaesner, Hans Joachim, & Sprung, Rudolf
Die Europäische Wirtschaftsgemeinschaft, Kommentar zum Vertrag, Berlin & Frankfurt am Main 1960.

Wuermeling, Joachim
Kooperatives Gemeinschaftsrecht, Kehl (*inter alia*) 1988.

Wyatt, Derrick, & Dashwood, Alan
European Community Law, 3rd ed., London 1993.

Zilioli, Chiara
The Recognition of Diplomas and its Impact on Educational Policies, in: de Witte, B. (ed.), European Community Law of Education, Baden-Baden 1989, 51-70.

Zuck, Rüdiger
Subsidiaritätsprinzip und Grundgesetz, Munich 1968.

Zuleeg, Manfred
Das *Recht der Europäischen Gemeinschaften* im innerstaatlichen Bereich, Cologne (*inter alia*) 1969.
Die Kompetenzen der Europäischen Gemeinschaften gegenüber den Mitgliedstaaten, *JöR 1971*, 1-64.
EG-Richtlinien auf dem Gebiete des Wasserrechts und ihre innerstaatlichen Auswirkungen, *ZfW 1975*, 133-147.

Der Verfassungsgrundsatz der Demokratie und die Europäischen
    Gemeinschaften, *Der Staat 1978*, 27–47.
Die Bedeutung des europäischen Gemeinschaftsrechts für das Ausländerrecht,
    NJW 1987, 2193–2199.
Vorbehaltene Kompetenzen der Mitgliedstaaten der Europäischen
    Gemeinschaft auf dem Gebiete des Umweltschutzes, *NVwZ 1987*, 280–286.
Die *Rechtsprechung* des Europäischen Gerichtshofes zum Europarecht im Lichte
    des Grundgesetzes und seiner Dogmatik, in: Battis, U. et al. (eds), Das
    Grundgesetz im internationalen Wirkungszusammenhang der
    Verfassungen, Berlin 1990, 227–245.
Die Stellung der Länder und Regionen im europäischen Integrationsprozeß,
    DVBl. 1992, 1329–1337.

INDEX